AF352714

Snorri Sturluson and the *Edda*

THE CONVERSION OF CULTURAL CAPITAL IN MEDIEVAL SCANDINAVIA

Snorri Sturluson and the *Edda*

THE CONVERSION OF CULTURAL CAPITAL IN MEDIEVAL SCANDINAVIA

KEVIN J. WANNER

UNIVERSITY OF TORONTO PRESS
Toronto   Buffalo   London

© University of Toronto Press 2008
Toronto Buffalo London
www.utppublishing.com

ISBN 978-0-8020-9801-6

Toronto Old Norse–Icelandic Series

Library and Archives Canada Cataloguing in Publication

Wanner, Kevin J.
    Snorri Sturluson and the Edda: the conversion of cultural capital in medieval
Scandinavia / Kevin J. Wanner.

(Toronto Old Norse and Icelandic studies)
Includes bibliographical references and index.
ISBN 978-0-8020-9801-6

1. Snorri Sturluson, 1179?–1241 – Criticism and interpretation. 2. Edda Snorra
Sturlusonar. I. Title. II. Series.

PT7335.Z5W36 2008   839'.61   C2008-902573-3

Jacket illustration: Gangleri stands in Valholl before the triple throne of Odin, who
appears here in the person of three kings named High, Equally-High, and Third. From
the Uppsala manuscript of the Prose Edda, Uppsala University Library, DG 11, f.26v.

University of Toronto Press gratefully acknowledges the financial assistance of the
Centre for Medieval Studies, University of Toronto, and of Western Michigan
University in the publication of this book.

University of Toronto Press acknowledges the financial assistance to its publishing
program of the Canada Council for the Arts and the Ontario Arts Council.

University of Toronto Press acknowledges the financial support for its publishing
activities of the Government of Canada through the Book Publishing Industry
Development Program (BPIDP).

For Angie

Contents

Acknowledgments

While of course no firm borders separate these spheres, the debts I have accumulated while working on this project can be acknowledged under three headings: intellectual, professional, and personal. Intellectually, my principle debt in this as in all my work is to my doctoral advisor and continuing mentor Bruce Lincoln. From the manuscript's beginnings as a seminar paper and through its development as a dissertation and now book, Bruce has been unfailingly generous with guidance and advice both academic and practical in nature. Simply put, this study would not exist without him. Special thanks are also due to Martin Riesebrodt and John Lindow, both of whom served as readers on my dissertation, and without whose input and encouragement this work would be much the poorer.

Professionally, I thank first my colleagues in Western Michigan University's Department of Comparative Religion for providing a supportive and stimulating atmosphere in which to teach and research. Special thanks are due in this regard to Stephen Covell, David Ede, and Brian Wilson. Second, I thank all at the University of Toronto Press who have worked to bring this book to print. Chief among these are Suzanne Rancourt, Andy Orchard, Robert E. Bjork, Roberta Frank, my copy-editor Miriam Skey, and two anonymous reviewers who provided many helpful comments and suggestions. Third, I wish to acknowledge the generous financial assistance provided towards publication of this book by the Centre for Medieval Studies in the University of Toronto and by Western Michigan University.

Personally, I thank my parents Jack and Diane Wanner (for support throughout my educational career, and for valiantly trying to explain to my other relatives what it is I do for a living), Friday, Elanor, and Astrid (for keeping me company at various stages of writing and rewriting this book, though I'm pretty sure that to them it just felt like being ignored), Jamonn

Campbell, Sam Wagner, and Bryan Mickle (for no reasons in particular), and finally and above all Angela Trupo, for, among other things, many years of feigning, mostly successfully, interest in something she should by all rights care nothing about.

Snorri Sturluson and the *Edda*

THE CONVERSION OF CULTURAL CAPITAL
IN MEDIEVAL SCANDINAVIA

1 The Paradox of Snorri Sturluson

Janus Faces: The Man, the Age, the Work

Snorri Sturluson has long proven a paradoxical figure for those who think and write about medieval Norse culture. Many scholars believe that a satisfactory understanding of Snorri and his work will only be possible once the contradictions that surround this most famous of medieval Icelanders have been resolved. Anthony Faulkes, editor and translator of Snorri's *Edda*, writes:

> Snorri Sturluson is the only medieval Icelandic author about whom we have sufficient biographical information and by whom a sufficient range of writings survives for it to be possible to write a comprehensive book about the author and his *œuvre*. There have, however, been remarkably few attempts to write such a book ... The reason is probably the immense difficulty of demonstrating a connection between the life of this turbulent and rather less than admirable political figure and the writings attributed to him which are so marked for their breadth of vision, sympathy, sense of humour, and delicate style ... No one who has written about him has succeeded in reconciling satisfactorily the picture of the man given by contemporary historical accounts of him with that which emerges from his works. Most have assumed, like Sigurður Nordal, who seems to have been dissatisfied with the explanation, that the writings were a compensation for the life: that Snorri sought to express in books the ideals he failed to live up to in reality.[1]

As Faulkes suggests, scholars have been more prone to draw attention to what they see as a fundamental incongruity between Snorri's personality and pursuits than to try to solve this dilemma. For example, Lee M. Hollander writes in introducing his translation of Snorri's *Heimskringla*: 'For his own contemporaries Snorri no doubt was the powerful chieftain known for his munificence as well as his avarice ... a ruthless intriguer whom it was dangerous to have as one's adversary.'[2] And yet, thanks to his literary legacy, Snorri appears to us more as 'a historian who in many ways can be compared with Thucydides and in some is in nowise inferior to his Greek counterpart.'[3] Elsewhere, Hollander underlines Snorri's dichotomous character even more: on the one hand, he was 'unscrupulous,' 'his life was anything but exemplary,' and he led 'a career of duplicity and tortuous politics'; on the other, he was a 'literary genius, all in all the greatest in ancient Scandinavia.'[4] Marlene Ciklamini, author of what has for some time been the only book-length survey in English of Snorri's life and writings, offers a similar opinion about her subject, describing a political career in which 'acts of injustice, indifference toward the obligations of friendship and kinship, and the instigation of disputes illustrate Snorri's disregard for right and wrong,' only to contrast this portrait with another Snorri, 'a man of charm, wit, and imagination, – the man, in short, we sense through his writings.'[5]

Sigurður Nordal, whose 1920 book on Snorri remains the most thorough treatment of its subject, suggests that Snorri's character combined contradictory family traits that were manifested more purely in his two elder brothers and their offspring:

> Where the family seems in one moment split into a calm and peaceful branch in Þórðr and his sons, and a severe and obstinate branch in Sighvatr and his sons, Snorri's temperament lies at the meeting of the branches. He is in one part a chieftain, covetous, ambitious, and eager for esteem, and yet timid in terms of courage, reflective, and not much of a leader, in the other a writer, scholarly, profound, and artistic, and yet with thought for earthly things.[6]

While Sigurður's description of Snorri's personality is more nuanced than most, in that it distinguishes between opposing facets of his opposing sides, it features the same bipolarity stressed by others, and indeed he separates Snorri's political and cultural halves more emphatically than have many. In this passage, negative aspects of Snorri's chieftainly and scholarly personas result from a contamination of one sphere by the other: his intellectual reserve produces a lack of political resolve, while his lust for power and wealth taints his literary pursuits. As Sigurður puts it, 'such fickle-mindedness, where contrary impulses struggle for power, weakens emotions and the strength of the will.'[7]

In many scholars' opinions, Snorri's conflicted character mirrored that of the entire era in which he lived, a period known as the Sturlung age (*Sturlungaöld*), after Snorri's own family. As Einar Ól. Sveinsson writes, this age was

> notorious for every kind of outrage – warfare, atrocities, murders and incendiarism, treachery and immorality ... But this is not its only visage; like Janus, it has two faces. For this was also an age of tremendous cultural activity. It is the age of

Snorri Sturluson and his *Edda* and *Heimskringla*, the age of all the anonymous masters who wrote the Icelandic sagas. The contrast between conscious, disciplined cultural achievement and the frenzy of unrestrained vitality is the outstanding characteristic of the age and the riddle of its life.[8]

While Snorri is here set against his period, he is himself characterized a few pages later by Einar as 'versatile and fickle, a man of wealth, aristocrat, scholar, poet, princely, and yet so avaricious,' as, in short, a microcosm of the contradictions of the society and time in which he lived.[9]

Such identification of Snorri and his age has proven durable. Paul Schach, writing in the 1980s, observes that the 'ambivalent and enigmatic' Snorri 'seems to have been a perfect embodiment of the vices and virtues of the Sturlung Age ... [H]e was ruthless and relentless in his pursuit of wealth and prestige. At the same time, he was one of the most significant and influential writers of medieval Europe.'[10] Still more recently, E. Paul Durrenberger has written of Snorri that he 'was not only a shrewd political maneuverer, an astute and cunning arranger of marriages and alliances, a keeper of Iceland's laws, and a past master at the accumulation of wealth and power, he was *also* the writer of a handbook of poetry,' and of his time period: 'While the Sturlung age was a period of internecine warfare, strife, cruelty, shortsighted selfishness, and violence, it was *also* an age of great writing.'[11] Passages such as these offer a perfect parallel between Snorri and his time: both are split in two, torn between base, worldly impulses and the desire to overcome these through the extra- or apolitical cultivation of art and literature. To quote Einar Sveinsson once more, 'Here we are back at the great riddle of the age: How could these two things go hand in hand, its intellectual culture and its savagery?'[12]

Scholars' tendency to imagine two Snorris, the one a power-grubbing, self-serving politician/lawyer, the other a literary-minded, aesthetically motivated producer of art, is often joined by an analogous division of his two most famous works. On one side is placed the overtly political *Heimskringla*, a monumental history of and, in many respects, tribute to the Norwegian monarchy. On the other is his *Edda*, usually described as, foremost, a handbook for skaldic verse, and second, a compendium of pagan Norse myth.[13] In relation to the first function, Faulkes, in introducing his popular translation of the *Edda*, writes:

It is likely that Snorri Sturluson, traditional aristocrat that he was, would have foreseen and regretted that the traditional poetry of the skalds was to be superseded ... It seems that he wrote his *Edda* as a treatise on traditional skaldic verse to try to keep interest in it alive and to encourage young poets to continue to compose in the traditional Scandinavian oral style.[14]

Given that he uses the word 'traditional' four times in these two sentences, Faulkes clearly understands Snorri's project as one of preserving and, if necessary, recuperating an ancient and beloved art form. Faulkes also comments on the *Edda*'s second focus, suggesting that Snorri's review of 'mythology is a scholarly and antiquarian attempt to record the beliefs of his ancestors ... beliefs which were outdated but still relevant for the proper understanding of an ancient kind of poetry which he wished should be preserved and continue to be produced as an important part of the contemporary culture of the Icelanders.'[15]

This view of the *Edda* as a product of antiquarian desire has become a more or less doxic assumption of critics, and on the face of things, there is little to argue against in this account of Snorri's purpose in writing this text. It does seem clear that his chief wish was to promote the continued production and appreciation of skaldic verse, and that the mythological material, while it gives the *Edda* most of its value for modern readers, was included mainly to provide needed background for the comprehension and crafting of this poetry. The problem, however, with this understanding of the *Edda*'s origins is that it leaves its author's motivations for wishing to preserve skaldic verse in the first place largely unexamined. Of those who have considered the source of Snorri's concern for this poetry, most have taken it for granted that he *should* be interested in saving such an important part of his cultural heritage. Given such tacit affirmation of the poetry's inherent worth, there is little need to probe Snorri's motives further: it is enough to say that he was 'a fine scholar and literary artist' with a 'didactic interest in' and 'love for a complex poetic genre' who, fearing 'that the technique of the ancient poets was falling into disuse,' felt 'the impetus to systematize and to narrate myth' and therefore wrote a 'detached and scholarly treatment both of religion and poetry.'[16] The *Edda* has thus become the emblematic marker of the absolute cultural pole of the several interlocking dichotomous pairs that are supposed to have revolved around this learned Icelander. The *Edda*, in short, has come to represent that which is most aesthetic, disinterested, apolitical, cultivated – in a word, positive – in the character of not only Snorri Sturluson but all of thirteenth-century Iceland.

This understanding of the *Edda* and its author seems to me to depend on two premises. The first concerns the norms that govern academic or cultural practice, the disinterested interests of which ought to lie in the preservation and expression of knowledge and/or culture in and of themselves. According to this way of thinking, scholarship and art are their own raisons d'être, and offer their practitioners alternatives to or respites from worldly and above all political concerns and cares. Second, it is assumed that this model of the relations of scholars and artists with their work applies not only in modern contexts, but to past societies and cultures. This imputation of the gratuitous, quietistic nature of the relationship of scholar and subject, or, what is the same thing, artist and work, abounds in the literature on Snorri and the Sturlung age. Einar Sveinsson, for example, states that it was in this era's 'moments of quiet and leisure' that its 'great achievements in learning and art' were born, and Sigurður Nordal avers that while Snorri's prose works are lively and entertaining, 'the undisturbed tranquillity of the scholar [is] continuously in the background.'[17] Further, Snorri, often described as an 'enlightened humanist' or 'something of a Renaissance man,' is again and again praised for his 'unfaltering objectivity,' his 'almost humanistic detachment and his respect for antiquity,' and his 'wonderful detachment' from the turmoil of his age, of which he was 'so serene an observer.'[18]

In my view, the application of a model of academic disinterestedness and cultural conservatism to Snorri's *Edda* is possible only when the conditions of its authorship are neglected. This book challenges prevailing interpretations of Snorri's literary practice, above all the tendency to dissociate Snorri the politician/lawyer from Snorri the aesthete/scholar, through application of the theory of practice of French sociologist Pierre Bourdieu (1930–2002). Bourdieu's work offers a model and method for understanding how social agents operate within and between fields or markets in which the strategic accumulation, protection, and deployment of field-specific but often interconvertible forms of capital, i.e., resources and powers or capacities, are at stake. I am not the only researcher to have recognized the usefulness of Bourdieu's theory for understanding Snorri and his context. Independently and to all appearances simultaneously with my initial work on this project, which culminated in my 2003 dissertation, Torfi H. Tulinius issued a number of studies in which he applies Bourdieu's theory to the practice of Snorri and other Sturlungar within what he characterizes as Iceland's economic, symbolic, and cultural fields of practice.[19] Some of the results of Torfi's work on Snorri are close to my own; this is particularly true of parts of my discussion in chapter 3. In most respects, however, our projects are quite different. Whereas Torfi's comparatively brief treatment focuses on Snorri's practice within his domestic sphere, his possible identity as author of *Egils saga Skallagrímssonar* and, in Torfi's view, his entry into and largely successful participation within a nascent field of literary production in medieval Iceland, my study aims to understand, within the context of Snorri's total practices and interests in the shared political/social field of Iceland and Norway, the reasons that lay behind and the process through which he produced his *Edda*. Despite these differences, I regard Torfi's application of Bourdieu's theory to Snorri and his context as a welcome and independent affirmation of my own approach.

By using Bourdieu's ideas concerning the circulation of forms of politically effective capital within social markets to understand Snorri's production of the *Edda* in the context of early thirteenth-century Scandinavia, I hope to cast the literary activity of this prominent Icelander in a different and more accurate light. Above all, I intend to demonstrate that Snorri was not invested in skaldic verse on antiquarian grounds, but rather that he strove through the creation of a novel literary product to preserve the capacity of this ancient art form to function as a marker of social prestige and tool of political power in the present. My aim is thus not so much to resolve the paradoxes that have surrounded the figure of Snorri as to dissolve them, by showing that the dilemma posed by the desire to reconcile the opposing halves of Snorri's character has had more to do with the assumptions of those who have written about this distinguished Icelander than with the relationship between the life and work of the man himself. The reason, in short, that scholars have had such trouble reuniting the two sides of Snorri Sturluson is that they are the ones who have torn him apart.

The Economics of Practice

A disgruntled anthropologist of Iceland wrote in 1992 that 'Old Norse scholars ... are notorious for their rejection of anything beyond their traditional closed realm of questions and sources.'[20] While this judgment was too harsh in its blanket condemnation, and has become less true in the intervening years, the explicit application of theory in works of history or literary criticism is probably more often lamented than welcomed by Scandinavianists. What often seems to lie behind efforts to discourage dependence upon a set of theoretical tools defined by a specific thinker or '-ism' is the conviction that the historian or critic is amply equipped for his or her task by a combination of common sense and contextualized data, by the capacity to interpret sources through straightforward application of reason to evidence. One of Bourdieu's major contributions, however, is to have shown that in order to gain anything like an objective perspective on the dynamics of a social world one must first break with the 'doxa' that governs it, the common-sensical principles of classification and division that determine how agents situated within that world perceive it.[21] For those analysing a foreign or long-vanished society, this admonition is twofold: one must avoid not only accepting native conceptions uncritically, but also inappropriately applying one's own common-sense categories to that society. The latter error results in what Bourdieu has called the 'scholastic fallacy,' the habit 'of unconsciously universalizing the vision of the world associated with the scholastic condition' by crediting 'agents with [the modern scholar's] own vision, and in particular an interest in pure knowledge and pure understanding which is normally alien to them.'[22] More to the point, it has led to the application of labels such as 'scholar,' 'antiquarian,' or 'intellectual' to medieval cultural producers such as Snorri, who would neither have recognized themselves or their practice in these categories, nor have played roles equivalent to these within their social contexts.

One benefit of Bourdieu's theory is that it provides a method for breaking with not only the subjective representations of those under analysis, but also outside observers' tendencies to reify and formalize the rules that govern social practice. It does so by seeking to understand social worlds as overlapping and fluid arenas for structurally determined yet strategically motivated action. This perspective is meant to overcome a set of false dichotomies, including subjectivism vs. objectivism, individual vs. society, agency vs. structure, autonomy vs. constraint, and consciousness vs. unconsciousness, that have plagued the social sciences. To this end, Bourdieu posed one overriding question in his work: how can one account for the regularity, predictability, and coordination of human practice without resorting to objective, rule-based models, or assuming that subjective, conscious deliberation continually shapes action?[23] In answer, he insisted that practice is best understood as strategic, as being guided by a 'feel for the game,' or, more technically, by agents' adaptation to objective conditions guided by the pursuit, though not necessarily conscious pursuit, of interests.

In seeking to analyse the strategic logic of practice, Bourdieu employed four key concepts: capital, field, social space, and habitus. The first is obviously borrowed from Karl Marx, and to some extent it is appropriate to view Bourdieu's project as an extension of Marx's ideas about the production, control, and circulation of economic capital to a much wider range of practices.[24] In his view, Marxist thinkers as well as many anthropologists and sociologists tend to employ

> a *restricted definition of economic interest*, which ... is the historical product of capitalism: the constitution of relatively autonomous areas of practice is accompanied by a process through which symbolic interests (often described as 'spiritual' or 'cultural') come to be set up in opposition to strictly economic interests as defined in the field of economic transactions by the fundamental tautology 'business is business'; strictly 'cultural' or 'aesthetic' interest, disinterested interest, is the paradoxical product of the ideological labour in which writers and artists, those most directly interested, have played an important part and in the course of which symbolic interests become autonomous by being opposed to material interests, i.e. by being symbolically nullified as interests.[25]

Acceptance of this opposition results in a model of practice in which economic practice is (correctly) understood as interest-driven, and symbolic/cultural practice is (incorrectly) understood as disinterested. As Bourdieu puts it:

> contrary to naively idyllic representations of 'pre-capitalist' societies (or of the 'cultural' sphere of capitalist societies), practice never ceases to conform to economic calculation even when it gives every appearance of disinterestedness by departing from the logic of interested calculation (in the narrow sense) and playing for stakes that are non-material and not easily quantified.[26]

Here, Bourdieu challenges any theory of practice that walls off and privileges economics as the central component of social existence while finding 'no place in its analyses, still less in its calculations, for the strictly symbolic interest which is occasionally recognized ... only to be reduced to the irrationality of feeling or passion.'[27] In like fashion, scholars of medieval Scandinavia have tended to situate the *Edda* outside of the realm of material, political, or even symbolic interest, preferring to view it as a leisurely labour of scholarly love, or, to repeat Bourdieu's formulation, a work whose genesis lies in 'the irrationality of feeling or passion.'

Bourdieu defines his second major concept, that of 'field,' as 'an independent social universe with its own laws of functioning, its specific relations of force, its dominants and its dominated ... where, in accordance with its particular laws, there accumulates a particular form of capital and where relations of force of a particular type are exerted.'[28] This definition makes clear that for Bourdieu neither capital nor interest can be defined abstractly – each exists, i.e., becomes a stake worth contesting, within a field, an arena of social interaction. One consequence of this interdependence is that there are potentially as many forms of capital as there are fields. In practice, however, Bourdieu boiled the kinds of capital down to four basic species: economic, cultural, social, and symbolic. The first three are the major types of capital under which most others can be filed. The first, economic capital, is easiest to conceptualize, as it corresponds to traditional notions of the term: simply put, economic capital is an individual's or group's material (tangible property and goods) and financial (money or whatever assets can be directly and simply converted into material wealth) holdings.

The second and third major categories of capital, cultural and social, while also fairly straightforward, have been subject to misunderstanding even among Bourdieu's sympathetic critics. In part, this confusion stems from the fact that Bourdieu uses the terms 'culture' and 'cultural' in a more restricted sense than is common. Most social scientists' notion of culture aligns with that of Clifford Geertz, who defined it as 'an historically transmitted pattern of meanings embodied in symbols, a system of inherited conceptions expressed in symbolic forms by means of which men communicate, perpetuate, and develop their knowledge about and attitudes toward life.'[29] This conception of culture as a symbolic system that conveys meaning and demands interpretation has led some interpreters of Bourdieu to confuse forms of capital that ought to remain distinct. Most often, they collapse cultural and social with symbolic capital, regarding each as forms used by dominant classes to legitimate their possession and retention of economic capital through misrecognition of the arbitrary distribution of wealth among social agents.[30] For Bourdieu, however, the first two varieties are to be regarded, like economic capital, as *species* of capital, subtypes of resources or powers holding value within specific fields. Thus, cultural capital is 'a form of knowledge, an internalized code or a cognitive acquisition which equips the social agent with empathy towards, appreciation for or competence in deciphering cultural relations and cultural artefacts,' and 'social capital is the sum of the resources, actual or virtual, that accrue to an individual or a group by virtue of possessing a durable network of more or less institutionalized relationships of mutual acquaintance and recognition.'[31]

The fourth and final major type of capital, symbolic, is not, strictly speaking, a variety or species of capital at all. Rather, it is a quality that types of capital assume when they are recognized, or, what is the same thing in Bourdieu's parlance, misrecognized, as legitimate. As Bourdieu puts it, 'A capital (or power) becomes symbolic capital ... only when it is *misrecognized* in its arbitrary truth as capital and [therefore] *recognized* as legitimate.'[32] In another passage, he writes more plainly that 'symbolic capital, commonly called prestige, reputation, fame, etc. ... is the form assumed by [the other] kinds of capital when they are perceived and recognized as legitimate.'[33] While such recognition is typically field-specific, Bourdieu also describes symbolic capital as 'one of the mechanisms which ... make capital go to capital.'[34] By this, he means not only that display of symbolic capital facilitates accumulation of resources, but that it permits conversions of capital, as when a diploma or certificate grants access to a stable and predictable level of monetary income in modern societies.

This capacity to convert capital, to transform one type of social power into another, comes into play when one shifts focus from autonomous fields of practice, wherein one or few kinds of capital are relevant and only a portion of the social group is active, to what Bourdieu calls the 'social space,' his third key concept. A social space, the boundaries of which vary according to context but which Bourdieu most often treats as coterminous with political, geographic, or cultural (in the Geertzian sense) boundaries, is multidimensional and relational. It can be envisioned as a set of points, each corresponding to an agent (individual or group) occupying a position according to its placement along axes in two dimensions: 'Agents are ... distributed, in the first dimension, according to the overall volume of the capital they possess and, in the second dimension, according to the composition of their capital.'[35] Thus, all agents possess a total volume of capital, specific to them in quantity and quality, that determines their position relative to other agents within the social space.

The ranking of agents according to possession of capital is never, however, a purely quantitative procedure. This is because the region of social space in which dominant agents reside, a region Bourdieu came to call a society's 'field of power,' is always 'the site of struggles between holders of different powers (or kinds of capital) which ... have at stake the transformation or conservation of the relative value of different kinds of capital.'[36] Thus, competition within the field of power to control the rate of conversion between fundamental species of capital (economic, cultural, and social) must be factored into any attempt to graph 'the state of the relations of power' in a given society.[37] Such struggles to regulate what amounts to the production and distribution of symbolic capital take a different form in societies that possess institutions capable of awarding and guaranteeing durable and universal signs of accomplishment and prestige, such as noble titles, technical certifications, or academic diplomas, than in those lacking such means. In the former, 'objectification guarantees the permanence and cumulativity of material and symbolic acquisitions which can then subsist without the agents having to recreate them continuously and in their entirety' through time-consuming, costly, and less predictable personal interactions.[38]

Having defined capital and field and the related notions of interest and field of power, and having discussed how these concepts interact within a social space, I now turn to the fourth concept used by Bourdieu to describe the forces that generate and condition practice. According to Bourdieu, two types of objectified history must be taken into account when analysing practice: the first is history objectified in the state of things, in the space of positions and position-takings that constitute a field. The second is history objectified, or incorporated, in people, in the dispositions, tastes, and capacities that agents carry into fields.[39] He calls this complex of attributes and abilities the 'habitus.' He defines habitus in one place as

> systems of durable, transposable dispositions, structured structures predisposed
> to function as structuring structures, that is, as principles which generate and

organize practices and representations that can be objectively adapted to their outcomes without presupposing a conscious aiming at ends or an express mastery of the operations necessary in order to attain them.[40]

Put more simply, Bourdieu here states that all agents inherit or acquire through early inculcation a volume and composition of capital which, by generating certain aspirations and expectations of success, predispose them to participate in particular fields of practice, and to adopt certain positions and strategies therein. Practices 'can therefore only be accounted for by relating the social conditions in which the *habitus* that generated them was constituted, to the social conditions in which it is implemented,' or, in other words, by relating the field in which an agent currently operates to those in which his or her habitus was formed.[41] The concept of habitus thus suggests not only that agents do not enter into fields of practice as self-aware participants for whom every position and strategy appears equally open and viable, but also that agents' choices and actions are not determined solely by rules or structures immanent in the field.

One of Bourdieu's more controversial assertions is that, in the normal course of things, the encounter of habitus and field is characterized by a more or less perfect adaptation of agents' expectations and behaviours to objective chances for success.[42] Such harmony preponderates because, '[h]abitus being linked to the field within which it functions (and within which, as is most often the case, it was formed) by a relationship of ontological complicity, the action of the "practical sense" amounts to an immediate encounter of history with itself.'[43] Even if this is so, however, there are instances of mismatch between the two forms of objectified history, when, that is, a habitus is confronted by a field radically different or transformed from that in which it arose. It is in such dissonant moments that the mechanistic functioning of the habitus is likely to fail and rational calculation (or ineffectual flailing) to take over.[44] Capital is a social power prone to fluctuations in worth: not only can agents lose capital by failing to exploit resources effectively or pursuing ill-conceived strategies, but the value of their stores can, through no fault or action of their own, be deflated or even obliterated by changes in the dynamics of a field, such as the introduction of new technologies into a medical or scientific field, or of novel products and practices into a cultural one. In such cases, agents who had recently occupied the upper reaches of a field can find themselves left with, quite literally, nothing of value on its market.

To summarize, Bourdieu offers a model of practice in which agents, as a function of their habitus, strategically accumulate, deploy, and convert forms of capital within and between fields of production, consumption, and competition, all of which, while to some degree autonomous, have profound effects upon one another and on the position agents occupy in the overall social space and its associated field of power. If in reaching this point I have dwelled at some length on Bourdieu's theory, this has not been for its own sake, but because of the role it will play in my efforts to elucidate the dynamics between author, text, and context surrounding production of Snorri's *Edda*. While some readers may find reliance on such a specific method or set of concepts unnecessary or distracting, I would insist that, even if reducing the explicit presence of Bourdieu's theory might lend my study an air of greater originality, there would be much lost in doing so. For example, while it might seem simpler to speak of 'skaldic poetry' rather than 'cultural capital,' the two terms are not interchangeable (the first is an artistic form that may or may not hold value within a field of practice; the latter by definition does), and to treat them or similar pairs as if they were would rob my analysis of precision and clarity. Moreover, I am confident that by the end of the book it will have become clear why this set of theoretical tools is eminently suited to illuminating the particular data in which I am interested.

Taken as a whole, this book provides an account of Snorri Sturluson's attempts to use, convert, and defend forms of capital within several fields, with a particular focus on the role played by his cultural practices and products, those that critics have tended, with a few significant exceptions, to dissociate from his worldly, political pursuits. Above all, I will consider the place of the *Edda*, long considered the paradigmatic marker of the cultural in Snorri's life, and even medieval Iceland as a whole, in this process. Chapter 2 lays further groundwork for this study by reviewing the sources for and offering a brief yet thorough account of Snorri's life. Chapter 3 begins with a discussion of the structure and operation of early thirteenth-century Icelandic society, moving on to an examination of Snorri's activities within his domestic sphere, of which he briefly reached the pinnacle. Chapters 4 and 5 then shift to an analysis of Snorri's forays into the foreign market of Norway's courts, and of his attempts to realize there the profits traditionally associated with expertise in skaldic verse, profits that ultimately, I will argue, did not meet his expectations. To contextualize Snorri's efforts to exploit this resource, these chapters will consider in some detail the historical development and role of skaldic verse in medieval Scandinavia, as well as the manner in which its mastery and monopolization provided Icelanders with a form of cultural or linguistic capital that could be readily converted into social and material benefits in court settings.

Chapters 6 through 8 provide close textual analyses of the three major parts of Snorri's *Edda* in the order in which they were probably written: *Háttatal*, *Skáldskaparmál*, and *Gylfaginning* (plus the *Formáli* or prologue). In these chapters, I argue that production of the *Edda* should be understood not as a disinterested act of antiquarian conservation, but as a strategic practice aimed at protecting the market value of an important but endangered source of capital, preservation of which would have served to maximize Snorri's overall position in domestic and foreign social and political fields. To argue for this conclusion, it will be necessary to break with the tendency to treat the *Edda* as a finished and autonomous work of art or scholarship. In Bourdieu's terms, we will need to move from perceiving this text as an artefact, an *opus operatum*, to viewing it as a practice, a *modus operandi*, that played out in time in strategic response to ever changing contexts and needs.[45]

2 *Snorra saga Sturlusonar*: A Short Biography of Snorri Sturluson

While he has long been the most famous Icelander of the Middle Ages, there is no saga dedicated to Snorri Sturluson (although his father has one, and even his nephew gets a *þáttr*). It is therefore up to us to assemble an account of his life from available sources. Mostly, we depend on information provided by Snorri's nephew Sturla Þórðarson (1214–84) in his *Íslendinga saga*, which in the course of describing the period of internal feuding leading up to Iceland's loss of independence in 1262–4 narrates the major events of Snorri's life, from his birth in 1179 to his murder by agents of Norway's king in 1241.[1] This saga, part of the *Sturlunga saga* compilation, was written towards the end of Sturla's life, sometime between 1271–84, and therefore some three decades or more after Snorri's death. The second major source for Snorri's life is *Hákonar saga Hákonarsonar*, a biography of the eponymous Norwegian king.[2] Since this saga too was written by Sturla Þórðarson, it is not of much use for verifying *Íslendinga saga*, though it does add certain details regarding Snorri's dealings with Hákon and his regent jarl Skúli. Aside from these works of Sturla Þórðarson, and a few others that depend upon them, information about Snorri in contemporary writings is scarce.[3] By far the most important additional source is the anonymous *Sturlu saga* (c. 1220), a text also from the *Sturlunga* compilation that centres on the rise to prominence of Snorri's father, whose name too was Sturla Þórðarson. Sturla's saga ends with his death in 1183, and so is most useful for information concerning Snorri's family and the first years of his life. Information on Snorri's ancestry as well as progeny can be found in *Ættartölur*, a set of genealogies in *Sturlunga saga*, and he is named as one of the poets in the line of Egill Skalla-Grímsson in *Gunnlaugs saga ormstungu*.[4] Finally, some scraps of information about Snorri can be gleaned from lists preserved in the *Uppsalabók* manuscript of his *Edda*: *Skáldatal*, a catalogue of names of court-poets and their patrons from the ninth to thirteenth centuries; *ættartala*, a Sturlungar genealogy; and *lögsögumannatal*, a list of Icelandic lawspeakers ending with Snorri's 1222–31 tenure.[5]

Generally, critics have viewed *Íslendinga saga* and other *samtíðarsögur*, or 'contemporary sagas,' as more reliable than the *Íslendingasögur* or 'sagas of Icelanders' that date from the same time but chronicle an earlier period of Iceland's history.[6] While confidence in Sturla's veracity proceeds as much from necessity as anything else – most scholarly accounts of Snorri's life are little more than Sturla's with dates added – there seems no compelling reason to challenge it here, except to note the trend in recent years of highlighting the ideological and literary dimensions of the *Sturlunga* compilation.[7] Sturla's bias or attitude towards his uncle has been judged variously, from highly positive to highly negative to, unsurprisingly, ambivalent.[8] In my view, 'ambivalent' is as good a word as any for Sturla's dispassionate portrayal of Snorri, so long as one bears in mind that this posture likely reflects forced equivocation rather than genuine indifference; while Sturla seems to have enjoyed a reasonably amicable relationship with his uncle and to have remained well disposed towards him after his death, he was after 1259 a sworn subject of jarl Gizurr Þorvaldsson, the man directly responsible for Snorri's assassination, and later of King Magnús Hákonarson, the son of the monarch whose letters provided the catalyst and justification for this act.[9]

My primary goal in this chapter is to offer a straightforward account of major events in Snorri's life, drawn from all available sources and unencumbered by commentary, to serve as a framework for the more detailed but piecemeal analyses of later chapters.[10] It is by no means meant to provide an exhaustive portrait of the man and his life, the lack of which Faulkes laments when he writes that 'there have … been remarkably few attempts to write … a comprehensive book about the author and his *œuvre*.'[11] My focus is not so much Snorri the human being as Snorri the social and political agent, a carrier of capital who participated in various fields of interaction and competition. By treating Snorri as an analytic construct in which only those variables relevant to the fields under examination are considered, we avoid treating him as a singular and thus enigmatic entity, one resistant to sociological study. It might be objected, of course, that this sort of analysis of Snorri (or anyone) is flawed because it is partial, or because the variables that are considered of interest are preselected. And indeed, anxiety over the reduction of persons to assemblages of interchangeable attributes seems borne out by Bourdieu's rather extreme suggestion that sociology ought to treat 'as identical all the biological individuals who, being the product of the same objective conditions, are the supports of the same habitus.'[12] In the present case, however, such misgivings are mitigated by the fact that few of the known events, situations, and actions of Snorri's life are irrelevant to his examination as a political agent. While, to be sure, many aspects of his person can be safely left aside, my analysis will demonstrate how extensively Snorri's varied pursuits, including literary practices and products, were implicated in his quest for power and prestige. In short, we will discover in Snorri the distance between agent and individual – or, more accurately, narrative representations of this individual – dwindling to the point of near imperceptibility.

The Life of Snorri

Snorri's lineage was distinguished, although one must go back a few generations to uncover the sources of this distinction. His grandfather Þórðr Gilsson was for much of his life a farmer, but rose to the rank of *goði* (pl. *goðar*), 'priest-chieftain,' when he inherited the Snorrungagoðorð, ancestral chieftaincy of the famed Snorri goði Þorgrímsson (d. 1031).[13] At Þórðr's death, his eldest son Sturla (1115–83) inherited this *goðorð* (sg. and pl.) and its body of *þingmenn*. Although Sturla began his career as his father had ended his, as a provincial authority, his wealth and influence grew owing to his skill in prosecuting lawsuits on behalf of himself and others. Unlike his sons, however, Sturla would never gain possession of more than one *goðorð*. In 1160, Sturla took as his second wife Snorri's future mother, Guðný Böðvarsdóttir, whose most notable ancestor was the famed tenth-century skald, Egill Skalla-Grímsson.

Snorri was born on Sturla's farmstead of Hvammr in western Iceland in 1179.[14] He was Guðný's and Sturla's third son, and the eleventh of his father's seven legitimate and seven illegitimate children.[15] Given the competition he would face for inheritance of his father's authority, wealth, and property, Snorri's chances for advancement would have seemed limited. His prospects unexpectedly improved, however, when he was just two years old. At this time, Sturla became embroiled in a protracted dispute in which he was wounded in the face by an opponent's wife, for which he demanded extravagant reparation through self-judgment. The dispute was settled only when Jón Loptsson, head of the powerful Oddaverjar family of southwestern Iceland, intervened and convinced Sturla to accept a greatly reduced settlement, but offered as alternative compensation to foster Sturla's young son Snorri.[16] So it was that, through what more than one scholar has regarded as 'a providential accident,' Snorri was raised and educated at Oddi, thirteenth-century Iceland's premier centre of learning and culture.[17]

Snorri was still living at Oddi when Jón Loptsson died in 1197. Now nineteen years old, the time had come for Snorri to marry and establish himself in society. His ability to do either was compromised, however, by his mother having squandered his inheritance.[18] Snorri recovered from his financial woes by marrying, with the help of Þórðr, his oldest full-brother, and his foster-brother Sæmundr Jónsson, now head of the Oddaverjar, into a wealthy family in 1199. Although Snorri originally planned to move with his wife Herdís Bersadóttir to Hvammr, they stayed at Oddi for several more years. In 1200, Snorri entered into his first lawsuit, a property dispute pitting himself and his foster-brother Sæmundr against a party allied to Snorri's other full-brother Sigvatr.[19] Snorri took a central role in prosecuting this case, and was victorious.[20] It was also around this time that Snorri first sent a poetic tribute abroad, to Norway's King Sverrir Sigurðarson.[21]

In 1202, Snorri inherited his father-in-law's property, including probably the Mýramannagoðorð, Snorri's first chieftaincy.[22] He and Herdís moved to Borg, former homestead of Egill Skalla-Grímsson.[23] From this time, Snorri began rapidly to collect *goðorð*s, and his authority soon stretched over nearly all of the Borgarfjörðr region. Around this same time, a dispute with a group of Orkney merchants brought Snorri into his first conflict with his foster-family. After Snorri had the merchants' meal seized and demanded to set his own price on the goods, the foreign traders killed one of his men and fled to Oddi, where Sæmundr Jónsson sheltered them. Despite his close relationship and past alliances with the Oddaverjar, it is told that 'Snorri sent three assassins together [to Oddi], but nothing came of it.'[24]

In 1206, Snorri took over the estate of Reykjaholt, where he would live for most of the rest of his life. Sturla recounts that just before Snorri moved to his new home, troubles lying in his future were foreshadowed in a dream of one of his Mýramannagoðorð *þingmenn*. In this dream, Egill Halldórsson is visited by the ghost of Egill Skalla-Grímsson. The dream Egill, 'greatly frowning,' asks the dreaming Egill:

'Does Snorri, our kinsman, intend to go away from here?' 'That's what is said,' says Egill. 'He intends to go away, and in that he does ill,' says the dream-man, 'because little have men got the best of us Mýramenn, when we thrived, and he ought not to have despised this land.' Egill recited a verse:
'A man spares with sword to strike,
snow-white is blood to behold,
an age of quarrels we are able to relate,
sharp blade got land for me,
sharp blade got land for me.'
And then he turned away. And Egill wakes up.[25]

Despite the shade's misgivings, things at first went well for Snorri following his move. As his nephew Sturla relates with typical understatement: 'He then became a great chieftain, because he was not short of property. Snorri was the most thrifty man.'[26] Sturla also lists Snorri's offspring at this point in *Íslendinga saga*. After naming Snorri's and Herdís's only two children to live past childhood, their son, Jón murtr 'the small,' and daughter, Hallbera, he continues:

> Snorri was ... fickle and had children with more women than Herdís. He had a son, who was called Órækja. Þúriðr, daughter of Hallr Órækjuson, was his mother. He also had children with Guðrún, daughter of Hreinn Hermundarson, but of those children only Ingibjörg made it out of childhood. Þórdís was Snorri's daughter. Her mother was called Oddný.[27]

Sometime after his move to Reykjaholt, Snorri was given part of the Eyvellinga-goðorð by Þorsteinn Ívarsson, who wished to block the growing power in the north quarter of the *goði* Kolbeinn Tumason.[28] When Kolbeinn, however, was killed by followers of Bishop Guðmundr Arason, whose efforts to enforce principles of Gregorian reform had alienated most of Iceland's *goðar*, Snorri, in a rare show of solidarity among members of all six of Iceland's leading families, joined in a 1209 attack on the farm/episcopal see of Hólar.[29] After the raid, Snorri invited the bishop to stay with him at Reykjaholt.

Over the next decade, Snorri's wealth and authority continued to grow, and the Sturlungar overtook the Oddaverjar as Iceland's leading family. Snorri's rise, like that of his father, can be largely attributed to his legal skills. Although rarely successful in preventing violence among his *þingmenn* or in his districts, Snorri proved adept at prosecuting offences and arbitrating settlements, to the increase of his wealth and reputation. His status as a legal expert was affirmed in his appointment to his first term as *lögsögumaðr* (1215–18), head of the *alþing* and commonwealth Iceland's only elective office. Snorri's most notable legal victory during his first term as lawspeaker occurred when he had Magnús Guðmundarson, the *allsherjargoði* or '*goði* of the supreme chieftaincy' sentenced to full outlawry.[30]

During his rise, Snorri had also cultivated foreign connections. By 1215, he had sent skaldic tributes abroad to King Ingi Bárðarson and his half-brother jarl Hákon galinn ('the mad').[31] The jarl responded by sending Snorri gifts and an invitation to visit him in Norway.[32] By the time Snorri found the opportunity to travel to Norway, however, both the jarl and his brother the king had died, and a new monarch, the fourteen-year-old Hákon Hákonarson, purported grandson of Sverrir and cousin of Ingi, had ascended to the throne. In the fall of 1218, Snorri, after giving his *goðorð*s to his brother Þórðr to administer and marrying his only legitimate daughter Hallbera to the minor chieftain Árni óreiða Magnússon, sailed for Norway.[33] It was also around this time that a long-building dispute between the Oddaverjar and Norway erupted. Páll Sæmundarson, a grandson of Jón Loptsson, had perished in 1216 in a storm off Norway's coast after being intimidated into sailing from Björgyn. In retaliation, Sæmundr Jónsson demanded compensation from all merchants from this city then in Iceland, and, in the same fall that Snorri set sail, Sæmundr's seizure of their property led to the killing of his brother Ormr and nephew Jón.[34] Snorri is reported to have been unaware of these killings when he left for Norway, where he was received hospitably by jarl Skúli, Hákon's regent and half-brother of the deceased King Ingi. Snorri first visited with Skúli, and then travelled east to visit a noblewoman to whom he delivered poetry.[35] After the summer of 1219, Snorri returned west to stay with Skúli.

Snorri does not appear to have actually met King Hákon until he had been in Norway well over a year. The first hint Sturla gives about dealings between the two is his statement that Snorri, after two winters with Skúli, received the title of *skutilsveinn* from the king and jarl, a substantial but not unheard of honour for a distinguished Icelandic guest.[36] In 1220, when Snorri was preparing to sail home, the conflict between the Oddaverjar and Norwegian merchants was still going strong, and Norway's rulers were giving serious thought to invading Iceland.[37] Though many opposed this action, it was, according to Sturla, Snorri's promise to sway his fellow chieftains to accept the king's sovereignty that proved decisive in dissuading Hákon and Skúli from this plan.[38] Snorri was now made a *lendr maðr* of the king's court – and this *was* an unprecedented honour for an Icelander – and it was agreed that he should deliver his son Jón as 'a hostage to the jarl, until matters turned out as had been stipulated.'[39] Before sailing home, Snorri composed poetry for Skúli, for which the jarl rewarded him richly.[40]

If upon his return Snorri was expecting gratitude for his efforts on Iceland's behalf, he was to be disappointed. Especially displeased by his dealings with Norway's rulers were relatives of the murdered Ormr Jónsson, led by Ormr's son-in-law Björn Þorvaldsson of the Haukdælir. In addition to physical intimidation, Snorri was met with lampoons of his poetry for Skúli. Snorri aligned himself in this conflict with a junior member of the Oddaverjar, who was responsible for Björn's death in 1221 and was sent into exile in the summer of 1222. In that same summer, Snorri fulfilled part of his pledge to the king by sending to Norway his son Jón, accompanied by his son-in-law Árni óreiða. Skúli took a liking to Jón and treated his 'hostage' well. Also in 1222, Snorri was elected to his second term as lawspeaker, a post he held until 1231.

This decade saw further expansion in the circles of Snorri's friends and enemies, as well as increased tensions within his family. By 1228, Snorri had as
sons-in-law prominent members of three of Iceland's leading families, Gizurr
Þorvaldsson of the Haukdælir, Þorvaldr Snorrason of the Vatnsfirðingar, and
Kolbeinn Arnórsson of the Ásbirningar, and had made for himself a lasting
'partnership' with Hallveig Ormsdóttir, widow of Björn Þorvaldsson, granddaughter of Jón Loptsson, and Iceland's richest woman. Probably Snorri's
chief adversary during this period of alliance building was another of his
nephews named Sturla, this one the son of Sigvatr. Though the course of
Snorri's and Sturla Sigvatsson's conflict is too complex to relate in detail, it is
worth describing a few of the more dramatic moments. In late 1222, Sæmundr
Jónsson died, and it was requested that Snorri direct the division of his
property. In fulfilling this duty, Snorri proved particularly zealous in securing
the inheritance of Sæmundr's youthful daughter Solveig. Whatever Snorri's
designs on Solveig, they were cut short when Sturla Sigvatsson married her.
As Sturla Þórðarson relates: 'Snorri became displeased when he learned of
Sturla's wife-taking, and it seemed to men that he had intended something different.'[41] In 1226, Snorri, bent on establishing his son Jón after his return from
Norway, joined his brother Þórðr in bringing a series of lawsuits against their
nephew Sturla Sigvatsson at the *alþing*, with the aim of regaining possession
of the Snorrungagoðorð. Their action ended successfully in 1227, when Þórðr
took over a third and Jón murtr two-thirds of the Sturlungar's ancestral chieftaincy. In the late summer of 1228, continuing resentment over the forced
transfer of the Snorrungagoðorð contributed to the death of one of Snorri's
eminent sons-in-law, when Þorvaldr Snorrason was burned in his hall by allies
of Sturla Sigvatsson. This crime was avenged in 1229 when Þorvaldr's sons
burned Sturla's own farmstead to the ground while he was away from home,
an attack that Snorri was suspected of helping to plan.[42]

Just as matters between uncle and nephew seemed to reach a point of no
return, their animosity unexpectedly cooled. Sturla and Þorvaldr's sons
reached a settlement, and 'now things improved between Snorri and Sturla,
and Sturla was then a long while in Reykjaholt and gave much thought to having saga-books written after those books, which Snorri had put together.'[43]
Peace proved fleeting, however. First, Snorri received word that his son Jón,
who had returned to Norway and Skúli's service, had been killed in a drunken
brawl in which Gizurr Þorvaldsson had played a suspicious part; perhaps
owing to this turn of events, Gizurr and Snorri's daughter Ingibjörg separated
in 1231. Next, Sturla Sigvatsson broke his truce with the sons of Þorvaldr
Snorrason, ambushing and killing them as they travelled to meet with Snorri in
1232. It is told that after the deed 'Sturla and his men ... talked about how

Snorri would like these killings, and whether he would compose [poetry] about them.'[44] While Snorri was livid, he took no action for these killings, and indeed he profited by them – his grandson Einarr inherited Þorvaldr's property and authority, both of which Snorri, as Einarr's guardian, gave in 1233 to his son Órækja to administer. This decision would prove, as Jón Jóhannesson puts it, 'highly injudicious.'[45]

At that summer's *alþing*, Snorri surprised everyone by allying with Kolbeinn ungi Arnórsson, who had always been a closer friend to Sigvatr and Sturla, Kolbeinn's neighbours in the north quarter, than to Snorri. Although Kolbeinn had separated from Snorri's daughter Hallbera before she died in 1231, he nonetheless acquiesced to the latter's audacious claims on his property and authority.[46] To redress the failure of the union that had linked them, the two also agreed to join Órækja to Kolbeinn's sister. This marriage was, however, nearly called off when Snorri refused to travel north for the event, probably to avoid his own brother and nephew. Though Snorri salvaged the match by agreeing to give Órækja and his bride wealth plus control over Stafaholt and its church, he in the end only angered Kolbeinn more by reneging on this promise, sending Órækja and his new daughter-in-law to live instead in Vatnsfjörðr, as mentioned above.

Also in 1232, a letter arrived from Norway's archbishop summoning Sigvatr and his son Sturla to answer for an assault on Bishop Guðmundr a decade earlier. It was decided that Sturla should go to answer the charges, and he set sail the next year. Sturla first stayed with Skúli, and then travelled to Denmark and Rome, where he received from Pope Gregory IX absolution for his and his father's sins. On his return trip, he was hosted by King Hákon and, according to his cousin's saga, 'talked with him about many things.'[47] During Sturla's two-year absence, a series of dizzying twists and reversals once again reconfigured Iceland's political landscape. Suffice it to say that Kolbeinn's and Snorri's alliance had withered, hostilities between Sigvatr and Kolbeinn had blossomed, and Órækja had been tramping through everyone's 'gardens,' including those of his father and uncles. The situation was simplified somewhat by the departure for Norway and then Rome of Kolbeinn ungi, whose absence in the north allowed the recently returned Sturla Sigvatsson to focus his energies southward, towards the territories of his kinsmen. In the spring of 1236, he and his father marched on Snorri, an action they justified by saying that they 'wanted that he should compensate them for those crimes which Órækja, his son, had done.'[48] Although Snorri gathered a force to defend his lands, he ended up fleeing southward, permitting Sturla and Sigvatr to seize Reykjaholt and lay claim to much of Snorri's holdings in March of 1236. Sturla then arranged a meeting with Órækja, but he betrayed Snorri's son and had him mutilated, leaving him wounded in the eyes and minus a testicle. Órækja fled to Norway just as Kolbeinn ungi returned.[49]

The year was now 1237, and with Kolbeinn only just back, the recent deaths of Þorvaldr Gizurarson of the Haukdælir (1235) and Þórðr Sturluson (1237), Órækja recovering abroad, and Snorri having essentially forfeited his realm, Sturla Sigvatsson and Gizurr Þorvaldsson had emerged as Iceland's most powerful *goðar*. Sturla's position was soon undermined, however, by his father's decision to restore Kolbeinn peacefully to his possessions in the north, and in the spring Snorri, his cousin Þorleifr Þórðarson of Garðar, and his nephew Óláfr Þórðarson gathered men for an attack on Sturla.[50] Snorri's resolve failed before the plan was carried out, however, and he withdrew even further south. Sturla easily defeated the force led by Þorleifr of Garðar and Óláfr and ordered both to go to Norway and submit themselves to the king.[51] They were joined on this journey by Snorri, who, having run out of land in the south to flee into, decided it was time he paid Norway another visit.

Snorri's second trip to Norway lasted from 1237 to 1239. He seems never to have met with Hákon during this time, but stayed in Niðaróss with Skúli's son Pétr and then with the duke himself (Skúli had been elevated to that rank in early 1237 by the king in a last-ditch effort to satisfy his growing ambitions).[52] Back in Iceland, Sturla Sigvatsson bullied Gizurr Þorvaldsson into pledging to sail to Norway as well.[53] But instead of going abroad, Gizurr made an alliance with Kolbeinn ungi. The clouds finally burst in the summer of 1238 at the battle of Örlygsstaðir, the largest ever fought on Icelandic soil, in which Sturla Sigvatsson, two of his brothers, and his father lost their lives.[54] When news of the slaughter of the Sturlungar reached Norway in the fall, Snorri was shaken, and King Hákon was particularly troubled by news of Sturla Sigvatsson's death, because 'Sturla and he had made those plans, that he should bring the land under King Hákon, and the king should make him chieftain over the land.'[55]

Despite the fact that Gizurr and Kolbeinn now controlled much of Iceland, Snorri resolved to sail home in 1239. This decision was in open defiance of Hákon, who, having lost his chief agent in Iceland, sent out letters in which he 'forbade all those Icelanders to sail that summer. They showed Snorri the letters, and he answers thus: "I will sail out."'[56] As Sigurður Nordal has observed, such conviction seems out of character for someone who had so recently, so readily, and so often fled before his foes, and it is likely that Snorri was emboldened by his renewed ties to Duke Skúli, who was on the brink of declaring himself king and openly rebelling against Hákon.[57] According to Sturla Þórðarson, it was now that rumours of Snorri having secretly received the title of jarl from Skúli began to circulate.[58] While Sturla claims not to believe these reports, he leaves little doubt as to which side his uncle had chosen in the impending contest for Norways's throne. Unfortunately for Snorri, it was to be the wrong side: Skúli was killed in May of 1240, freeing the king to turn his attention to any intractable Icelanders who had managed to escape his grasp.[59]

Upon arriving back in Iceland, Snorri moved back to Reykjaholt with Hallveig, and even resumed his role as legal arbitrator, helping to reach a settlement between Þorleifr of Garðar, who along with Óraækja had returned with Snorri, and Sturla Sigvatsson's surviving supporters. Even after news of Skúli's defeat and death must have reached Iceland, Snorri gave no outward sign that he feared unwanted attention from Hákon or Gizurr Þorvaldsson, the king's new favourite in Iceland. However, the death of Hallveig in the summer of 1241 set in motion a chain of events that would lead to Snorri's own. When Hallveig's sons Klængr and Ormr came to Snorri to divide their mother's property, he proved difficult to deal with. The brothers turned for aid to their uncle Gizurr, who had in the previous summer received letters from Hákon (delivered by Árni óreiða, another of Snorri's former sons-in-law) in which the king commanded

> that Gizurr should force Snorri to go abroad, whether that seemed to him acceptable or not, or, as another choice, kill him because he had left against the ban of the king. King Hákon called Snorri a traitor against him. Gizurr said that he wanted on no account to disobey the king's letter, but says he knows that Snorri would not willingly go abroad.[60]

Spurred to action by his nephews, Gizurr moved to execute the king's orders, and on the night of 23 September 1241 he led a troop of men stealthily into Reykjaholt. Snorri was alerted by the sound of Gizurr's men breaking into the house in which he slept. He managed to slip out and hide in the cellar of a nearby storehouse, where, however, he was betrayed by the priest Arnbjörn. Gizurr, who seems never to have intended to offer Snorri the king's choice between exile or death, nevertheless excused himself from performing the deed, sending a group of otherwise unremarkable men to deal with Snorri. Sturla offers this blunt account of his uncle's last moments:

> After that they became aware of where Snorri was. And they, Markús Marðarson, Símon knútr, Árni beiskr, Þorsteinn Guðinason, and Þórarinn Ásgrímsson, went into the cellar. Símon knútr bade Árni to strike him. 'You shall not strike,' said Snorri. 'Strike,' said Símon. 'You shall not strike,' said Snorri. After that, Árni gave him his death-blow, and both he and Þorsteinn struck at him.[61]

Snorri the Author

By now, one yawning gap in my account of Snorri's life is surely apparent, namely the near absence of any discussion of his production of prose texts. The reason for this is that, aside from Sturla Þórðarson's mention of Sturla Sigvatsson's desire to copy some of his uncle's 'saga-books,' he says nothing about Snorri's literary activities or products. This silence has long sustained, as Faulkes puts it, 'the sneaking suspicion that Snorri may not in fact be the author, or even the compiler, of the works attributed to him.'[62] Aside from Sturla's isolated reference to Snorri's sagas – which might refer to material associated with *Heimskringla* or perhaps *Egils saga*, but almost certainly not the *Edda* – our only real documentation for Snorri's involvement with 'his' texts is found in manuscripts containing those works. Even this evidence, however, is sporadic and ambiguous. Of the manuscripts containing all four parts of the *Edda*, only *Codex Upsaliensis*, or *Uppsalabók*, attributes the work as a whole to Snorri: 'This book is called *Edda*. Snorri Sturluson has set it together according to that manner in which it is here arranged. First is [told] about the *æsir* and Ymir, next *Skáldskaparmál* and the names of many things, last *Háttatal* which Snorri has composed about King Hákon and Duke Skúli.'[63] The phrase used here to describe Snorri's activity, *setja saman*, is the same used by Sturla in *Íslendinga saga*. Literally it means 'to set together,' and its vagueness has given rise to disagreement over the nature of Snorri's role in the *Edda*'s production. While some translate *setja saman* simply as 'to compose,' others understand it in the sense of 'to compile,' implying that Snorri did not so much create the *Edda* as edit and arrange previously existing material, and still others take it to mean that Snorri *had* the *Edda* put together, and thus regard him as supervisor or patron of those who actually produced the text. [64] Even more pronounced doubts exist concerning Snorri's responsibility for his other purported works. The earliest explicit testimony we possess for *Heimskringla*'s authorship comes from two sixteenth-century Norwegian translations, both of which twice ascribe the collection to Snorri.[65] In the case of *Egils saga*, evidence for Snorri's authorship is entirely circumstantial.[66]

Setting aside questions about Snorri's responsibility for the last two works, I wish to argue that the use of *setja saman* to describe Snorri's role in the *Edda*'s production in no way obligates us to regard him as a supervisor of scribes or assistants, or mere patron or commissioner of this text. In the passage from *Uppsalabók* given above, different terms describe Snorri's production of *Háttatal* and that of the *Edda* as a whole. In the former case, it is not said that Snorri *saman setta* the poem, but that he *hefir ort*, 'has composed' it. These phrases were used by medieval Icelanders to distinguish between the production of prose versus poetry. In neither case, as M.I. Steblin-Kamenskij has argued, do producers receive credit for the material of which they spoke.[67] The form of one's speech, however, and the style of one's work were viewed as individual and artistic feats that, if done well, were worthy of recognition. It was too bad for saga writers, then, that their creations lacked form or, more accurately, employed the unremarkable language of everyday speech. Poetry, however, was regarded as exceptional and distinguished speech; thus, while poets received no more credit than did saga writers for their work's content, they were admired for their ability to cloak that of which they spoke in memorable and pleasing form.[68] It is owing to this differential evaluation of form that skaldic compositions are almost always and sagas almost never credited to named producers.[69] More to the point, this explains why Sturla Þórðarson frequently describes Snorri's composing of poetry, both his praise-poems for Norway's elite and the *lausavísur*, or 'occasional verses,' he recited at home, while virtually ignoring his writing of prose. Not only did Snorri's prose works, unlike his poetic ones, play little appreciable role in the events and feuds of which he was part, they were not considered truly distinctive and therefore noteworthy creations of their producer.

Thus, even if the *Uppsalabók* compiler's use of the phrase *setja saman* cannot help us determine with any precision the nature of Snorri's role in the *Edda*'s creation, it does not preclude identification of Snorri as the text's primary producer. I find little cause, therefore, not to join most scholars in giving Snorri the benefit of the doubt in this matter. I am not, of course, insisting that Snorri personally selected and/or physically recorded every word of the *Edda* as it now exists in any of its manuscript forms. On the contrary, it is entirely possible and, considering the sheer bulk of *Heimskringla*, probable that Snorri employed the services of scribes or 'research assistants.' What I am suggesting is that it ultimately makes little difference whether Snorri wrote the *Edda* in isolation, dictated it to scribes, or collaborated with others, so long as we can assume that his was the guiding will behind its production. Margaret Clunies Ross has suggested that 'most of us who write about *Snorra Edda* probably use the name "Snorri Sturluson" as a kind of shorthand to refer to a shaping unity of purpose that we detect in the works attributed to the man so named.'[70] While this statement comes near to articulating the position I am advocating, there are two reasons that I cannot include myself among those it describes. First, Clunies Ross's suggestion that a 'unity of purpose' or, as she also describes it, an 'intellectual integrity' underlies the *Edda* conflicts with my claim that Snorri's purposes and strategies evolved over the course of producing this text.[71] I will insist and seek to show that a single agent does not entail a singular purpose. Second, the way in which I intend to work the *Edda* into Snorri's biography requires a much stronger affirmation than Clunies Ross gives that the figure responsible for this text was the man named Snorri Sturluson, and none other. Most scholars have been unwilling to make this strong a claim because of the contradictions they perceive between the Snorri depicted in contemporary sagas and the personality and interests they find in the works attributed to him. It is my intention, however, to dissolve such contradictions by demonstrating that a close and explicable relationship existed between Snorri's literary and extra-literary practices. Rather than attempt vainly to establish at the outset of my analysis that Snorri is author of the *Edda*, however, I will simply suggest at this point that my entire project is a contribution to the case for Snorri's more-or-less direct authorship (i.e., composition and/or close supervision) of this product.

Finally, I will suggest where I think Snorri's literary activity best fits into the biographical sketch that I have given above. In spite of the lack of hard evidence linking Snorri to his works, scholars have been far from shy about speculating about when, in what order, and under what circumstances he wrote them. Generally, the *Edda* is considered to have been the first of Snorri's literary products.[72] For a long while, it was assumed that the *Edda*'s sections were written in the order in which they appear in manuscripts containing all four parts, but since Elias Wessén's groundbreaking 1940 study the consensus has been that Snorri wrote its parts in reverse order: *Háttatal*, *Skáldskaparmál*, *Gylfaginning*, *Formáli*.[73] According to this view, Snorri began to compose *Háttatal* shortly after his return from Norway in 1220, probably finishing it and its commentary sometime in 1222–3. While many have suggested that the rest of the *Edda* was completed in short order, say by 1225, others, most notably Faulkes, have argued that work on the text continued on and off for the rest of Snorri's life, and that he may have left parts of it in an unfinished state at the time of his sudden demise.[74] As for *Heimskringla*, Snorri is thought to have begun work on his compilation of *konungasögur* also during the years 1220–5 and to have finished this project by early 1236, when he was driven from Reykjaholt by Sturla and Sigvatr. The dates that have been suggested for *Egils saga* are, like most everything else associated with this text, little more than guesses; while many believe it too was a work of the 1220s, it has been dated as early as 1200 and as late as 1239–41.[75]

The bulk, then, of Snorri's prose is believed to have been produced in the decade and a half following his return from his first voyage abroad. These were years during which Snorri served his second term as *lögsögumaðr*, managed vast estates, participated in numerous altercations, lawsuits, and property divisions, supervised three marriages and four separations between his daughters and various notables (not to mention the partnerships he arranged for himself and Órækja), reached the height of his authority, wealth, and influence, and ultimately had most of this power torn from his grasp. Given all this, it is difficult to subscribe to Sigurður Nordal's description of 'those thirty years, when [Snorri] had his home at Reykjaholt, and was allowed to sit there in good peace, 1206–1236,' a period that supposedly afforded him the opportunity to produce his works and turn his home into a centre of learning and culture to rival Oddi.[76] Indeed, this statement seems to owe more to Bourdieu's scholastic fallacy, the idea that works of culture spring from leisure and disinterest rather than competition and self-interest, than to its author's extensive knowledge of Snorri's life. This book will demonstrate that Snorri's cultural/literary activity cannot be treated in isolation or as a respite from the worldly pursuits and interests that dominated his life during his years at Reykjaholt. It will show that the production of the *Edda* had as much to do with Snorri's political aspirations, and was therefore deemed as worthy of his time and energy, as the shady lawsuits, shaky alliances, and cynical marriage arrangements that otherwise filled his time. First, however, chapter 3 will examine more closely the latter set of activities, those that comprised Snorri's attempts to accrue, deploy, convert, and defend his politically effective forms of capital in the domestic field of Iceland, where his store of cultural and poetic capital, while still relevant, was of less importance.

3 Snorri at Home: Converting Capital in Commonwealth Iceland

As chapter 2 made clear, Snorri was throughout his life committed to gaining power and influence in the political arenas of Iceland and Norway. While this chapter focuses on Snorri's domestic practice, it must be borne in mind that he was active and invested in two overlapping arenas wherein different forms of capital, only some of which were transferable from one arena to the other, were effective. Of these forms, two in particular, both of which can be treated as varieties of cultural/linguistic capital, are critical to an examination of Snorri's practice: in Iceland, this was legal capital, and in Norway poetic/literary capital.

William Ian Miller remarks in his book on Icelandic feud and law:

> Historians of medieval England and continental Europe have the luxury of being able to assume that their intended audience is conversant with some of the basics of their topics ... But historians whose field is early Iceland are granted no such grace ... Even the few specialists in the field expect to be reminded with each book they read when Iceland was settled and what a family saga is.[1]

Despite appreciating Miller's irony, I do think it necessary before examining Snorri's accumulation, expenditure, and conversion of capital in his domestic sphere to provide some historical and cultural context. My selective review will focus on the functions and role of *goðar* in Icelandic governance and law, particularly on the semi-official duties and privileges that distinguished them from other members of the Icelandic polity. I will also, before turning to Snorri, scrutinize important episodes in the career of his father, Sturla Þórðarson. Contrasting the strategies and resources available to and exploited by each will prove instructive in two respects. First, since the two decades separating the end of Sturla's and the beginning of Snorri's careers correspond roughly with the inauguration of the so-called Sturlung age, this comparison provides an efficient means of highlighting transformations in Iceland's political field that emerged during this period. Second, setting father's and son's careers side by side will permit us to perceive differences between them that result not only from the contours of the fields in which they operated, but also from their early exposure to and accumulation of forms of capital, in short, those attributable to their divergent habitus.

Goðar and the Law: The Icelandic Context

The most distinctive feature of Icelandic society from the settlement period of 870–930 to its loss of independence in 1262–4 was its lack of a king.[2] What it had instead was a body of law, of an intricacy perhaps unmatched in medieval Europe. The commonwealth's central institution was the *alþing*, an annual assembly, market, and social event, the legislative court of which, the *lögrétta*, formulated and reviewed Iceland's laws.[3] Its voting members were called *goðar* (this term is often translated as 'chieftain,' though its literal meaning is closer to 'priest'),[4] the holders of thirty-six *goðorð*s ('chieftaincies'), and it was presided over by the *lögsögumaðr* or lawspeaker.[5] Early Icelandic government's most important judicial forums were the *várþing*s, spring assemblies convened by sets of three *goðar*, each of whom selected twelve *bœndr* (sg. *bóndi*), or farmers, to serve as judges on an ad hoc basis. Around 965, increasingly apparent flaws in this system compelled the *lögrétta* to divide Iceland into judicial quarters and to establish quarter-courts (*fjórðungsdómar*) at the *alþing*.[6] Their judges were still chosen by *goðar*, but were assigned to quarter-courts by lot, ensuring less regional bias in their findings. *Várþing*s remained in operation, and three were assigned to each quarter except for the north, which for demographic reasons received four. To address this imbalance, three 'honorary' *goðar*, who held no *goðorð* and could not select jurors for quarter-courts but who held voting rights in the *lögrétta*, were assigned to the other three quarters.[7] The last major adjustment to the system was the creation c. 1005 of the *fimtardómr*, a 'fifth-court' of appeals.[8] Iceland's conversion to Christianity at the *alþing* of 999 or 1000 had, aside from the addition of its two bishops (sans advisors) to the *lögrétta* in the early 1100s, little effect upon legal structures. After this final modification, Iceland's political system remained essentially unaltered until its loss of independence to the Norwegian monarchy in the mid-thirteenth century.[9]

Clearly, *goðar* occupied the theoretical and practical centre of Iceland's legal system. A *goði* was, simply, any *bóndi* who owned all or part of a *goðorð*. *Goðorð*s, while assigned to specific quarters, were not defined in terms of land, but were property that could be transferred or divided through inheritance, sale, etc. Possession of a *goðorð* entitled its owner to three prerogatives, two of which, the right to vote in the *lögrétta* and to appoint *várþing* and quarter-court juries, have been described. The third and perhaps most important was allegiance of a *mannaforráð* or body of *þingmenn*. In Iccland, every *bóndi* owning a certain amount of wealth was obliged to attach himself and his household to a chieftain residing in the same quarter, and in this way all members of society were attached directly or indirectly to a *goði*.[10] This pact was significant given commonwealth Iceland's lack of an executive power. The enforcement of law was a private rather than a state responsibility, and success in legal matters often depended upon the manpower one could muster. Possession of a chieftaincy thus brought several advantages: first and foremost, a *goði* was guaranteed to enter into conflicts with ready-made bands of supporters; second, they were in a better position to enlist the aid of other *goðar* and their bodies of *þingmenn*; and third, although there was no social fraction or institution endowed with a monopoly on the legitimate use of violence in medieval Iceland, 'certain people had a presumption of legitimacy,' and these, more often than not, were *goðar*.[11] In sum, the commonwealth's legal system was constituted in such a way that non-*goðar* who sought redress through the courts or less formal mechanisms nearly always found it necessary to secure the support of one or more *goðar* if they were to have any hope of winning their cases, or of enforcing any victories won.[12]

Goðar intervened in others' conflicts as advocates or as arbitrators. Cases in which *goðar* acted as the former could involve comprehensive acts of delegation: often, the advocate became the principal litigant, with all potential winnings (and risks) falling to him.[13] That Icelanders quarrelling over land or seeking compensation for insults and injuries were willing to hand over these very spoils to proxies suggests that such conflicts had intangible as well as tangible stakes, and that to defend the former one often had to sacrifice the latter. The principal intangible prize was honour. Old Norse has several terms for this concept, *sæmð*, *sómi*, and *virðing* being the most common. While it is not always easy to tease out the semantic distinctions being made in uses of these terms, the importance of gaining and maintaining honour in medieval Iceland is beyond dispute.[14] As Miller observes, 'one's status depended on the condition of one's honor, for it was in the game of honor that rank and reputation was attained and retained. Honor was at stake in virtually every social interaction.'[15] The need to defend not only one's person and property but also one's honour applied to non-*goðar* as well as *goðar*, and one of the surest ways to lose honour was to ignore offences or forfeit one's rights. This game of honour forced non-*goðar* into an especially precarious position: with little hope of winning suits or enforcing claims without the support of *goðar*, low-ranking Icelanders were effectively forced to choose between the options of preserving their honour by sacrificing potential material winnings, or of losing both.

Based on the foregoing, one might assume that, once advocates were selected and support gathered, most disputes ended with a ruling by a jury of *goðar*-appointed *bœndr*. In reality, this was the less usual outcome. Just as lawsuits tended to become disputes between *goðar*, resolution of conflicts typically ended up in the hands of chieftains. This occurred through arbitration, the submission of a dispute to a third party by opponents who have agreed, often with conditions, to accept the decision reached.[16] The factor that most encouraged litigants to appeal to arbitration was the broader range of compromises and sanctions available. In serious disputes permitted to run their course through the courts, there were only two likely outcomes for defendants: exoneration or a sentence of lesser or full outlawry. In arbitration, however, fines and less stringent forms of outlawry (with loss of neither property nor *goðorðs*) were common.[17] Such flexibility made it easier for arbitrators to satisfy honour on both sides of a conflict.

There were three major types of benefits available to *goðar* who acted as advocates or arbitrators. First, there were irregular but potentially substantial material profits.[18] Second, these roles provided *goðar* with a means to acquire and defend their own honour. Quarrels between farmers often served as pretexts for bouts of honour between *goðar*, and the talent to effect peaceful resolutions between litigants was highly respected. Performance of these functions was not without risk, however: while being asked to serve as advocate or arbitrator acknowledged one's skills, tact, and honourable (i.e., disinterested) purposes, it was also always a public test of these abilities and intentions, and could, if the job were botched, lead to considerable loss of prestige. The third benefit for *goðar* acting as advocates or arbitrators were these roles' capacity to legitimate their disproportionate possession of wealth, power, and influence. As Miller notes,

> the most noteworthy feature of ranking and class in Iceland was the paucity of objective, external, and unambiguous juridical markers of status and hierarchy. Except for ecclesiastical office, there were no titles beyond Lawspeaker and *goði*, and even the latter was not without ambiguities occasioned by the fractured ownership of the office and the real power of some local big *bœndr*.[19]

Thus, while *goðorðs* granted owners a title and, in a limited sense, office, *goðar* did not enjoy a clearly defined quantum of power, but had personally to forge and renew ties of obligation and domination with social inferiors. In addition to legal practices, *goðar* maintained such ties through protection, feasts, gifts, loans, and other kinds of hospitality and charity, all forms of what Bourdieu calls 'symbolic violence':

> In a society in which overt violence ... meets with collective reprobation ... symbolic violence, the gentle, invisible form of violence, which is never recognized as such ... the violence of credit, confidence, obligation, personal loyalty, hospitality, gifts, gratitude, piety – in short, all the virtues honoured by the code of honour – cannot fail to be seen as the most economical mode of domination.[20]

While many of a *goði*'s activities involved misrecognition of domination, this was particularly true of their legal practices. As Jesse Byock argues, 'advocacy ... had both overt and covert functions. The overt function was to provide clients and their leaders with a mechanism for arriving at the consensus necessary to settle disputes in a way that satisfied law and honor. The covert function was to allow leaders to maintain or increase their own power.'[21] Similarly, arbitration allowed *goðar* to earn prestige and rewards while acting in the name of universal interests such as the satisfaction of justice and promotion of peace – and if their intentions were sincere, this in no way alters the nature of these acts as acts of self-promotion. On the contrary, part of the collective, subjective misrecognition of these practices that made their objective truth as mechanisms of domination possible was the inclination of both *goðar* and those they exploited to perceive the symbolic violence exercised through legal mediation as altruism.

Goðar's privileged access to legal capital rested on two foundations, one objective (rooted in institutions and structures) and one embodied (rooted in the habitus of agents). As for the first, *goðar*, merely by possessing the name, were guaranteed legal prerogatives. *Goðar* could also, however, go beyond institutionally defined rights and duties by using their skills and knowledge to reap profits in juridical markets. Here, we are no longer talking about privileges attached to a rank or title, but rather exploitation of competencies, cognitive as well as performative, typically acquired by (future) *goðar* through formative exposure and experience.[22] Possession and deployment of such skills were ultimately, however, less important for their role in determining the outcome of disputes than in restricting the pool of agents who could engage in legal practice in the first place. In short, the performative demands coupled with the Byzantine complexity of commonwealth law ensured that only those with long-standing exposure to or extensive training in the legal sphere could become full participants in it.

Typically, the institutional and embodied forms of legal privilege went hand in hand. Since profit deriving from control over a set of linguistic skills

> results from the fact that the supply of products (or speakers) corresponding to a given level of linguistic (or, more generally, cultural) qualification is lower than it would be if all speakers had benefited from the conditions of acquisition of the legitimate competence to the same extent as the holders of the rarest competence, [profits are] ... logically distributed as a function of the chances of access to these conditions, that is, as a function of the position occupied in the social structure.[23]

Put simply, access to scarce cultural/linguistic competencies correlates with elevated social status. It is important to note, however, that the habitus and name of *goði* are not the same thing, and that ownership of one does not guarantee ownership of the other. An agent who buys rather than inherits a *goðorð* would hold the legal rights of a *goði*, but might lack the skills to inspire others to seek him out as an advocate. On the other hand, there were certainly agents who did not own a *goðorð* but possessed a high degree of legal expertise; although lacking certain privileges, such agents could enjoy profits associated with legal mediation.

It was, however, when the name and habitus of a *goði* converged in a single agent that optimal conditions were met for the conversion of legal into symbolic capital in Iceland. Such men, endowed with the social and cultural capital needed to dominate the legal field, held the greatest advantage in the *þing*, the market wherein political alliances were negotiated with greatest regularity and forms of politically effective capital most often exchanged hands, and where both interactions unfolded in a manner perceived as legitimate.[24] Inheritors of *goðorð*s, then, were in the best position, owing to their dominance over institutional and embodied forms of legal capital, to regulate and profit from the legitimate conversion and transfer of most other forms of capital effective in Iceland's field of power. This is an observation to bear in mind as we turn to our analysis of the careers of two *goðar* and skilled lawmen alike, Sturla Þórðarson and his son Snorri.

Sturla: Pursuing the Intangible

Stephen Tranter considers Sturla's career to epitomize a period of drastic transformation of Icelandic society. In his eponymous saga, 'Sturla uses lawsuits as a means of aggrandizing his own power, and that of his family ...

Power has become more important than considerations of justice.'[25] Whether justice ever truly trumped power in medieval Iceland, the twelfth century was a time when the stability of *goðar/þingmenn* bonds and the capacity of law to regulate conflict weakened, and the stage was set for the rise of chieftains whose authority was more territorial and dictatorial in nature. During Sturla's life, however, such changes remained largely beneath the surface, and he operated, or saw himself operating, in essentially the political and legal context described above.[26]

Sturla was not an especially rich or important man at the outset of his career. As depicted in his saga, his rise in Iceland's political sphere depended, to a degree unrivalled in saga literature, on his legal talents. Even so, his saga gives us no sense of the manner in which Sturla acquired this expertise. About all that can be said on this matter is that Sturla, as the son of a *goði*, was in a position to learn the rules, procedures, and loopholes of Icelandic law from an early age, and that he proved adroit at exploiting this knowledge. His legal practice was characterized by a two-front strategy. In the first place, he courted the allegiance and admiration of social inferiors, his own *þingmenn* as well as others, through his willingness to promote their interests in disputes. In a manner consistent with the discussion of advocacy above, material as well as symbolic gains resulted from these interventions. In the first suit in which Sturla is known to have participated, he vigorously prosecuted the killing of one of his *þingmenn*, succeeding in winning not only a sentence of full outlawry but a large payment from those, including a powerful *goði*, who had harboured the killer.[27] In another episode, Sturla took up the defence of a son-in-law who had wounded another man. Despite the boast of Einarr Þorgilsson, the injured man's *goði*, that others 'would not often harm his *þingmenn*,' Sturla was able to bring a greater troop to their meeting, and Einarr ended up paying him a horse and ox in compensation.[28] Sturla later achieved a more significant victory over this same opponent when Álfr Örnólfsson appealed to Einarr, his *goði*, to help him obtain compensation for the wounding of his son by another of Einarr's *þingmenn*. As *goði* of both parties, Einarr should have worked to reach an amicable settlement; instead, he refused to support Álfr's action, and the farmer turned to Sturla for support. Sturla won the case and 'Álfr then shifted to *þing*-allegiance under Sturla.'[29] Here, we see Sturla, as Tranter describes, 'making a name for himself as a *goði* to whom one can turn for assistance and from whom one can expect effective help.'[30]

In the second place, Sturla used others' disputes as opportunities to challenge his social betters. Like most *goðar*, his aim in such instances was to increase his own prestige. If Sturla was at all atypical in this respect, it was in his eagerness to confront opponents whom most would have considered out of his league. Although in his prime Sturla was according to most objective standards the equal or near-equal of his opponents, he lagged behind rival *goðar* in the more subjective realm of public opinion, reputation, honour, etc. It therefore comes as no surprise that such measures of social standing became for Sturla the most attractive prizes to be won through legal action. Sturla's interest in less tangible stakes, and his willingness to sacrifice material profits in order to obtain them, are explicitly acknowledged in his saga. Both traits are on display in the first of his many disputes with the aforementioned Einarr Þorgilsson, son of one of the more powerful *goðar* of the time. In 1157, Einarr's sister Yngvildr was trying to hide from her brother the birth of an illegitimate daughter by Sturla's brother-in-law. In exchange for his aid in helping the couple abscond to Norway, Yngvildr transferred to Sturla all claims for money owed to her, and appointed him the principal in any cases brought against her or her estate. Einarr brought suit against Sturla for his role in the conspiracy, and in response Sturla charged Einarr with failing to pay a previous fine. Each managed to have the other sentenced to minor outlawry.[31] As litigants were responsible for enforcing sentences, each was obliged to hold a court of confiscation (*féránsdómr*) at the other's farmstead, or else admit defeat. Sturla was still a minor *goði* at this time, and he was only able to gather sixty men to attend the court at Einarr's farm. Einarr, however, brought over 350 men to Hvammr, and left one hundred at home. Although both courts were held without incident, Sturla took a great risk by going forth so outmanned. When chided for his rashness, 'Sturla said that he would not be thought the equal of Einarr, if he sat at home and would not hold courts of confiscation, and he said that it was hard to know which of them would there get the larger share.'[32] Of course, whatever people may have thought, Sturla was not Einarr's equal at that time. Even so, his determination to enforce his rights in this affair surely influenced public perception and contributed to the gradual reversal in their relative standing over the next few years.

The current dispute was far from over, however. The *féránsdómar* had been largely symbolic: no property was seized, and both outlaws remained at home. The next summer, after Sturla had already left for the *alþing*, Einarr attacked Hvammr, burning much of it to the ground. With matters getting so out of hand, pressure for reconciliation mounted at the *þing*. It was finally agreed that Bishop Klængr Þorsteinsson would arbitrate a settlement, although Sturla, suspecting the bishop of prejudice, insisted that he take 'the fifth-court's oath, that he had arbitrated an agreement on equal terms.'[33] The bishop ended up awarding Sturla a token judgment, after which Sturla made the following pronouncement: 'I esteem the bishop's oath as much as the Easter mass. I cannot measure that in wealth, but that is an honour for us. But most will call the fines not large and the arbitrations not lucrative.'[34] Clearly, what was more important for Sturla was not the sum awarded, but that the bishop, one of Iceland's most distinguished figures, had sworn that he had judged Einarr and Sturla as equals in the case submitted before him. Here again, we find Sturla displaying a canny awareness of the capacity of subjective measures – honour, esteem, and reputation – to balance, even outweigh, more tangible measures of social rank.

The last of Sturla's suits that I shall consider began with the deaths of Þórir inn auðgi ('the wealthy') Þorsteinsson and his wife Þorlaug overseas. The couple's inheritance was disputed by Þorlaug's father, the well-connected priest and *goði* Páll Sölvason, and Þórir's sister, who was supported by, among others, Sturla.[35] Sturla was attacked during a reconciliation meeting in 1180 by the hot-tempered, knife-wielding wife of Páll, Þorbjörg Bjarnadóttir, who tried to put out one of his eyes while shouting: 'Why should I not make you most like that one, whom you want most to be like – and that is Óðinn?'[36] Fortunately for Sturla, Þorbjörg's stroke was off, and he was wounded in the cheek. Demonstrating calculated restraint, Sturla agreed to delay seeking compensation and called for the negotiations to continue. But when Páll later granted him self-judgment Sturla proved less conciliatory, demanding a sum so outrageous that it 'seemed to all men a great wonder, when it came into his mind to pronounce such [a sum].'[37] Páll refused to pay, and further violence seemed inevitable.

Enter Jón Loptsson of Oddi, regarded by our sources and modern critics alike as medieval Iceland's most effective peace-maker.[38] Jón first joined this case as a supporter of Páll, because he 'did not find it fitting for powerful chieftains to contend against old and noble clerics.'[39] He also expressed readiness to intervene, threatening to have three of Sturla's associates killed for every one of Páll's who might be slain.[40] According to Peter Foote, Jón viewed Páll as a fellow 'member of a distinguished class … [whose] connections are with the "clerical gentry" … the old *goðar* who had adopted the new authority of the Church into their midst,' and so wished to check Sturla's outsized ambitions.[41] And yet, despite Jón's obvious bias against him, Sturla was urged by many to permit the Oddaverjar leader to arbitrate the dispute. The saga tells us that Sturla announced his decision in a remarkable speech at the *alþing*:

'The case was settled and self-judgment was granted to me by Páll. But now the most prominent men in Iceland are sought out so that this case might now be put to arbitration, which before was submitted to self-judgment. Now if an example can be found, that men have done such before, then it might be worth considering. But [taking into account] those men, who now involve themselves with the suit – I name first in this Jón Loptsson, who is the most distinguished man in this land, and all refer their lawsuits to him – then I do not know how else honour is now to be expected than to try whatever honour he will give me. Now it may be, that I lack the wits to look out for myself, but I would want to hold on to my honour.'[42]

Here again, Sturla is shown submitting his case to someone better disposed towards his opponent than himself, and willing to forgo material winnings in exchange for the honour that cooperation will bring him (and we need not puzzle over which shade of honour Sturla was most worried about, *virðing, sómi,* or *sæmð,* since he names them all in this speech). In effect, Sturla redefined a forced concession to an illegality as a free and unprecedented gesture of concern for the public good, a risky but shrewd bid to trade claims on material wealth for prestige.

To all appearances, the gamble worked. Jón lauded Sturla's high-mindedness, remarking that he 'spoke wisely and looked out for the interest of many. "But the fines," says Jón, "on Páll's side will be set aside, because they were raised [too] high."'[43] To soften the blow, however, Jón offered to foster Sturla's son Snorri at Oddi. Part of Jón's motive in this was surely to ensure that the deal held. For Sturla's part, however, Jón's gesture provided him with additional sources of honour that even he could hardly have anticipated. While the purpose and significance of fostering arrangements varied, the offer to foster another's son was most often viewed as a sign of submission; as a proverb from *Laxdæla saga* states, 'and that one is always called the lesser man, who fosters another's child.'[44] Still, in this case the arrangement was likely viewed, as Ciklamini has recognized, as 'a gesture of magnanimity' through which Iceland's most powerful *goði* recognized the rising status of Sturla and his family, and called upon others to do the same.[45]

Snorri: The Value of a Head Start

Sturla's 1181 deal with Jón Loptsson abruptly and radically altered the course of his youngest son's life. As a consequence of this bargain, Snorri's habitus became something altogether different from and, in terms of potential for social advancement, superior to that of his father (who had been fostered by a *bóndi*) or those of his siblings.[46] Sturla's lack of cultural acumen and the weakness of his ties to the social elite have often been noted. Ciklamini calls him 'an upstart chieftain,' and Foote observes that Sturla, in relation to Iceland's 'social and cultural aristocracy … is an upstart in the one, and apparently a total stranger in the other.'[47] This aristocracy, dubbed by Foote the 'clerical gentry,' was composed of families with close connections to the church and Norwegian royalty, and with cultural distinction derived from their capacity to combine native culture with continental literary models, both through study abroad and the establishment and patronage of centres of learning at home. Sturla's lack of privileged social connections, any sort of formal education, and the resulting want of cultural competency effectively denied him, no matter the stockpile of wealth, *þingmenn*, and legal victories he amassed, entry into this gentry. Sturla's marginal position resonates with Bourdieu's discussion of the nouveau riche in modern France, those who, while economically on a par with the upper bourgeoisie, did not receive a habitus that inculcated in them the tastes and dispositions of the social elite.[48] Sturla's not having been born into the position he eventually occupied in Iceland's social field cheapened the value of that position, prompting those who preceded him there to resist recognizing the legitimacy of his presence among them.

For Sturla, the effects of such cultural snobbery were lifelong – even Jón's recognition of his honour and goodwill could not compensate fully for his lack of legitimate culture and connections. Jón's gesture could do considerably more for Sturla's son, however. Sturla's arrangement to have the third son of his second wife fostered at Iceland's 'center of ecclesiastical and worldly learning' emerges as a clear case of intergenerational capital conversion.[49] The most obvious gains for Snorri were cultural. Through his transaction with Jón, Sturla effectively co-opted the cultural capital of a more distinguished family than his own, so as to combine in his son the amassed capital of two separate lineages.

The nature of the cultural resources available at Oddi and the extent to which Snorri exploited them are complex issues, and will be dealt with in chapters 4 and 5, which focus on the value of Snorri's cultural talents within the Norwegian market. In this chapter's discussion, it is more useful to treat the capital amassed through Snorri's fosterage as social, rather than cultural, gains. In other words, whatever the extent of Snorri's precocious internalization or mature realization of the cultural resources made available to him at Oddi, the more important point for examining his domestic career is that he was recognized by others as having had sustained and legitimate access to such resources. It was this recognition that afforded him a degree of access to the ranks of the Icelandic elite unrealizable for his father and less well-connected kin.

The relationships Snorri forged during the eighteen years he lived at Oddi were a resource only so long as his interests remained aligned with those of his foster-kin, and for the first stage of his career this alignment held. As mentioned in chapter 2, Snorri was just about *félauss*, penniless, when the time came for him to leave Oddi.[50] To remedy his situation, Snorri had recourse to marriage and law. His marriage to the daughter and heiress of Bersi inn auðgi Vermundarson was probably the most advantageous move he made in early adulthood, as it would result in his first *goðorð* and a huge increase in his material wealth. Since both his brother Þórðr and his foster-brother Sæmundr helped him to secure this match, Snorri in this instance made use of both his foster-family's long-standing social connections and his birth-family's rising status to extricate himself from a difficult situation.

The first true test of Snorri's loyalties came in 1200, when he entered into his first lawsuit, a property dispute between Snorri's foster-brother Sæmundr and Sigurðr Ormsson, a *goði* of the east quarter. Sigurðr enlisted the support of Kolbeinn Tumason of the Ásbirningar and Snorri's other full-brother Sigvatr, both of whom were based in the north. Snorri, now twenty years old, acted as the main representative of Oddaverjar interests in the preparation and execution of the case; it was he who summoned Sigurðr to court, and whom Sæmundr sent 'to Borgarfjörðr to call up his *þingmenn*, those who Jón, his father, had had, both many and good farmers.'[51] After Kolbeinn and Sigvatr failed to fulfil their promises of aid, Sigurðr Ormsson was sentenced to minor outlawry. Both parties gathered forces after this verdict, but Sigurðr was soon persuaded by the superior strength of Sæmundr's troop to submit the case to arbitration. In the end, arbitrators (including Páll, bishop of Skálholt and Sæmundr's half-brother) awarded the contested property to Sæmundr.

Sturla Þórðarson sums up the results of this contest thus: 'Sæmundr had honour from these cases. Kolbeinn Tumason liked these cases' outcomes ill, but Sigvatr worse.'[52] Sturla does not state what Snorri thought about this case, or what he gained from it, but we can surmise both. In this conflict, Snorri joined with his foster-family against his own kin, and it is not difficult to understand why. At this early point in his career, Snorri still controlled little in the way of politically effective resources. The material and social benefits of his marriage were as yet unrealized, and he and his wife still lived under Sæmundr's roof. Moreover, neither the case that Snorri prosecuted nor the men he led were his, but Sæmundr's. In letting Snorri act as his proxy in this dispute, Sæmundr probably meant to test the young man's abilities and loyalties alike; if so, Snorri passed with flying colours. For Snorri, this case was his first real opportunity to establish a name for himself in Iceland's legal field. And while Snorri's ability to take a central role in this dispute partly resulted from the legal training he must have received at Oddi, it was also made possible, like his marriage, by the social capital his upbringing had earned for him, a resource that authorized him to enter into a dispute among the upper echelon of Icelandic society as, if not quite an equal, then a trusted ally and delegate.

This dispute also provided a way for Snorri to get ahead in the contest for dominance in his own family. As Bourdieu writes: 'Among the determinants of dispositions one must take into account ... is the position ... within the family itself as a field.'[53] Under more normal circumstances – that is, if the opportunity for Sturla's act of intergenerational conversion had never presented itself – Snorri, the youngest of Sturla's sons, ought to have been struggling as a young adult merely to compensate for his material and social deficits vis-à-vis his older brothers. As things stood, it was his brothers who had to keep up with him. Recognizing the source of Snorri's advantages within the field of his birth-family permits us to account for his alignment with Oddaverjar and against Sturlungar interests in his first lawsuit. But even though one of Snorri's brothers was on the other side of the dispute, his success in defending Oddaverjar interests was likely facilitated by his ties of kinship to one of his opponent's key allies, whose support he may have undermined. But if Sigvatr may have contributed to Snorri's triumph, he did not share in its spoils. Rather, the case resulted in a diminution of his honour.

The next major turning point in Snorri's career was the death of Bersi inn auðgi. When Bersi died in 1202, Snorri took control of his father-in-law's farm, wealth (over 800 hundreds, a huge sum, particularly when one considers that Snorri's father probably only had 120 hundreds when he died),[54] and *goðorð*, thereby securing the objective means to make good on his social and cultural advantages. From this point forward, the interests Snorri looked after were his own, and it was up to others to join or oppose him. The rest of his domestic career, until he was driven from Reykjaholt in 1236, can be characterized as one long, continuous cycle of conversion, with increasing returns, of material, social, and legal capital. As was true for his father, Snorri's legal expertise provided the means as well as the legitimation for much of his accumulation of capital. It must be kept in mind, however, that not only did Snorri enter the political game from a more elevated position than Sturla ever achieved, but the entire field in which Snorri operated was greatly transformed from what his father had known. The changes undergone by Iceland's political field and the factors lying behind them are complex. While I cannot address these issues adequately in this short discussion, it is necessary before examining further Snorri's activities within his domestic sphere to sketch in broad outline the processes that reshaped this context.

Some have argued that contrasts between the 'saga' and 'Sturlung' ages should not be exaggerated, and that much of their seeming difference stems from idealized depictions of the former produced by thirteenth-century authors entangled in the latter. However much this is true, undeniable and systemic changes emerged in Iceland's political and legal sphere around the year

1200, the most striking of which was the consolidation of power into fewer hands. By 1220, control and ownership of most *goðorð*s had been monopolized by members of six families.[55] The quality and type of power exercised by this shrinking Icelandic elite was also changing. While throughout the commonwealth era *goðorð*s had often functioned as regional units of power, there is no question that the authority of *goðar* became in the 1200s more openly and fully territorial.[56] It was also in this period that, perhaps for the first time, single *goðar* took possession of more than one *goðorð*. As Jón Jóhannesson observes, the ambitions of early thirteenth-century *stórgoðar* ('big-*goðar*') or *höfðingjar* (sg. *höfðingi*, 'chieftains') far outstripped those of their forerunners, 'none of [whom] ... ever entertained the idea of imposing his authority upon large areas, much less upon the entire country.'[57] This new brand of chieftain also made more stringent demands upon subordinates: they began to require *þingmenn* to swear oaths of fealty patterned after continental custom, and grew less tolerant of *bœndr* who resided in their areas of control but remained attached to rival *goðar*.[58] The methods *stórgoðar* used to enlarge their holdings were also growing more predatory, and their strategies and aims less often cloaked in pretences of disinterestedness or altruism.

Alongside this concentration of power came a reduction in the capacity of law and the courts to regulate, restrain, and resolve disputes. As Tranter observes, this era is marked by 'the emergence of a small number of people who are in a position so strong that they are beyond the reach of the limited executive power of the Alþing.'[59] Neither the law nor *alþing* became irrelevant, however. As Miller insists, the 'ideal of obeying the law was ... part of the repertoire of legitimating discourse,' and this remained true even for *goðar* who, practically speaking, no longer needed the law to further their pursuit of wealth and power.[60] Obtaining the validation of law and public opinion, even after the fact and in ever more artless fashion, remained an efficient means of legitimizing predatory practices. Even so, the traditional system of *goðar-þingmenn* coalitions engaging in disputes regulated by courts and arbitration had become something of an anachronistic shell overlaying a transformed political field.

Snorri was positioned both to benefit from and influence these patterns. For example, it is difficult to judge whether he was among the first beneficiaries of the new permissiveness regarding individual accumulation of *goðorð*s, or whether he helped inaugurate this trend. Following his inheritance of Bersi's property in 1202, Snorri began to acquire *goðorð*s with astonishing rapidity: around 1205, his maternal uncle Þórðr Böðvarsson gave him half of the Lundarmannagoðorð (which, like Bersi's Mýramannagoðorð, was based in Borgarfjörðr) so as to keep Snorri's brother Þórðr from siphoning off his *þingmenn*; shortly afterward, Snorri was given half of the Æverlingagoðorð, located to his north; he attained his second full *goðorð* along with the estate at Reykjaholt, former home of his father's old nemesis, Páll Sölvason, which he bought in 1206; there may have been more.[61] While there was likely more work involved in this process than Sturla's account of his uncle's career suggests, its relative ease can be attributed to Snorri's spatial and social positions in the Icelandic field. After establishing himself in Borgarfjörðr, Snorri was poised between areas controlled by the Haukdælir and Oddaverjar to the south, and his own kin and the Ásbirningar to the north. Snorri's situation between the most powerful families in his half of Iceland positioned him, in a manner similar to his social suspension between the Oddaverjar and Sturlungar, to exploit rivalries. For example, when Snorri played off his uncle's anxiety about his brother to gain a share in the Lundarmannagoðorð, he was able, as in the legal case of 1200, simultaneously to exploit and subvert family connections in pursuit of personal standing.

After receiving half of the Æverlingagoðorð, Snorri had *þingmenn* in all of Iceland's quarters but the east.[62] But even if the scope of Snorri's power was unprecedented, and perhaps illegal,[63] his supporters still called upon him to fulfil the traditional roles of arbitrator and advocate. Such demands placed Snorri in a precarious but potentially very profitable position. The most well-documented instance of Snorri's arbitration occurred in the context of a 1216 feud between men of Miðfjörðr and Víðidalr. As offences mounted, people looked to Snorri for help, since he 'had the most *þingmenn* in each of the two districts, and it seemed to men up to him to get them to reconcile.'[64] Snorri dutifully summoned the rival leaders to negotiate a settlement. Both sides arrived with large forces and fighting broke out immediately. Sturla describes what happened next:

> Snorri called to them, that they should not fight. No one paid attention to what he said. Then Þorljótr from Bretalækr went to Snorri and asked him to go between them. Snorri says that he does not have the men for this on account of their folly and fury. Þorljótr directed hard words at Snorri. Then Þorljótr ran among the horses and untied them and drove them between [the fighting men].[65]

As Sigurður Nordal has observed, Snorri and his troop could have broken up this fight at least as easily as the lone Þorljótr.[66] His reluctance, however, to enter the fray is further underscored as the Víðdælir fled: 'the Miðfirðingar then egged Snorri to ride after them, and Teitr [Þorbjarnarson] directed great reproof at him, when he did not want to add to their difficulty.'[67] But despite shame being twice heaped on his head during this incident, it was Snorri who,

when the two sides were ready to come to terms, 'accomplished a settlement ...
and arbitrated all cases which had arisen.'[68] This episode provides a clear
example of the way in which Snorri could use his social and legal capital to
turn a complete debacle, even one that he had helped cause, to his advantage.

Having achieved dominance in his own family and districts, Snorri spent
much of 1206–18, from his move to Reykjaholt to his first journey abroad,
challenging Oddaverjar supremacy. Most of his attacks on his foster-kin were
made indirectly, by antagonizing Oddaverjar allies and supporters rather than
members. As Helgi Þorláksson has shown, Snorri's 1202 harassment of
Orkney merchants, whose favour the Oddaverjar had long courted to combat
the monopolization of foreign trade by Norwegian merchants backed by the
king, was an early sign that Snorri had turned on his foster family.[69] A later
episode also attests to this shift. At the *alþing* of 1216, Snorri's booths sat next
to those of Magnús Guðmundarson, his neighbour to the south, holder of the
allsherjargoðorð, and sister's son of Sæmundr Jónsson. In a brawl over timber
that broke out between Snorri's and Magnús's men the latter was wounded,
and the Sturlungar and Oddaverjar assembled men in Þingvellir. Sæmundr's
force was larger, and the case was submitted for arbitration to Þorvaldr
Gizurarson, who awarded Sæmundr self-judgment, provided he declared no
sentences of outlawry. Afterwards, one of Sæmundr's men said to him that, as
usual, he 'alone had honour from this case,' to which the Oddaverjar chieftain
retorted: 'What good is that to say, since these brothers push themselves forward such that nearly no men hold their own against them?'[70]

'Snorri was ill-pleased' with this outcome, but he soon had the chance to
assuage his disappointment.[71] Sometime after the *þing*, Jórunn in auðga died
without an heir, and having assigned no one the authority to divide her property. Since, however, she was 'in *þing* with Magnús ... he intended [to take]
her property for himself, and to divide it among her relatives as to him seemed
fit.'[72] Snorri, sensing an opportunity, sent one of his men to investigate: 'And
when he came from the south, he had with him that man, who was called
Koðrán, a vagrant, and Snorri declared him Jórunn's heir, and he took the
money-suit from Koðrán.'[73] Snorri then 'summoned Magnús to full outlawry
at the Þverárþing. Magnús declared himself an *útanþingsmaðr* there [i.e.,
declared the summons invalid because he did not reside in that district]. But
Snorri bade him to bring forward his defence there. After that Snorri went
home and his case went forward at the Þverárþing, and Magnús was sentenced
as a full outlaw.'[74] Defying his conviction, Magnús brought a large force to the
next *alþing*, where he was confronted by Snorri's force of 'six hundred men,
and there were eighty Norwegians in his flock, all armed with shields. His
brothers were both there with a great troop'; in the end, Bishop Magnús

Gizurarson arbitrated a settlement, ruling that the land should be leased to Jórunn's partner Atli, but that rent should be paid to Snorri.[75]

Sturla sums up this dispute's outcome thus: 'Snorri had honour from these suits. And in these suits, his honour became the greatest here in the land.'[76] While Sturla does not specify why this affair was so productive of honour for Snorri, it seems unlikely that it derived solely from his having got the better of Magnús, who, even if he held a fancy title, was not one of Iceland's more powerful citizens. To understand the import of this victory we have to see the case for what it was: Snorri's retaliation for his humiliation at the previous year's *alþing*. Snorri earned such honour not by defeating Magnús but rather his own foster-kin the Oddaverjar, who were no longer able, as Sæmundr had admitted and this case now confirmed, to defend themselves or their friends from the Sturlusynir's strength, which in this case was augmented from abroad. Sturla's mention of Norwegians is significant. As described in chapter 2, the Oddaverjar had since 1215 been feuding with Norwegian merchants, a conflict that would result in jarl Skúli's trade embargo against Iceland in 1218. Given these circumstances, it is likely, as Helgi Þorláksson has argued, that the Norwegians in Snorri's troop were merchants who, with or without the knowledge of King Hákon and his regent, aided Snorri out of animosity towards the Oddaverjar and their allies.[77]

Even after recognizing the nature of Snorri's triumph, however, it may still seem odd that Sturla would speak of an increase in his uncle's honour or *virðing*, rather than power or *vald*. As Sturla more or less acknowledges, the legality of every move made by Snorri in this dispute was questionable.[78] And yet, it is telling that Snorri went through the motions (making the summons on the proper day, holding a trial, settling the case through arbitration, etc.), and that Sturla and the public ratified his actions and the suit's outcome by recognizing the increase to his honour. That such transparently illicit tactics, ones performed, moreover, by the current lawspeaker, could make Snorri the most 'honourable' man in Iceland confirms that, as objective forms of capital were monopolized by fewer agents in the 1200s, the need for such agents to generate legitimacy through symbolic violence proved less crucial to their retention and exercise of power. In short, the meaning of 'honour' had changed somewhat since the elder Sturla's day.

From 1218–20 Snorri was in Norway. After his return, he resumed his post as *lögsögumaðr* and his use of the law to further his interests. Over the next fifteen years, Snorri went to great efforts to thwart the ambitions of his increasingly assertive nephew Sturla Sigvatsson. As described in chapter 2, Snorri and Sturla faced off in a series of legal confrontations during these years. But while the law continued to be an important part of Snorri's arsenal, he had, as in his early career, another weapon that he could use to increase his social and material standing, namely marriage. Snorri had separated from Herdís around the time he moved to Reykjaholt in 1206, and some sixteen years passed before he seems to have given serious thought to another union in his abortive attempt to woo Solveig Sæmundardóttir. Less than two years after Solveig married Sturla Sigvatsson, however, Snorri had established his 'partnership' with another granddaughter of Jón Loptsson, and a richer one to boot. Sturla writes: 'Snorri brought Hallveig Ormsdóttir home and joined her property to his, and took into his custody the wealth of her sons, Klængr and Ormr, 800 hundreds. Snorri had then much more wealth than anyone else in Iceland.'[79] The emphasis Sturla places on the material outcome of this match indicates the reversal in position of the Oddaverjar and Sturlungar clans. The Oddaverjar's standing had long been on the wane, and after Sæmundr's death in 1222 they were probably the weakest of Iceland's leading families. Snorri no longer looked to his foster-family as a source of superior social capital, but rather as one more route to material prosperity.[80]

There were other families, however, with whom Snorri was more interested in building lasting relations, and for this, his children were his most precious asset. Snorri's sons played a minor role in this respect: the legitimate Jón never married, while Órækja's 1232 union was a semi-successful attempt to repair a previous match gone wrong.[81] His daughters proved useful, however. The first union Snorri arranged was between his sole legitimate daughter Hallbera and Árni óreiða Magnússon, a minor *goði* from Kjalarnes, southwest of Snorri's home. When the couple separated in 1224, Snorri vigorously enforced his rights, demanding and receiving an estate and perhaps a share of Árni's *goðorð*.[82] In the same year, Snorri made ambitious matches for his other two daughters, giving Þórdís to Þorvaldr Snorrason of the Vatnsfirðingar and Ingibjörg to Gizurr Þorvaldsson of the Haukdælir. In 1228, Hallbera was again married, this time to Kolbeinn ungi of the Ásbirningar. Because Snorri was now connected through marriage with four of Iceland's six major families, Jón Jóhannesson pinpoints this as the year in which he 'reached the height of his power.'[83] And yet, while this web of social ties was an undeniable source of strength, it also burdened Snorri with often irreconcilable obligations. This impression is shared by Sturla, who foreshadows the problems his uncle's sons-in-law would bring him in the future:

That was one evening, when Snorri sat in [his] bath, that the *höfðingjar* were discussed. Men said that no *höfðingi* was then such as Snorri and that no *höfðingi* could compete with him because of those in-laws which he had. Snorri agreed that

his in-laws were not small men. Sturla Bárðarson had kept watch over the bath, and
Snorri led him home, and he spoke forth this ditty, so that Snorri heard:
You have similar in-laws
as had aforetime
  – injustice always proves
ill – the clever king of Hleiðr [Hrólfr kraki]. [84]

The poet's warnings were borne out. Within a few years, all three of the Snor-
radœtr's marriages had failed: Þórdís's ended with Þorvaldr's murder in 1229; at
that summer's *alþing* Kolbeinn, who supported Sigvatr and Sturla in this incident, rode in with Hallbera but went home without her; and in 1231, in the aftermath of the death of Jón murtr in Norway, Gizurr and Ingibjörg called it quits.

Just because these marriages failed, however, does not mean that they were
unproductive. Snorri, in fact, came into a great deal of property and power as
a result of their failure. After the killing of Þorvaldr, and of his sons in 1232,
Snorri placed first Þórdís as guardian of her son Einarr, and then Órækja in
charge of the Vatnsfirðingr's land and authority. In the case of Hallbera,
Snorri brought multiple suits against Kolbeinn for having abandoned his
daughter. In the end it was agreed that 'Snorri should own half of those
*goðorð*s which Kolbeinn rightfully had, and Kolbeinn should travel with and
support Snorri at *þing*s.'[85] In contrast, Snorri seems to have been eager to
maintain the ties established with the Haukdælir through Gizurr's and
Ingibjörg's union: at one point, he and Þorvaldr, Gizurr's father, each gave
the couple money to try to keep them together. But while the terms reached
after their separation are not described, it is unlikely that, given his track
record, Snorri came away empty-handed.

A pattern emerges from this trail of broken marriages and property divisions.
In each case, the initial intent of these unions was to augment Snorri's social
capital through the creation of durable alliances with those who would otherwise be his principal foes in Iceland's field of power. The only one of these
attempts to come close to realizing this long-term objective was Þórdís's marriage, mainly because it was the only one to produce offspring.[86] In the other
cases, Snorri's social gains were quickly forfeited – indeed, he ended up losing
social capital as the unpleasant dissolution of these marriages transformed
potential enemies into real ones. And yet, when all was said and done, Snorri
came away with a substantial net gain in wealth, property, and authority. He did
so by adopting decidedly asocial and even predatory practices when these
unions dissolved. This shift in tactics permitted Snorri to derive material or else
asymmetrical brands of social capital from the failure of these marriages.

While this sort of strategic adaptation may have helped Snorri cut his short-term losses, however, it was also part of what eventually did him in. After all, three of Snorri's four former sons-in-law (all but the dead one!) took part in planning and executing his murder in September 1241. By then, Snorri, after the loss of his authority and property in 1236, the slaughter of his most powerful kin and son's exile in 1238, and the deaths of Skúli in 1240 and Hallveig in 1241, had become isolated from his social equals or near-equals. The estates, lands, and support that he regained following his return from Norway in 1239 could do him little good now that his supply of social capital was virtually exhausted. Even after he was dead, however, Snorri was not free of the Icelandic game of honour, in which, as Miller has observed, there was no rest, not even for a corpse.[87] Snorri's corpse, as things turned out, did pretty well for itself: the honour attached to his name was sufficient for Órækja and Snorri's nephew Sturla Þórðarson to exact 200 hundreds from Gizurr, the highest compensation assessed for any killing in the Sturlung age.[88] And so, we find Snorri's terminal balance of symbolic capital sufficient to support one final and profitable act of conversion.

Like Father, Like Son?

In comparing Snorri's and his father's careers, the most pronounced differences that emerge are the sorts of ends and rewards pursued by each. Sturla was singularly and self-consciously intent on raising the level of his honour, an aim for which he was almost always willing to sacrifice actual or potential material gains. Snorri followed a nearly opposite policy: he appears to have focused more on the condition of his material wealth and personal authority than on the state of his honour and reputation, and in numerous instances he proved perfectly willing to trade the latter for the former. Put simply, Snorri was oriented towards securing and conserving objective rather than subjective forms of politically effective capital, and most of his successes lay in this direction.

Several factors help account for this divergence in the aims and motives of father and son. One is the less mystified or more cynical notion of 'honour' operative in Snorri's era. Another, more significant factor was the dissimilar composition of resources afforded Sturla and Snorri as young *goðar*. From the start of his career, Sturla was not accorded the recognition by the Icelandic elite that his store of objective capital warranted, and this remained true no matter how great his wealth and influence grew. Snorri's early career was also marked by dissonance, only in his case it was his abundant store of symbolic capital that belied his conspicuous lack of objective measures of power, such as wealth, land, and supporters. Received and treated as a peer by the social elite from the start, Snorri never developed the compulsion to seek and hoard symbolic capital that governed his father's tactics in Iceland's field of power.

The most important factor, however, contributing to Sturla's and Snorri's differing strategic orientations was the fragmented character of Snorri's social identity. In terms of resources, Snorri was an heir of the Oddaverjar: even if ties to his birth-family proved crucial assets throughout his career, Snorri's early stores of social, material, and legal capital overwhelmingly derived from his foster-family. To understand Snorri's disposition towards his inherited resources, however, it is necessary to consider the liminal position into which he was thrust by his fostering. Whereas most foster-children in medieval Iceland were raised in social, material, and cultural environments roughly equivalent to that of their birth-family (or else comparatively impoverished), Snorri was relocated at a very young age into a more capital-rich context than any afforded his near kin. And yet, though he enjoyed legitimate access to his foster-family's resources, he seems never to have attained the sense of comfort with his position or the resources at his command that characterized the practice of his foster-father, Jón Loptsson. As Sigurður Nordal observes, 'Jón sat in the patrimony of his forefathers, his power at the *þing* and in his district was deeply rooted, his *þingmenn* were his father's followers and all the people of the land acknowledged the Oddaverjar's authority. Jón was born to power, with which he was well contented'; Snorri, however, 'had in his nature an ambition, which could never be fully satisfied,' and 'his effort to increase his wealth and power is the major part of all that is said about him.'[89]

Although I have been at pains to integrate rather than disjoin Snorri's character, this disparity between his capital and his disposition towards it, an incongruity that contributed to his persistent and ultimately counterproductive efforts to enlarge his already ample resources, is best explained as a result of his suspension between two social units. Snorri was neither entirely Sturlungar nor entirely Oddaverjar, but both at once, and while he inherited the social, cultural, and (eventually) material advantages attached to the latter name, he did not receive the corresponding disposition that marks legitimate heirs to such resources. Rather, he was disposed to exploit them like a Sturlung, to use them to enlarge rather than maintain his social position. In sum, Snorri seems never to have got over the sense that his inherited capital – capital that permitted him to participate at the highest level of the political game from the beginning of his career, before he had actually achieved any victories or earned any rewards of his own – was anything other than borrowed, and hence illegitimate.

Though I have so far discussed only differences in Snorri's and his father's careers, it should be noted that they shared one crucial similarity. Each employed the same mechanism to acquire and hold onto much of his power, wealth, and support: the law. Both knew the ins and outs of Icelandic law, and were able to use advocacy to exploit the conflicts of supporters and the courts to launch or to justify attacks against opponents. Given that legal capital was instrumental to both Sturla's and Snorri's success, it cannot have been the case that this resource was available to the latter only by virtue of his presence at Oddi – he could have acquired it at home. The difference between the legal capital Snorri accumulated at Oddi and that which he could have obtained at Hvammr was thus quantitative rather than qualitative. In other words, while Snorri's fosterage afforded him greater and more potent resources for use in Iceland's political field, it does not seem to have offered him anything completely new in this regard. This raises the question: were there any sorts of capital acquired at Oddi that would have been utterly unavailable to him had he remained at home?

The answer, which has been touched on briefly, is that Snorri was afforded access at Oddi to varieties of cultural capital that allowed for appreciation and production of literature, poetry, and art. While his father was deficient or utterly lacking in such capacities, they were necessary for recognized admittance to the ranks of Iceland's elite. And yet, despite the importance of such competencies, I have found little cause to tie Snorri's ascent in his domestic sphere to his possession of forms of cultural capital other than legal. Rather, it has proven possible to discuss the benefits afforded Snorri by his fosterage almost entirely in social terms, as interpersonal ties of affinity and allegiance with members and factions of the Icelandic elite. This emphasis, moreover, is borne out by our sources. In narrating Snorri's domestic practice, Sturla Þórðarson's only references to his cultural production are the saga-books Sturla Sigvatsson is said to have perused, and some verses that Snorri recited in the course of conflicts – and more often than not, such poetry generated scorn rather than prestige for Snorri, contributing to his reputation as a man of words rather than of action.[90] It seems, then, that cultural capital in the form of literary/poetic skill or appreciation played a rather insignificant role in Snorri's domestic career, except as a foundation upon which his social capital rested. And yet, if we are to characterize the cultural acumen and skills acquired by Snorri at Oddi as capital, it is necessary to identify an arena or field wherein these capacities did not lie dormant, but were put into play. In order, therefore, to assess the full impact and value of Snorri's cultural instruction at Oddi, we need to shift focus outside of Iceland, and to look at the relations that Icelanders established and maintained with the courts and elite circles of Norway, and the types of capital they found most useful in that context.

4 Snorri Abroad: Icelandic Exploitation of Cultural Capital

In the fall of 1218, Snorri Sturluson was arguably Iceland's most powerful citizen. His only true rival for several years had been his foster-brother, Sæmundr Jónsson, but Snorri's defeat of the *allsherjargoði* and his Oddaverjar backers at the 1217 *alþing* did much to tilt the balance of power in his favour. That Snorri chose to visit Norway at a time when his pre-eminence in Iceland was newly won and vulnerable seems at first a surprising move. It is well, however, to recall the aid provided Snorri at the *alþing* by the troop of eighty Norwegians, a wellspring of support that could be fortified by a cordial visit to its source. It also pays to consider the types of capital that contributed to Snorri's elevation to the pinnacle of his society. Snorri was by 1218 the largest single shareholder of three of Iceland's most valuable forms of capital – legal (his position as lawspeaker and recent judicial victories), social (his large, widely dispersed body of kin, allies, and supporters), and symbolic (his recent designation as the most 'honourable' man in the land) – and not far from achieving dominance in the fourth, material.[1] This meant, however, that there was little left for Snorri to achieve, aside from maintaining his status, in his domestic context, and indeed that further attempts to expand his powers, resources, or associations could be counterproductive. Norway's court was, then, the nearest untapped source of social capital available to Snorri, as well as a setting wherein the only form of capital that he held in abundant supply but had not yet fully exploited, cultural capital in the form of artistic/literary/poetic skill, could prove extremely valuable.

By way of background to Snorri's efforts to deploy his cultural resources in Norway, I will describe in this chapter's first section the broader movement of agents and capital between Iceland and Norway, focusing primarily on the art form known as skaldic poetry and those who produced and consumed it. In surveying the four centuries during which skaldic verse functioned as cultural capital, I will discuss its origins and development in elite circles of ninth-century Norway, its later monopolization by Icelanders, the formal qualities that enabled its use as a tool for generating prestige and legitimacy, and the religious ideology that informed its production in pagan times. Because skaldic poetry survived the advent of Christianity, I will also touch upon the post-conversion practice of this art in Norway's courts, as well as its status in the learned milieu of twelfth-century Iceland, where Snorri learned it. Finally, I will discuss Snorri's attempts to profit by his poetic talents both before and during his visit to Norway in 1218–20, and the responses that his praise elicited from its subjects.

There and Back Again: Interactions of Norway and Commonwealth Iceland

Throughout the era of Iceland's independence, people, goods, and communication passed often between Norway and its colony. Norwegians' motives for maintaining contact with Iceland were straightforward – they came to trade and, for a brief time, to proselytize. Norway's kings also periodically sought to exert influence over Iceland, though typically from a distance. As for Icelanders, they too made the trip for commercial reasons, but also to visit its rulers. Despite their general aversion to overbearing royal authority, kingship continued to inspire a certain fascination in Icelanders, and from the beginning of the commonwealth its prominent citizens were frequent guests at court, where they gathered gifts and reputations. The most sought-after prize for such visitors was the title of *hirðmaðr*, given those who attended the king and served as his advisors and bodyguards. While the title held no official status in Iceland, it was a source of prestige for those who carried it home. Most of our information concerning how often and under what circumstances kings admitted Icelanders into their *hirð* comes from sagas. In these accounts, Icelanders, often *goðar* or their sons, are accepted by kings as *hirðmenn* based upon their distinguished lineage or reputation. The bestowal of this honour is depicted, however, as an act of munificence – since the Icelander has nothing that the king *needs*, which could compel rather than merely dispose him to honour the foreigner, it is a gift given at his discretion.

In stories and reality, this imbalance derived from the fact that relative to the Norwegian elite Icelanders possessed an inferior quantity and quality of most every form of capital – material, social, martial, and symbolic – of value in Scandinavia's field of power. Iceland had neither an army nor a true aristocracy, and while it could offer certain rare goods, it is certain that, in matters of trade, Icelanders needed Norway more than they were needed by that country.[2] And yet, there was one type of capital that medieval Icelanders amassed more effectively than Norwegians: this was cultural capital, the most potent source of which was mastery of skaldic verse. From the mid-tenth until the turn of the fourteenth century, Icelanders delivered poetic tributes, most composed in the prestigious *dróttkvætt* metre (short for *dróttkvæðr háttr*, or 'court metre'), to aristocratic hosts in Norway and other parts of Scandinavia. Icelanders' dominance in the cultural production of the medieval north extended well beyond skaldic verse, however; to this, we must add their recording of all extant eddic poetry and the invention of most branches of saga literature, including their exclusive production of *konungasögur*, which Norwegian kings came to rely upon for the recording of their history and deeds.[3]

The relationship of medieval Iceland's cultural producers and Norway's aristocrats exhibits a strong structural homology with that which pertains between modern French artists/intellectuals/scholars and commercial/industrial leaders as described by Bourdieu in his book *Distinction*.[4] In France, Bourdieu writes, 'the dominant class is organized in a chiastic structure,' in which 'the structure of the distribution of economic capital is symmetrical and opposite to that of cultural capital.'[5] This division results in a social configuration wherein intellectuals, artists, and scholars, because their chief resource is, compared with that of commercial and business leaders, less quantifiable, convertible, and universally recognized, form what Bourdieu often refers to as the dominated fraction of the dominant class. This unequal allocation of economic and cultural capital between two sets of agents becomes the defining feature of Bourdieu's general notion of a field of power, which he defines at one point as

> a space of play and competition in which the social agents and institutions which all possess the determinate quantity of specific capital (economic and cultural capital in particular) sufficient to occupy the dominant positions within their respective fields ... confront one another in strategies aimed at preserving or transforming this balance of forces ... The distribution according to the dominant principle of hierarchization (economic capital) is [in this field] inversely symmetrical to the distribution according to the dominated principle of hierarchization (cultural capital).[6]

Thus, a field of power is occupied by agents clustered around two poles: + cultural capital, − economic capital (dominated); − cultural capital, + economic capital (dominant).

Bourdieu's model is remarkably useful for analysing the practices of elite medieval Icelanders in Norway's courts, wherein they are best understood as the dominated fraction of a politically dominant class. Icelanders' use of culture to compensate for their lack of more tangible resources was recognized by Saxo Grammaticus, who in the prologue to his *Gesta Danorum* (c. 1210) writes:

> Nor may the pains of the men of Thule be blotted in oblivion; for though they lack all that can foster luxury (so naturally barren is their soil), yet they make up for their neediness by their wit, by ... devoting every instant of their lives to perfecting our knowledge of the deeds of foreigners. Indeed, they account it a delight to learn and to consign to remembrance the history of all nations, deeming it as great a glory to set forth the excellences of others as to display their own.[7]

Here, Saxo perceives the roots of medieval Icelanders' cultural preoccupations better than have most modern scholars. For example, a recent volume of essays tries to solve the problem of 'why and how a materially poor, remote part of medieval European society was able to produce such a rich and diverse literature.'[8] This question seems to me to supply its own answer: Iceland produced such a literature *because* it was materially deprived and geographically isolated. The question would be better posed by asking how this poor and peripheral region of medieval Scandinavia produced such a literary output. Yet such a narrowing of focus only deepens the puzzle for many, causing them to wonder why Iceland's literary boom should have coincided with a period of intense cultural, economic, and political contact with Norway. As one scholar asks: '[If] in Norway the conditions for the development of literature were obviously nearly the same as in Iceland ... what are the reasons for such a different development of literature?'[9] Again, the answer is to be found in the question: Iceland produced its literature *because* of its close ties with Norway. To reach this conclusion, however, one must acknowledge that 'the conditions for the development of literature' were anything but identical for Icelanders and Norwegians, owing to the unbalanced distribution of forms of capital between them, a disparity made all the more obvious by their intensified interaction in the twelfth and thirteenth centuries.

Bourdieu has written that

> the literary field is so attractive and so welcoming to all those who possess all the characteristics of the dominants *minus one*: to 'poor relations' of the great bourgeois dynasties, aristocrats ruined or in decline, members of minorities ... those whose uncertain and contradictory social identity predisposes them ... to occupy the contradictory position of dominated among the dominants.[10]

For Iceland's elite, we need to create another category: those possessing all of the qualities of the dominants, *only less*. With this group, we are confronted by a social fraction that within its own land was politically, economically, and socially dominant, but which, when placed within the larger Scandinavian context, was dominated in all of these measures of power and distinction. In other words, the Icelandic elite occupied opposite poles of the overlapping fields of power in which they operated: dominant in their immediate sphere, dominated in the wider sphere into which the first was subsumed. In this, Icelanders were unique: nowhere else in medieval Europe do we find a group that maintained such close cultural, social, and political ties with a neighbouring society from such a physical and material remove; in no other do we find the divide between agents occupying the culturally dominant pole and those occupying the economically, militarily, and socially dominant pole falling so neatly along geographical and 'national' borders. In sum, elite Icelanders' cultural interests ought to be understood as a focusing of energies necessitated by their situation at the dominated pole of the Scandinavian field of power. This assertion can best be demonstrated through an analysis of the long-standing role of Icelandic skalds as the semi-official historiographers, spokesmen, and propagandists of the Norwegian court.

Skaldic Verse as Cultural Capital

Skaldic verse production was not always dominated by Icelanders. This art form first emerged in western Norway in the mid-800s, not long before Haraldr hárfagri's consolidation of royal authority and Iceland's settlement.[11] As with these events, a mythic air surrounds the origins of this poetry. The first skald whose work survives, Bragi Boddason, was apotheosized as an eponymous god of poetry, and scholars have long remarked upon the skaldic style's seemingly instantaneous birth in his verse.[12] This pioneering poet plied his trade in what was to become the skald's customary milieu, Norway's courts. For the next century, all court poets of record were Norwegian, but this ended in the mid-900s. Indeed, after Eyvindr skáldaspillir Finnsson, a poet in the service of Hákon inn góði Haraldsson (c. 946–61), all were Icelandic.[13] While the fact of this transition is universally recognized, scholars have had difficulty explaining it. Most attempts to do so have been too broad, chalking it up to Icelanders' general cultural predilections, or too narrow, crediting the charisma and influence of individual poetic geniuses.[14] My line of analysis suggests, however, that the monopolization of this art form should be understood as part of a program by Icelanders to establish a majority share in the cultural capital available in west Norse society, and thereby to counter Norwegian dominance over other politically effective resources.

While many have correlated skaldic verse's intricacy with its use in elite circles, few have been willing to view its exclusionary function as more than an unproven and probably unprovable hypothesis, and fewer still have made it their special analytic focus. Most have tended to downplay the poetry's social function while emphasizing its artistic and intellectual worth. One critic writes that 'scaldic poetry is above all an exploration of and a play with basic human categorising powers within restricted semantic domains. As the favourite pastime of an intellectual elite, first in Norway and then in colonial Iceland, its literary and aesthetic as well as its purely intellectual appeal are easier to understand.'[15] Those who produced and consumed skaldic verse were not just an intellectual elite, however, but also a social/political one, and skaldic poetry was not just a form of aesthetic play, but a discursive tool capable of erecting and maintaining social and political distinctions. This assertion is not so controversial as to require proof at the outset of my discussion – invariably, people's cultural intake and output serve to demarcate existing or emerging political, economic, and, in the broadest sense of the word, cultural boundaries. Indeed, cultural preferences, when perceived as freely chosen and politically disinterested, are one of the more effective and insidious ways in which social classificatory systems are naturalized. As such, the task at hand is to describe the precise manner in which skaldic verse distinguished and generated profits for specific social fragments in medieval Scandinavia.

While it is a relatively simple matter to identify those among whom the skaldic art emerged – as noted, the first skalds appeared in the courts of western Norway – most have looked farther afield for its 'causes.' Stephen Tranter, for example, asks: 'What induced Icelandic poets to adopt a marked increase of stylisation in their panegyric lyric during a period starting somewhere around the middle of the ninth century?'[16] Finding in the immediate context no 'single cultural impulse of [sufficient] magnitude' to account for this development, Tranter turns for explanation to cultural contacts occasioned by Viking-age exploration, concluding that the advent of skaldic verse is 'proof of little more than the Norseman's openness of mind.'[17] Such inclination to look for foreign rather than domestic catalysts for skaldic poetry's invention seems to me to depend on the idea that the roots of cultural practices must themselves be cultural as opposed to social or political. What tends to get overlooked in such quests for skaldic verse's origins is that this highly stylized poetic form appeared at precisely the historic moment when sets of agents emerged in Norway who were in need of mechanisms for legitimating a rapid expansion of their power. In the mid-800s, the courts of both King Haraldr hárfagri and his most powerful ally/rival the jarl of Hlaðir were home to 'a dynamic representative of a power-seeking dynasty ... in need of ideological support for his soaring ambitions.'[18] A primary impetus, then, for the development of this ornate praise-poetry was the native emergence of concentrated, and competing, centres of authority.

Skaldic poetry's value in this context would have derived from its ability to generate what Bourdieu calls a 'profit of distinction,' the capacity of prestigious cultural practices to contribute to the status of elite agents, groups, or institutions. This capacity often depends upon the difficulty or degree of artificiality of the art form in question, and the consequent amount of exposure and training needed to produce or consume it. In the case of skaldic poetry, this profit was originally generated through oral recitation in the court. Skaldic poetry, therefore, like legal expertise in the Icelandic *þing*, was not just cultural but also linguistic capital. As Bourdieu writes: 'The constitution of a linguistic market creates the conditions for an objective competition in and through which the legitimate competence can function as linguistic capital, producing a *profit of distinction* on the occasion of each social exchange.'[19] Within such linguistic markets

> linguistic exchange – a relation of communication between a sender and a receiver, based on enciphering and deciphering, and therefore on the implementation of a code or a generative competence – is also an economic exchange which is established within a particular symbolic relation of power between a producer, endowed with a certain linguistic capital, and a consumer (or a market), and which is capable of procuring a certain material or symbolic profit.[20]

Cultivation of an intricate, artificial form, as measured by distance from everyday speech, is a primary means through which discursive practice generates profit. As Bourdieu writes in an especially apt passage: 'The exercise of symbolic power is accompanied by work on the *form* of discourse which, as is clearly demonstrated in the case of poets in archaic societies, has the purpose of demonstrating the orator's mastery and gaining him the recognition of the group.'[21]

As many have rightfully observed, one would be hard-pressed to find a type of poetry more intricate than that of the skalds: it is 'one of the most esoteric art forms that Western man has produced,' 'a revelling in *form*, an overemphasis on it,' a 'poetry [that] revels in obscurity ... [and] a desire to outdo all competitors in wit and craftsmanship ... Few meters are more intricate, subtle, or like a straightjacket than *dróttkvætt*.'[22] I will try here to give some sense of the metrical constraints under which skalds laboured.[23] Like all Germanic verse, that of the skalds is alliterative, and its structure is stanzaic. Beyond these features, skaldic verse, particularly its most common but also most demanding metre, *dróttkvætt*, added a host of prescriptions that grew more restrictive over time. The basic unit of skaldic composition is the four-line *helmingr* (pl. *helmingar*), or half-stanza, a self-contained metrical and often syntactic unit. Regular *dróttkvætt* features sets of three alliterating syllables in every two-line pair, two in the odd line plus one in the first syllable of the following even line. Each line additionally has two rhyming syllables. Both alliterating and rhyming syllables are stressed. Unlike in Anglo-Saxon or eddic poetry, unstressed as well as stressed syllables are counted in skaldic lines.[24] Finally, a periodic two-line *stef*, or refrain, may be added to knit *dróttkvætt* stanzas together to create the prestigious form known as a *drápa* (pl. *drápur*).[25] While skalds' tortured syntax was long considered a lamentable consequence of their having to force content into the structure demanded by alliteration, rhyme, stress, and syllable-count, recent critics have preferred to see it as an aesthetic choice of the poets.[26] In either case, word order was another feature that served to distinguish skalds' products from those of less accomplished artisans.

A further source of the poetry's difficulty is its diction. Skaldic verse commonly employs two sorts of metaphoric devices, the *heiti* (sg. and pl.), an archaic or sometimes strictly poetic noun,[27] and the *kenning* (pl. *kenningar*, from *kenna* e-t *við* e-t, 'to make e-t known by e-t'),[28] which Kari Ellen Gade defines as 'a nominal phrase consisting of a base word (noun) modified by one or more genitival or adjectival attributives (qualifiers).'[29] Two kennings for battle are *Hugins teiti*, 'joy of Huginn (i.e., ravens),' and *Hárs veðr*, 'weather of Hárr (Óðinn).'[30] Skalds often employed such circumlocutions to the point of seeming absurdity, exhibiting what one scholar calls 'a mania for kennings, so that in extreme cases virtually nothing is mentioned by its own name or designated by an everyday word.'[31] The examples of kennings above represent their simplest possible form – any such kenning (base word + modifier) can be lengthened by splitting its modifier into a new kenning, initiating a chain of allusions that, in theory, could extend infinitely. Skalds were also singularly indifferent to the semantic dissonance occasioned by their juxtaposition of images, calling, for example, the heart the 'acorn of the spirit' or a warrior the 'bush of the beast of the waves.'[32] Such jarring combinations result in a vocabulary wherein, in the words of Einar Ól. Sveinsson, 'all things are other than they seem or are said to be.'[33] In combination with skaldic verse's metrical requirements and stereotyped content, this zeal for metaphoric devices resulted in an extremely (almost maximally) artificial form of linguistic practice, whose production and consumption relied upon a producer's mastery and an audience's familiarity with a highly refined style of discourse.

While *heiti* and kennings are usually discussed as artistic means of exploring semantic boundaries, their use was crucial to making skaldic verse an exclusive form of linguistic practice. Like other specialized languages – those of science or theology, for example – that lay claim to a privileged position in the hierarchy of discourses, skaldic poetry had to 'produce the illusion of independence through strategies which create a false break' with ordinary language.[34] Such a break is effected through the constitution of a quasi-independent sphere of language wherein technical terms, that is, 'ennobled forms of ordinary words,' receive new meanings by virtue of their placement within this bounded structure.[35] Thus armed with a vocabulary to which they alone hold the code, specialists in these purportedly autonomous discourses can generate statements imbued with an authority greater than that warranted by their content, greater, that is, than identical statements of fact or opinion expressed in more mundane form would hold.

In the case of skaldic poetry, however, it has long been debated whether its form may not have actually hampered its communication of content. How much authority, after all, could skalds' words have held if most who heard them could not understand them? While the majority of scholars have tried to preserve the verse's authority by arguing for its comprehensibility to its original auditors, ultimately the question of whether or not skalds' contemporaries could understand their poetry is not all that relevant to determining its effects.[36] What those who insist on skaldic verse's lucidity in its original context tend to overlook is that a specialized discourse's authority does not necessarily depend on effective communication of its content. Indeed, the reverse is often true; as Bruce Lincoln notes, the authority of 'experts' opinions ... may be enhanced by a certain incomprehensibility.'[37] Bourdieu speaks to this same point when describing 'the gap between acknowledgement and knowledge' that characterizes different sets of agents' relations to their society's 'legitimate culture,' or what Lincoln calls its 'Capital-C Culture ... the "choice" works and the "select" genres that enjoy greatest aesthetic privilege, social cachet, and official support.'[38] For a form of cultural or linguistic practice to attain such status, it is sufficient, and usually preferable, that most are able to recognize it and its products as prestigious or authoritative, while remaining unable to grasp or articulate, let alone reproduce, the features of their form and content that make them so. Those agents, however, who possess both recognition and knowledge of legitimate culture are typically elite members of the society whose habitus afforded them formative exposure to the required codes, or whose other resources, primarily material, provided them with the leisure to gain such expertise through secondary means.

The assumption that skaldic discourse's effectiveness depended on communication of content also assumes that there was something to be communicated. And yet, as Roberta Frank observes, the information offered in praise-poetry usually amounted to 'what the audience already knew,' and its unadorned content often boils down to generic tributes to its subject's prowess in battle or generosity with gold.[39] Bjarne Fidjestøl has suggested that skaldic poetry fulfils a function very different from that of regular speech:

> The ordinary user of language aims to be able to produce and communicate an unlimited number of units of meaning with the aid of a small and limited number of signifying units (phonemes). The skald, on the other hand, needs to produce an unlimited number of signifying units (kennings) on the foundation of a small and comparatively limited number of units of meaning (sense-words) ... The skald appears to be the polar opposite, as it were, of the ordinary language-user, because his need for means of expression is of a peculiar kind. Although he is a professional user of language, he has in fact little he needs to say.[40]

Although skaldic verse is not really unique in this respect – rather, it is one of a number of ritualized discourses, such as political speeches, sermons, and academic addresses, whose purpose often is, in Lincoln's words, 'to say inconsequential and platitudinous things in a way that makes them sound fresh and stimulating'[41] – Fidjestøl does here call attention to the fact that, unlike less formal modes of speech, skaldic verse was not suited for communicating information so much as demonstrating mastery over form. As discussed in chapter 2, cultural artistry in medieval Scandinavia lay not in invention of content, but in the ability to give a pleasing form to ostensibly objective information. As Sverre Bagge puts it, the art of composing skaldic verse 'did not consist in telling a story, but in the particular, highly developed verbal embroidery, which needed a real craftsman.'[42] *Hirðskálds* in particular lacked responsibility for the content of their work; to quote Fidjestøl again, the 'skald was handed his subject-matter ... by his princely patron – its historical content and ideology – and his task was a technical, professional one – to give it form in well-wrought verse ... The skalds' task was to give expression to the official ideology of the monarchy.'[43]

The sparseness of skaldic verse's content does not mean, however, that it lacked value. First, a court-poem provided facts about its subject: name, identity of foes, sites of important battles, genealogy and kin, and, in the case of elegies, place and manner of death. Second, it served as a vehicle of praise or, less often, blame, by providing judgments on its subject's character and deeds. In effect, court-poems painted factual and evaluative portraits for posterity.

The clearest of many expressions of the importance attached by Norse society to the preservation of memory and fame is found in these oft-quoted lines from the eddic poem *Hávamál*: 'Cattle die, kinsmen die, you yourself will die the same; but fame will never die, for him who wins it.'[44] In Norse society as in the archaic Greece described by Marcel Detienne, blame was not the only, nor the most forbidding, antithesis of praise. Like Greek heroes, what the northern warrior or king feared most was that his life and deeds would fall into oblivion – and, like the Greek bard, it was the skald's job to make sure his patron did not suffer this fate.[45]

Parallels between Greek and Scandinavian poetic practice run still deeper. In both contexts, the poet's role as cultural curator was in part due to necessity. In oral cultures, poetry provides, because of its conservative and mnemonic qualities, one of the more reliable means of effecting the transmission of knowledge, and the masters of poetic form often become their society's default historiographers, biographers, and mythographers. The poet's role as royal historiographer, genealogist, and judge was founded on more than utility, however. In Greece, the poet's capacity to pronounce truth was tied to the belief that he possessed 'direct access to the Beyond'; his speech, according to Detienne,

> eludes temporality because it is at one with forces beyond human ones, forces that are completely autonomous and lay claim to an absolute power. The poet's speech never solicits agreement from its listeners or assent from a social group ... To the extent that magicoreligious speech transcends human time, it also transcends human beings. It is not the manifestation of an individual's will or thought, nor does it constitute the expression of any particular agent or individual. It is the attribute and privilege of a social function.[46]

As with the Greek bard, much of the authority of pagan skalds' speech derived from its purportedly extra-human inspiration. In Norse myth, poetic skill was dispensed to chosen individuals in the form of mead by the supreme god Óðinn, who stole this liquid from the *jötnar* (sg. *jötunn*) or giants, foes of the *æsir* (sg. *áss*) or gods. This myth is best known from Snorri's *Edda*, and an analysis of his prose version will be offered in the discussion of *Skáldskaparmál* in chapter 7. Other than Snorri, sources for this story are limited to the poetry itself: the myth is referenced in many skaldic kennings – most of them variations on 'mead/liquid of Óðinn = poetry' – and parts of its narrative are recounted in *Hávamál*.[47] As is often the case, the kennings for poetry can only be decoded by an audience familiar with the characters, motifs, and events of pagan myth. Prior to the appearance of the *Edda*, the major means for the transmission of such information was eddic verse. As E.O.G. Turville-Petre writes, 'Scaldic poetry was dependent upon the Eddaic. No one could understand the scaldic kennings unless he knew the myths and legends to which the scalds alluded. These myths and legends lived in their most coherent form in the Eddaic lays.'[48]

Skaldic verse relied on eddic for more than comprehension, however. The latter also provided an ideological foundation for the former's generation of prestige and legitimacy. While skaldic verse is complex, usually ascribed to named poets, and, in terms of content and circumstances of composition, anchored in specific, historical contexts, eddic verse is simpler in form and diction, anonymous, and timeless, dealing with mythic or legendary settings and figures.[49] Given these qualities, many have assumed that eddic verse was a popular rather than courtly art form.[50] As several scholars have argued, however, there is no evidence for, and several facts that speak against, the existence of separate classes of poets in medieval Scandinavia; it is most likely that both forms of poetry were produced by essentially the same set of elite practitioners (and were ultimately targeted towards the same audience), and that their divergences in form and character should be attributed to their fulfilment of different functions.[51]

As we have seen, the primary functions of skaldic court-poetry were to praise, commemorate, and legitimize patrons. Its capacity to perform such functions relied in part on the idea that poetic speech was divinely inspired. This ideology is primarily expressed in eddic rather than skaldic verse, however. As several critics have suggested, eddic poetry in many ways relates to skaldic verse as prose does to poetic speech in general: like prose, eddic verse is relatively straightforward, easy to follow, focused on narrative and content rather than style or form, and is regarded as a collective rather than an individual product.[52] These impersonal and atemporal qualities of eddic poetry foster a sense, which it shares with saga literature, that its content is objective, rather than formulated by specific agents for specific purposes. Thus, eddic poetry, product of no named or nameable person, place, or time, could establish a divine basis for the authority of poetic speech in a way that context-bound skaldic compositions could not.

Otherworldly accounts of the origin of poetic skill and its transfer to humans are also found in sagas about poets. These provide practically no information on the training of skalds – in the sagas, skalds are born, not made.[53] The most famous precocious skald is Egill Skalla-Grímsson, who is depicted as spouting impromptu *dróttkvætt* at age three.[54] Even in the cases of those who start composing at more realistic ages, sagas portray their skill as something inborn rather than acquired, simply stating that so-and-so *var gott skáld*,[55] or providing supernatural explanations for the emergence of this talent.[56] Furthermore, many sources insist that skaldic speech, especially when used in conjunction with runic inscriptions, held an inherent, magical efficacy.[57] With the extra-human origin and power of their speech thus grounded in two forms of 'authorless' narrative, eddic verse and sagas, the praise (or blame) of kings dispensed by skalds was tantamount to a manifestation of divine approval (or censure).

Looming behind any discussion of the religious dimensions of skaldic speech is the arrival in northern society of Christianity. If the inspiration of Óðinn and other sorts of extra-human forces was central to a skald's claim to authority, how was this claim affected by conversion? While the victory of Christianity seems as if it should have marked the end of the court skald's profession, this was in fact not the case. To be sure, conversion necessitated changes in the way that *dróttkvætt* was practised: in particular, mythological kennings, especially those referring to rulers as pagan deities, were rejected by missionary kings such as Óláfr Tryggvason and Óláfr Haraldsson.[58] And yet, despite their aversion to aspects of the skaldic art, neither of the Óláfrs nor the kings who followed them got rid of their poets altogether. The continued lack of written culture was probably the deciding factor in *dróttkvætt*'s endurance. While its kings were solidly Christian from the late 900s, Norway's church remained for some time in a primitive state. It was not, in fact, until the institution of an archbishopric in Niðaróss in 1152/3 that the Norwegian court had anything like the literate and bureaucratic clerical staffs enjoyed by monarchs of other Christian nations. The roles that such staffs fulfilled for continental courts (secretary, diplomat, counsellor, propagandist, etc.) remained largely the province of skalds during the interim. Similarly, the *hirðskálds*' products continued to serve as kings' chief means of preserving the history of their reigns until the mid-1100s, when Latin and vernacular annals began to appear. Even if, therefore, the claim to divine inspiration provided a basis for the authority of *hirðskálds*' speech in the pagan era, its loss was not enough to finish *dróttkvætt* off. The verse's distinguished form, coupled with the lack of a viable alternative means of commemorating the deeds and character of kings, proved sufficient to safeguard this art form's value to monarchs for some two centuries after the conversion.

The Education and Early Cultural Production of Snorri Sturluson

While Icelanders continued to compose *dróttkvætt* for Norway's kings in the twelfth century, skaldic poetry began during this time to play a more varied and vital role in the culture of Iceland itself. This century is often labelled a 'skaldic renaissance' in which the ornate form and mythological kennings of an earlier era gained a new lease on life.[59] It was also when Iceland began to produce written texts. Both developments must be considered in light of the rise of what Peter Foote calls the clerical gentry, a coalition of church and secular authorities who constituted twelfth-century Iceland's highest social and political stratum, as well as its chief producers and consumers of culture.[60] As Guðrún Nordal has shown, skaldic verse's popularity among this elite grew out of its use as exempla for the study of *grammatica*, the cornerstone of clerical education.[61] She also argues that a rise in interest in skaldic verse 'coincided with the leaning of the Icelandic ruling families towards aristocratic codes of behaviour,' a development parallelling the situation in Norway around the time of *dróttkvætt*'s first appearance, when an ascendant elite had required cultural products to naturalize its rising status.[62] Members of this Icelandic oligarchy were not just consumers of skaldic verse, but themselves used it in interactions and altercations to banter, comment upon events, or taunt enemies.[63] The capacity to recite such *lausavísur* was, like clerical education and involvement in the production of written texts, a mark of distinction. Most of these elite poets were what Guðrún Nordal calls non-professionals; they shared the poetic field in twelfth- and thirteenth-century Iceland with the more traditional, remunerated *hirðskáld*s, and an emerging group of religious poets who used pagan metres to praise the Christian God and his saints.[64]

Most, then, who produced prose literature or skaldic verse in twelfth-century Iceland were either clerics, monks, or *goðar* with clerical training. Not surprisingly, such agents' products were either amalgams of native culture and Latin models, like the law codes, genealogies, and annalistic histories that were Iceland's earliest written texts, or adaptations of native art forms to new purposes, like their verse. The first sites to offer anything like formal instruction in Iceland were the sees of Skálholt and Hólar, where many *goðar*'s sons were educated. The bishops' seats were not the only educational choices available, however. Both the Haukdælir and Oddaverjar, families with long-standing ties to the clerical hierarchy and wealth founded on ownership of prosperous churches, ran schools of instruction at their homesteads.[65] Of these four centres of learning, Oddi is considered to have achieved the most perfect balance of continental and native culture, and Jón Loptsson is thought of as the clearest embodiment of this syncretism. Foote and David M. Wilson write: 'Jón can be said to epitomize the situation of the Icelandic chieftain, who since the conversion had made the Church and its learning and literature a part of their lives, but had done so essentially on independent, native terms.'[66]

The same cannot be said of Jón's foster-son. Turville-Petre writes: 'Snorri's education, unlike that of his foster-father ... was the education of a layman.'[67] The cause of Snorri's break with the cultural milieu and interests of the clerical gentry can be traced to a single year and document, both of which mark the climax of a gradual estrangement of religious and secular authority in Iceland. For most of the 1100s, clergy were weakly differentiated in Iceland, where priests could be and often were *goðar*, participated in lawsuits and combat, married, and had children. In this century's last decades, however, the ripples of Gregorian reform made themselves felt in Iceland, finding champions in its bishops, and a string of edicts from Norway's archbishops succeeded in drawing a sharper line between clergy and laity than had previously existed in Iceland. The last and most important of these directives, issued in 1190, forbade ordination of *goðar*.[68] Although never made into law, this ban was extremely effective – after 1190, there is no record of an Icelandic *goði* ever again entering the priesthood.[69]

Snorri was around eleven years old when this ban, which forced elite Icelanders to make an unaccustomed choice between pursuing religious versus secular authority, went into effect. Snorri's choice was unequivocal: unlike his foster-father and foster-brother, both deacons, or his brother Þórðr, a subdeacon, Snorri never held nor seems to have aspired to hold even a minor church office. Since 'Snorri was the first Icelandic prose writer whose background is known who was not a cleric,' we encounter something new in his cultural production.[70] Unlike earlier Icelandic writers, Snorri's basis of authority, the focus of his pursuits, and the interests he took in native culture were overwhelmingly secular. While an aspiration to integrate Norse poetics into the study of grammar may have inspired the clerical gentry's enthusiasm for this art, Snorri's work on poetry was born of a more conservative impulse, namely, his desire to preserve its capacity to generate profits for Icelanders in Norway's courts. I will deal shortly with Snorri's lack of expertise and/or interest in continental, Latin learning. Here, I wish only to insist that scholars have underestimated the effect that the archbishop's foreclosure of the possibility of joint religious and secular authority had upon the strategic interests that Snorri, in comparison with his immediate predecessors in Iceland's young textual culture, took in the kinds of resources available to him at Oddi.

There is no doubt that the deal reached between Sturla Þórðarson and Jón Loptsson afforded Snorri access to forms of cultural and linguistic capital that would have been unavailable to him had he remained at home. Foote has characterized this arrangement as 'an offer and an acceptance of a share for one member of Sturla's family in the cultural gifts which seemed an indispensable heritage in those who were to belong amongst the greatest members of the commonwealth.'[71] But if Snorri's early exposure to legitimate culture is beyond question, our sources are vague on the particulars of his education. The younger Sturla Þórðarson provides few details concerning Snorri's years at Oddi, and scholars have long debated the content, range, and formality of his training. All agree that he was in a position to receive the best education that late twelfth-century Iceland had to offer – the library at Oddi must have contained (in Latin and Icelandic) annals, poetry, law codes, genealogies, saints' lives, grammatical treatises, religious exegesis, and hymn and homily collections. What remains contested is the extent to which Snorri realized the opportunities presented by this material. Since Oddi was not comparable to the cathedral schools or nascent universities of continental Europe, and thus Snorri is unlikely to have followed a set course of study mirroring the trivium and quadrivium, his education was probably informal, and our clearest window into its particulars lies in his own cultural output. Based on this alone, Snorri was clearly conversant in commonwealth law, Scandinavian (particularly royal) history, genealogical lists, pagan myth, skaldic verse in all its forms, and, for lack of a better term, local lore.

Snorri's works provide much less certainty, however, about his conversance with Oddi's Latin resources or contemporary ecclesiastical culture. On this question, I follow the judgment of Anthony Faulkes, who feels that the search for Snorri's Latin influences has run somewhat amok in recent years, and that direct influences from Latin texts are hardly to be found in his work.[72] Like Faulkes, I doubt that Snorri was widely read or even proficient in Latin, and I agree with his opinion that traces of Latin learning in Snorri's works can be accounted for by his knowledge of vernacular translations or by concluding 'that Snorri gained all this knowledge orally from people who had read Latin works.'[73] At any rate, even if one wishes to argue that Snorri knew Latin, it must be conceded, given that he 'nowhere refers to Latin writers or claims (even falsely) to be quoting them ... [and is] the only major medieval historiographer of whom it can be said that he made hardly any use of Latin sources,' that he was singularly averse to making this talent known.[74] To Faulkes's reasons for doubting Snorri's Latin learning, I would add only my suggestion that, whatever his capacity for using Latin texts may have been, the interests he would have had in exploiting such resources were severely curbed by the archiepiscopal decree of 1190.

The first brand of cultural capital other than legal that Snorri exploited in early adulthood was skaldic verse. Like early Icelanders, Snorri quickly recognized poetry as a resource that could be converted in foreign markets. Unlike his predecessors, however, he did not travel to Norway to exploit this skill, at least not at first. Instead, he sent poems in written form to his objects of praise.[75] According to *Skáldatal*, a list of court poets and patrons in a manuscript of Snorri's *Edda*, the first panegyric that Snorri sent abroad was dedicated to Norway's King Sverrir Sigurðarson. Sverrir died in 1202, and it is thought that Snorri composed and sent his tribute in this same year. Snorri's offering of praise to this monarch was by no means a neutral act, but one that, if publicized, could have alienated at least two powerful factions in Iceland. The first of these was Snorri's own foster-family, who were not on good terms with Sverrir. As Helgi Þorláksson describes the situation, the Oddaverjar had, in the course of combating Norwegian dominance over Icelandic trade, sought alliance with an Orkney jarl who had supported rivals in Norway of Sverrir and his followers.[76] If Snorri's poem can be dated to 1202, it was contemporary with two events – his harassment of Sæmundr's Orkney merchant friends and his inheritance of Bersi's authority and property – that marked his emerging independence from his foster-family. In similar fashion, Snorri's poem signalled his willingness to align himself with Sverrir against the Oddaverjar. The other faction Snorri risked offending were churchmen in Iceland and elsewhere. Sverrir, a Faroese priest claiming to be an illegitimate son of King Sigurðr munnr, clashed with church agents at home and abroad for his entire reign. Whereas the monarch whom Sverrir usurped and killed was the first to be crowned by Norway's archbishop, Sverrir drove two successive archbishops and all five of Norway's bishops into exile, revoked virtually all of the clerical privileges his predecessor had granted, and died under a papal ban.[77] Snorri's willingness to praise such a king signals at the very least a lack of regard for ecclesiastical sensibilities, and perhaps resentment over the church's growing assertiveness in northern politics.[78]

Over the next quarter century, Snorri continued to demonstrate support for Sverrir's dynasty through his poetry. While there is no record of Snorri having praised Sverrir's two immediate successors, both of whom died in 1204, he dispatched praise to Sverrir's nephews, the half-brothers King Ingi Bárðarson and jarl Hákon galinn Fólkviðarson. Only one response to this poetry has been recorded, but it was a positive one. According to *Íslendinga saga*, jarl Hákon repaid Snorri's gesture with 'a sword and shield and mail-coat,' rewards so impressive that another skald praised Snorri just for having received them.[79] But tragedy intruded on Snorri's triumph: 'The jarl wrote to Snorri, that he should travel abroad, and promised that he would show great honours to him. And that was much to Snorri's liking. But the jarl died in that time, and that delayed his journey abroad for some years.'[80] This was in 1214, and the jarl's brother the king died not long after, in 1217. With some of Norway's aristocrats dying too quickly for Snorri to capitalize on the connections forged by his tributes, and some, it seems, even faster than he could compose and deliver poems in their honour, a less persistent skald might have decided it was not worth his trouble. Snorri, however, knew the advantages that powerful Norwegian allies could provide him in Iceland's field of power, and so, when he finally sailed to Norway in the autumn of 1218, he came ready to deliver more skaldic paeans to his hosts.

The King, the Jarl, the Lady, and the Poet

Snorri arrived in a country with two rulers. Upon Ingi's death, his half-brother Skúli Bárðarson, jarl and inheritor of the king's *hirð* and wealth, had seemed the strongest contender for the throne.[81] It was, however, their younger cousin, the fourteen-year-old Hákon Hákonarson, who became king: as illegitimate son of Sverrir's first short-lived heir, Hákon's claim to be a direct descendent of this popular monarch was enough to gain him the support of the Birkibeinar faction in 1217.[82] The following year, after his mother underwent an ordeal to confirm his royal pedigree, Hákon secured the belated blessing of Archbishop Guttormr, and he and Skúli reached an agreement in which the jarl would control one-third of the country and serve as regent during the king's minority.[83] Of Snorri's arrival in Norway, *Íslendinga saga* tells that 'the jarl received Snorri exceedingly well, and he went to [stay with] the jarl.'[84] Skúli must have known Snorri by reputation and from the poetry sent to his late relatives, and he hosted the Icelander throughout the winter of 1218–19 in Túnsberg, where Hákon was also in residence.[85] It is not mentioned, however, in either of Sturla's two accounts of Snorri's trip to Norway that he met with the king during this time.

In the spring of 1219, Snorri travelled east to visit the lawman Áskell Magnússon and his wife *frú* Kristín Nikulássdóttir, widow of Hákon galinn and niece of King Sverrir.[86] No trace remains of a poem, entitled *Andvaka* ('Wakefulness'), that Snorri is said to have composed for Kristín at her late husband's request, and it is uncertain whether he presented it to her at this meeting or had sent it earlier.[87] Whichever was the case, *Íslendinga saga* tells that Kristín 'received Snorri honourably and gave him many honourable gifts. She gave him the standard, which Eiríkr Knútsson, king of the Swedes, had owned. He had that when he killed King Sörkvir at Gestilsrein.'[88] Sturla's detailed account of this standard suggests that Snorri brought it back to Iceland, where it was much admired. The gift also held a more pointed significance; as Helgi Þorláksson writes, 'This is an unusual poetic reward. The Birkibeinar had been favoured by Eiríkr but Sörkvir gave his support to the Danes ... Kristín perhaps thought that Snorri, as a zealous proponent of the Birkibeinar, was deserving of this, to bear the standard of Eiríkr, who had died in 1216.'[89] Kristín's reward for Snorri's poetry was thus chosen as a token of thanks for his support of the reigning dynasty, as evidenced by his recent opposition to his foster-family, current adversaries in Iceland of the king and his friends.

Snorri, Skúli, and Hákon were all in Þrándheimr in the winter of 1219–20, but there is no hint that Snorri and the king met until the spring.[90] At this time, Snorri wished to sail home, but was delayed by deteriorating foreign relations, of which Sturla writes: 'the men of Norway were still great enemies of the Icelanders and most of all the Oddaverjar.'[91] By this time, the dispute of the Norwegian merchants and Oddaverjar had led to several deaths.[92] Skúli went so far as to prepare to invade Iceland, but was persuaded to cancel this expedition. Sturla's sagas agree on this outcome, but they differ as to how it was reached. In *Íslendinga saga*, 'the wiser men' among the Norwegians speak out against the plan, and an Icelander, Guðmundr Oddsson, advises Skúli to abandon his plans with a verse.[93] Snorri's intervention, however, is said to have been decisive:

Snorri greatly opposed the expedition and advised them to make friends with the best men in Iceland, and declared that as soon as he could come to them with his words, it would seem best to men to turn with obedience to the Norwegian rulers. He also said this, that there were not then other men in Iceland greater than his brothers, except Sæmundr, and declared that they would follow his advice ... And with such persuasions the jarl's mood was rather softened, and he made that plan, that the Icelanders should ask King Hákon that he might intercede for them, so that the invasion would not occur. The king was young then, but Dagfinnr the lawman, who was his advisor, was the Icelanders' greatest friend. And that came to pass, as the king decided, that the invasion did not take place.[94]

In *Hákonar saga*, this chain of intercessions is nearly reversed. Here, 'Snorri Sturluson and those Icelandic men, who were there, asked Dagfinnr *bóndi* to plead with the king that this plan might be abandoned.'[95] Dagfinnr succeeded, and Hákon is said to have then appealed to Skúli, who 'then gave up this design. That plan was made, that Snorri Sturluson was sent abroad to intercede for the Norwegians. King Hákon gave him the title of *lendr maðr* ... Then for the first time that was discussed with the jarl, that Snorri should bring the land under the king.'[96] While in *Hákonar saga*, this unprecedented honour is said to have come from the king, in *Íslendinga saga* Sturla says that, while the title was given by both king and jarl, 'that was mostly the doing of the jarl and Snorri.'[97]

Snorri finally sailed for Iceland in the autumn of 1220. Sturla tells that before he left, 'Snorri had composed two poems about [the] jarl.'[98] Both were *drápur*, the most distinctive form of skaldic composition, and one normally reserved for praising kings. In response, Skúli gave Snorri 'the ship, that he went abroad in, and fifteen big gifts'; as Jón Jóhannesson remarks, 'there are no other instances of an Icelander having had so many honours heaped upon him by a foreign sovereign.'[99] In ways, this parting exchange echoes Snorri's dealings with Kristín during the preceding summer. In both instances, Snorri received lavish gifts in return for poetic gestures, but what was also being rewarded was his willingness to support royal interests back home. In each case, we find the agents involved following a sort of script: rather than openly acknowledging the political nature of their dealings, both nobles postpone any material or symbolic reward until Snorri has extended to them a cultural gift in the form of a poetic tribute.

The conduct of Snorri and his patrons mirrors a well-attested literary motif, that of the Icelander who travels to a foreign court to obtain favour through demonstration of verbal skill. While present in early *skáldasögur*,[100] this motif emerges most clearly in the *þættir* (sg. *þáttr*), or short stories, that are mostly preserved in *Morkinskinna*, a collection of kings' sagas dating to c. 1220. As Joseph Harris writes, such *þættir* typically 'chart the relationship between two main characters, a king and a commoner, usually an Icelander: the Icelander is the hero with whom the reader identifies, and his relation to the king is normally one of relative dependence and powerlessness.'[101] But while the hero is initially met with suspicion or contempt, he invariably proves himself 'cleverer and more tough-minded than the Norwegian in spite of his disadvantages as a provincial.'[102] Given Icelanders' historical monopolization of court-poetry, such tales were clearly more than literary fancy. They are best regarded as dramatic distillations of the historical relations and interactions of Icelandic poets and foreign rulers – they are an instance of art imitating life. Since most critics agree that these *þættir* of travelling poets existed as independent and probably oral tales prior to their incorporation into sagas,[103] there is no reason to doubt that Snorri was familiar with them, or that they conditioned him to approach his hosts with certain expectations regarding his (and their) proper roles and conduct. His hosts, moreover, seem to have shared his expectations – Snorri's dealings with Skúli and Kristín are instances of life imitating art imitating life. Whatever else was at stake in their interactions, Snorri approached these nobles first and foremost as a skald bearing poetic gifts, and they, at least on the surface, rewarded him as such.

There was, however, one crucial figure whose interactions with Snorri did not conform to this literary/historical pattern: King Hákon. Based on Sturla's accounts, the recitation and reward of poetry had no place in their dealings – the only thing Snorri is said to have received from the king was (perhaps) the title of *lendr maðr*, for which he offered only his cooperation and (perhaps) loyalty. Few have found it significant that the ritualistic exchange that Snorri performed with other nobles seems not to have occurred with the king. Most simply assume, as Sturla's silence suggests, that Snorri did not dedicate or perform any verse for Hákon while in Norway. I find it hard, however, to accept that Snorri, in light of his sensitivity to form in his dealings with other rulers, as well as the fact that he recited *drápur* for Hákon's recent rival to the throne, offered no praise to the king. The reason for Sturla's silence on this matter is not, I would suggest, that Snorri did not offer Hákon any verse, but rather that his gift was not reciprocated. This argument is supported by Sturla's general tendencies in writing about his uncle's practice as court-poet. *Skáldatal* lists Snorri as *hirðskáld* of six Norwegian notables: the kings Sverrir, Ingi, and Hákon, the jarls Hákon and Skúli, and the lady Kristín. Of these six, Sturla mentions only Snorri's praise of the three lowest-ranked, nowhere referring to his poems in honour of kings.[104] It is critical to observe, however, that whenever Sturla does refer to Snorri's praise-poetry, he focuses not on the verse itself, which he hardly quotes, but on the rewards that were received for it.[105] In short, Sturla was not impressed by his uncle's poetic skill so much as by what it was capable of being converted into. Sturla's silence regarding Snorri's poetry for kings suggests that these attempts at conversion failed.

While Snorri's first trip abroad seems to have been a generally successful and profitable undertaking, it likely fell short of his expectations in at least one significant respect. While the poetic capital Snorri had acquired at Oddi had proven its worth within Norway's political field, there remained one, particularly crucial agent who appears to have been impervious to the charms of his artistic displays. Hákon's indifference to Snorri's poetic wares was not the only cloud dotting this skald's horizon, however. In the next chapter, I will discuss not only the factors that lay behind the evolving cultural tastes of the early thirteenth-century Norwegian monarchy, and what such shifts meant for Snorri and Iceland's other cultural producers, but additional developments and trends in the Scandinavian political and cultural sphere that would have given Snorri reason to suspect that the ability of his poetic capital to continue generating political, social, and economic profit was fading, and not likely to last much longer.

5 A Poet in Search of an Audience: The Diminishing Prestige-Value of Skaldic Poetry

The newly appointed *lendr maðr* Snorri Sturluson returned to Iceland in his new ship, laden with gifts from jarl Skúli and *frú* Kristín, in the fall of 1220. As Sturla relates, news of Snorri's 'arrival spread quickly inland and he was received with all kinds of honours.'[1] Already the man with the 'greatest' honour in Iceland when he departed in 1218, Snorri had taken his resources and practices into a new market, the Norwegian court, where he had effected a conversion of cultural into material capital, which was then reconverted into symbolic capital upon his homecoming. And yet, Snorri failed to bring back tangible tokens of appreciation from the king, which, as proof of Norway's most powerful agent's recognition of himself and his talents, would have provided the greatest symbolic profits. Whether one concludes, as I have argued, that Hákon failed to appreciate and compensate the products that Snorri offered him, or that Snorri, perceiving the king as an unlikely source of profit, had focused on more promising prospects, poetry appears to have played no significant role in their interactions.

Most scholars, rather than try to account for Hákon's insensitivity to Snorri's verse, have affirmed the king's reaction (or lack thereof) through their own negative appraisals of Snorri's art. For many, he simply was not very gifted. Ciklamini, for example, feels that Snorri 'lacked the makings of a great skald,' while Sigurður Nordal laments that he 'was not given the temper and feelings of Egill Skalla-Grímsson.'[2] According to this view, Hákon's reaction was only natural – if Snorri's poetry had been better, the response might have been more favourable. A variation on the claim that Snorri lacked poetic charisma holds that his relationship to skaldic verse was too academic to yield great art. As Turville-Petre writes, 'Snorri knew better how to interpret poetry than to compose it,' while Hollander describes his poems as 'essentially "products of the library."'[3] Such opinions are often not grounded in any detailed comparison of Snorri's work with that of the geniuses against whom he is found wanting, but depend, as Bourdieu writes, upon an opposition 'of "authentic" culture to "scholastic" knowledge, which as such is devalued.'[4] Snorri's poetry has been judged, in short, in line with the maxim: those who can't do, teach (or those who teach, couldn't possibly do). In any case, as I will show, the relative aesthetic worth of Snorri's poetry, as measured by medieval or modern standards, had nothing to do with the failure of his cultural wares to capture the attention of his most desired patron.

For the most part, those who go beyond aesthetic or charismatic explanations for Hákon's disregard of Snorri's verse have rightly viewed it as part of a wider shift in cultural tastes. As is well known, in the late twelfth and thirteenth centuries skaldic poetry experienced, particularly in Norway's court, a reduction in audience that led to its virtual extinction by the early 1300s. During this same time, the importation, translation, and adaptation of foreign culture rapidly increased, again most visibly in and through Norway's court. Given this backdrop, Snorri's efforts to interest the Norwegian elite in his verse, and to encourage the practice of this art form by writing the *Edda*, have been viewed as a lonely struggle against the poetry's ineluctable displacement by facile but ever more popular foreign literature. Snorri's resistance to this trend has been understood as an attempt to preserve the poetry for its own sake. Just as Snorri's motivations are seen as primarily artistic, the shifts in taste that spurred his efforts have been understood mainly in cultural terms. Faulkes, for example, describes the threats posed to skaldic poetry as if they were mainly a result of the introduction of novel literary genres into the north:

> As a means of preserving the memory of historical events, as well as as an organ of royal propaganda, skaldic poetry was being superseded by the written prose saga ... and as a part of the ritual and entertainment of the court was being superseded by various kinds of prose narrative, including translated romances; taste in poetry was moving to favour the ballad and its derivatives; in Iceland a new genre, the *rímur*, was to replace skaldic verse as a medium of entertainment both written and oral.[5]

In this chapter, I provide an account of not only the cultural but also the social and political factors that contributed to the waning interest in native poetry, thus laying the groundwork for later examinations of Snorri's response to this decrease in the value of his cultural capital. Faulkes's list of genres, while inadequate as an explanation for the *Edda*, offers a useful schema for organizing this survey: first, I will look at changes that impacted the overall sociocultural sphere of medieval Scandinavia, not only the appearance of prose works such as the saga, but of literacy itself, and the preconditions to the emergence of this technology, the conversion, and the establishment of ecclesiastical institutions; second, I will discuss developments specific to early thirteenth-century Norway, particularly the importation of romance at the court of Hákon Hákonarson; finally, I will examine the infiltration of foreign cultural impulses, above all the ballad metres that would give rise to the genres of *danzar* and *rímur*, into Iceland, and how this impacted the position and status of skalds in that country.

Literacy and Legitimacy

As mentioned in chapter 4, Christianity's victory did not spell the immediate doom of skaldic poetry in Iceland or Norway. Conversion did, however, introduce changes that contributed over time to the marginalization and ultimate extinction of this art form. The earliest and most obvious of these was the challenge that conversion posed to the continued dissemination of pagan mythology, the stories and characters of which provided source material for kennings, the building-blocks of skalds' speech. As I have noted, the discrediting of pagan myth resulted in an initial impoverishment of skaldic diction, until the so-called skaldic renaissance of the twelfth century reinvigorated to some extent the use of mythological kennings. It is no coincidence that this revival was roughly contemporary with the first application, at least in writing, of euhemerism, the theory that beings now or once regarded as gods were in fact originally ancient kings and heroes, to pre-Christian Norse religion.[6] While literal belief in pagan deities was not an option for twelfth-century Icelanders, euhemerism provided them as well as other Scandinavians with a way to talk about the gods of their past, even to extend some measure of reality to them, without contradicting Christian belief.[7] And yet, despite the new interest in and possibility of speaking about pagan gods, there are signs that by the time Snorri was trying to make his way as a skald, knowledge of myth and its characters was, at least in some sectors of society, precariously low.[8] A full discussion of the extent of thirteenth-century Icelanders' and Norwegians' familiarity with pagan myth, and the steps taken by Snorri to reacquaint contemporaries with this heritage, will be postponed until chapter 8 where an analysis of *Gylfaginning* and the *Formáli* will be presented. Here, I will focus on two other sociocultural developments for which conversion paved the way, but the effects of which upon the practice and reception of skaldic verse were not truly felt until the mid-1100s: these were the introduction of, first, literacy and written prose works, and, second, ecclesiastical legitimation of Scandinavian kings.

From the start, a major focus of written culture in Iceland and Norway was history, especially royal history. Sæmundr Sigfússon, Iceland's first known writer, was renowned as an authority on the history of Norway's monarchs.[9] The first prose work that we possess is Ari Þorgilsson's *Íslendingabók* (c. 1122–3), a vernacular account of Iceland's settlement and first several centuries. While Ari's extant work does not describe Norwegian royalty except insofar as it impacted important moments in Iceland's history, he makes reference in his prologue to a longer version of his text in which the history of Norway's kings figures prominently.[10] As for Norway, texts dealing with native royal history, sometimes called the 'Norwegian synoptics,' began to appear in Latin and the vernacular in the 1170s.[11] Production of such works by Norwegians was relatively short-lived, however; as with the composition of skaldic poetry, it was not long before Icelanders had all but monopolized the writing of prose, historical works.

During the time when Icelanders established their dominance over prose history, the texts themselves evolved from a bare-bones, annalistic style towards the greater characterization and narrative detail that would typify sagas. The first sagas appear during the last half of the twelfth century, and deal almost exclusively with lives of kings, mostly Norwegian.[12] The earliest extant *konungasaga* is *Sverris saga*, a work commissioned and in part supervised by its subject, Sverrir Sigurðarson.[13] Like all Icelandic or Norwegian texts before Snorri's, *Sverris saga* was written by a churchman, in this case Karl Jónsson of Þingeyrar monastery.[14] This text marks a turning point in the clerical or monastic scribe's usurpation of the *hirðskáld*'s position as privileged recorder of royal history. Indeed, while eleven skalds are attached to Sverrir in *Skáldatal*, only two lines of their poetry about him have survived, and these only in Snorri's *Edda*.[15] One factor accounting for the ready embrace of this new medium by kings is that sagas allowed them to take possession of the vehicles of their praise and commemoration in ways not possible with skaldic verse. As written products, sagas were presented to kings as objects rather than performances. Unlike with oral encomia, the presence of the producer was no longer necessary to the transmission of the product. The saga writer thus had less opportunity for conversion of cultural goods into material rewards or symbolic recognition, exchanges that face-to-face delivery of praise-poetry had rendered all but obligatory. There are also formal differences to consider. As discussed in earlier chapters, authorship in the medieval north was a function of form, not content. Thus, while neither skalds nor saga writers held an intellectual copyright on the matter of which they told, the former, owing to their mastery over rarefied speech, held a greater claim to their products than the latter, who worked in the undistinguished medium of quotidian speech.[16] In sum, saga writing was a very different kind of cultural practice from skaldic composition: it produced works with greater clarity and claims to objectivity, both traits benefiting its subjects, but held less possibility for conversion into immediate reward or enduring prestige for its practitioners.

The second factor associated with conversion that negatively impacted skaldic practice in Norway's courts was a growing reliance on ecclesiastical modes of legitimation to buttress the authority of not just individual kings but monarchy itself. As discussed in chapter 4, even when skaldic verse lost its claim to divine inspiration with the eclipse of paganism, its practitioners continued to laud kings' generosity, honour, and warrior prowess. Skaldic poetry's post-conversion viability thus depended upon the continued relevance of kings' personal traits and deeds to their legitimacy. However, as Sverre Bagge has demonstrated, Norwegian society's fundamental notions of kingship underwent dramatic changes from the mid-twelfth to mid-thirteenth centuries, during which time 'the royal office largely replaces the individual person.'[17] Whereas royal power had previously been regarded as personal, charismatic, and resting upon support from below, it was now conceptualized as a position filled by God. No longer a divisible estate to which all sons of earlier kings, legitimately born or not, held equal claim, the kingship was now viewed as a divinely instituted office whose single occupant was to conform to the Augustinian ideal of the *rex iustus*, and be selected in accordance with the church-sanctioned standards of legitimate birth, primogeniture, and Christian virtue.[18]

Alongside this new ideology came new methods for selecting and installing kings, above all the ceremonies of coronation and anointing. Performance of these rituals was made possible by the establishment of an archdiocese in Norway in 1152/3.[19] About a decade later, in 1163 or 1164, the first coronation of a Norwegian king, the young Magnús Erlingsson, was performed by Eysteinn Erlendsson, second archbishop at Niðaróss.[20] An account that Snorri offers of this event suggests that he was conscious as well as wary of the challenge that ecclesiastical legitimation posed to the traditional functions of Icelandic court skalds.[21] Whether or not he was aware of this threat, however, it was certainly real – while Magnús's reign and dynastic hopes alike were ended by Sverrir's rebellion, subsequent kings, including the usurper himself, recognized the advantages inherent in unitary kingship and the possibility of anchoring their rule in God's will, and actively sought archiepiscopal support before and after attaining the throne.

At the end of chapter 4, I suggested that while Snorri is known to have praised six Norwegian notables, Sturla never mentions his uncle's tributes to kings because of their failure to reciprocate.[22] One way to account for this is to assume that kings, having attained the pinnacle of society, saw little to be gained from encouraging Icelandic poets vying for attention and largesse. Still, this had not stopped kings from patronizing skalds for centuries. What, then, was it that made a nobleman into a king during Snorri's period? What did those candidates who gained the throne possess that the others lacked? One answer, and probably the most significant, is the support of Norway's archbishop. Of course, things were not as simple as this; all of the nobles with whom we are dealing had complicated relationships with the church. Sverrir, for instance, seized the throne in defiance of Norway's bishops; but since he was probably dead when Snorri's tribute arrived, it seems best to leave him out of a consideration of responses to Snorri's poetry.[23] Then there is Skúli, who, while he was an enthusiastic consumer of Snorri's verse, initially enjoyed, as legitimately born heir of the previous king, episcopal backing in his bid for the throne. Ultimately, however, the archbishop supported Hákon, bowing to his popularity among the Birkibeinar.[24] Our last two contenders, Ingi and Hákon galinn, fit our pattern neatly: Ingi was chosen king over his older half-brother largely because of his legitimate birth and the resulting approval of the archbishop.[25] Whatever, therefore, the particulars of each case, the basic point holds: those whose aspirations to the throne were stymied by a lack of church support responded to Snorri's poems, while those who reached that goal with the aid of episcopal endorsement did not. It seems that Norway's kings no longer invested in skaldic verse as a generator of legitimacy and prestige in part because they had access to a more potent source of both in the sanction of God, as manifested through the approval of Norway's highest church official.

In sum, Snorri's efforts to interest kings in his poetry had to compete from the outset against two trends in the Icelandic/Norwegian social space that powerfully compromised skaldic verse's capacity to function as cultural capital. During the same period when Snorri was receiving his education at Oddi, King Sverrir was promoting the adoption of sagas as a preferred instrument of royal celebration as well as acceptance of ecclesiastical measures of royal power. Ultimately, the ascendancy of prose texts and church-sanctioned standards and rituals of royal legitimation were not just the earliest but also, given the extent to which they rendered the practical and ideological functions of skaldic verse obsolete or redundant, they were the most devastating of the factors that contributed to this art form's extinction in Norway's court. Nevertheless, there are other factors that more immediately impacted Snorri's efforts to deploy his poetic talents at the highest level of Norwegian society, the most important of which was the importation of foreign and above all French literary products into the court of Hákon Hákonarson.

Keeping up with the Angevins:
King Hákon and the Importation of Romance

Continental culture's infiltration into Scandinavia's courts predated Hákon's reign by centuries, and skalds had long been jealous of kings' divided attentions. In a poem composed c. 940 by Þorbjörn hornklofi for Haraldr hárfagri, the skald complains about having to compete with continental entertainers:

> About jesters [or fiddlers] and jugglers have I said little to you: what cheer is there from Andaðr [a jester] and those others in Haraldr's halls? Andaðr is loved by an earless hound and commits folly and makes a king laugh; those and others, who of old had to bear a burning spoon, with burning caps dragged under their belts, are men deserving to be kicked.[26]

Such professional rivalry is echoed in later times. In 1149, Einarr Skúlason – an ancestor of Snorri and 'the most important skald of his century'[27] – was driven by the failure of his verse to elicit a reward to compose a satire in which he reproved a Danish king's preference for 'fiddles and pipes to *dróttkvætt*.'[28] Thirty-some years later, the skald Máni tried to distract Magnús Erlingsson, Norway's first crowned king, from his own band of jugglers, jesters, and minstrels.[29] For all of the anxiety these entertainers aroused, however, the threat they posed to skalds' livelihood was never very serious – in the face of the latter's ornate disdain, the piping, miming, and dog-tricks of the former could not help but seem frivolous. More importantly, these foreign entertainments were incapable, owing to their essentially non-discursive nature, of directly undermining skaldic poetry's laudatory, propagandistic, and historiographical functions.

Nevertheless, as we have seen, the time did come when skaldic verse's centuries-old position of cultural supremacy was seriously jeopardized. It was not, however, until Hákon Hákonarson's reign that skaldic poetry was forced to cede its dominant status in Norway's court. As Einar Sveinsson writes, it was in the early years of Hákon's rule that 'the country was flooded with the currents of chivalry ... [and after his] time the victory of the chivalric spirit in Norway was completed.'[30] More than just witnesses to or participants in a shift in consumption patterns, Hákon and his court drove skaldic verse's displacement as the 'legitimate' or 'capital-C' cultural product in Norway. In order to avoid the language of volition and value judgment that has typified past discussion of Hákon's cultural predilections, I will stress in what follows that propensities for cultural consumption need not arise, any more than potential for cultural production, from deliberation, but rather are functions of the environment in which agents' tastes and capacities are formed. To explore adequately, then, Hákon's attraction to continental culture, I will discuss several topics: first, the form and nature of the king's education; second, the web of international political, social, and economic relations into which he entered upon assuming the throne; and finally, what can only be described as his and his court's programmatic importation, translation, and adaptation of Anglo-Norman cultural products, models, and values.

'The education,' Rudolf Meissner writes, 'that King Hákon Hákonarson received was a clerical-courtly one, modern for his time and his land, essentially defined by foreign ideas.'[31] As with Snorri, however, details on Hákon's schooling are hard to come by. The information available suggests that there was some disagreement over the kind of education this king's son ought to receive. For most of his first decade, Hákon was raised by jarl Hákon galinn and his wife Kristín. According to Sturla, 'When Hákon the king's son was seven years old the jarl had him set to book-learning. But when he had been studying for awhile, the jarl asked: "What are you studying, Hákon?" ... "I am studying chanting, my lord," he said. The jarl answers: "You shall not study chanting – you shall be neither a priest nor a bishop."'[32] If at all true, this anecdote testifies to jarl Hákon's bitterness towards the church that in 1204 had delivered the crown to his younger but legitimately born half-brother, feelings that may have translated into resistance to his young charge's clerical indoctrination. The jarl, however, died in 1214, and Hákon was transferred into the care of King Ingi, who had him educated alongside his own son at Niðaróss's cathedral school, where Hákon remained a student into the early years of his reign.[33] By all accounts, Hákon emerged from Niðaróss the most educated king Norway had yet seen, well-read in Latin and the vernacular, and probably having some knowledge of Old French as well. The most frequently cited proof we possess for the king's erudition is Matthew Paris's description, made after a 1248 embassy to Norway's court on behalf of France's Louis IX, of Hákon as *bene literatus*.[34]

Hákon's metropolitan education provided preparation for the sustained contact with foreign courts that marked his lengthy reign. Above all, this interaction was with England. This was, of course, nothing new – from Haraldr hárfagri's ninth-century consolidation of power to the death of Haraldr harðráði ('hard-ruler') in battle near York in 1066, all of Norway's kings had spent a good deal of time residing in or worrying about the British Isles. But while these early kings' interests in Britain were largely predatory, the relationship that developed between England's and Norway's royalty in the twelfth and thirteenth centuries was more amicable. One early high point of this association was Henry I's hosting of King Sigurðr Jorsalafári ('Jerusalem-farer') as the latter journeyed to crusade in 1107.[35] This friendship was renewed when Sigurðr's (purported) grandson came to power in 1184, and even Pope Innocent III could not dissuade John I of England from associating with the excommunicated Sverrir or providing him with aid in his struggle against the church-sponsored Baglar rebellion.[36] From this time, commercial, cultural, ecclesiastical, and diplomatic relations between these countries intensified. Aside from the military and political support that the Angevins continued to supply for Sverrir's successors, and the organizational models and training that Canterbury provided for Norway's church, Norway's king and archbishop profited enormously from preferential trade arrangements reached with the English crown.[37]

As a student in the port city of Niðaróss, Hákon spent most of his teen years at a nexus of Anglo-Norwegian intercourse, positioned to observe the advantages that relations with England held for Norway's crown and church. Capitalizing and building on this relationship became the principal agenda of the early years of his reign. One of the first actions taken by Hákon after his 1217 election was to establish ties with the equally recently appointed and young Henry III.[38] Letters sent at this time, Knut Helle writes, 'struck a note that was to resound throughout the long reigns of both monarchs: Norway wanted peace and friendship with England.'[39] Of the 'more than fifty state documents relating to trade, travel, and negotiations between the two nations' preserved in English records, three are letters addressed to Henry from Hákon, and four are letters from Skúli.[40] Gifts were also exchanged: among the exotic items Hákon sent Henry were Icelandic falcons, whale tusks, furs, a live elk in 1222, and, thirty years later, a live polar bear.[41] Both kings and their chancelleries also issued frequent writs of passage granting merchants from the other country special protection and status within their borders, and in 1223 a formal trade agreement, the first of its kind for either nation, was reached between their courts.[42]

Of course, Hákon's foreign interests were not restricted to England. As Helle observes, '*Hákonar saga* makes much out of these contacts with foreign lands and the supposedly flattering attention which the king received from there.'[43] Hákon's dealings with powers from the mainland (and beyond) include correspondence with Emperor Frederick II, an invitation to go crusading with France's Louis IX, the marriage of his daughter Kristín to the brother of the king of Castile, exchanges of gifts with the sultan of Tunis, and the several decades' worth of negotiations with Rome that culminated in his 1247 coronation by a papal legate.[44] Most of this far-flung diplomacy was concentrated, however, in the latter half of Hákon's reign, when, after Skúli's defeat, Norway was unified under his rule. During the period with which we are primarily concerned, 1217 to the mid-1220s, England remained the primary diplomatic focus of his court. It is no surprise, then, that England is the first place scholars have looked for the cultural impulses that entered Norway during these years. As Henry Goddard Leach writes:

> The Norwegians who visited England in the twelfth and thirteenth centuries ... carried home chivalric ideas that changed the character of the Norwegian court, and they bore from England manuscripts (in Latin or Anglo-Norman or Middle English) of the best mediæval literature, to be translated into the vernacular of the North.[45]

Looking to trace the import of a specific text, Paul Schach writes: 'It was in the summer of [1225] ... that the Norwegian monarch sent Henry III a brace of falcons ... and the Angevin monarch in return sent King Hákon a gift of grain. It is tempting to connect the *Tristran* manuscript with this exchange of gifts.'[46] The *Tristran* (c. 1175) of Thomas de Bretagne, a French poet active in Henry II's court, was the first Anglo-Norman literary product adapted at Hákon's court. According to the prologue of this first translated *riddarasaga*, or 'saga of knights,' entitled *Tristrams saga ok Ísöndar*, 'It was when 1226 years had passed since the birth of Christ, that this saga was translated into the Norse language at the behest and request of the honourable lord King Hákon. Brother Robert prepared and wrote it up.'[47] This saga was followed by a string of translations/adaptations of French metrical romances, chansons de geste, and *lais*. Four more of the resulting works refer explicitly to Hákon as patron or commissioner, and one also names 'Roðbert ábóti,' presumably the same man responsible for *Tristrams saga*, as its author.[48] There are a number of other translated *riddarasögur* that, while they identify neither author nor patron, are also believed to have been produced during Hákon's lengthy reign.[49]

Given the unprecedented scope of this translation effort, it is clear that by the mid-1220s Hákon was deliberately seeking to cultivate at his court a cultural milieu to match those of continental rulers. The proximate model for this effort, as well as Hákon's main source for imported literature, was the court of his lifelong friend, Henry III. And yet, Henry's court can be considered neither the ultimate source of these cultural innovations nor the true object of Hákon's emulation. The origin of the political, social, and moral ideals with which Hákon wished to associate himself and his court – ideals that can be lumped under the term 'chivalry' – must be located in the Parisian rather than the Angevin court.[50] Like most European rulers of the high Middle Ages, Hákon sought to imitate social mores and literary models that 'originated in France ... among the noblest and wealthiest class of what was at that time the greatest center ... of European culture.'[51] That Hákon could look to England for French literary goods was due to the fact that by the early 1200s the former had become, in the words of E.F. Halvorsen, 'in matters of literary culture, a French province.'[52]

Hákon's motives in sponsoring importation of French culture are clear. As Meissner writes,

> Hákon first wanted to see Norway recognized as, to use a modern expression, a European superpower, but secondly – and this was for him certainly the more important – through these associations with dazzling foreign courts to raise the reputation and dignity of the Norwegian monarchy at home ... [and if] the court of the strengthened Norwegian monarchy should stand equal to foreign courts, so must also the same intellectual and social culture be found there as abroad.[53]

Meissner's conclusions are affirmed by Susanne Kramarz-Bein, who writes:

> As no other Norwegian king before him, Hákon Hákonarson oriented himself in his courtly cultural/educational-policy towards England and the European conti-nent ... Behind the didactic intent of the *riddarasögur* ... stands an ideological goal. The translated *riddarasögur* make in a more fictional form their contribution to the formulation and strengthening of the feudal-aristocratic idea of kingship.[54]

By 'didactic intent,' Kramarz-Bein refers to how the *riddarasögur* produced for Hákon served as guides to chivalric practice for Norwegian courtiers. As Geraldine Barnes has argued, some of Hákon's adaptations focus even more attention than their source material does on the training of noblemen, and they drop the ironic tone of poets like Chrétien de Troyes, whose work often paro-dies the contradictions of the courtly ideal.[55] In sum, *riddarasögur* supplied Hákon and his men with narrative exempla of chivalric ideals that would later be laid out more systematically in texts like the *Konungs skuggsjá* or *King's Mirror*, an anonymous work of the late 1240s, and *Hirðskrá*, a product of Magnús Hákonarson's court.[56]

To some, it may seem that I have to this point presented a one-sided portrait of the formation of Hákon's tastes and patterns of patronage and consumption. Hákon was not, after all, a complete philistine when it came to Scandinavian (or Icelandic) culture. One piece of evidence for this claim is the story of the king's death in *Hákonar saga*. The saga tells that in his last sickness Hákon

> first had Latin books read to himself. But then he found it very wearisome to follow after what [those] said. He then had read for him books in the Norse

language, night and day, first saints' sagas; and when those ran out, he had read to him tales of kings from Hálfdan svarti, and afterwards about all Norwegian kings, one after another ... up to Sverrir. Near midnight *Sverris saga* was finished. But as midnight passed, almighty God called King Hákon from this world's life.[57]

Given that this account was written by a Sturlung, it might be suspected of speaking more about the desire of Icelandic cultural producers than the reality of the king's death-bed consumption. Still, even if this report's authenticity is granted, it attests only to Hákon's appreciation for sagas, native works of prose, not for traditional praise-poetry. And kings' sagas, as I have argued, were hardly less of an innovation in the Norwegian court than translations of French romance, and posed a similar threat to the value of skaldic verse within that space.

There are, however, other facts that suggest that Hákon was not uninterested in skaldic verse. First, as I have noted, he spent his early years in the care of Hákon galinn, in whose court skaldic verse was valued. Hákon may even have been at the jarl's court when Snorri's tribute was delivered sometime before 1214, and he was likely there at the same time as the skald Máni, from whom we hear no complaints about his treatment there.[58] Hákon's tastes, therefore, were formed in an environment favourable to skaldic practice. There is reason to think, however, that the jarl's regard for this verse had little impact on his charge, except perhaps to dissuade him from its consumption. Although the jarl may have resisted Hákon's clerical schooling, he was probably not seen by his ward as a primary role model: Hákon galinn's rank and status were not ones for which Hákon was socially destined. Hákon, his mother, and his aristocratic and clerical handlers had their eyes on the kingship, a position for which, in the early 1200s, training in Latin, ecclesiastical curricula, and foreign literature held meaning. Skaldic verse, however, had become an outmoded art form whose appeal was limited to those occupying a very specific social position – the royal aspirant who had been denied the throne but in a prior state of the political field would have been a preferred candidate. Hákon galinn was one such agent, and his half-brother Skúli would be another. It is no coincidence that both were eager to consume and reward an art form that had been closely linked to royal legitimacy and prestige before the triumph of the clerical standards and rituals that conspired, not least by precluding the possibility of joint rule, to keep them from the throne.[59] To the young Hákon, however, patronizing skaldic poetry, an art form consumed by runners-up and also-rans, must have appeared politically and culturally pointless.

Another fact that could potentially speak for Hákon's appreciation of skaldic verse is that the names of eight skalds, a high number for any period, are attached to his in *Skáldatal*.[60] Before concluding from this, however, that skaldic production and performance occurred in Hákon's court, we must consider the identity of these poets, their relationships, if known, with the king, and the ways in which their praise was produced and transmitted. *Skáldatal* lists the following skalds as Hákon's: Snorri, his nephews Óláfr and Sturla Þórðarsynir, Gizurr Þorvaldsson, Játgeirr Torfason, Árni langi, Óláfr svartaskáld Leggsson, and Guttormr körtr Helgason.[61] As Guðrún Nordal observes, this list is more representative than the verse cited in *Hákonar saga*, in which Sturla's 'selective presentation of Hákon Hákonarson's poets ... reveals his manipulation of his sources; he cites only a half-stanza by Gizurr and Játgeirr ... and chooses to ignore Guttormr körtr, Óláfr Leggsson, and Árni ... [His selection] does not represent skaldic activity around Hákon as suggested by *Skáldatal*.'[62] But what, exactly, does *Skáldatal* suggest? While *Hákonar saga* gives a more Sturlungar-centric portrait of Hákon's poets than *Skáldatal*, I would caution against accepting either text as accurately representing skaldic activity at Hákon's court. Two of the listed poets, Sturla and Óláfr, never met Hákon, and most if not all of their poetry about the king was composed after his death.[63] There is, as we know, no evidence that Snorri's verse (assuming he ever presented it to the king) was rewarded by Hákon. Játgeirr's relations with Hákon were, sadly for him, much like Snorri's: as his extant verse attests, he was mainly a follower of Skúli, never seems to have been recognized as a poet by the king, and was killed by Hákon's agents in the aftermath of Skúli's rebellion.[64] Gizurr knew the king, but there is no record of his having recited poetry before him; like other powerful Icelanders, he was valued by Hákon as a political agent, not a cultural producer.[65] About Árni, we know nothing; Óláfr Leggsson, whose work appears in grammatical treatises, is not said to have delivered poetry before Hákon; and Guttormr's activities in Iceland alone, not Norway, are described, and his one extant stanza deals with domestic matters.[66] There is, then, no positive evidence that Hákon encouraged, rewarded, or even permitted recitation of poetry within his hall by any of 'his' skalds listed in *Skáldatal*, even those whose relations with the king Sturla would have had most reason to highlight.[67]

One last point to be made is that Snorri's first trip to Norway occurred before Hákon began the program of importing and translating continental culture that would continue to the end of his reign. He visited at a time, therefore, when it might still have been possible to lure the king's interests to native poetry. Nothing suggests, however, that Snorri (or anyone else) had any success in altering the trajectory of Hákon's patterns of consumption. At the time when Snorri could have done so, an integral nexus already existed between Hákon's tastes, education, and aspirations. When Snorri arrived in 1218, Hákon was still a student of Niðaróss's cathedral school, was struggling to maintain his tenuous grip on the throne with the aid of Norway's bishops, and had already begun to direct his energies and ambitions beyond Scandinavia. Over the next decade, as Hákon's communications with foreign courts increased, as he and the archbishop arranged a national assembly at which his sovereignty was affirmed and the power-sharing arrangement with Skúli renegotiated, and as he embarked on a decades-long quest to be crowned by a representative of Rome, the king's alliance with and reliance upon the church only intensified.[68] It was into this context and developing relationship that Snorri intruded as a peddler of skaldic verse, a form of cultural goods that could celebrate the king's deeds and character but no longer assure him of divine approbation. Snorri came, in short, with none of the cultural resources or capacities to which Hákon had grown accustomed to look to augment his power and distinction. Despite the chance, therefore, that his visit afforded for face-to-face interaction with a king, Snorri was unable to improve his record for garnering specifically royal recognition for his poetic talents. But the final blow to Snorri's sense of poetic self-worth was still to come – this time, however, it would strike at home.

Hard-Mouthed Jarls and Defecating Eagles: Waging Poetic Warfare in Iceland

To date, Snorri's most profitable transactions involving poetry had been with Skúli Bárðarson. As he had done some years earlier with Skúli's older brother, Snorri used his poetic talents to elicit tangible and intangible gifts from the jarl. Both enhanced Snorri's honour at home. Signs of favour from Skúli, however, were not automatically advantageous in Iceland in the early 1220s, when factions of two leading families, the Oddaverjar and Haukdælir, still feuded with Norway's merchants and rulers. While Sturla is careful in *Íslendinga saga* to describe the accolades with which his uncle was met upon landing in Iceland, he admits that not everyone was pleased to hear of Snorri's return, or of the results of his trip. This was especially true of the relatives of one of Snorri's foster-brothers and a high-profile casualty of the feud: 'The Southlanders then bristled much against [Snorri], and most of all the in-laws of Ormr Jónsson ... Foremost in this was Björn Þorvaldsson.'[69] As husband of Ormr's daughter Hallveig (who would later become Snorri's domestic partner), Björn (whose brother Gizurr would later mastermind Snorri's assassination) was convinced that Snorri's alliance with Norway's rulers would prevent him from seeking compensation for his father-in-law, and he refused Snorri's protests of innocence when the two met at Skálholt.[70]

Snorri was well protected during this meeting, and no violence occurred. The first attack had already been made against him, however, with words rather than swords. Snorri, as we know, composed two *drápur* for Skúli before leaving Norway. Sturla quotes three lines from one of these: 'Hard-mouthed was Skúli, created the very greatest of jarls, with the high-country's strong-beam [gold].'[71] By referring to him as 'hard-mouthed' (*harðmúlaðr*), Snorri meant to describe the jarl's generosity. The term was put, however, to different use by his enemies:

> The Southlanders made great mockery of those poems that Snorri had composed about the jarl, and they perverted them. Þóroddr in Selvágr paid a sheep to a man who composed this:
> To us it seems ill to kiss a jarl,
> that one who rules a country,
> the lip is too sharp on the lord,
> hard-mouthed is Skúli.
>
> Never has more mud of a
> carrion-vulture of the sea [eagle]
> come before wise lords –
> people find fault in the poems.[72]

This parody was the first in a series of physical and verbal volleys exchanged between Snorri's and Björn's parties. Snorri's chief ally in this conflict was Loptr, son of Snorri's foster-brother Bishop Páll Jónsson, and one of several Oddaverjar who resented the fact that Björn, a member of the Haukdælir, had gained a foothold in their region on account of Ormr's death.[73] Even so, after Björn was killed, Loptr was abandoned by Sæmundr Jónsson and most of his family, who wished to avoid extending the feud. Snorri, however, 'was very much determined to aid Loptr, because things had been bad between him and Björn. He was also ill-pleased by that mockery, which the Southlanders had made of his poems.'[74] Not only must Snorri have been incensed over the satire's thinly veiled suggestion that his relationship with the jarl was inappropriately close, but also that 'an anonymous hack' had dared to denigrate publicly the merit of what he and, based on his response, Skúli considered a distinguished poetic product.[75] Indeed, there was little worse one's poetry could be called than *leir hrægamms sævar*, 'mud of the carrion-vulture of the sea' or 'eagle crap.' As Snorri himself will relate in *Skáldskaparmál*, in pagan myth the poems of non-professionals, the ditties of uninspired rhymesters, were not, like skalds' verse, regarded as gifts from Óðinn, but rather were thought to derive from the remnants of the poetic mead which the god was forced to evacuate rearward as he fled in eagle's form from the *jötunn* Suttungr.

Given Snorri's displeasure over his enemies' scorn, it is only fitting that his most conspicuous action in this affair was poetic in form. Though widely suspected of instigating and aiding Loptr before and after Björn's death, Snorri was never directly implicated in any violent action. Sturla reports, however, that after Björn had been killed and Loptr had sought protection at Stafaholt, where Snorri had gone to avoid contact with the Southlanders, the following verse issued from that location: 'I heard Björn was struck in the windpipe – a good trick was that – with sharpened iron; Guðlaugr [Eyjólfsson, a follower of Loptr] did the man enormous harm. The unhappy wealth-hoarder gave up his life on account of Grásíða [Guðlaugr's sword]. She was rather difficult to kiss – hard-mouthed was Skúli.'[76] Although Sturla does not name this stanza's composer, he implies that it was Snorri.[77] Whoever composed it, the verse clearly illustrates, through its turning of the parody of Snorri's *drápa* back against his enemies, that this battle was for Snorri as much over the worth of his poetry as over territory, honour, or anything else.

While the altercation I have been considering was between agents whose enmity grew out of their divergent relations with Norway's rulers, the portion of the contest waged through poetry can be viewed as a manifestation of transformations in Iceland's cultural market. Long before the currents of French romance and chivalry spread from Norway to Iceland, the island felt the influence of cultural trends of continental origin, some of which heavily impacted poetic practice and consumption during the twelfth and thirteenth centuries. The earliest and clearest evidence we have for such influence derives from the testimony of Gunnlaugr Leifsson (d. 1218/19) of Þingeyrar, who places the appearance in Iceland of metrical ballad forms of French origin in the early 1100s.[78] The products that emerged from this importation of ballad metres, known as *danzar* (sg. *danz*, a name of transparently French derivation), grew increasingly popular among the lay elite over the next century and a half, and there are numerous references in the *Sturlunga* compilation to dance-making in this period.[79] For some time, skaldic verse and *danzar*, whose differences in style and metre are evident even to those completely unversed in Norse poetics, coexisted in the domestic market, with the former continuing to enjoy somewhat higher status, particularly among the clergy and literate elite. A turning point in the contest of these art forms for prestige and popularity came, however, during the transition between Snorri's generation and the next. As Einar Sveinsson observes, the Norwegian court's 'chivalric influences' became a defining ethos for the Icelandic elite 'after 1230, and then especially among those who [went] abroad ... while still young'; conversely, the 'attitudes of the older generations were formed earlier and did not change through contact with life at the court or even the assumption of official functions there.'[80] While the contrast drawn here is perhaps too rigid, the chivalric ideals flowing through Norway certainly left a greater impression on the tastes and dispositions of Icelanders who became active political players about a generation after Snorri. With this trend came a lessened attachment to native poetic forms and a growing preference for foreign ones. Ultimately, the victory of balladry in Iceland, like that of French romance in Norway, was decisive: whereas skaldic verse stopped being produced by the middle of the fourteenth century, *danzar* would persist in Iceland in 'exactly the same' form into the seventeenth.[81] And while *rímur*, metrical romances from the 1300s that remained one of Iceland's chief cultural products into the modern era, preserve some of skaldic verse's stylistic features, their metre is largely an extension of the less demanding rhythm of *danzar*.[82]

Neither the cultural displacement that occurred in Norway nor that which followed in Iceland was simply a result of shifts in taste among the relevant elite. Rather, each was a symptom of staggered relations of domination and submission between social elites from different regions: dominant Icelanders borrowed culture from dominant Norwegians, who borrowed from the English, who borrowed from the French. What the Icelanders who mimicked trends then in vogue in Norway's court could not have realized, of course, was that in so doing they were effectively dispossessing themselves of their long-standing position as the dominant cultural producers of the north. By turning to French balladry, romance, and their northern derivatives, Icelanders adopted cultural practices that they were less well-equipped than their counterparts in Norway to manufacture. Thus elite Icelanders contributed to the devaluation of the only form of capital that for centuries they had held in greater abundance than Norwegians, the only thing which they, as the dominated fraction of the Norwegian/Icelandic dominant class, had to offer those on the other pole of that spectrum.

Given the detrimental impact of *danzar* and their offspring on skaldic practice in Iceland, it is reasonable to think that Snorri's production of the *Edda* was partly a response to the increasing popularity of this art form. As Sigurður Nordal writes:

> The popularity of the dance poems threatened to revolutionize Icelandic poetical art and taste and to make Icelandic poetry conform to the poetical usage of other European nations. The master of the ancient skaldic craft during the early part of the thirteenth century, Snorri Sturluson, sounded the alarm for the defense of skaldic poetry.[83]

Still, it seems doubtful that Snorri was worried enough by the popularity of *danz* forms among his contemporaries for this to have been a major impetus for his work. After all, dances had been popular in Iceland for well over a century, mainly as a form of entertainment at feasts, including, according to *Sturlu saga*, ones held by Snorri's father; and the fact that Snorri kept a man named Dansa-Bergr in his following during the mid-1220s, the very years when he was writing the *Edda*, speaks against the conclusion that he felt directly threatened by the proliferation of this poetic form.[84]

If Snorri can be said to have experienced deleterious effects from expansion in the practice of *danzar*, this did not occur so much in the cultural register as in the context of feuding, as seen in the incident discussed above. The verbal assaults that figured into Snorri's feud with Björn and other Southlanders were unprecedented in several respects. As Frank has observed, the 'literary satire represented by [the] stanza [directed at Snorri] ... sophisticated and witty, is a late development in skaldic tradition,' one that runs counter to the gravity with which skaldic praise and blame were treated in earlier periods.[85] Two things in particular make this instance of mockery stand out: first, while Icelanders had long used verse to taunt their enemies, it was not so usual for a praise-poem, as opposed to *lausavísur*, to be implicated in such bantering; second, not just the poet but the poetry itself was here the target of derision – it was the value of Snorri's cultural capital that was under attack. What is more, this assault on the most prestigious possible type of skaldic verse-making – *dróttkvætt* metre in *drápa* form – was not the only novel pairing of mockery and verse that figured into this conflict. During the winter of 1220–1, as hostilities were heating up, followers of Björn 'sneered at Loptr in lampoons and directed at him many dances and other mockery of many kinds.'[86] This is the first evidence of the use of *danz* metres to taunt enemies during a feud, something that grew, however, more common as the thirteenth century progressed.[87] Sturla goes on to quote one of these stanzas, which was targeted not just at Loptr, who had gone into hiding after Björn's killing, but also Sæmundr Jónsson, who, despite his refusal to succour his nephew, had fled Oddi to avoid the forces of the Haukdælir: 'Then this was recited: Loptr is in the islands, he bites a puffin bone, Sæmundr is in the lowlands, and eats the berries alone.'[88] The possibility realized here of using *danz* rather than skaldic metres to insult one's adversaries had far-reaching consequences for the waging of poetic warfare in Iceland. The use of poetry as a weapon had always been treated seriously in this society: by law, poetic libel, particularly when used to impugn an opponent's masculinity, was held equivalent to a physical assault, and was subject to punishment by full outlawry.[89] But whereas one once had to be a virtuoso (or at least an initiate) in the rarefied skaldic art to score points in the verbal arena, the introduction of simplistic *danz* metres widened the pool of potential combatants. In this shift, the potency of all verbal attacks was diluted: if everyone could compose ditties at enemies' expense, words could no longer command the same respect or fear. Thus, even though *danz* metres are not reported to have been used directly against Snorri during this conflict, the democratization of the poetic battlefield through the deployment of *danz* forms certainly helped make possible the degree of mockery to which Snorri, an accomplished practitioner of what had become, however, just one among several poetic forms, was subjected.

Crisis of Distinction, Cultural Dissonance, and Mismatch of Habitus and Field

In the first decades of the thirteenth century, practitioners of skaldic verse were undergoing a crisis of distinction – a radical diminution in the capacity of their art form to generate for themselves and their consumers honour, legitimacy, prestige, and other sorts of profits related to social standing and recognition. As an agent who received through early education substantial expertise in skaldic poetry, a type of capital that, at the time when he acquired it, held the potential for conversion into many other forms in Iceland's and Norway's political fields, Snorri's actual and potential social standing was impacted adversely by any development that eroded the prestige value of this art form within either or both of these fields. As things turned out, Snorri was confronted by the early 1220s with a host of circumstances, events (the deaths of some of those who were most likely to reward, Hákon's indifference to, and mockery of his poetry) as well as processes (the ascendancy of literacy and clerical modes of legitimation, the growing popularity of sagas and ballad metres, the imminent flood of Anglo-Norman romance and its associated chivalric ethos), that were causes or symptoms of such erosion. 'Most people,' Bourdieu asserts, 'are statistically bound to encounter circumstances that tend to agree with those that originally fashioned their habitus.'[90] In such cases, social ambitions and possibilities remain in harmony. If, however, agents encounter fields radically different from that in which their habitus was formed and capital acquired, aspirations are likely to be frustrated. In Snorri's case, the fields of habitus origination and capital application were one and the same: the Norwegian/Icelandic field of power. And yet, owing to the developments traced in this chapter, there was a fundamental shift over time in the valuation of forms of cultural capital within this field. According to Bourdieu, agents whose capital stores are negatively impacted by field discord typically respond in one of two ways: with resignation, which leads to inactivity, or with rebellion, in which case they adopt 'extremely varied and extraordinarily inventive strategies, whose aim is to maintain their [social] position,' or, to put it another way, 'to valorize the species of capital they preferentially possess.'[91]

The *Edda*, as a product of the cultural dissonance generated in Snorri by the mismatch between the field of power of the formation of his habitus and that in which he was active and invested in the 1210s and 1220s, was, as I will argue in the following chapters, the latter type of response. This treatise was Snorri's attempt, in the face of forces and circumstances that threatened the value of his cultural resources, to preserve and, if possible, reinvigorate the capacity of skaldic verse to act as capital within Scandinavian circles of power. The *Edda* did not begin, however, as so ambitious and comprehensive a project – rather, its design and purpose emerged over time in a series of accumulative stages or texts, each of which responded to different immediate needs and was oriented towards its own, limited aims. The first of these stages/products was a last attempt by Snorri to interest his patrons directly in his traditional cultural wares, to persuade the king and jarl at once of the contributions which he, as a practitioner of the skaldic art, could make to their power, legitimacy, and prestige. In the next chapter, I will examine the strategic intent that lay behind Snorri's production of *Háttatal* and its commentary, and the ways in which this work's union of poetry and prose laid the foundation for the parts of the *Edda* that followed.

6 *Háttatal*: Beginning and End of the *Edda*

Preliminaries to a Reading of the *Edda* as a Strategic Practice

It has long been recognized that the *Edda* is first and foremost a treatise on skaldic verse. In the words of Elias Wessén, 'the Edda as a whole is a manual on the art of poetry. It is this object which has determined its contents and composition. The Edda contains precisely what in Snorri's opinion a native skald required to know so as to be able to practice his art in a proper manner: mythology, stylistics, and metrics.'[1] While most scholars today would still accept Wessén's judgment, there has been a growing determination in recent decades to move beyond this simple and pragmatic formulation of the *Edda*'s purpose, and to identify more sophisticated and subtle theoretical projects that can be shown to carry through, ideally, all four parts of Snorri's text. This trend has resulted in two general theses. Some have argued that Snorri's project was essentially cultural, that he sought with his *Edda* to integrate Norse poetics into the study of grammar, and thereby assert the equal dignity of skaldic verse to the classical poetry that provided traditional exempla for this branch of Latin learning.[2] Others have argued that his project was essentially religious, that he designed his text to demonstrate how the beliefs of his pagan ancestors fit into the Christian world view. These theses have sometimes been joined, in which case the *Edda* is perceived as Snorri's attempt to preserve and validate pagan poetry and mythology alike as expressions of his forebears' estimable if naive groping towards a truth that can finally be attained only through Christian revelation. As one scholar summarizes this perspective: 'Skaldic poetry ... experienced a renaissance as a genuine expression of the language, religion and conception of the world of the Icelanders' heathen forefathers. It is from this point of view that Snorri Sturluson wrote a poetics of skaldic verse and reproduced the myths of the gods in his *Edda*.'[3]

While such efforts to pinpoint Snorri's concern with his subject matter are preferable to those offering no reason aside from antiquarian desire, they too succumb to the scholastic fallacies that have plagued *Edda* studies. One way they do so is by approaching the *Edda* as an atemporal whole, the plan for which was present in its creator's mind before or from early in the stages of its production. Rather than assume a transcendent blueprint that existed prior to the *Edda*'s realization and directed its evolution, I will examine this text as the unfolding product of a strategic intent, which, while it may have involved conscious design on the part of its producer, need not assume it. Another way in which recent readings of the *Edda* have fallen prey to the scholastic fallacy is by imputing to Snorri an interest in disinterestedness that exists as a motivating factor for modern academic, cultural, or religious practice, but did not exist within the fields in which this medieval Icelandic agent was implicated. Those who make of Snorri a grammarian whose desire was to elevate the academic cachet of a native art form, or a theologian who sought to bestow dignity and truth-value on the religious intuitions of his ancestors ignore the fact that, given what we know of his social positions and spheres of activity, he would have had no interest in pursuing such ends. It is this apparent contradiction that has, of course, posed the major obstacle to a confident ascription of the *Edda* to Snorri: why, scholars continue to ask, should this individual, who in accounts of his life is deeply involved in the pursuit of political, material, and legal gain, but seems to have lacked academic or religious sensibilities, have produced a treatise on poetry and myth? It does not make sense – at least until we recognize that skaldic verse and, by extension, pagan myth were not important to Snorri as 'cultural' or 'religious' artefacts, but as convertible resources with the potential to generate social, symbolic, and material profit within the Icelandic-Norwegian field of power in which he was active and invested.

I am not the first to suggest that self-interest lay behind Snorri's desire to recuperate the value of skaldic poetry. The scholar who has come nearest to articulating the perspective on the *Edda* that I am advocating is Kari Ellen Gade, who in 1995 wrote that

> there is reason to believe that Snorri's attempt to reawaken interest in the composition and understanding of the old *dróttkvætt* was not solely rooted in his antiquarian curiosity ... It is possible that Snorri, fueled by political ambition, was prompted to compose his poetic exegeses by the desire to credit his own poetic production, that is, the tool by which he, in the spirit of ancient Icelandic court poets, hoped to gain allies and reward at the Norwegian court.[4]

Gade revisited this suggestion in a 2000 paper, proposing that in the 1200s the Sturlungar 'brought their own panegyrics to Norwegian dignitaries to obtain political advantages.'[5] It is my intention to investigate systematically and in the end validate the suggestion that there is more to Snorri's writing of the *Edda* than most scholars have allowed. It is telling to look at the reaction to Gade's ideas by Margaret Clunies Ross, editor of the volume in which her 2000 paper appears. Outlining possible purposes behind the *Edda*, Clunies Ross writes:

> It has often been assumed that Snorri wrote in part to revive what he may have perceived as a flagging or ill-informed interest in skaldic verse among young Icelanders of his day. This may well have been one of his motivations, but his vision went far beyond that particular pedagogical aim. He was apparently concerned to legitimate Icelandic vernacular poetry and poetics, and its underpinning ideology, in the face of antique classical models as medieval Christian learning presented them. He may also have had personal motives, in the political climate of his day, for promoting his own abilities as a skald and a scholar, as Gade suggests.[6]

While this passage acknowledges a strategic intent behind the *Edda*'s production, it also reiterates the dichotomous view of Snorri's practice that I am challenging. In listing the *Edda*'s potential aims, Clunies Ross introduces Snorri's political motives after his pedagogical motives and what we may call theological/grammatical interests, and with the words 'may also,' suggesting that one can leave the question of his political investment in skaldic poetry open, and treat his scholarly interests in this art apart from them. Moreover, in characterizing Snorri's political aims in writing the *Edda* as 'personal,' that is to say, interested, Clunies Ross places them in contrast to what she understands to have been his scholarly, that is to say, disinterested, interests. In my view, no facet of Snorri's treatment of these topics can be understood apart from his political – which are, indeed, his personal – interests in this skill and body of knowledge.[7]

Finally, while I will preface my analysis of each of the *Edda*'s parts with a discussion of its manuscript history, it is necessary here to describe how I will approach a work that has come down to us in drastically different forms. In recent years, there has been a shift in the favoured approach of scholars to the text of the *Edda*. Instead of reconstruction through manuscript conflation and emendation, more and more scholars have adopted a 'codicological' method, in which each of the preserved versions is examined on its own terms and in relation to other texts with which it has been transmitted. While there is much to be said for this manuscript-centred approach, it is unsuited to the aims of my project. Whereas the codicological method seeks to uncover 'the attitudes and planning behind the production of each codex containing [a] text' rather than its 'one authorial original,'[8] it is my purpose to recover the original, if not strictly 'authorial' then strategic intent that directed the *Edda*'s production. My focus on the *Edda*'s origins, as opposed to its transmission or reception, obliges me to raise the old-fashioned question of which of the two major manuscript traditions provides a better (i.e., closer to Snorri) model: the longer branch represented by Codex Regius (early 1300s; hereafter 'R'), along with Codices Wormianus (mid-1300s; hereafter 'W') and Trajectinus (c. 1600; hereafter 'T'), or the shorter version of Codex Upsaliensis (c. 1300; hereafter 'U').[9] While all of these manuscripts contain at least portions of the *Edda*'s four major sections in the same order – *Formáli*, *Gylfaginning*, *Skáldskaparmál*, and *Háttatal* – the two branches differ considerably in style: that of RTW is more expansive, coherent, and has generally been preferred, while U is truncated, at times confused or incoherent, and has been regarded, with notable exceptions, as an awkward abridgement and reordering of the text. R in particular has been singled out as the version most likely to have preserved some of the style, content, and format of Snorri's original, and has served as the basis for all major editions of the *Edda*, including Anthony Faulkes's four-volume edition, which will provide the main text for my investigation.[10] I will, however, discuss at certain points material from U, a manuscript that, despite its differences from and (as most think) inferiority to texts of the longer branch, may preserve an alternate version of Snorri's own work.[11]

Deciding which manuscripts of the *Edda* to use does nothing to alter the fact, however, that we lack assurance that anything in these version(s) actually came from the pen, as it were, of Snorri. As Faulkes writes: 'Taking into account … the span of time and possible number of copies between the author's original and the earliest extant manuscripts, it is clear that it is impossible to reconstruct an archetype with any confidence.'[12] Our inability to recover the precise text of Snorri's *Edda* (at least of its prose sections; *Háttatal*, as we will see below, is another matter) might seem to pose an insurmountable hurdle to the fulfilment of my project. If, after all, we cannot be certain that any passage, phrase, or word of our text(s) is to be attributed to Snorri rather than some later scribe or editor, how can the thesis that the *Edda* was a product of this agent's efforts to protect the value of a variety of his cultural capital be demonstrated?

In ways, this problem is the same as that faced in the earlier, biographical chapters, in which information about Snorri's life was drawn from a few texts, all written by or derived from the work of Sturla Þórðarson. Just as we cannot verify that anything appearing in the prose sections of our versions of the *Edda* was written by Snorri, or that much of what he wrote has not been lost, there is no guarantee that anything that Sturla says happened in Snorri's life occurred, or occurred in the way he says it did, or that he did not leave anything important out of his accounts. While neither problem is amenable to an easy solution, I wish to suggest that, once completed, the two sides of my investigation will reinforce each other's authenticity. This has not, admittedly, been the usual conclusion when Snorri's life and work have been considered side by side. As Lois Bragg has written of the relationship between Snorri's literary and extra-literary pursuits:

> The difficulty we have in accepting that the Snorri we see in *Sturlunga* – a wealthy, unscrupulous politician with no aesthetic interests apparent – and the Snorri we know as a scholar and artist are one and the same person – and they certainly are – suggests just how selectively and consistently the compilation has been shaped.[13]

In Bragg's view, the fact that the Snorri whom we find in contemporary sagas does not resemble the one we imagine we find in the works that he produced raises doubts about the veracity of Sturla's portrait of Snorri. This conclusion depends, however, upon assumptions about what a scholar or artist ought or, better, ought not to be (not a politician, not unscrupulous, and certainly not wealthy). If, however, it can be demonstrated that Snorri did not write the *Edda* as a scholar or artist, with, that is, a disinterested interest in preserving and presenting knowledge and art, and if this text can be shown to exhibit the same strategic intent as the political, legal, and social activities with which he is known to have occupied himself, then these two sets of data, the biographical and textual, may finally be seen to support rather than undermine each other's value as accurate representations of the life, work, and interests of Snorri Sturluson.

Introduction to *Háttatal*: Praise, Pedagogy, and Scholarly Neglect

Háttatal, or 'List of Metres,' is a composition of 102 stanzas, divided into three poems or *kvæði* (sg. and pl.) of near equal length, accompanied by a running prose commentary. While Snorri's authorship of the commentary, which appears in all manuscripts, is debated, I assume in my analysis that he wrote it, while reserving discussion of its role in the *Edda*'s development until the end of the chapter. Attribution of *Háttatal*'s verse component has been far less controversial – indeed, of all of 'his' texts, this poem can be ascribed to Snorri with most confidence.[14] *Háttatal* is also of Snorri's works the one that we can be most sure has been transmitted in a form reasonably faithful to its original.

All of its stanzas have been preserved, and Faulkes concludes in the introduction to his edition that 'there is not often reason to doubt the essential accuracy
of the text of the poem itself.'[15] Still, some reconstruction and guesswork has
been necessary: all 102 stanzas are preserved only in R, and some of the spots
where this text is illegible cannot be supplemented using other manuscripts.[16]

Háttatal's date of composition has also been fixed with a rare degree of precision and consensus. In 1869, Konráð Gíslason argued that it was written in
the winter of 1222–3, a conclusion accepted by many since.[17] Most of the
poem's few references to identifiable events are to military actions led by
Skúli, the latest of which is the jarl's defeat of Ribbungar forces in late 1221.[18]
Snorri fails, however, to mention Skúli's more impressive accomplishments of
early 1223, when he negotiated a truce with these rebels.[19] If, it is argued,
Snorri had not yet completed *Háttatal* when he heard of this event, he would
surely have incorporated it into the jarl's tribute. Early 1223, therefore, is the
latest time when Snorri is likely to have been at work on *Háttatal*. The opinion
that Snorri did not begin his poem before late 1222 seems less certain. There is
no need to suppose, after all, that *Háttatal* was not begun until after Skúli's
exploits of 1221–2, since Snorri could have worked these into his ongoing
composition once he had got word of them, as most assume he would have
done had he learned of the jarl's 1223 achievements in time.[20] At any rate, I
find it likely that Snorri had at least conceived of his plan to produce an
unmatched panegyric for the king and jarl not long after returning from
Norway in the autumn of 1220.

The period of *Háttatal*'s composition can confidently be assigned, then, to
between the fall of 1220 and early 1223. But does this dating place the poem
at the beginning or the end of the *Edda*'s course of production? Scholars long
assumed that the *Edda*'s major parts were written in the order in which they
appear in manuscripts: *Gylfaginning* (plus the *Formáli*), *Skáldskaparmál*,
and, lastly, *Háttatal*. Sigurður Nordal, for example, thought that Snorri wrote
Gylfaginning and *Skáldskaparmál* before his 1218–20 visit to Norway, and
upon his return conceived of *Háttatal* as a way to kill 'two birds in one blow ...
to add the third and last part to his *Edda* and ... to praise Hákon and Skúli.'[21]
According to this view, *Háttatal* is best regarded as an execution of principles
which had been formulated and assembled before the poem was conceived, let
alone composed.

This understanding of the *Edda*'s evolution reigned without much question
until 1940, when Wessén argued in an unassuming but revolutionary essay
that the most logical way for Snorri to have written the *Edda* was in reverse
order, beginning, that is, with *Háttatal*.[22] In considering how Snorri came to
formulate the plan for and went about producing the *Edda*, Wessén asked:

'How is it that he begins with a mythology, and passes on to stylistics and metrics? Can Snorri be imagined to have had the plan clearly before him already from the beginning?'[23] Wessén's response to the latter question was no, Snorri did not have a clear vision in his mind of the *Edda* as it would exist when he began writing it. Rather, the work grew out of the composition of *Háttatal*, a poem designed to demonstrate the continuing relevance and viability of the skaldic art through its dual aims of praise and pedagogy. Owing to the complexity of his poem and the nescience of his contemporaries, Snorri was obliged to attach to *Háttatal* a commentary on metre, which was then supplemented by discussions of, first, poetic diction and, second, northern myth, and, finally, by a prologue that placed the entire text's treatment of pagan art and religion within a theologically acceptable frame. According to Wessén, then, the *Edda* began not with theory but with execution.

While Wessén's hypotheses about the *Edda*'s evolution have been widely accepted, few seem fully to appreciate one implication of his insights, namely, that *Háttatal*, as the seed from which the *Edda*'s other parts emerged, ought to have a central place in any attempt to understand the entire text and its intention. Neglect of *Háttatal* has been most marked among those who seek, as Klaus von See describes it, to 'theologize' the *Edda*.[24] Building on the work of Walter Baetke, such scholars, among whom are Ursula Dronke and Peter Dronke, Anne Holtsmark, Lars Lönnroth, Clunies Ross, and Gerd Wolfgang Weber, have tried in a variety of ways to demonstrate that Snorri's chief concern in writing the *Edda* was to situate, historically and doctrinally, pagan myth and religion within and in relation to what he, as 'not only an important scholar ... but also a believing Christian,' accepted as truth.[25] Because they focus on myth and religion, *Gylfaginning* and its *Formáli* have been of most interest to these scholars; the *Formáli* in particular has been treated as the lens through which the rest of the *Edda* must be read. In 1987, Clunies Ross made the first sustained attempt to read *Skáldskaparmál* in a theological register: Snorri's interest in diction and the kenning-system, she argues, stemmed from his conviction that his ancestors' religious conceptions had been enshrined and preserved in the language of the skalds.[26] The *Edda*'s first three sections can thus be understood as Snorri's attempt 'to explain and justify the poetic technique of the pagan skalds – especially their use of Norse myth – in terms of his own Christian world view and medieval theories about poetic language.'[27]

Then, however, we come to *Háttatal*, and the theologizing abruptly stops. Indeed, champions of the above theory of the *Edda*'s purpose have tended to dismiss or ignore its climactic section altogether.[28] An emblematic illustration of this attitude is Weber's entry for 'Edda, Jüngere' in the *Reallexikon der germanischen Altertumskunde*, in which the following amounts of space are allotted to each part of the work: the *Formáli* receives 4½ columns of text, *Gylfaginning* 10, *Skáldskaparmál* 6, and *Háttatal* 1. About a third of *Háttatal*'s lone column, moreover, is used to downplay its significance: 'The assumption,' Weber writes, 'that Snorri in 1220 after his journey to Norway ... first composed *Háttatal*, before he seized on the plan of *Gylfaginning* and *Skáldskaparmál* ... is unproven and, in view of the theoretical and didactic unity of the entire *Edda*, superfluous.'[29] The *Edda*'s development is not so easily divorced from its overall plan and purpose, however. If one agrees with Wessén that *Háttatal* was the first part written, it is difficult to accept any arguments that claim to provide a comprehensive theory of the *Edda* while neglecting what is not only the treatise's evolutionary origin, but its structural destination. This explains Weber's need to challenge *Háttatal*'s temporal priority. And yet, to resurrect the possibility that Snorri began the *Edda* not with this poem but with *Gylfaginning* or its *Formáli* obliges one also to revisit the problem of why Snorri, given who he was, the interests he held, and the activities he pursued, would have written a work the purpose of which was to vindicate beliefs of his ancestors, and in which skaldic verse was of concern insofar as it contributed to this theological project. The answers avoided by not asking this question are that Snorri would not have written such a work, and that it is less likely that his interests in skaldic verse derived from its association with pagan myth/religion than that he was interested in the latter owing to its relevance to the production and comprehension of the former. And just as these scholars have got Snorri's interests and emphases backward, so too they have misjudged the relative importance of the *Edda*'s outlying sections: it is not the *Formáli* that is the key to the text and *Háttatal* its afterthought, but the other way around.

As noted above, *Háttatal* is a poem designed to fulfil the dual purposes of praise and pedagogy: it is a work celebrating the king, jarl, and in some cases the skill of its composer, as well as a demonstration and explication of metrical variation within the skaldic stanza. While *Edda* scholars universally affirm that *Háttatal* has these two functions, most focus their analyses on only one. For a long while, its pedagogic dimensions were of greater interest to scholars, who used *Háttatal* to further their own understanding of skaldic metrics, or sought for its models in native and Latin culture.[30] In recent decades, investigations of the poem's panegyric content have begun to appear, but its two functions continue to be treated largely separately. Different audiences for these functions have also been assumed: while as a praise-poem, *Háttatal* was clearly intended for those to whom it was dedicated, it is thought that insofar as it served as a treatise on metrics Snorri must have had another audience in mind, namely young prospective skalds in Iceland. As Hermann Pálsson writes, critics can choose to study *Háttatal* as a panegyric or

> in a much narrower context by dealing with it primarily as an integral part of Snorri's *Edda* taken as a whole … instead of treating *Háttatal* simply as one of many laudatory poems in Old Icelandic, the main emphasis would then be placed on its instructional value; the praise of King Hákon and Earl Skúli is then set aside and subordinated to the principal aims of Snorri's *Edda*: to entertain and educate young people who want to master the noble art of making verse.[31]

Given, however, that each of *Háttatal*'s 102 stanzas demonstrates a possible metrical or stylistic variation in skaldic verse-making, the poem was clearly intended from its inception, and apart from its commentary, to serve simultaneously as a vehicle of praise and a tool of instruction. The poem's inherent didacticism suggests that Snorri considered not only his fellow countrymen but also, and perhaps in the first instance, the king and jarl to be among those who would benefit from its metrical instruction. In my analysis, therefore, I will highlight the ways in which not only *Háttatal*'s content but also its pedagogic design have been tailored to address the needs, capacities, and sensibilities of his would-be patrons.

Another commonly held conception about *Háttatal* has to do with its intentions. Most have assumed that Snorri's purpose in composing this tribute was to thank Hákon and Skúli for the hospitality he had been shown during his visit to Norway.[32] As my discussions of Snorri's trip in chapters 4 and 5 suggest, however, there is reason to doubt that matters were so simple. The most effective way, after all, for Snorri to have shown gratitude to as well as enhance his standing with his hosts would have been to work to fulfil the charge they had given him: to persuade his fellow chieftains to accept Hákon's overlordship. This is not, however, what Snorri did – instead, he sat down and composed the longest skaldic praise-poem on record. He did this, moreover, despite the fact that Hákon does not seem to have shown interest in his verse while he was actually in Norway; and even Skúli surely valued him more as a political ally than a cultural producer. In this light, *Háttatal* begins to look like an ill-considered gift on Snorri's part, one as likely to irk its recipients as to please them.

The motives behind *Háttatal* become clearer if the work is understood not as an expression of Snorri's satisfaction with his time spent in Norway but of his dissatisfaction with aspects of that experience and its aftermath, above all Hákon's indifference to his poetry and the mockery that was made of his verse for Skúli upon his return home. *Háttatal* is best seen as a product of the dissonance generated in Snorri by the failure of his poetic skills to realize the profits that he believed them capable of producing in the Scandinavian political sphere. It does not seem to have been enough for Snorri that the king and jarl recognize and reward him as one of Iceland's superior social, economic, and symbolic capital-holders. It is as if, having acquired in his youth a mastery of skaldic verse as well as a knowledge of the contexts in which this resource could be used and converted, Snorri was compelled to realize, irrespective of his chances for success, his potential as a poetic producer for Norway's court. *Háttatal* was more, therefore, than a simple if monumental thank-you note: it was also Snorri's attempt to extend or repeat a transaction of cultural for material and symbolic goods with one of his hosts, and a last-ditch bid to forge a poet/patron bond with the other. Neither goal was assured of success. *Háttatal* was a gift uncertain of its own reception, and had to achieve several things if it was to make good on its potential for profit: it had to demonstrate to its subjects that skaldic verse remained a distinguished art form, to persuade them of its continued relevance and worth to their own careers and reputations, and to provide them with some of the tools needed to become more enthusiastic and effective consumers of this poetry. Snorri launched his efforts – as he probably had to – at the point of greatest resistance and with the most difficult task, by dedicating the first section of his poem to the praise and blandishment of the young, and thus far unreceptive, King Hákon.

Poem One: Praise for Hákon

Háttatal's distribution of praise is often schematized as follows: stt. 1–30 (*kvæði* one) are dedicated to Hákon, stt. 31–66 and 68–95 (the bulk of *kvæði* two and three) to Skúli, and stt. 67 and 96–102 (the ends of *kvæði* two and three) celebrate both patrons along with Snorri's talents as a skald.[33] Accordingly, *Háttatal* appears to most as more of a tribute to the jarl than to the king. Recently, some have gone further by arguing that Snorri's intention in *Háttatal* was not to praise the king at all, but rather to thrust him deeper into the shadow of his more accomplished regent.[34] Guðrún Nordal writes, 'It is not only the unfavourable proportion of praise that is offered to Hákon, which could have offended the young king, but the praise is very difficult to find in the first thirty stanzas.'[35] Snorri only took this 'incredible risk,' she reasons, because he could 'wrap the praise about Hákon in so difficult a form.'[36] On this view, *Háttatal* becomes a joke at Hákon's expense shared by Snorri and Skúli, one made possible by the king's inability to understand it. While there is no question that quantitatively *Háttatal*'s panegyric balance tilts in Skúli's favour, I do not agree that the work as a whole was meant to belittle or antagonize Hákon. Whatever Snorri's factional biases, it remained in his interests to enlist not only the jarl but the king as a patron of his verse. Stanzas 1–30 ought to be read, therefore, as a sincere attempt to compliment Hákon and entice him to consume skaldic praise-poetry. This was, to be sure, no simple task – paying tribute to this particular king raised a host of complications. In tracing Snorri's efforts to ingratiate himself and his verse to Hákon, I will discuss the following facets of stt. 1–30: a) the form in which Snorri casts his praise; b) the content of this praise, particularly that relating to warfare; c) the use of mythological and legendary elements; and d) the manner in which Snorri uses the final stanzas of *kvæði* one to segue from praise of Hákon to praise of Skúli, and, in so doing, to attempt to implicate the former in the poet/patron relationship that he had forged with the latter.

The poem *Háttatal* begins with the following stanza:

Lætr sár Hákun heitir
(hann rekkir lið) bannat
(jörð kann frelsa) fyrðum
friðrofs konungr ofsa;

sjálfr ræðr allt ok Elfar,
ungr stillir sá, milli
(gramr á gipt at fremri)
Gandvíkr jöfurr landi.

That one who is called King Hákon (he emboldens the host) causes peace-breaking violence to be banned among men (he knows how to free the land); the prince himself, that young ruler, rules the land all the way between Gandvík and the Elfr (the lord has the greater fortune).[37]

This stanza offers a textbook example of basic *dróttkvætt*, which in the commentary is called 'the beginning of all metres' and the metre in which 'most [poetry] that is elaborately wrought is composed.'[38] *Háttatal*'s next seven stanzas do not deviate from this form, and are designed to answer the question: 'How shall the verse-forms be varied and the same metre be kept?'[39] It is not, therefore, until st. 9 that we encounter what Snorri considered to be a formal variation on *dróttkvætt* form.[40] Even after this point, the metrical variety on display in *Háttatal*'s first *kvæði* is minimal: it is not until st. 28 that we meet, according to the commentary, 'the first verse-form that can be written of those which are changed from *dróttkvætt* by a complete alteration of form ... according to alliteration and rhyme or line-length,' and in Hans Kuhn's judgment it is not until st. 33, at the start, that is, of the first *kvæði* for Skúli, that a significant metrical departure from *dróttkvætt* appears.[41] Most of the diversity on display in *kvæði* one, then, is stylistic, rhetorical, or syntactic as opposed to metrical.[42] As a result, *Háttatal* is in its first section something less, but also something more, than what its title implies: while *kvæði* one falls short of being a true 'List of Metres,' it does provide a fairly comprehensive illustration of non-metrical experimentation within basic *dróttkvætt* form. Snorri's focus on the metre of the court and its possibilities in the section of *Háttatal* devoted to Hákon was, I believe, no accident, but was meant to drill into the young monarch's head the verse form most suited to the praise of kings. Thus, while *Háttatal*'s first *kvæði* employs a difficult and complex metre, there is little reason to conclude, given the repetition with which this metre is not only used but explicated, that Hákon was not intended to comprehend it.

As to the content of Snorri's poem for Hákon, most judge its praise sincere if uninspired. In the thirty stanzas devoted to Hákon, all of the skaldic stereotypes of kingship are present: the king is the land's protector, a just ruler, a warrior and war-leader, a skilled seafarer, and a host generous with gifts, food, and drink. The formulaic quality of Snorri's praise for Hákon has most often been blamed on the king's thus-far uneventful career: lacking adequate substance, it is argued, Snorri was forced to fall back on convention.[43] Alternatively, some view the pallid quality of the praise for Hákon as an attempt by a partisan of Skúli to diminish or antagonize the king. Whatever its intention, a joint encomium such as *Háttatal* runs the risk of its audience measuring the deeds and character of one of its subjects against those of the other. In *Háttatal*'s case, the winner of such a comparison would have been clear. While the king and jarl could be praised for attributes such as generosity, hospitality, and pedigree in like proportion without raising too many eyebrows, there was one domain in which parity of acclaim was out of the question: experience and accomplishments. When *Háttatal* was composed, Skúli was in his early thirties, had been a player at the highest political level for over a decade, had served as Norway's de facto ruler since 1217, and had recently won major military and diplomatic victories over rebel camps. Hákon, while he was ambitious, surrounded by powerful noble and clerical allies, and, most crucially, sitting on the throne, had barely reached adulthood. Guðrún Nordal suggests that the fact that Snorri chose implicitly to compare two patrons with such uneven levels of experience signalled his intent 'to insult Hákon' and perhaps even 'start a fight between Hákon and Skúli.'[44] Contrary to this view, I will argue that both the metre and content of the first *kvæði* were chosen with the same purposes in mind: to please the king, and to educate him in the basic conventions of the skaldic art. In short, Snorri's selection of praise for Hákon was neither perfunctory nor disingenuous, but a painstaking effort to manufacture a tribute that would offer the king neither too little nor too much praise.

The need for skalds to strike this balance was something of which Snorri was well aware. As he writes in a famous passage in *Heimskringla*'s prologue: 'And that is the custom of skalds to praise that one most who they are then before, but none would dare to speak directly to him about those deeds of his which all those who heard, as well as he himself, knew to be falsehoods and fables. That would then be mockery, and not praise.'[45] While Snorri had likely not yet written these words while he was at work on *Háttatal*, the thought behind them seems to have informed his praise for Hákon. Nowhere is this more evident than in his persistent efforts to link the young monarch with matters of battle and warfare.

Faced with the task of inflating Hákon's martial reputation while steering clear of fabrication, Snorri turned to skaldic convention. This proved a less than perfect solution: relying on battle clichés could lead to absurd results when these were applied to a subject who, so far as we know, had yet to experience warfare at firsthand. Consider st. 7: 'The bold helmet-provider makes men quiet with Vindhlér's helmet-filler [Vindhlér's (i.e., Heimdallr's) head = sword]; he does with a thin sword make corpse-rivers flow; the terrible helmet-provider makes men have a blood-stained shield; the strong ruler reddens the iron-grey coat of tumult for lords.'[46] But if the praise is in this case overblown, there are instances where Snorri seems to avoid attributing too much warrior prowess to Hákon. One way he does so is by embedding praise for the king in generic descriptions of battle: 'Severe wounds increase greatly, strong edge cuts sharply trusty shields for bold men. The high prince lives honourably. Each warrior dyes clean swords mightily. The noble ruler, bright, rejoices in a bold heart. The fine shield is furrowed amazingly.'[47] He also stresses Hákon's role as mover of warriors under his command, by saying that the king 'lets snakes of battle [swords] slide along scabbard-path' or 'lets the white spear be driven forth over the army.'[48] Such devices have the effect of removing Hákon from the scene of battle while assigning him credit for what is achieved there.[49] In stanzas linking Hákon to warfare, Snorri is also sometimes vague about whether he is describing this king in particular, or traits and behaviours befitting kings in general. Stanza 10, for instance, reads: 'A ruler defends the land with swords. Spears rip wounds apart. Coloured shield is cut in tumult. Skull flies loose from the body. People fall on the field. A generous lord wages battle. Edge bites deformities on limbs. Scalp lies sliced by sword.'[50] As graphic as this litany of mutilations may be, it is not actually said that Hákon has done all (or any) of these things, only that these are the kinds of things kings ought to do. This stanza is normative or exhortative rather than descriptive. Taken together, use of these rhetorical strategies allows Snorri to connect Hákon with warfare in a manner that obeys the principle expressed in *Heimskringla*'s prologue – namely, that it does no good to praise a lord by attributing to him deeds that all know to be false.

Mythical and legendary motifs are both employed sparingly in *kvæði* one, in which seven stanzas refer, mostly using kennings, to myth and four to legend. The first of these kennings is *Hamðis fang* or 'Hamðir's tunic,' in st. 2; the reference is to a hero of the Völsung legend, and the kenning's referent is 'mail-coat,' the shirt of a warrior.[51] This kenning is straightforward and requires only a rudimentary knowledge of northern legend to decode. The same is true of the first *kvæði*'s two other clear legendary kennings, *Róða stóð* (steed of Róði [a sea-king] = ship) and *Rínar röf* (amber of the Rhine = gold), as well as many of its mythological kennings, including *Hlakkar haukr* (hawk of Hlökk [a valkyrie] = raven) and *unna Gyllir* (Gyllir [a mythical horse] of the waves = ship).[52] Based on such examples, Snorri seems to have been taking it easy on the king in terms of his use of skaldic diction. There are, however, several kennings in stt. 1–30 that are more complex as well as obscure: one that I have already cited is *Vindhlés hjálms fyllr* (filler of the helmet of Heimdallr = Heimdallr's head = sword), and another is *gríma grundar gjaldseiðs* (helmet of the payment-fish of the ground), an apparent reference to the dragon Fáfnir, from whose hoard the *ægishjálmr*, 'helm of terror,' was claimed by Sigurðr Fáfnisbani.[53] Then, there is st. 3, the first in *Háttatal* in which mythological kennings appear. The commentary states that this stanza illustrates the use of extended kennings, those comprised of three or more elements, and Snorri chooses as examples four tripartite mythological kennings:

Úlfs bága verr ægis
ítr báls hati málu;
sett eru börð fyrir bratta
brún Míms vinar rúnu;

orms váða kann eiðu
allvaldr göfugr halda;
menstríðir njót móður
mellu dólgs til elli.

> The noble hater of the fire of the sea defends the woman-friend of the enemy of the wolf; prows are set before the steep brow of the confidante of the friend of Mímir. The noble, all-powerful one knows how to protect the mother of the attacker of the worm; enjoy, enemy of neck-rings, the mother of the troll-wife's enemy until old age.[54]

For those lacking the erudition to comprehend this stanza – familiarity with five mythological narratives, knowledge of the family relations of two gods, and some experience with skaldic convention is needed – its content must appear fairly nonsensical. But for those who possess such knowledge, it is easily deciphered: Hákon is the 'noble hater of the fire of the sea' and 'enemy of neck-rings,' both typical kennings for a 'generous lord,' and all four extended mythological kennings have the same referent, *jörð*, 'earth' or, in this case, 'the land,' which as personified in myth is the mistress of Óðinn ('enemy of the wolf' and 'Mímir's friend') and mother of Þórr (foe of the 'worm' and 'troll-wife'). Doing away, then, with all poetic embroidery, st. 3 reads: 'Hákon defends the land; prows are set before the steep edge of the land. Hákon knows how to protect the land; may Hákon enjoy the land until old age.'

Having grasped this stanza's unadorned meaning, the question arises: Would the king, the target of the praise offered, have been able to do so? As my discussion of Hákon's education and cultural background in chapter 5 suggests, there is reason to doubt that he would have been able to decipher this verse unaided. Indeed, it is easy to imagine the king reading or listening to Snorri's poem in the mid-1220s, reaching st. 3 with its dense mythological allusions, throwing up his hands, and turning to something more accessible – like, say, his translated copy of *Tristrams saga*. Here again, however, I doubt that this stanza was designed to bewilder or alienate the king. Rather, this verse served a purpose similar to the preoccupation of stt. 1–30 with *dróttkvætt*: to call attention to its producer's mastery over and to educate its consumer on how to appreciate the skaldic art. Form, not content, is the point of st. 3; or, more precisely, its content serves as a demonstration of formal artistry. Even if everyone knows and anyone can say that a king rules and protects his land, only a skald can proclaim this fact in four distinctive and distinguished ways in a space of eight lines. The skald's ability to vary and ennoble such a mundane sentiment depends above all else on the use of kennings, devices that, as the commentary states, increase the *orðfjöldi*, 'word-store,' at a poet's disposal.[55] Kennings, in turn, rely on pagan myth as quarry for their material. Neither kennings nor references to myth are of value, however, to a poet whose audience cannot decode them. In this light, st. 3 is Snorri's attempt to introduce the king at the outset of the poem dedicated to him to what a skald, employing his arsenal of poetic diction and most distinctive metre, was capable of doing with even the most simple and redundant of content.

Lastly, I will look at stt. 27–30, those containing the only references in *Háttatal*'s first poem to identifiable events. These stanzas refer to Snorri's 1218–20 trip to Norway, and as such are as much about the poet as the king; they are also, I will argue, about the jarl. Stanza 27 recounts Snorri's journey to meet the king and his reception of a title. He then describes further gifts and honours he received in Norway: in st. 28, he thanks his host for a *skipreiða*, a 'ship-levy estate,' and *unna dýr* (animals of the waves = ships), and in st. 29 for hospitality and *margdýrar hnossir*, 'very valuable treasures.'[56] There are several discrepancies between the account Snorri offers here of his dealings with the king and what we know from Sturla Þórðarson's sagas. Most obviously, st. 28's claim that the king gave a ship to Snorri contradicts Sturla's statement in *Íslendinga saga* that 'the jarl had given [Snorri] the ship, that he went abroad in.'[57] Few have commented on this inconsistency, but most appear to accept Sturla's testimony, and, given what we know of Snorri's dealings in Norway, this judgment seems sound.

If Sturla's report is accepted as authentic, how is Snorri's account of this instance of gift-giving in st. 28 of *Háttatal* to be explained? A clue may lie in st. 27, where we are told that while in Norway Snorri was given the title of *hersir*[58] by *jarla prýði*, a kenning with two possible readings: on the one hand, *prýði* may be the dative singular of the masculine noun *prýðir*, in which case the kenning is 'adorner of jarls,' and refers, presumably, to the king; conversely, the term could be the dative singular of the feminine noun *prýði*, in which case it would read 'ornament among jarls,' and the logical referent would be Skúli. This kenning has long caused editors and translators difficulty: Faulkes, for instance, opts for 'ornament of earls' in his 1987 translation of *Háttatal*, but switches to 'adorner, one who dispenses honour to' jarls in his 1991 edition.[59] Given, however, that this kenning would have been as ambiguous to a thirteenth-century reader of Snorri's poem as it is to us, choosing between its meanings may be neither necessary nor appropriate. Snorri may, in short, have designed this kenning so that either the king or jarl could see himself in it. The motive for employing such a tactic emerges from *Íslendinga saga*'s description of this event: 'When King Hákon and jarl Skúli made Snorri their *lendr maðr*, that was mostly the doing of the jarl and Snorri.'[60] If Sturla is believed, Snorri had cause to be circumspect in expressing gratitude for this gift: even if Skúli was chiefly responsible for securing this honour, the authority to bestow titles within the royal *hirð* ought to rest with the king. Under such circumstances, the use of an equivocal referent would allow Snorri to implicate the king in the giving of a gift for which he was not directly responsible, thereby giving himself something concrete for which to thank Hákon at the close of the poem devoted to his praise. Thus, this may be another instance where Snorri discreetly lauds the king for things he has not technically done. This argument may also apply to st. 28, where Snorri claims, contrary to Sturla, that a ship was given to him by the king. Although none of the appellations for 'ruler' used in this stanza are as ambiguous as *jarla prýði*, they are still too vague to tell precisely whom Snorri is thanking; and it may be significant that one of the terms employed here is *skyli*, 'protector,' a *heiti* that, in *Skáldskaparmál*, Snorri will identify with the proper name Skúli.[61] At any rate, a ship is a big enough gift to accommodate two donors, and it does not seem unreasonable to suppose that both stt. 27 and 28 seek to include the king in acts that were, in reality, 'mostly the doing of the jarl and Snorri.'

Finally, we come to st. 30, the last of the poem for Hákon. Here, Snorri turns, as he will at the close of each *kvæði*, to his own relationship with his patron or patrons: 'I beg that the fir of the green shields [man = Snorri] may keep the helmet-provider's favour, Hrungnir's sole-plank ash [man = Snorri] gained advancement from that; wielder of the wand of the battle-land [Hákon], enjoy power over many lands – you are beneficial to us – until noble old age, feller of enemies.'[62] While it is not unusual for a praise-poem to end with an appeal for recognition, there are several things that set this stanza apart. In the first place, Snorri does not speak of his talent or the composition that he has just delivered; there is, in fact, no mention of poetry in this stanza or in any that come before it, and no sense, therefore, that a poet/patron relationship has been forged, through this or previous works, between Snorri and Hákon. Second, there is something uncommonly plaintive in the way that this stanza begs for the king's approval, reassuring him not once but twice that any support he deigns to show is appreciated and valued. The close of Hákon's panegyric is not the triumphant vaunting of the poet's skill and call for reward that we expect from a skaldic encomium, but a muted, tentative plea for recognition, one born, I believe, of its composer's fear that the value of his product was in the hands of a consumer who was not in the market for what he was selling.

Poems Two and Three: Praise for Skúli

The first stanza of Snorri's first *kvæði* for Skúli reads:

> Stáls dynblakka støkkvi
> stinngeðs samir minnask
> (álms bifsœki aukum
> Yggs feng) á lof þengils;

odds bláferla jarli
örbrjót ne skal þrjóta
(Hárs saltunnu hrannir
hrœrum) óð at stœra.

It befits the impeller of the noisy-horses of the prow [controller of ships = Snorri] to recall the firm-minded prince's praise (we augment Yggr's booty [Óðinn's mead = poetry] for the quiverer of the elm-bow [warrior = Skúli]); the eager-breaker of arrow's dark paths [breaker of shields = warrior = Snorri] shall not cease to increase poetry for the jarl (we stir the waves of Hárr's hall-vat [poetry]).[63]

Unlike any in Hákon's poem, this stanza suggests a history of successful transactions between the skald and his patron. By recalling the *lof* that he has already raised for the jarl,[64] and by reassuring him that there is more to come, Snorri introduces his current tribute to Skúli as the latest stage in an ongoing relationship. Snorri also reflects in this stanza, for the first time in *Háttatal*'s poetic portions, on his own practice as a skald, congratulating himself not just for enhancing the jarl's fame, but for enriching the canon of skaldic verse – as he boasts, he augments *Yggs fengr*, 'Óðinn's mead.' Whereas the poem for Hákon closed on a note of anxiety, Skúli's encomium opens with an air of confidence.

Snorri's newfound temerity extends to his use of metre in praising Skúli. Around the start of *kvæði* two, Snorri grows bolder in his variation of form. This upswing in metrical experimentation no doubt signals the poet's faith in his second patron's capacity to respond to a wider range of verse-forms; in didactic terms, Snorri regarded Skúli as a more advanced pupil of skaldic metrics than Hákon. Even so, the metres employed in stt. 31–67 remain, as the commentary repeatedly stresses, essentially *dróttkvætt*. The jarl could rest assured, therefore, that his praise was cast in a form as distinguished as that used to applaud the king. With the close of *kvæði* two, however, Snorri's use of *dróttkvætt* ends. As the commentary following st. 67 states: 'Now shall the third poem begin, that which is composed from the lesser metres, and yet those metres are frequent in the past in praise-poems.'[65] This last comment reassures the poem's patrons (both of whom are addressed in st. 67) that these lesser forms, while perhaps not strictly court metres, are suitable for lauding lords such as themselves.

Kvæði three, which immediately reverts to praise of the jarl alone, begins with a trio of interconnected stanzas that conclude with this line: 'Many a poetic metre of mine has never before been composed in about a wise point-clash meeter [warrior].'[66] In contrast to the commentary, where the poem's praise is accorded worth because its form is traditional, its value is here traced to its metrical novelty. Such contradiction could be taken to suggest that these parts of *Háttatal* were not written by the same individual. I would argue, however, that these claims reflect different facets of Snorri's strategy to interest and educate his patrons. On the one hand, he has shown a proclivity to stick to *dróttkvætt*, the most well-attested skaldic verse-form. Such conservatism is particularly evident in stanzas dedicated to Hákon and stems, I have argued, not only from the poem's organizational logic, but from Snorri's justified doubt about the king's facility with this art form. As we leave the portion of the poem devoted to the king, however, Snorri grows more adventurous in his use of metre, and more willing to tout his own inventiveness. This development climaxes in st. 100, which states that a 'man must not be called unworthy of renown if he is able to compose in all verse-forms,' an interesting claim given that, as he admits to having invented many of the forms used in *Háttatal*, Snorri is necessarily the only skald to have thus far accomplished this grand feat.[67] The conflicting appeals, then, to tradition at the end of *kvæði* two versus innovation at the beginning of *kvæði* three are consequences of the fact that Snorri has had to address himself to two patrons, each of whom comes to the cultural product on offer with markedly unequal levels of experience, competence, and interest.

Just as Snorri seems more secure in his metrical abilities in his pair of *kvæði* for Skúli, he is also more comfortable extending certain kinds of praise to the jarl, particularly when it comes to warfare. This is surely because in Skúli's case he actually had something to work with. Snorri takes immediate advantage of his more mature patron's experience in this arena, incorporating into stt. 32–7 details from Skúli's early deeds in the service of his brother Ingi.[68] At several points in these stanzas, Snorri strongly emphasizes Skúli's fraternal relationship with Hákon's predecessor on the throne, and in st. 39 recounts his reception of the title of jarl from Ingi in 1217.[69] Snorri also includes concrete events from Skúli's career in stt. 63–6, which make mention of the jarl's victories of 1221–2. But despite having more material with which to praise Skúli, Snorri continued to rely heavily on convention in *kvæði* two and three. Stanzas 41–8, for example, are given over to stereotypical acclamation of the jarl's generosity, 49–62 to the kind of hyperbolic but generic descriptions of 'showers-of-spears' and 'feasts-of-wolves' that would be right at home in Hákon's panegyric, and 71–9 to portraits of Skúli urgently driving fleets of ships to nowhere in particular. But if the jarl's praise is often as hackneyed as the king's, Snorri often seems more enthusiastic about offering it, making heavy use of superlatives, and reiterating compliments to near the point of absurdity.[70]

Another telling difference separating Hákon's praise from Skúli's is the heavier use of mythological and legendary kennings in the latter. Skúli's first poem begins, as we have seen, with several kennings for poetry, and the stanzas describing his early career contain references to myth and legend. It is in st. 41, however, that Snorri's use of such content truly intensifies. This stanza, the first of a string praising Skúli's generosity, contains four kennings for gold that all refer to the Völsung legend: *otrgjöld* (otter's payment), *Grana þungfarmr* (Grani's heavy burden), *Gnitaheiðar reiðmálmr* (loaded-metal of Gnita-heath), and *Niflunga skattr* (Niflungar's treasure).[71] These are followed by *fagrregn Mardallar hvarma* (fair rain of Mardöll's [Freyja's] eyelids) in st. 42, and in st. 43 by a trio of gold kennings – *Grotta glaðdript* (joyful snow of Grotti), *Fróða friðbygg* (Fróði's peace-barley), and *Fenju meldr* (Fenja's meal) – that refer to King Fróði's gold-producing mill.[72] More nods to myth and legend appear as Snorri returns to the topic of war: st. 49 alone contains four kennings for battle, all of which, like those in stt. 41 and 43, derive from a single legend, in this case that of Hildr, a maiden who nightly raises the dead from among the armies of her feuding husband and father.[73] From here until the end of *kvæði* two, there are eleven stanzas that contain clear mythological or legendary kennings, and multiple references to Skúli using the names of the gods Baldr, Týr, and Gautr (Óðinn).[74]

In *Háttatal*'s third *kvæði*, the occurrence of mythological and legendary material falls off sharply: in part, this is because the simpler metres and shorter line-lengths found in this section are ill-suited to the use of complex kennings. There are two references to myth in st. 85, which comments on Skúli's warrior skills, and allusions to legend are dictated by this section's major themes, Skúli's maritime expertise and his generosity/hospitality. By far the most significant use of such material is in st. 94, which places Skúli in the company of four illustrious heroes of northern legend, the Danish Hrólfr kraki, the sea-king Haki, the dragon-slayer Sigurðr, and the Viking-leader Ragnarr loðbrók.[75] Despite this tapering off of mythological and legendary material, its relative presence in Skúli's poems is much larger than in Hákon's: in total, there are eleven clear mythological and three legendary references in the thirty stanzas devoted to the king, as compared to thirty-three mythological and eighteen legendary in Skúli's sixty-four stanzas. As with Snorri's more ambitious use of metre and praise, the greater presence of Norse myth and legend in the sections of *Háttatal* devoted to the jarl reflects a confidence that Skúli possessed the cultural background needed to recognize and appreciate this material. That Snorri credited Skúli with such is evident from those stanzas in which multiple kennings are drawn from a single myth or legend; much of their artistic effect, particularly in cases like st. 41, where the order of the kennings parallels the plot of the story in question, would be lost on someone lacking such knowledge.

Finally, I turn to the concluding stanzas of *kvæði* two and three, which, like the final stanza of *kvæði* one, focus on the skald's relations with his patron(s).

Stanza 67, the last of *kvæði* two and the first in which Skúli and Hákon are praised together, reads: 'I composed with six tens of metres as a memorial for men about brave rulers, those whom I knew to be the most outstanding. Not at all have the princes thrown into the ancient sea the glory or gold with which they have honoured me (that is for us an advancement).'[76] As in many of the verses directed at Skúli, the poet here expresses confidence in his skill and versatility. Also in this stanza, however, is a return of the anxiety of st. 30. As there, Snorri's unease manifests in a declaration that any rewards – tangible or intangible, past or future – his labours might earn him are neither wasted nor unappreciated. This juxtaposition of bravado and humility may reflect uncertainty over how best to address simultaneously two patrons whose attitudes and reactions towards the product being offered are liable to be, if past experience is any judge, quite different.

Despite st. 67's assurances about the worth of Snorri's art, it is not until the close of *kvæði* three that he spells out what its sponsors can expect to receive in return. As Fidjestøl puts it, 'The praise-poem about the princes ends by becoming a praise-poem about the praise-poem.'[77] More than this, *Háttatal* becomes at its end a disquisition on the reciprocal benefits of a successful skaldic transaction. Stanza 95 reads: 'I remembered fifteen large gifts from the lord, when to the helmet-provider of the Mærir I presented four poems. Where might a man know of praise previously composed with nobler metres for a destroyer of neck-rings under the sheets of the sky?'[78] As we ought to expect by now when Snorri addresses the jarl alone, this stanza exhibits great confidence in the quality of his verse – fifteen gifts for four poems is more than a fair trade.[79] However, in the next stanza, where Snorri addresses both Skúli and Hákon, his pride does not, as we might expect, abate. Rather, the poet here makes his boldest claim yet for his work: 'That will live forever, the princes' praise, unless humanity passes away, or the worlds perish.'[80] This sentiment is echoed in *Háttatal*'s last stanza: 'May king and jarl enjoy old-age and halls of wealth. That is the poem's end. May the land, supported by stone, fall into the sea before the rulers' praise.'[81]

Here, at the end of his tribute, Snorri finally tempts the king and jarl with what court poets the world over dangle before their patrons: the promise of undying fame. This is not offered for free, however – there are reminders to his patrons of what they must do to fulfil their end of the deal: 'I raised bright praise of the people's king, the jarl's glory is borne up before men. What man would hear praise thus recited of one who is slow to give gold and treasures?'[82] Whether these statements exhibit more self-doubt or self-assurance makes little difference, as both manifest the poet's anxiety that his elaborate gift may be rejected by one or both of its subjects. In this, Snorri is not so different from his forebears. To extend a praise-poem was a threatening act – a skaldic gift not only demanded a return, but tested, often publicly, the taste and discernment of its recipient, who was called on to process the work presented, judge whether it was well or poorly made, and decide how best to respond to it. For these reasons, the prudent skald begged the lord's leave before reciting in his honour.[83] For Snorri, things were more complicated and more risky; in seeking to extend the value of what was becoming an obsolete cultural resource, he had composed a tribute, unparalleled in length and complexity, that had to be sent, if at all, long-distance and unsolicited to two patrons, one of whom lacked the capacity and incentive to absorb it, the other of whom had already rewarded his poetry to excess, and both of whom would have been better pleased by news of his progress in bringing Iceland under their control. It was under these circumstances that Snorri had to pursue the goals that I identified at the start of my analysis: to convince his patrons that his poetry remained the most prestigious art form of the north, to persuade them of its continued relevance to them as elite social actors, and to provide them with enough pointers to appreciate the artistry on display and, if possible, develop or deepen their tastes for it. The manner in which the metre, diction, and content for *Háttatal*'s various sections were tailored to the needs of its patrons provides evidence of its composer's efforts to achieve these aims. Given, however, the number and magnitude of the obstacles Snorri faced, it is little wonder if, even at the end of 102 stanzas, he does not seem so sure that he has succeeded.

Some Comments on the Commentary

While scholars continue to find inconsistencies between *Háttatal*'s verse and its commentary, these are not so extreme as to rule out Snorri's responsibility for both.[84] There are, moreover, several facts supporting Snorri's authorship of the commentary: first, it is found, whole or in part, in all *Edda* manuscripts containing *Háttatal*;[85] second, there is a possible reference to the commentary in st. 100 of the poem, which would suggest not only that the same person wrote both, but that work on them was carried out simultaneously;[86] and third, W's scribe seems to identify Snorri as its author.[87] Most conclude, then, that the weight of the evidence supports Snorri's identification as producer of the commentary, although many leave open the possibility that he worked with one or more collaborators, or that his work was altered or expanded by later hands.

Aside from passages that I have already discussed, I have little to say about the commentary's content or its classification of skaldic metre. Instead, I wish here to address the question of why Snorri found it necessary to attach explanatory remarks to what was already a didactic work. As in my analysis of the poem, it is my view that the commentary was not designed solely for use by young Icelandic skalds, but also for the king and jarl. This presumes, of course, that Snorri planned to deliver poetry and commentary together to Hákon and Skúli. While most agree that Snorri must have sent or tried to send the poem at least to its subjects, there is no record of *Háttatal*'s delivery or reception, and so no way of knowing in what form or by what means it was transmitted, if at all. I doubt, however, that Snorri would have gone to the trouble of composing a work like *Háttatal* and then not have delivered it. As for our sources' silence on this matter, this would not be the first time that one of Snorri's tributes to a Norwegian king was ignored by his chief biographer Sturla, who was inclined, as I have argued, to report only those poetic gifts of his uncle that were reciprocated. In any event, without proof that Snorri sent his poem and/or commentary to the king and jarl, the most that can be done in analysing either is to identify its producer's aspirations and the strategies of the work designed to fulfil these.

It is usually assumed that Snorri patterned *Háttatal*'s commentary after Latin treatises on poetry, grammar, and rhetoric. Even those who doubt that Snorri's knowledge of such treatises went very far concede that he was likely inspired by what he knew of such works to attach a learned commentary to his poem.[88] Signs of Latin influence are most prominent in the commentary's opening section, which is structured as a master-and-pupil dialogue: 'What are the forms of poetic speech? Three. Which are? Rule, licence, prohibition. What are the rules of the forms? Two. Which are? Regular and varied,' and so on.[89] All attempts, however, to identify a specific model for this or any other portion of the commentary have proven, in Roberta Frank's words, 'infuriatingly difficult.'[90] Unlike the earlier and later Icelandic grammarians, Snorri does not seem to have worked from any known or unknown Latin template.[91] Thus, the commentary remains chiefly concerned with and indebted to principles of analysis based in and drawn from native poetic practice. To some, this intrusion of oral tradition into the work of 'a product of Christian-Latin written learning' is surprising.[92] Tranter, who has written much on this matter, states: 'The vitality of this [oral] tradition is demonstrated in this, that it still survived in the analysis of literate scholars.'[93] Such reasoning strikes me as backwards: rather than a still kicking oral tradition insinuating itself into a treatise on poetry planned and written along classical lines, it seems to me more likely that Latin style and analytic methods were enlisted to help resuscitate a failing oral tradition. What Tranter takes as evidence of skaldic vitality in Snorri's treatise are rather signs of its author's determination to reinstil life into a moribund art form.[94]

If, however, Snorri's knowledge of Latin texts was superficial and his interests lay in oral/native rather than literate/foreign poetics, why did he even attempt in *Háttatal*'s commentary to mimic the 'manner and style and approach of the learned Latin treatises'?[95] In responding, it pays to recall the clerical education of King Hákon, the principal target of not only the praise but perhaps also the metrical instruction of *Háttatal*'s first section. Hákon was certainly instructed in grammar and rhetoric, probably using the same kinds of texts that directly or indirectly influenced *Háttatal*'s commentary. After visiting Norway, Snorri would have been aware of his younger host's educational background, and it may be that his inconsistent and often clumsy efforts to reproduce something of the style and format of Latin treatises was motivated by a desire to attract Hákon to his poetry, by placing it in the kind of didactic frame with which the king was familiar. That Snorri had Hákon foremost in mind when crafting his commentary is suggested by the fact that its quasi-Latinate features are much less pronounced after the end of *kvæði* one; indeed, its dialogic format is abandoned altogether after st. 24. Nowhere in the pair of *kvæði* aimed mainly at Skúli do we hear again from the first section's enthusiastic pupil, a role that Snorri likely hoped Hákon would identify with and adopt.

Of course, if Hákon was to become an apprentice in the study of skaldic metrics, Snorri had first to adopt the role of master. In this respect, *Háttatal*'s commentary marks a crucial benchmark not only in the *Edda*'s production, but in Snorri's cultural output as a whole. In writing or having this commentary written, Snorri moved from being a simple producer to an instructor and exegete of culture. This is not to say that he suddenly became a scholar, someone with a genuine stake in fostering and disseminating knowledge and culture for their own sakes. It is to say that it became in his interests, as an agent seeking to defend the value of a substantial stockpile of politically relevant capital, to begin to behave something like one. The commentary is a sign that *Háttatal* could not be trusted to accomplish on its own the aims that its producer had set for it, that the king would not be swayed to consume a product that his education and occupational interests did not dispose him to view as a form of legitimate culture solely by persuasions deployed from within the poem itself. It also marks the moment when Snorri recognized on some level that it was not enough to focus his efforts to rehabilitate the worth of his poetic talent only on those agents from whom he hoped to elicit direct rewards. The forces eroding skaldic verse's capacity to function as capital stretched far beyond Hákon and his court, and any project that hoped to counteract or reverse this process had to confront them all. Snorri was faced, in short, with the task of reconstituting the field or market wherein skaldic verse had held value and a capacity for conversion. *Háttatal*'s commentary, the first of Snorri's works in which he addressed an audience wider than his immediate patrons, represented a first, tentative step in this direction. *Skáldskaparmál*, the subject of the next chapter, is where this work really began.

7 *Skáldskaparmál*: Salvaging the Market for Skaldic Verse

In composing *Háttatal*, Snorri's aspirations were undoubtedly little different from those motivating his and others' prior panegyrics: to convert a distinguished cultural product into symbolic and material profits. That *Háttatal* had, however, to pursue this end under less favourable conditions than its forebears is attested by the work's extravagant length, hyperbolic praise, and overblown claims for its own worth. Almost everything about Snorri's poem is scaled to compensate for, or deny, the fact that skaldic verse was no longer the most in-demand cultural good in the medieval north. But if *Háttatal* was a direct and sometimes blunt attempt to insist on the continued value of the skaldic art, Snorri's writing of a commentary for his poem signalled his adoption of a more sophisticated and expansive approach. Here, Snorri's strategy shifted from an effort to persuade desired sponsors within the field in which he was operating to consume his product to an attempt to reconstitute the conditions of the market wherein this product had held high value. As Bourdieu writes: 'Those who seek to defend a threatened linguistic capital ... are obliged to wage a total struggle. One cannot save the *value* of a competence unless one saves the market, in other words, the whole set of political and social conditions of production of the producers/consumers.'[1] By the early 1220s, Snorri was confronted by a decline in both of the populations vital to the continuing operation of such a market. While he retained the competence and clung to the desire to produce and deploy skaldic poetry, potential consumers within the market, particularly the royal consumer seated at its apex, were losing their capacity to appreciate this product. At the same time, there were ever fewer Icelanders, traditional producers and suppliers of skaldic goods, investing the time and energy needed to master this art, no doubt as a consequence of the diminishing returns such expertise could earn them. If Snorri was to have any hope of preserving the worth of his poetry, he had to develop a strategy that would not only increase the number of interested and informed consumers of skaldic verse, but produce other competent producers of this art form.

Skáldskaparmál is the part of the *Edda* in which Snorri's efforts to salvage the market for skaldic verse are most evident. Still, scholars' understandings of how this text pursued this end have been remarkably one-sided. Most regard *Skáldskaparmál* as having been designed by Snorri mainly or even exclusively for use by other skaldic producers, principally fellow Icelanders. This perspective on *Skáldskaparmál*'s audience receives some verification from its author, who in the so-called *Eptirmáli* or 'Afterword,' which, while likely among the last portions of the *Edda* written, is placed near the start of *Skáldskaparmál* in all manuscripts, writes: 'And this is now to be told to those young skalds who desire to take the language of poetry and to make for themselves a word-store with old names, or those who desire to know how to understand that which is spoken obscurely: then he should take this book as knowledge and entertainment.'[2] Here, Snorri explicitly identifies an audience for *Skáldskaparmál*, and there is no reason to doubt his desire to encourage younger Icelanders' interest in skaldic diction. Too often, however, critics have imagined Snorri as instructor to a set of fledgling poets, an image that at once feeds off of and reinforces the normative view of Snorri (at least of his non-political half) as a scholar/artist whose interests in skaldic verse were primarily aesthetic and antiquarian. And yet, there is scant evidence that Snorri founded or sought to establish any sort of school around himself. Whatever Eugen Mogk and others have argued, Snorri cannot be numbered among Icelanders like Eyjólfr Sæmundarson, founder of Oddi's school and possible author of the *First Grammatical Treatise*, or his nephew Óláfr, who set up a school at Stafaholt and wrote the *Third Grammatical Treatise*.[3] At any rate, Snorri did not need students – he needed competitors, those who through their rival skaldic production would further his efforts to resuscitate the market wherein his own store of poetic expertise could continue to function as a convertible resource. The other thing needed to stimulate this market was a set of active consumers. Though it has gone little noticed, there is alongside Snorri's explicit address to *ungum skáldum* in the *Eptirmáli* a more subtle appeal to consumers of skaldic verse in his comment that his work is offered to those who would also *skilja*, 'understand,' the skalds' secret language.

By focusing on diction rather than metre, *Skáldskaparmál* continues the project begun with *Háttatal* – to encourage interest in Snorri's brand of poetic goods, and to supply tools that would enable his audience to respond to his work. Indeed, there is a closer connection than is generally acknowledged between the instruction presented in *Skáldskaparmál* and the skaldic 'demonstration' that is *Háttatal*; as I will show, the *Edda*'s middle portion is a supplement to a reading of *Háttatal*, a key of sorts to its comprehension and appreciation. In line with this understanding of the text, I regard as one of its principal targets Snorri's most desired but least responsive patron, King Hákon. In this, I differ from previous critics of *Skáldskaparmál*, few of whom even mention the king or his court when discussing this text, an omission that seems to me to have obscured its many points of connection with *Háttatal*. *Skáldskaparmál* should also be recognized for introducing a new dimension into Snorri's ongoing quest to protect his skaldic investment. Much of the text consists of illustrations from the work of *höfuðskálds*, the 'chief-poets' of the north. In compiling an anthology of the verse of skaldic luminaries, much of which he excerpted from eulogies for Norwegian kings and jarls, Snorri aimed not only to preserve the tradition, or to assist others in understanding kennings and admiring their application in his work, but also to display skaldic poetry's four-hundred-year history as the chief repository for the memory of the characters and deeds of the ancestors of his two most desired patrons.

Tackling the Tangled Text(s) of *Skáldskaparmál*

Skáldskaparmál, or 'The Language of Poetry,' is the longest and most hetero-geneous portion of Snorri's *Edda*, comprising in its fuller versions extended narratives, enumerations of kennings, hundreds of illustrative stanzas and half-stanzas from the skaldic corpus, lengthy extracts from single poems, and lists of poetic synonyms, all loosely bound together by a frame dialogue. *Skáldskaparmál* also appears to be the part of the *Edda* that was least precisely planned or fully realized by its author – its organization is muddled and uncertain, its division of *heiti* from kennings is inconsistent, its definitions and illustrations are often inadequate or inappropriate to the kenning-types being explicated, its narratives sometimes appear randomly placed or awkwardly integrated, and its framing dialogue is erratically employed. Its history of transmission is also the most tangled of any of the *Edda*'s parts. *Skáldskap-armál* was clearly the most interesting to later generations, and the most freely reworked by redactors: versions of it are found in seven manuscripts, the four (R, T, W, and U) that include all parts of the *Edda*, as well as three that present portions of *Skáldskaparmál* alongside other Icelandic works on poetry or grammar.[4] In several manuscripts, *Skáldskaparmál* is broken up by ancillary material, and it is likely that in all of its extant versions the text has been heav-ily emended and interpolated by hands later than Snorri's.

As with the *Edda* as a whole, R's text of *Skáldskaparmál* is widely regarded as that which most nearly approximates Snorri's original vision.[5] *Skáldskaparmál*'s contents in R can be summarized as follows: first appears the so-called *Bragarœður*, or 'Speeches of Bragi,' in which the framing device of a conversation between Ægir (god or perhaps giant of the sea) and Bragi (god of poetry and likely apotheosis of history's first remembered skald, Bragi Boddasson) is established.[6] Included here are a number of narratives that are discussed below. Chapter 1 of what many consider to be *Skáldskaparmál* proper finds Bragi instructing Ægir on different categories of poetic speech. Next comes the *Eptirmáli*, which offers a statement on the text's purpose, a warning to Christian readers on how they ought to understand the pagan material being presented, and a passage in which the *æsir* are euhemerized as Trojan heroes. *Skáldskaparmál* then continues with ch. 2 (exemplifying kennings for Óðinn), ch. 3 (kennings for poetry), and chs 4–16 (kennings for other gods, beginning with Þórr and ending with Loki). Chapters 17–18 relate Þórr's fights with the *jötnar* Hrungnir and Geirrøðr, and provide excerpts from the skaldic sources for these tales, Þjóðólfr of Hvinir's *Haustlöng* and Eilífr Guðrúnarson's *Þórsdrápa*. Chapters 19–32 deal with kennings for the *ásynjur*, nature, men and women, and gold. Chapters 33–45 narrate myths and legends from which gold-kennings derive. Chapters 46–53 complete the section on kenning-types with those that relate men and women to gold and refer to them as trees, followed by kennings for battle, weapons and armour, ships, Christ, and kings and noblemen. Chapters 54–74 deal mostly with *ókent heiti*, or simple poetic synonyms, for a wide range of concepts, although kennings continue to appear as examples. Chapters 67–8 turn attention briefly to several other types of poetic diction: *fornöfn* (sg. *fornafn*), *viðkenningar*, and *sannkenningar*. Finally, *Skáldskaparmál* in R ends with ch. 75, made up of 106 stanzas of *þulur*, versified lists of simple terms for use in poetry. Of the other manuscripts that contain all parts of the *Edda*, only that of U diverges from R in ways that are significant for my analysis. Stylistically, U is much more condensed. As for content, U omits *fornöfn* from its classification of diction in ch. 1, the Trojan material from the *Eptirmáli*, most of the longer skaldic excerpts, several chapters of kenning-types, and the *þulur*. In terms of organization, U places the narratives of Þórr's giant-fights (R chs 17–18) immediately after the material corresponding to R ch. 1 and the *Eptirmáli*, and inserts between these and R ch. 2 three lists with obvious significance for Snorri and his family: *Skáldatal*, a Sturlungar genealogy extending into the early 1300s, and a list of lawspeakers ending with Snorri's second term.[7] Finally, U places some of the narratives exemplifying gold-kennings in shortened form at the end rather than in the middle of *Skáldskaparmál*.

As past scholarship has amply demonstrated, the complex relations of *Skáldskaparmál*'s manuscripts to one another as well as postulated forebears can be envisioned in a host of (often contradictory) ways.[8] In light of this uncertainty, I have chosen to focus my analysis on what may be called three modules – broadly defined units that few or no scholars would refuse to ascribe to Snorri – and the way in which these contribute to the strategic aims that motivated production of this second major portion of the *Edda*. These modules are 1) *Skáldskaparmál* 'proper,' i.e., enumerations of kennings and *heiti* with illustrative verses drawn from skaldic tradition, including passages in which Snorri defines and systematizes categories of poetic diction; 2) extended narratives; and 3) the frame dialogue and *Eptirmáli*.[9] Adopting this modular approach in my analysis allows me to do several things. First, it permits me to disregard much of the disagreement in detail between manuscripts, such as differences in wording or presence versus absence of specific stanzas. Second, since my investigation will be largely neutral in respect to the ordering of material, much of the manuscripts' divergence at the level of organization may be set aside. In downplaying the importance of structure, my analysis departs rather severely from recent investigations of *Skáldskaparmál* that treat it, as one critic puts it, as a work of 'high theoretical unity.'[10] The most prominent such study is Clunies Ross's 1987 book, in which her main hypothesis – that Snorri intended *Skáldskaparmál* to further the theological agenda of the *Formáli* and *Gylfaginning* by setting forth the world view of his pagan ancestors as embodied in the language of skalds – is supported largely through reference to the text's organization, above all by its ordering of kenning and *heiti* categories, in which Clunies Ross perceives the influence of medieval encyclopedic tradition.[11] I do not find the organization of *Skáldskaparmál*'s content anywhere near as subtle or meticulous as Clunies Ross perceives it to be. In my view, *Skáldskaparmál* is an eminently practical, strategically oriented, but not particularly orderly text: it is not a systematic treatise but a conglomerate of disparate materials that could be (and was, by later copyists as well as probably by Snorri himself) reordered and reworked without fundamentally altering its focus or purpose. Along with Sigurður Nordal and Faulkes, I doubt that *Skáldskaparmál* ever received a form that its producer was fully satisfied with.[12] The fact, as I argued in chapter 6, that in composing *Háttatal* Snorri had to persuade two patrons with unequal levels of interest and competence of the worth of his poetry required him to adopt diverse, at times conflicting, tactics. As he moved on to *Skáldskaparmál*, his intended audience grew wider, and his task more complex. Heterogeneity of audience led to a heterogeneity of material, which was selected to address, sometimes simultaneously and sometimes serially, the interests and needs of all those necessary to the maintenance or reconstitution of a market for skaldic verse.

The third advantage of a modular approach is that it allows me to attempt to draw out the temporal development of *Skáldskaparmál*. This progression

is reflected in the order in which I will discuss its modules: first, illustrations/
explication of categories of poetic diction, second, stories, and, third, the
frame and *Eptirmáli*. While this model of *Skáldskaparmál*'s evolution is neither very novel nor controversial, it is incapable of proof.[13] Nevertheless, I
will seek to support it by appealing to the evidence of the ordering of material
in U. For over a century, scholars have entertained or rejected the idea that U
may derive from a provisional stage of the *Edda*, from notes or a 'rough-draft'
that remained in the keeping of the Sturlungar, while the fuller forms of RTW
stem from a more polished version later produced by Snorri.[14] Given my view
of *Skáldskaparmál* as a text that progressed in an uncertain fashion, it seems to
me not unlikely that different manuscript versions reflect different stages in
Snorri's own work. The concluding section of this chapter will depart from
this chronological examination by focusing on what I consider to be the central narrative of *Skáldskaparmál*, and perhaps of the entire *Edda*, Snorri's
myth of the origin of the poetic mead. Here, I will seek to determine why
Snorri went to such lengths to compose, synthesize, and, if certain critics are
correct, partially invent this lengthy, elaborate, and peculiar story. I will also
argue that the composing of this narrative, and the desire to make others,
among whom we may include the king, the jarl, Norwegian courtiers, and
actual and potential Icelandic skalds, take it seriously, supplied a major impetus to the production of the sweeping overview of pagan myth and euhemeristic frame narrative that comprise the *Edda*'s two final sections, *Gylfaginning*
and the *Formáli*.

Kennings, *Heiti*, Myths and the Skalds Who Use Them

The greater part of *Skáldskaparmál* consists of single and half-stanzas, culled
from the work of more than sixty named and unnamed skalds of the ninth
through twelfth centuries, that illustrate the use of kennings and *heiti* in
poetry. In structure, this component of *Skáldskaparmál* closely resembles
Háttatal: both consist of brief snippets of verse embedded in prose commen-
taries, and both are given a dialogic form reminiscent of classical and medieval Latin textbooks. The opening dialogue of *Skáldskaparmál* ch. 1 reads:

> Then says Ægir: 'In how many ways do you vary the word-choices of poetry, or
> how many kinds of poetry are there?' Then says Bragi: 'Two are those kinds
> which divide all poetry.' Ægir asks: 'Which two?' Bragi says: 'Language and
> metre.' 'What choice of language is used in poetry?' 'Three are the categories of
> poetic speech.' 'Which are? ...'[15]

As with *Háttatal*'s commentary, scholars have not identified a specific Latin template upon which this exchange or its analysis of poetic speech depend, and it may be that Snorri chose to continue with this mode of presentation – which, despite ch. 1's identification of the speakers as Bragi and Ægir, runs throughout most of *Skáldskaparmál* as a dialogue between an anonymous master and pupil – so as to maintain the textbook feel of his treatise and retain the king's interest in its subject-matter.[16] At any rate, it seems clear that this module of *Skáldskaparmál* was conceived as a straightforward complement to what had already been achieved in *Háttatal*, and that, once united, these were intended to form a primer to the most distinctive and difficult of skaldic verse's technical features, its metre and diction.

I see Snorri as having had two purposes in producing his guide to skaldic diction: first, to introduce and explicate the kenning- and *heiti*-types of most relevance to the composition and comprehension of skaldic praise-poetry; and second, to establish a set of definitions for use in categorizing kinds of poetic substitution. Thus, there are in *Skáldskaparmál* two systems for classifying poetic diction, the first organized around common referents ('king,' 'Óðinn,' 'battle,' 'gold,' etc.), the second around types of formulae available for expressing these referents (simple versus compound terms, according to accidental versus essential qualities, etc.). Of these two purposes/levels of classification, the second was certainly subordinate to the first. In other words, Snorri developed *Skáldskaparmál*'s formal categories and terminology to facilitate presentation of what seemed to him the most important conceptual categories for the understanding and composition of praise-poetry, not least his own. Snorri's focus here was, in short, practical as opposed to theoretical. Since it would be difficult, however, to discuss Snorri's groupings of kennings and *heiti* by reference to objects, entities, and persons without having addressed his use and understanding of these and related terms, I will first describe his terminology and attempts at a formal categorization of skaldic diction, and then move to a discussion of his major conceptual categories.

That Snorri was never very committed to providing young skalds with an exhaustive system for classifying skaldic diction is suggested by how little space he actually dedicates to discussing his categories and terminology: aside from a few refinements of his definition for kennings, he does so in only two places. This sharply contrasts with what we find in Iceland's grammatical treatises, each of which is principally dedicated to formulating and systematizing grammatical and poetic terminology and rules. Snorri's main statement on such matters is found in ch. 1, where he has Bragi list three categories of poetic language: the first is 'to call each thing according to its name; another category is that which is called *fornöfn*; the third category of speech is that which is called a kenning.'[17] Only the first and third categories are of real consequence in *Skáldskaparmál*. The second, *fornöfn*, is only mentioned here and in chs 67–8, and does not, since it refers to either simple or compound terms that substitute for proper names, constitute its own distinct category of poetic diction.[18] It is also the only term in *Skáldskaparmál* that is clearly derived from Latin, being as Clunies Ross states 'a calque on the Latin *pronomen*,' and seems, based upon its treatment in several manuscripts, to be either a late addition to Snorri's taxonomy of skaldic speech, or else one that users of the *Edda* rejected.[19] The inclusion of this underdeveloped and poorly integrated component of Snorri's classificatory system is perhaps best explained, like the dialogic format given both *Háttatal* and the portion of *Skáldskaparmál* with which we are dealing, as an attempt to impress those of his readers who possessed more classical learning than he did by working into his text features of transparent, if superficial, Latin derivation.

Essentially, then, Snorri divides his treatise on diction according to two formal categories, which largely accord with those employed by modern scholars: chs 2–53 are devoted to terms expressed as kennings or, as Snorri often calls them, *kent heiti*, compound constructions of a base-word plus one or more determinants, while chs 54–74 are (except for 67–8) dedicated to simple poetic synonyms, what scholars call *heiti* and Snorri *ókent heiti*, terms that, lacking a qualifier or determinant, tend to refer to themselves rather than to some other entity.[20] But while modern scholars have adopted this binary scheme, they are often troubled by what they see as two flaws in Snorri's execution of it. The first of these has to do with his definitions of kennings, the earliest of which appears in ch. 1:

> and that category is so arranged that we speak of Óðinn or Þórr or Týr or any of the *æsir* or elves, so that with each of those whom I name, I then attach the name of a possession [or attribute] of another of the *æsir*, or I mention any of his deeds. Then he, and not that one who was named, takes possession of the name, so that when we say Sigtýr or Hangatýr or Farmatýr, that is then Óðinn's name, and we call that a *kent heiti*.[21]

As many have observed, this definition, aside from not being a very good one for kennings in general, does not even adequately define those that immediately follow it, of which few utilize this type of name-substitution.[22] Subsequent attempts to refine this definition fare little better: in these, Snorri says that kennings refer to a deity, man, or woman through his or her actions, possessions, attributes, or family relations.[23] Here, Snorri, while not insisting on name-substitution, remains fixated on the construction of kennings that refer to specific persons or beings, as opposed to objects or classes of people. While Clunies Ross argues that Snorri's preoccupation with these sorts of referents is evidence of his immersion in 'the intellectual discipline of medieval grammar,' in which 'kennings whose referents were proper names constituted a grammatical and philosophical problem,' and further that his focus on kennings for animate beings reflects his belief, as established in the *Formáli*, that the natural religion of the pagan north was animistic,[24] a simpler and better explanation is offered by Faulkes:

> Snorri's emphasis on kennings and *heiti* for persons is probably due to his seeing skaldic poetry as mainly concerned with the praise of persons (human and divine), and kennings and *heiti* principally as means of referring to the subjects of the poems. This is in fact the commonest use he himself makes of kennings in *Háttatal*, where the majority of his kennings refer to King Hákon and Earl Skúli.[25]

To this I would add that the technique of name-substitution is prominently displayed in *Háttatal*, in which Hákon is referred to using names of pagan gods in two instances, and Skúli in six – and, as Snorri mentions in *Skáldskaparmál*, 'it is correct to refer to a man with the names of all of the *æsir*.'[26] It seems, then, that Snorri's kenning definitions were not meant to be general, but were formulated, consciously or not, to explicate the types of kennings most used in the skaldic subgenre that he was interested in preserving and promoting. We will find this same tendency to focus on the kenning-types most often employed in praise-poems, and in *Háttatal* in particular, in Snorri's explanations and illustrations of conceptual kenning categories.

The second defect perceived in Snorri's organization is his failure to observe a strict division of *kent* from *ókent heiti* – in all manuscripts, numerous kennings seep into chapters dedicated to *ókent heiti*, and vice versa. This confusion has been accounted for in two ways: either Snorri began without separating his categories and later only partially reorganized his text, or else later redactors distorted his original plan.[27] Though there is likely truth in both explanations, what each misses is that this confusion of categories may signal the secondary importance of formal principles in *Skáldskaparmál*'s construction. It is remarkable how eager critics have been to regard material as interpolated when it seems to them to violate the schematic logic of the text. Finnur Jónsson, for example, who was firmly of the opinion that Snorri scrupulously separated kennings from *heiti*, takes the blending of these categories in *Skáldskaparmál*'s penultimate chapters, which deal with terms for body parts, as evidence of the work of careless redactors.[28] What he overlooks, however, is how useful many of these kennings are for understanding references to body parts in *Háttatal*: in st. 2, for example, Snorri refers to hair or the scalp as *holt heila bœs*, 'wood of the dwelling of the brain,' a kenning for which *Skáldskaparmál* ch. 69 provides clear exegesis: 'Hair is *kent* by calling it "forest" or some other name for a tree, and qualifying it with "skull" or "cranium" or "head,"' terms that are themselves *kent* by referring to them as *heila land*, 'land of the brain.'[29] Another kenning explanation whose authenticity has come under fire is 'Heimdallr's head = sword,' which R.C. Boer finds incongruous in ch. 8, the focus of which is kennings referring to this god, not of which his name forms part.[30] The inclusion of this gloss is hardly surprising, however, when we recall the use to which this kenning was put in *Háttatal*, where Snorri refers to a sword as *Vindhlés hjálms fyllr*, 'Vindhlér's helmet-filler.'[31] As I have noted, this is one of the more obscure kennings in Hákon's poem, and its inclusion seems to have caused Snorri some anxiety by the time he produced the *Edda*'s other parts: he explains it not only in *Skáldskaparmál* ch. 8 (where he helpfully states that Heimdallr 'is also called Vindlér'),[32] but in reverse form in ch. 69 (Heimdallr's sword = head), and even in *Gylfaginning* ch. 27, where Eugen Mogk and Faulkes consider it out of place.[33] Even if the items under consideration seem to clash with or disrupt the flow of surrounding material, this should not lead us automatically to assume that Snorri was not responsible for their inclusion. On the contrary, their incongruity speaks for their origination with Snorri, for whom an opportunity to explain one of his more cryptic circumlocutions was more important than the formal integrity of his text. Instead of looking, in short, for organizational consistency from Snorri, scholars ought rather to ask what strategies and concerns motivated him to include (and sometimes repeat) what seems to them ill-fitted material.

I turn now to *Skáldskaparmál*'s conceptual or referential system of classification. It is generally agreed that the referents to which Snorri gives most attention were those most crucial for composing skaldic encomia: these include terms for kings and rulers, warriors and things of war, the sea and ships, and gold. But while few would deny that *Skáldskaparmál*'s content was at least partly chosen to facilitate understanding and production of this skaldic genre, scholars have underestimated how much Snorri's selection of material works to make his own praise-poetry accessible. In the appendix, I have sought to list all of *Háttatal*'s kennings, grouping them by concept or referent and then according to form or means of reference, and to show where each is (or is not) explicated in *Skáldskaparmál*. Having done so, it is immediately clear that there are very few kennings in *Háttatal* that are not explained in its companion text. More important, in assembling this data I have been able to classify all of the kennings that Snorri uses in *Háttatal* into types according to their possession of three sets of oppositional qualities:

Literal	Metaphorical
Non-mythological/legendary	Mythological/legendary
Defined by action/deed	Defined by attribute, possession, or relationship

Thus, 'dealer of battle' (*styrjar deilir*) is classified according to these criteria as a literal, non-mythological kenning for 'warrior' defined by action, while 'fair rain of Mardöll's lids' (*fagrregn Mardallar hvarma*) is a metaphorical, mythological kenning for 'gold' defined by possession.[34] As these examples suggest, the more qualities from the left column that a kenning possesses, the easier it is, on average, to decipher. This fact, as I will argue, strongly impacted Snorri's design for *Skáldskaparmál*, as attested by the space, extent of explanation, and number of illustrations that he devoted to each kenning-type. For example, while of the 366 kennings from *Háttatal* that I have identified,[35] ninety-seven or just over one-fourth are defined by action/deed, only five chapters of *Skáldskaparmál* (31, 47, 49, 53, 71) are used to explain how this type of kenning works; most of the rest of the text is devoted to explaining or illustrating how kennings defined by attribute, possession, or relation are to be decoded. This disparity stems from the fact that kennings defined by action or deed are more easily understood, and that they refer overwhelmingly to animate beings, particularly men, and so can be explained using blanket instructions, such as when Snorri says that 'it is correct to refer to all kings by calling them land-rulers or land's defender or land's conqueror.'[36]

A similar contrast emerges from the treatments accorded kennings that are literal as opposed to metaphorical. This disparity is seen clearly by comparing the set of *Háttatal*'s kennings that receives the least attention with that which receives the most in *Skáldskaparmál*. By my count, twenty-two kennings in *Háttatal* are not explicated by Snorri.[37] Of these, twelve are literal, and include kennings such as *samþykkjar søkkvir* (destroyer of unity = battle) and *jarðar skarð* (cleft of land = *fjörðr*), while the remaining ten employ visual and easily comprehended metaphors, such as *hunangs öldur* (waves of honey = mead).[38] On the other end of the spectrum, all but one of the twenty-four kenning-types from *Háttatal* that are given an extended narrative explanation in *Skáldskaparmál* are metaphorical.[39] To judge by this evidence, the amount as well as style of explanation that Snorri supplied in *Skáldskaparmál* for particular kenning-types did not depend upon the number of times he used them in *Háttatal*, but rather upon the difficulty they were likely to pose to key members of his audience.

This pattern grows more striking when we look at how Snorri treats mythological versus non-mythological kenning-types. If we apply the same test here as used to compare his handling of literal versus metaphorical kennings, we arrive at even more dramatic results: all of the twenty-two kennings from *Háttatal* that are given no explanation in *Skáldskaparmál* are non-mythological, while every one of those that are supplied with a narrative back-story is mythological. There are, in other words, no mythological or legendary allusions in *Háttatal* that are not referenced at least once in *Skáldskaparmál*, and the vast majority are glossed many times. To be more precise, if we tally the fifty-seven distinct mythological kenning-types found in *Háttatal* together with the nine figures of myth and legend mentioned outside of kennings, we find that fifty-seven of *Háttatal*'s sixty-six mythological allusions (86.36 per cent) are explicated more than once in *Skáldskaparmál*. Of the nine mythological/legendary kenning-types, moreover, that are provided with only one explanation, three (*hildigöltr*, 'battle-boar = helmet,' *gríma grundar gjaldseiðs*, 'payment-fish of the ground = dragon' and 'helmet of the dragon = the *ægishjálmr* (helm of terror) of Völsung legend')[40] contain no specific names or allusions, while five others (*Yggs drósar eisa*, 'valkyrie's fire = sword,' and the two kennings each for Óðinn and Þórr in st. 3)[41] are either extended kennings or parts of extended kennings the other elements of which receive thorough interpretation elsewhere in the text.[42] The most striking results, however, are reached by calculating the average number of explanations/illustrations that Snorri provides for mythological as opposed to non-mythological kenning-types: *Háttatal*'s fifty-seven mythological kenning-types are explicated and/or illustrated a total of 199 times in *Skáldskaparmál*, for an average of 3.49 instances of interpretation per kenning-type, while its sixty-seven non-mythological kenning-types are elucidated fifty-nine times, averaging only 0.88 instances of interpretation each.

In light of these calculations, it seems clear that a substantial part of *Skáldskaparmál* was devoted to making *Háttatal*'s mythological allusions legible. That scholars have not appreciated the extent of Snorri's efforts in this direction is understandable, since many of the specific kennings and *heiti* appearing in the latter text are nowhere to be found in the former. Even when, however, *Skáldskaparmál* gives no direct explanation for a kenning used in *Háttatal*, there is usually more than enough information in the former text to puzzle out its meaning. For example, while st. 59's *Göndlar glygg*, 'tempest of Göndul = battle,' is not in *Skáldskaparmál*, its referent can be ascertained by reading ch. 48, where 'battle' is called *valkyrju veðr*, 'valkyrie's weather,' and

Göndul is listed as a valkyrie's name, alongside ch. 59, where *glygg* is given as a *heiti* for *veðr*.[43] There are also good reasons why Snorri would not have supplied precise keys to too many of his kennings. For one, exact matches for the kennings in *Háttatal* would often not have been available in the work of earlier skalds whose work Snorri used as illustration in *Skáldskaparmál*. It seems doubtful, moreover, that Snorri would always have presented such examples when he was able to locate them. While part of *Skáldskaparmál*'s task was to render kennings employed in *Háttatal* intelligible, these also had to maintain a certain measure of esotericism – to explain them too clearly would blunt their effectiveness, and to cite too many parallels from the skaldic corpus would risk making his magnum opus appear unoriginal.

Nonetheless, there are places in *Skáldskaparmál* where Snorri's efforts to clarify his own praise-poetry are glaringly obvious. This occurs most often where he explains mythological kennings from *Háttatal*'s first thirty stanzas, the poem for the king. As noted in chapter 6, in comparison with what is found in his panegyrics for Skúli, Snorri uses few mythological or legendary kennings in his poem for Hákon. Many of these, however, are illustrated with uncommon explicitness in *Skáldskaparmál*. Snorri takes particular care, for instance, to explain the extended kennings from the mythologically dense st. 3. In *Skáldskaparmál*, he interrupts his list of stanzas illustrating kennings for Óðinn only twice, once to remark, 'Here is that example that earth (*jörð*) is called Óðinn's wife in poetry,' and then to stress, 'Here he is called gods' defence and Mímir's friend (*Míms vinr*) and wolf's enemy (*úlfs bági*).'[44] These are the precise terms used for Óðinn in *Háttatal* st. 3. Similar, if not quite so exact, commentary is provided for this stanza's Þórr kennings: *Háttatal* calls Þórr *orms váði* (worm's attacker) and *mellu dólgr* (troll-wife's enemy), while *Skáldskaparmál* explains that this god is referred to as *dólgr ok bani jötna ok tröllkvinna* and *dólgr Miðgarðsorms*.[45] There are other close illustrations of kennings from *Háttatal*'s first *kvæði*: the trouble Snorri took to explicate *Vindhlés hjálms fyllr* has been noted several times; st. 2's *Hamðis fang*, 'Hamðir's tunic,' is closely glossed by the example *Hamðis skyrta*; and *þilja Hrungnis ilja* (Hrungnir's sole-plank = shield), a kenning from st. 30, the last of Hákon's poem, is both explained and illustrated in nearly the same form in *Skáldskaparmál* ch. 49, while the mythic episode underlying it is narrated in ch. 17.[46] Whereas, then, Snorri was often reluctant to explain *Háttatal*'s kennings too clearly in *Skáldskaparmál*, spreading clues to their comprehension over several chapters, he departed from this practice in the case of mythological kennings aimed specifically at the king. In explaining these, Snorri cut down on noise versus signal so as to insure that Hákon would get the message.

Finally, I will look at a group of kennings and *heiti* that were of central importance in praise-poetry, those for kings and rulers. In two long chapters in which he treats these terms, Snorri seems to want to minimize the distance between the ranks of king and jarl, while avoiding any insult to the former's dignity. In ch. 64, he declares that 'the first and the highest *heiti* for "man" is to call a man emperor, after that king, after that jarl.'[47] He goes on, however, to collapse these categories, stating that 'these three [classes of] men together possess all these *heiti*.'[48] Similarly, Snorri writes in ch. 53 that after *keisari* and *konungr* come 'those men who are called jarls or *skattkonungar* (tributary kings), and they are equal in kennings with a king, except one may not call those *þjóðkonungar* (kings of a people or nation) who are *skattkonungar*.'[49] Snorri continues this guarded conflation of ranks when he writes:

> There next are in kennings in poetry those men who are called *hersir*. They may be referred to like a king or jarl by calling them gold-breakers and generous-with-wealth ... because each *þjóðkonungr* who rules many lands appoints as governors with himself *skattkonungar* and jarls to administer the land's laws ... and these judgments and sentences should there be equally as valid as those of the king himself.[50]

Hersir, we recall, is the title Snorri assigns himself in *Háttatal*.[51] In ch. 64, Snorri offers an account of the origin of various *heiti* for 'ruler.' He writes that the legendary king Hálfdan gamli had two sets of nine sons, the first set of whom were childless, but 'became so excellent in warfare that afterward in all sources their names are used as titles of nobility just like the name of king or the name of jarl,' while the second gave rise to the northern dynasties to which they lent their names.[52] As Heinz Klingenberg has shown, these passages represent one of Snorri's bolder attempts to level Hákon's and Skúli's prestige: not only does he extend many appellations normally reserved for kings to jarls, but he introduces an alternative spelling of the name of one of Hálfdan's first nine sons, *Skyli eða Skúli*, that makes the jarl's name into an honorific term for ruler.[53] Finally, we may note that Snorri again introduces material here that works himself into the company of those he lauds: one of the dynasties founded by Hálfdan's second set of sons are the Danish Skjöldungar, from whom the Sturlungar are said to descend in the genealogy, which may in origin stem from Snorri himself, found in the middle of *Skáldskaparmál* in U.[54]

Snorri Tells Stories

Skáldskaparmál's narratives are part of a third stage in the *Edda*'s evolution, one tied more closely to *Gylfaginning* and its *Formáli* than to *Háttatal*. What had begun as a praise-poem and grown into a technical treatise on metre and diction now became, in the words of the *Eptirmáli, fróðleikr ok skemtun,* 'knowledge and entertainment.'[55] Narratives were not worked in just for amusement, however – these too had a pragmatic purpose. At some point during collation of the material that became *Skáldskaparmál,* Snorri must have come to realize that, no matter how many illustrations he supplied of kenning-types, many could not be understood without knowledge of the stories on which they were based. Even a compilation of eddic poems, something Snorri may have considered and has even been credited with, would not have sufficed, for while many of these deal directly with myth and are easier to understand than most skaldic compositions, they recount few narratives with anything approaching clarity.[56] The only thing that could provide Snorri's audience with enough mythological knowledge to admire the allusive vocabulary employed in his and others' poetry probably did not exist at this time, and he therefore had to manufacture it himself – written, prose retellings of pagan mythological and legendary narratives.

Skáldskaparmál contains what may be identified as ten narrative sections: 1) the theft of Iðunn and her apples by the *jötunn* Þjazi, and the seeking of compensation by his aggrieved daughter, Skaði, after he is slain by the *æsir* (G56); 2) the origin of the mead of poetry (G57); 3) Þórr's battles with Hrungnir and Geirrøðr (chs 17–18); 4) Ægir's feast for the *æsir* (ch. 33; this is distinct from the frame, in which Ægir attends a feast given by the *æsir*); 5) the smithying of the gods' treasures and weapons by dwarves (ch. 35); 6) the otter's ransom (ch. 39); 7) the Völsung cycle (chs 40–2); 8) Fróði's mill (ch. 43); 9) two stories about Hrólfr kraki (chs 43–4) ; and 10) Hildr and the never-ending battle of the Hjaðningar (ch. 50). These narratives can be divided into two groups, based upon their placement and role in the text: narratives 1–3 stand apart from and do not always seem to have been selected to illustrate directly Snorri's kenning- and *heiti*-types, while 4–10 are more integrated with the technical portion of *Skáldskaparmál* and have clearly been chosen to further its purposes.

Much of this narrative material is bound together by its focus on a single concept. Specifically, 4–9 all provide background for kennings for gold, one of the most thoroughly covered conceptual categories in *Skáldskaparmál* as well as the most common referents in *Háttatal*.[57] Gold was central, of course, not only to Snorri's poem but to all skaldic encomia, and not simply because it 'was much in the thought of those greedy Norsemen of that age.'[58] 'Generous-with-gold' was, like 'courageous-in-battle,' an essential trait of a praiseworthy lord, one that skalds were practically obligated to assign their patrons. Having many kennings for this concept in their lexicon not only allowed skalds to vary their means of expression when referring to gold, it also served as a tool of euphemism when insisting on reward for one's verse. Kennings for gold that were tied to mythological and legendary figures and stories may also have helped to confer a measure of dignity on this conversion of cultural into material capital.

In looking at *Háttatal*, it seems at first that Snorri was not as reticent as many of his forebears about expressing an open longing for gold. Though he employed his share of kennings for this concept, Snorri was far from sheepish about naming gold outright in *Háttatal*: he uses the term *gull* in ten stanzas, and *seimr* and *vell, heiti* for gold, in ten.[59] Still, it seems doubtful that Snorri, when presenting himself as a cultural producer in Norway's court, was very intent on acquiring gold per se – he was, after all, short of neither money nor possessions at the time of his 1218–20 trip. And while it is possible that some of the gifts given to Snorri by Skúli in 1220 were of gold, those that receive most attention in our sources held as much or more symbolic value as material, such as the weaponry sent by Hákon galinn, the standard offered by Kristín, or even the ship given by Skúli. It may be, then, that Snorri did not need to euphemize gold in his poetry because this concept itself acted for him as a kind of euphemism. More precisely, gold serves in *Háttatal* as a symbol or token of what Snorri was really interested in obtaining – the recognition, esteem, and friendship of his patrons, and the social and political gains these could generate for him at home.

Snorri also seems to have found the rich legacy of gold-kennings and gold-stories available to him useful in demonstrating his technical mastery over skaldic diction. Thus, he may have included so many gold narratives in *Skáldskaparmál* partly to draw attention to his use of gold-kennings in *Háttatal*. For instance, narratives 6–8, those telling of the otter's ransom, the Völsungar, and Fróði's gold-producing mill, flesh out two focal stanzas in *Háttatal*'s first *kvæði* for Skúli, 41 and 44, both of which use four kennings to present parts of these stories in concentrated form. While I suggested in chapter 6 that Snorri counted on Skúli having some familiarity with these narratives, reconstituting them in prose form in *Skáldskaparmál* ensured that the full resonance of his kennings, and the artistry he put into their arrangement, would be appreciated by the jarl and whoever else might encounter them. The same argument can be made for the story of Hildr, which acts as a direct guide to the four kennings related to warfare in *Háttatal*'s st. 49.[60] As for the remaining gold-narratives, 4, 5, and 9, while these are not as closely wedded to particular stanzas in *Háttatal*, they nonetheless explicate kennings for gold found within and outside of Snorri's poem.[61]

Accounting for the presence of narratives 1 and 3 (2 is discussed in this chapter's concluding section) is more difficult. As already noted, these stories are less fully integrated with the kenning and *heiti* lists that likely formed the original *Skáldskaparmál*. This separation is especially evident in U, where chs 17–18 (group 3) are appended directly to *Bragarœður* (containing 1–2) and clearly split off from *Skáldskaparmál* proper, which begins after the ancillary lists with the heading: *Hér hefr Skáldskapar mál ok heiti margra hluta.*[62] While there are many possible explanations for U's idiosyncratic arrangement, it may, if Faulkes's suggestion that U 'is derived from an unfinished draft' of the *Edda* has any merit, reflect a stage in Snorri's work when placement of these narratives was still up in the air.[63] At any rate, narratives 1–3 are in all manuscripts somewhat clumsily suspended between *Skáldskaparmál* and *Gylfaginning*, suggesting that Snorri and/or later redactors were in doubt as to which text they should belong. Narrative 1, for instance, could easily have been incorporated into *Gylfaginning*, which contains an epilogue to this story in its account of the failure of Skaði's marriage to Njörðr, a union which, as things stand, we do not learn resulted from the settlement over her father's slaying until *Bragarœður*.[64] Nevertheless, there are two possible reasons for why this story was placed in *Skáldskaparmál*: first, it is based on a skaldic rather than eddic poem, Þjóðólfr's *Haustlöng*, part of which is quoted in ch. 22.[65] Second, it concludes by describing how the kenning 'speech of giants = gold' derives from Þjazi's and his brothers' use of their mouths to divide their father's estate.[66] It is in response to Ægir's questions about this anecdote that Bragi's discourse on poetic diction begins.[67] Narrative group 3, Þórr's fights with giants, are the most out of place of *Skáldskaparmál*'s stories, and it may be that Snorri intended to include a row of tales to illustrate the many *æsir*-kennings of chs 4–16 but, possibly because he had begun to work on *Gylfaginning*, never got beyond this pair. At any rate, Snorri's main sources for both of these stories were again not eddic but skaldic poems, both of which are quoted at length in R, T, and W.[68]

Finally, we come to what I believe was the last module to be added to *Skáldskaparmál*, the frame dialogue and *Eptirmáli*. *Skáldskaparmál* was almost certainly cast in dialogue form from its inception, but the identification of its master and pupil with Bragi and Ægir seems to have been a late addition resulting in only partial revision: the formulae *Ægir mælir* and *Bragi svarar* appear only in *Bragarœður* and at the start of chs 1 and 18, and at times Snorri ruptures the frame by referring directly to these characters' discussion, or by narrating in the third person stories in which they play a part.[69] Snorri's likely reason for introducing a conversation that takes place in the gods' hall in Ásgarðr was his need for a mediating device with which to present the mythological narratives he had begun to write. His choice of setting and interlocutors was pragmatic: influenced by the eddic poem *Lokasenna*, in which the *æsir* feast in Ægir's hall, Snorri chose Bragi as the best god to speak on the subject of poetry, and Ægir because, as an amicable outsider of ambiguous status, he made a likely candidate for instruction in the language and history of the gods. It is to *Gylfaginning*'s frame, and probably the *Formáli* as well, that the *Eptirmáli* refers when in its address to young skalds it states: 'These stories should not be forgotten or regarded as falsehoods, so as to take from the language of poetry those old kennings which the chief skalds liked to use. But Christian men should not believe in heathen gods or in the truthfulness of this account in any other way than what is found here in this book's beginning.'[70] Here, in what must be one of the final passages of the *Edda* written by Snorri, he is clearly worried about the reception his treatise will meet from contemporaries. Discussion of his strategies for dealing with this anxiety will be postponed until chapter 8 where I examine *Gylfaginning* and its *Formáli*. First, I will look at one final, central narrative from *Skáldskaparmál*, that of the origin of the mead of poetry, and assess the role it may have played in spurring Snorri to devise the historicizing perspective on pagan myth and religion that he will lay out in his 'book's beginning.'

Where Does Poetry Come From?

The supernatural origins of poetic skill and its conveyance to human practitioners are dominant themes in the works of skalds. In *Skáldskaparmál*, there are, outside of its chapters devoted specifically to poetry and ways of referring to it, around twenty allusions in illustrative stanzas to poetic skill as a mead possessed by Óðinn.[71] Snorri's version of the myth from which this idea derives is one of the longest and most complex tales in *Skáldskaparmál* or *Gylfaginning*. His myth begins with the end of the war of the *æsir* and *vanir*, two divine tribes who as part of their truce spit into a vat and shape from their collected saliva Kvasir, wisest of all beings. Kvasir is killed by two dwarves who mix his blood with honey to make a mead that imparts poetic skill and wisdom to whoever drinks it. The murder-prone dwarves next do away with a giant Gillingr and his wife. The giants' son Suttungr takes from the dwarves in atonement for their deed the mead, which he stores in a mountain stronghold inhabited by his daughter Gunnlöð. The story then turns to Óðinn, who after killing nine slaves of the giant Baugi, Suttungr's brother, offers, under the name of Bölverkr, 'evil-worker,' to perform their labour for the space of a summer. In exchange, Óðinn demands a drink of the mead and, after Suttungr refuses, he and Baugi drill into the mountain a hole through which Óðinn creeps in snake's form. Once inside, he sleeps with Gunnlöð for three nights and she allows him three drinks of the mead. Óðinn empties the vessels with these draughts and flees with Suttungr in pursuit; both are in eagle's form. Óðinn manages to reach Ásgarðr and to deposit most of the mead into tubs which the other gods have set out, but with Suttungr so close behind he is forced to send 'some of the mead backwards, and of that nothing was saved. Anyone had that who wanted it, and we call that the rhymesters' portion. But Óðinn gave Suttungr's mead to the *æsir* and to those men who know how to compose. Thus we call poetry Óðinn's booty and find, and his drink and his gift, and drink of the *æsir*.'[72]

Snorri's tale of the poetic mead has been singled out as one of his more imaginative efforts, and the evidence does suggest that he exercised a good deal of creative licence when manufacturing this story.[73] I am less interested, however, in how Snorri constructed his version of this myth than in what it was meant to accomplish in the context of the *Edda*. Those addressing this issue have basically agreed that the story was included, like most in *Skáldskaparmál*, to provide background for a major category of kennings, in this case those for 'poetry' or the 'poetic mead.'[74] While this conclusion is sound, it is worth noting that Snorri uses few circumlocutions for poetry in his own verse; only two kennings that refer to poetry as Óðinn's mead appear in *Háttatal*.[75] Snorri is much more likely to refer to poetry using *ókent heiti* such as *mærð*, *lof*, or *hróðr*, terms which literally signify 'glory,' 'praise,' 'honour,' or the like.[76] While Arthur Brodeur describes the use of such *heiti* for poetry as 'mild trope[s]' I would suggest that Snorri meant for Hákon and Skúli to take this association very literally.[77] Poetry, Snorri suggests, is 'praise,' 'honour,' etc., because it automatically engenders these things: just as a lord's fame inspires poetic laudation, poetic laudation augments and secures his fame. Snorri uses this same sort of chicken-and-egg logic in the myth of poetry's origins, in which he says that Óðinn confers his mead on those who *yrkja kunnu*, 'know [already?] how to compose,' and who, as a result of this inborn talent/ divine gift, become a *skáld eða fræðamaðr*.[78] The claim that those who imbibe the mead become *fróðr*, 'wise,' was not common,[79] and though *fræðamaðr* as used here has often been translated as 'scholar,' it seems to me better rendered as a 'learned' or 'well-rounded man,' one familiar with the sum of his native tradition and history. This is the kind of man that Snorri fancied himself to be, but which he may have feared the king would never become.

Given that the image of poetry as a divine liquid is of less importance in *Háttatal* than the identification of this skill with the qualities of honour, fame, and wisdom, why is the myth of the poetic mead's origins so fully developed and prominently featured in *Skáldskaparmál*? To answer this question, I wish to consider this story apart (for a change) from its usefulness for comprehending

Háttatal, and to emphasize the fact that its subject, rather than being just another category of kenning, is the primary focus of the entire treatise in which it is presented. In this light, the story invites interpretation as a metacommentary, and the question becomes: By telling this myth what was Snorri trying to communicate to his readers concerning the origins, nature, and authority of poetry, and, by extension, those who practise it? Taken at face value, his myth informs (or seeks to persuade) readers that poetic skill is an otherworldly substance that is transmitted to skalds through the mediation of Óðinn. The problem, however, with ascribing such a message to Snorri is that no one believes he could himself have taken it seriously: as a thirteenth-century Christian, Snorri could not possibly have believed that poetic talent was dispensed by a pagan god. To circumvent this difficulty, scholars have sometimes observed that Snorri's tale has at its core the same idea that likely gave rise to the myth in the first place – that of the inspirational effects of intoxicating beverages.[80] And yet, nowhere in the *Edda* does Snorri treat poetry as a craft that can be acquired through ecstatic practices or hallucinatory states as opposed to training and apprenticeship.[81] Indeed, the metaphoric as well as the literal meanings of the myth are belied by the mere existence of the treatise in which it is found – recipients of inspiration, divine or alcoholic in origin, should not require a textbook. More important, Snorri places less emphasis in his myth on the identification of poetry with an inebriating if supernatural drink than on the figures who serially possess it, and particularly its final owner, Óðinn, around whom Snorri weaves a more complex and engaging adventure than probably existed in his sources. Snorri's story, in short, is principally concerned to establish how the mead/poetry came into the possession of the Norse pantheon's chief deity.

This observation raises, however, the same objection stated above, namely that the story Snorri tells could hold no truth-value in the Christian era. This is not to say that the idea of divine inspiration was unavailable in Snorri's time. Its use ordinarily required, however, a substitution of the Christian God or his proxies for Óðinn. This move is attested in the most significant *dróttkvætt* compositions of the twelfth century, Gamli kanoki's *Harmsól*, the anonymous *Leiðarvísan*, and the priest (and Snorri's ancestor) Einarr Skúlason's *Geisli*, all of which appeal to God or the holy spirit for inspiration.[82] It is certain, then, that the tactic of swapping God for Óðinn was known to Snorri, and that he could have used it to restore to skaldic verse some of the religious authority which it had lost with conversion. That he did not do so, either in *Háttatal* or *Skáldskaparmál*, underscores Snorri's lack of religious authority/capital, and his disinclination to try to abrogate any such power to himself or his products. In effect, Snorri stuck to the old, pagan notion of Óðinn as source of poetic skill, a choice that seems as if it would have hindered rather than helped his efforts to convince his contemporaries of skaldic verse's worth. In other words, by refusing to metaphorize or theologize the myth of Óðinn's mead, Snorri appears to have squandered any chance he had to furnish this or a parallel story with a kind of 'truth' that would hold force for his audience, particularly the church-educated and church-supported king of Norway. As such, most critics have concluded that Snorri was not, in fact, trying to say anything true with this story, but that he offered it as a mythographer or even a parodist.[83] As Gert Kreutzer states: 'It is hardly to be accepted, that Snorri or any other skald so far into the Christian era, still actually felt himself to be obligated to Óðinn.'[84]

To this, I would respond that Snorri not only felt himself as a skald deeply obligated to Óðinn, but that he spent a good deal of his literary career trying to convince others of the reality and significance of this obligation. Scholars are right to insist that Snorri could not have believed in a literal myth in which gods, dwarves, and giants vie for possession of liquefied eloquence and wisdom. But to say that Snorri did not 'believe' in this myth is not to rule out the possibility that he took the chain of transmission it symbolizes seriously, or that he wished others to do so. In order, however, for this to happen, it was necessary for this story, or elements of it, to undergo translation from the register of myth to that of history. More precisely, if Óðinn was to retain his status as founder of northern culture as well as kingship, roles which, as I will argue, Snorri keenly wished him to retain and thereby conjoin, he had to be transformed from a god into a man. Snorri's first serious efforts to historicize pagan myth, and thereby preserve the intimate relationship between poets, nobles, and Óðinn posited in pagan ideology, are found in *Gylfaginning* and its *Formáli*, the final parts of the *Edda* to have been written, and the subjects of the next chapter.

8 *Gylfaginning* and *Formáli*: Myth, History, and Theology

In *Gylfaginning*, or 'The Deluding of Gylfi,' Snorri provides a pagan history of the cosmos from its fashioning from the body of the primordial *jötunn* Ymir by the brothers Óðinn, Vili, and Vé, to its destruction in *ragnarøkr*, the 'doom' or (according to Snorri) 'twilight of the gods,' and on into its paradisal rebirth.[1] This material is framed by a dialogue between Gylfi, a king of Sweden, and Hár, Jafnhár, and Þriði (High, Just-as-High, and Third), figures widely regarded as hypostases of Óðinn, here historicized as chieftain of the *æsir*, powerful and sorcerous migrants from Asia. Preceding *Gylfaginning* in all manuscripts is a *Formáli* or prologue,[2] which provides background for this frame narrative in the form of an account, drawn largely from Genesis, of the early history of the world, including its creation, humanity's fall away from God, and the rise of natural religion, and a description of the major regions of the earth and of the *æsir*'s origins in Tyrkland, specifically Troy, and their journey to and conquest of the north.

Compared to other parts of the *Edda*, textual problems encountered when working with *Gylfaginning* and its *Formáli* are slight. Although there are again differences in style between U (laconic and epigrammatic) and RTW (animated and prolix), the tellings of the myths in all manuscripts share the same essential content and structure; as in chapters 6 and 7, R will supply my main text. As for questions of authorship, to my knowledge no one has seriously disputed Snorri's responsibility for the bulk of the myths in *Gylfaginning*, although there have been doubts about parts of the text absent from U.[3] Conversely, Snorri's identity as author of the *Formáli* has regularly and sometimes vehemently been denied.[4] Without directly entering into this controversy, I will suggest how this text worked with *Gylfaginning* to contribute to the *Edda*'s overarching aims.[5]

In my view, *Gylfaginning*'s and the *Formáli*'s shared purpose was to contrive 'true' portraits of pagan mythological tradition, the origins of Scandinavian royalty and culture, and the working out of Christian history in the north. They operated, in short, on three distinct but interwoven levels: mythological (or mythographic), historical (or historicizing), and theological (or, as the German term best expresses it, *religionsgeschichtlich*). Scholars have recognized each of these levels at work in these texts, but have disagreed over their relative importance. Those who see the *Edda* as primarily a poetic textbook have tended to downplay *Gylfaginning*'s and the *Formáli*'s historical and theological layers, seeing both principally as tools for deflecting pious criticism of the survey of Norse myth that Snorri has offered to facilitate understanding of skaldic diction. Those who view the *Edda* as Snorri's bid to redeem pagan mythology as a carrier of natural religious conceptions partaking in Christian truth have emphasized the theological dimension of the *Formáli* and frame to *Gylfaginning*, while treating their historical and mythographic elements (and sometimes even the poetic guidelines in the rest of the *Edda*) as ancillary to this mission.[6] What these perspectives have in common is their assessment of the importance of the historicizing dimension, which they both regard as a means to another end, the erection of a frame within which a neutral or valorous portrait of pagan myth could be offered. I will argue, however, that establishing the reality of Óðinn and the *æsir* from Troy as founders of northern kingship, politics, culture, and language was a primary rather than secondary concern of Snorri, one that contributed to his efforts to entice King Hákon to become a consumer of skaldic verse, and which occasioned the need for his foray into theology/religious history. In sum, I will demonstrate that while critics have generally accurately gauged Snorri's interest in and reasons for relating pagan myth, they have on the one hand underestimated the significance for his plan of the historical scheme of *Gylfaginning* and the *Formáli*, and on the other exaggerated the weight he attached to these texts' theological speculations.

Resurrecting Myth

While *Gylfaginning*'s synopsis of pagan myth will certainly remain the portion of the *Edda* with the widest appeal and readership, little needs to be said about this material here. Snorri's purpose in recording myth is evident, and has often been remarked upon. Faulkes describes *Gylfaginning*'s origins and purpose: 'It is likely that it is an extension of the narratives included in *Skáldskaparmál*, and is intended to present in a systematic way the entire mythological background to the numerous mythological terms that form part of the poetic language discussed in *Skáldskaparmál*.'[7] To furnish this backdrop, Snorri adhered in his tellings of myth to two essential but in some ways incompatible principles: authenticity and accessibility. On the one hand, if he was to offer an effective guide to the interpretation of his and other skalds' diction, his account of the myths had to be reasonably objective – excessive euhemerization, allegorization, etc. would impede this aim, and so such techniques were relegated to the frame and *Formáli*. On the other hand, Snorri did not include every variant of every myth known to him, nor was he above refining his sources. Indeed, tinkering in the name of systemicity and coherence was entailed by his project, which required him to clarify the mythology for uninformed readers rather than confuse them with unnecessary or conflicting detail. That Snorri was willing to compromise his survey's fidelity to tradition for pedagogical expedience calls, as many have recognized, for caution when using *Gylfaginning* as a guide to pre-Christian Germanic religion.

As simple and sound as this explanation for *Gylfaginning*'s production is, there has long been a suspicion that something more is needed to account for the wealth of mythic material this text covers. As Faulkes adds by way of qualification to his above statement: 'Nevertheless it is true that many of the stories in *Gylfaginning* have little to do with poetry and must have been included mainly for the sake of completeness, or even just to provide entertainment.'[8] This remark applies to many of its narrative set-pieces; stories like Freyr's wooing of Gerðr, the binding of Fenrisúlfr and the loss of Týr's hand, the giant-builder, and Þórr's adventures with Útgarða-Loki and Hymir, while mostly deriving from eddic poems, are of little use in comprehending extant kennings, including those in *Háttatal*. What is often overlooked, however, is that narratives actually make up the smaller part of *Gylfaginning*. Much of it consists of material more properly labelled descriptive or classificatory: lists of names for gods and other beings, their dwellings, natural phenomena, and celestial bodies.[9] Even the celebrated accounts of creation and apocalypse that bookend *Gylfaginning* are more catalogues of names and deeds than true stories. This focus on mythological nomenclature at the expense of narrative is of course fitting for a textbook on skaldic verse. As for why Snorri would include at all stories that were of little use for instruction on this subject, Wessén seems on the right track when he writes, 'In the course of the work Snorri's interests underwent a considerable change, perhaps more than he himself was conscious of … He began as a scholar, but he finished as an artist.'[10] While I have argued that Snorri was neither of these, his interests and focus did evolve as work on the *Edda* progressed, and the tactics he adopted broadened and diversified. Even, then, if portions of *Gylfaginning* do not directly advance the aims of the *Edda*'s previously written sections, this should not lead us to conclude that this material did not contribute to the effort to reconstitute a market for skaldic verse. One essential ingredient of this market (at least of the sort Snorri was determined to revive) was a general familiarity with and sympathetic appraisal of the figures and events of pagan myth, not just knowledge among only skaldic producers of only those myths useful for crafting kennings.

Snorri's reeducation program was, however, targeted as well as general. Though he has sometimes been cast as a saviour of Norse myth from culture-wide neglect and oblivion, there is reason to think that Snorri's efforts to salvage this tradition were not so much for the benefit of his entire society or posterity as aimed at edifying a select group of contemporaries. While estimating the extent of early thirteenth-century Icelanders' and Norwegians' acquaintance with their religious past is difficult, the evidence speaks against the imminent disappearance of knowledge of pagan myth at the time when Snorri wrote the *Edda*. Evidence for Icelanders' continuing familiarity with myth comes from several sources, one of which is *Gylfaginning* itself. In writing this text, Snorri seems to have relied on two main sets of material: poetry, eddic and skaldic, and 'folk' traditions, i.e., stories about the gods that continued to circulate, mainly orally, at various levels of society.[11] Of these sources, eddic poetry had the greatest influence on *Gylfaginning*.[12] Skaldic poems had less for a number of reasons, the most important of which was that, since they were usually ascribed to named poets, they ill fit the frame conceit of a conversation between the gods' pre-historic doppelgangers and a legendary king. The extent to which folk tradition is reflected in *Gylfaginning* is harder to judge, but I suspect that it contributed much to this text; at any rate, many think that Snorri used oral prose tales to craft its livelier episodes, such as those of the giant-builder or Þórr's journey to Útgarðr.[13] Further evidence for knowledge of myth among at least the literate class of thirteenth-century Iceland is the recording of such material prior to and in the wake of Snorri's mythographic activity, above all the eddic poems collected in the Codex Regius manuscript c. 1270.[14] There were also sagas with mythological material circulating at this time, such as *Skjöldunga saga* and *Völsunga saga*, as well as numerous *Íslendingasögur* that describe aspects of pagan belief and practice. Perhaps the most important testament outside of the *Edda* to the endurance of knowledge of pagan myth is the work of Saxo Grammaticus. Though his myths undergo more extensive reinterpretation than Snorri's, Saxo's *Gesta Danorum* contains nearly as much mythological material as the *Edda*, and is about a decade older.[15] Aside from identifying the *Tylenses*, or Icelanders, and their 'ancient lore' as a source in his prologue, Saxo writes:

Danes of an older age, filled with a desire to echo the glory when notable braveries had been performed, alluded in the Roman manner to the splendour of their nobly-wrought achievements with choice compositions of a poetical nature; not only that, but they engraved the letters of their own language on rocks and stones to retell those feats of their ancestors which had been made popular in the songs of their mother tongue. Adhering to these tracks ... I have assiduously rendered one metre by another.[16]

While some doubt that Saxo possessed genuine Danish compositions of this sort, his comments are enough to persuade one that the knowledge of pagan myth underlying the early books of his history was circulating in the early 1200s not only among Icelanders other than Snorri and his circle, but also among Danes.

It is not clear, however, that the same can be said of Norwegians. From Norway there is no evidence, from before or after Snorri's time, of mythographic activity, and little textual trace of pagan religion at all. One notable exception is the anonymous *Historia Norwegiae*, which looks far enough back in time to mention euhemerized versions of Njörðr and Freyr.[17] In this, its author probably imitated Ari Þorgilsson, and thus ultimately *Ynglingatal*, but he otherwise demonstrates no knowledge of pagan myth.[18] But if Norwegian interest in such material was negligible prior to the time of Hákon Hákonarson, it must have dropped even lower during his reign, when, as I described in chapter 5, the court's cultural focus was oriented southward; indeed, no text that can be reliably traced to Hákon's milieu so much as mentions a pagan god or myth. And while the heavily allegorized and continentally flavoured accounts of the *Gesta Danorum* may provide some hint as to the state of the contemporary Norwegian elite's knowledge and estimation of pagan myth, Norway's kings and bishops never conscripted their own Saxo to work the old mythology into a history of national origins, and, among Icelanders who wrote sagas of and for Norway's kings, Snorri was the only one to attempt to do so.[19] While it cannot be claimed, then, that pagan myth ceased to circulate in written or oral culture in Norway of the early 1200s, there is nothing to indicate that this country's increasingly cosmopolitan elite were much invested or involved in collecting and preserving whatever knowledge or interest remained.

I find, then, no definite sign of the kind of drastic or sudden society-wide decline in knowledge of pagan traditions in early thirteenth-century Iceland and Norway that many believe spurred Snorri to write *Gylfaginning*. What we find, rather, is the perpetuation of a fairly stable pattern of the distribution of such knowledge in west Norse society since the advent of written culture:

Oral Culture	Written Culture
+ Mythological Knowledge −	
Icelandic Culture	Norwegian Culture

Once this pattern is recognized, it is clear that *Gylfaginning* was not so much an attempt to preserve pagan myth for posterity as to transform or balance the distribution of mythological knowledge in Snorri's own context. In short, Snorri took something existing mainly at the level of oral culture, in a form that Gísli Sigurðsson following Carol Clover has recently called an 'immanent whole,' and which had been especially preserved and cultivated by Icelanders, and transformed it into a written product suitable for export to and absorption by Norway's elite.[20]

Such repackaging of Icelandic oral culture for aristocratic Norwegian consumption was, of course, nothing new. As described in chapter 4, Icelanders had for centuries used the anonymous, collective, and ever-circulating raw material of eddic poetry and folk narrative to manufacture for Norwegians individual, unique, and convertible skaldic compositions. This traditional system of capital exchange, which prevailed from the mid-tenth into the twelfth centuries, is presented graphically in figure 1. By the time, however, when Snorri was seeking to market his poetry this system of exchange had experienced drastic changes. Most significantly, skaldic verse was no longer the end result of the chain of production, the good that was offered to Norway's elite in hopes of reward. Rather, it had become a chief ingredient of another cultural product – written kings' sagas, many of which amounted to prose recasts of skaldic encomia. But despite his prodigious knowledge of the skaldic canon, Snorri does not seem to have been very attracted to this tactic of cultural conversion, at least not when he was writing the *Edda*. It was, at any rate, an operation with comparatively limited prospects for profit. An event or a life could be told in prose by a single cultural producer just once, or at most a few times; in verse, however, one could say next to nothing in literally thousands of ways. And so, Snorri remained for some time determined – shrewdly, in terms of protecting his cultural investments – to exploit the traditional system of capital exchange.

As described in chapters 4 and 5, however, Snorri had by the early 1220s unsuccessfully tried to trade poetic for material and symbolic goods with three Norwegian kings. These failures cast the value of not just one, but all three types of Icelandic oral cultural product – skaldic verse, eddic verse, and folk tradition – into doubt, and *Gylfaginning*'s synopsis of pagan myth was nothing less than an attempt to salvage the worth of them all. Like skaldic verse in the traditional system of exchange, this product drew mainly from eddic poetry and oral tales. But unlike skaldic verse, *Gylfaginning* held no conversion value of its own in the system of exchange into which it was deployed, nor was it intended to. In terms of capital conversion, *Gylfaginning*'s purpose was to reactivate among the king and his courtiers, by providing them with a digestible guide to pagan myth,

Figure 1: Traditional System of Capital Exchange/Conversion

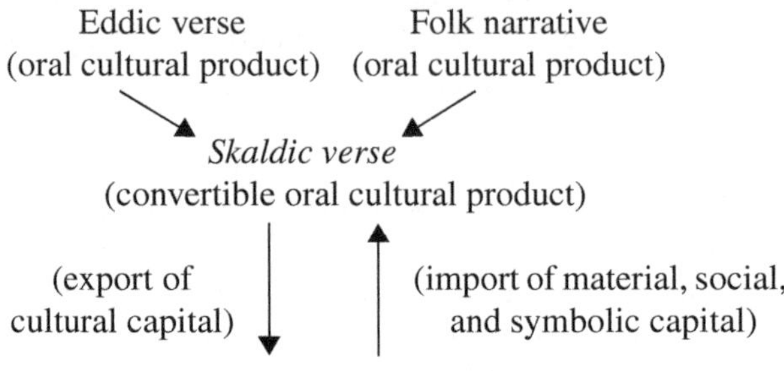

interest in skaldic verse, Icelanders' chief and only truly renewable cultural resource. But whether or not Snorri's abstract of Norse myth ever reached Hákon and his court, it would have come too late to achieve this aim. The traditional system of exchange that Snorri was struggling to restore was still in place, only it had shifted sharply and irrevocably southward; instead of looking to Icelanders plying cultural products rooted in native history and religion, Norway's primary cultural trading partners were now the translators and importers of continental and ecclesiastical literature, purveyors of products steeped in the chivalric ethos of the French and English courts and the ideology of the church (see figure 2).

Historicizing Óðinn

A perennial problem in *Edda* scholarship is how the historicizing frame within which Snorri's account of pagan myth is situated ought to be understood. It has probably most often been viewed as a means of damage control necessitated by Snorri's desire to narrate pagan myths objectively. Andreas Heusler, author of the most in-depth survey of the 'gelehrte Urgeschichte im isländischen Schrifttum,' regards it as a tool by which 'the most pious person could be appeased, and yet the stories could stand in their heathen vigour.'[21] In short, the frame's historical scheme has been viewed as a response to a theological problem generated by *Gylfaginning*'s mythological content. I will argue that, while it may be appropriate to regard the frame as a theological response to complications generated by the *Edda*'s depiction of pagan religion, its historicization of myth and mythic figures served a purpose separate from religious

Figure 2: New System of Capital Exchange/Conversion

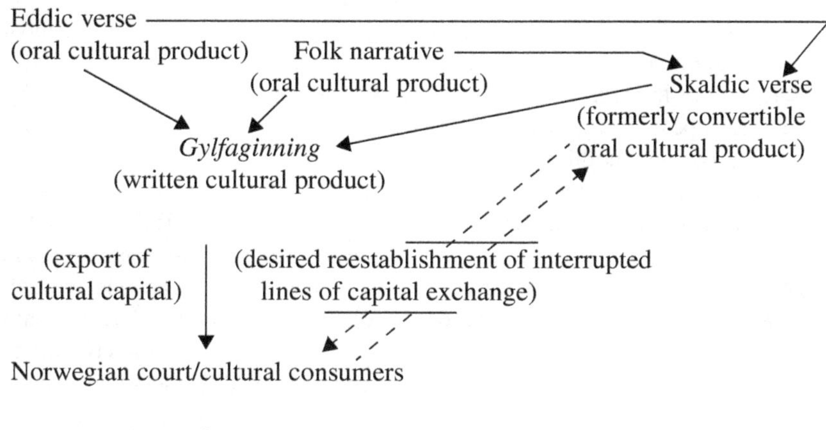

motivations or fears of clerical backlash. This purpose, which I touched on briefly at the close of chapter 7, was to establish Óðinn as an historical figure who, as founder of northern monarchy as well as culture, could link in a quasi-genealogical sense Norwegian kings and Icelandic poets.

Scholars have identified three main traditions linking Scandinavian royal and noble houses to euhemerized pagan gods.[22] Perhaps the oldest of these, surviving in Ari's work, traced the Ynglingar, ancient kings of Sweden, to Yngvi, from whom followed Njörðr and Freyr.[23] A second tradition informs the *Edda*'s *Formáli*, where it is told that Óðinn set a son to rule over 'that kingdom which is now called Norway. He is called Sæmingr, and Norway's kings, and also jarls and other noblemen, trace their ancestries to him.'[24] The third, represented by the lost but partially recoverable *Skjöldunga saga*, traced the line of the Skjöldungar, legendary kings of Denmark and reputed ancestors of Iceland's Oddaverjar and Sturlungar families, to Óðinn.[25] According to Faulkes, these three ancestries were combined in Iceland around 1200 into a line of descent that also incorporated material from Anglo-Saxon regnal lists. This composite scheme, preserved in a number of late manuscripts, introduced several changes around the figure of Óðinn/Woden, including giving him ancestors going back to biblical figures and finally to Adam.[26]

The *Edda*'s *Formáli* drew on all of these traditions to produce the most complex and encompassing genealogy yet. This text's second half opens with a description of the world's three regions, Africa, which 'is hot and burned by the sun,' Europe or Enea, of which 'the more northern part is so cold that grass does not grow and nothing can dwell there,' and Asia, where there 'is all beauty and splendour and wealth of earth's growth, gold and gemstones. There is also the middle of the world.'[27] Here, in Tyrkland (Turkey), lay the city of Troja (Troy), where there lived Munon or Mennon, husband of Troan daughter of Priamus, king of Troy.[28] Their son was Tror, 'the one we call Þórr,' who was fostered in Thracia, or 'Þrúðheimr,' by Loricus.[29] Tror is said at age twelve to have killed his foster-father and seized control of his realm; he then 'explored all parts of the world and defeated alone all berserks and giants and one of the greatest dragons and many beasts. In the northern part of the world he met a prophetess who was called Sibil, whom we call Sif, and married her.'[30] From Tror and Sibil came eighteen generations of sons, the last of whom was 'Voden, the one whom we call Óðinn.'[31] An 'excellent man with respect to wisdom and all accomplishments,' Óðinn married Frigida (Frigg), and with her and a large following migrated north, subduing lands and installing sons as kings.[32] Óðinn's travels ended in Svíþjóð, or Sweden, where he was given leave by King Gylfi 'to have as much power in his kingdom as he himself wanted,' a statement that anticipates the outcome of the encounter that frames *Gylfaginning*.[33] Óðinn founded the city of Sigtúnir in Sweden, which his son Yngvi inherited. The *Formáli* ends with an account of how the language brought by Óðinn and the *æsir* out of Asia became dominant in the north, so that it 'was the native-tongue through all these lands.'[34]

The *Formáli*'s major additions to this learned prehistory pivot around the figure of Óðinn. While this text joins others in placing Óðinn rather than Njörðr or Freyr at the centre of its genealogical plan, it gives him six sons, more than in the other sources combined, who establish royal houses in all of Europe's major regions.[35] Beyond expanding his progeny and influence, the *Formáli* includes a line leading back from Óðinn to Troy, and a migration narrative; while common in pseudohistories from many parts of Europe, these motifs are not found in earlier Icelandic texts. Some *Edda* scholars are openly offended by this back-story, lamenting that an historian of Snorri's calibre should be associated with such an unlikely fable.[36] Even those who feel that the Troy material ought probably to be ascribed to Snorri can be taken aback by its illogicality. As Faulkes writes: 'All the references to the Troy story in *Snorra Edda* are ... a strange mixture of genuine tradition and fantasy or ignorance' for which the 'author had no excuse.'[37]

While questions about Snorri's authorship of the *Formáli* or the *Edda*'s scattered Trojan material are unlikely to be resolved, there are reasons why he might have found it useful to employ the Trojan hypothesis. By establishing a connection between the euhemerized *æsir* and Troy, he might have hoped not only to flatter Hákon and the Norwegian elite by drawing them into the circle of European monarchs whose ancestry had been traced to this fabled city, but to attach skaldic poetry to the wellsprings of classical culture.[38] The links forged through Óðinn between the ruling houses of northern and central Europe might have made this scheme even more attractive to Hákon, who by the early 1220s was keen on fostering relations with neighbouring governments. As for how Snorri could have become familiar with the Trojan hypothesis, it seems likely that he had some acquaintance with early versions of *Trójumanna saga* and *Breta sögur*, translations/reworkings of Dares Phrygius's *De excidio Troiae* and Geoffrey of Monmouth's *Historia Britanniae*.[39] Alternatively, he could have learned of the Trojan legend and the uses to which it was put by European historiography through conversations in Iceland or Norway with those who had read such works. In any case, the *Formáli*'s author seems to have been rather free with the Trojan material he did know – scholars have remarked, for instance, on the fact that the figures at the nexus of this text's posited connection between the cultures of the north and of Asia, figures like Tror, Troan, and Loricus, lack clear equivalents elsewhere.[40] Such fabrication of tangential links using invented characters may have been a strategic move on Snorri's part. By placing the *æsir* into the stream of Trojan (and thereby world) history at a position of one remove, as it were, from the well-known figures and events of the Trojan war, he may have sought to create a prestigious pedigree for the founders of northern culture and kingship that could not easily be refuted by already established 'history.'

With whatever intentions Snorri may have devised his pseudohistorical recoding of Norse myth, it has seemed to some self-evident that his attempts to do so responded to the expectations and desires of his audience. Leach writes: as 'self-sufficient and national as was his method, even Snorri had to make one concession to the foreign fashion of the day. He must needs provide the Northern kingdoms with letters patent of divine right. He was obliged to establish for them, like the English, a Trojan ancestry.'[41] Still, as Leach admits, the Trojan 'theory was not current in the North, for it does not appear until his [Snorri's] time,' and it seems, moreover, never to have gained real purchase in Scandinavia outside of Iceland, where it continued to appear only in texts directly influenced by the *Edda*.[42] In order to determine what theories of royal origins Snorri was competing against and to consider why these were found preferable to that championed in his frame narrative, I will look at two texts that have, perhaps, the best claims to representing the ideology of the courts for which they were written: the *Gesta Danorum*, Saxo's history of Danish kingship completed c. 1215 and dedicated to King Valdemar II and the archbishops Absalon and Anders Sunesøn, and the *Konungs skuggsjá*, or 'King's Mirror,' a Norwegian text that probably reached its final form between Skúli's death in 1240 and Hákon's coronation in 1247.[43]

Although he was Snorri's contemporary, Saxo was more in touch with continental fashions and ecclesiastical conventions. He wrote in Latin, and used typology to make Danish history conform to a 'Romano-Christian concept of universal history.'[44] It is all the more interesting, then, that it was Saxo rather than Snorri who rejected the theory that northern kingship could trace its origins to the ancient world. As he writes at the start of Book One of the *Gesta Danorum*:

> The Danes trace their beginnings from Dan and Angul ... who were not merely the founders of our race but its guides also. Dudo however, who wrote a history of France, believes that the Danes sprang from the Danaans and were named after them ... Tradition has it, however, that it was from Dan that our royal pedigree flowed in glorious lines of succession, like channels drawn from a spring.[45]

Saxo, as Inge Skovgaard-Petersen observes, 'disposes very briefly of the theory that the Danes were descendants of the Greek Danai – whereby he foregoes the chance of linking the history of his people with the Trojan legends.'[46] It has been argued that Saxo's purpose in opting for a local rather than exotic heritage for his nation's monarchy was to craft for the Danes a history that would parallel rather than be subordinate to that of the Romans. Lars Boje Mortensen writes:

> Dan did not descend from Trojan royal stock like everyone else. Saxo probably wanted his readers to feel that even when served on a silver plate by Dudo, a fanciful origin from Troy was not necessary to assert claims of Danish grandeur. No important 'translatio' had taken place from the classical to the Nordic world in order to give rise to the Danish kingdom or to inspire the development of Danish culture ... His Danes are the Romans of the North ... The theory of autochthonous origin is one prop in this literary construction of independent Danes forming an alternative Roman empire.[47]

Saxo offers, then, a different vision of Scandinavian prehistory than Snorri, one that stresses native kings' aboriginal connections to their land and lessens the north's debt to antique culture. It is likely, moreover, that Saxo's ideas were more attuned than those of Snorri to the wants and needs of contemporary Scandinavian kings and courts, with whom he had more direct and sustained contact.

It should be observed, however, that Snorri never pushes Scandinavia's association with Asia so far that its independent achievements and excellence are entirely effaced. This is true with respect to both the lineage and arts of the *æsir*. As for the first, Snorri writes of Þórr/Tror's wife that, while 'no one can tell the ancestry of Sif,' she came from the *norðrhálfu heims*.[48] This statement, which seems to be original to Snorri, claims that Þórr's and Sif's descendants are not only scions of Asia but also of the north. The especial gift of Sif to her progeny, moreover, was *spádómr*, prophecy, a trait that Snorri does not ascribe to Þórr, but which Óðinn holds in abundance. Indeed, it is largely to this skill, a birthright of Óðinn's northern heritage, that Snorri credits his successes in that region:

> Óðinn had *spádómr* and so did his wife, and from that knowledge he discovered that his name would be remembered in the northern part of the world and honoured above all kings. For this reason he became eager to set off from Tyrkland and took with him a very great following ... And whatever countries they passed through, great glory was spoken of them, so that they seemed more like gods than men.[49]

As for the *æsir*'s culture, Snorri does not regard Norse poetry as identical to or derivative of Asian, i.e., classical, verse. In *Ynglinga saga*, he writes that Óðinn 'spoke all in rhymes, just as now that is recited which is called *skáldskapr*. He and his temple-chieftains are called song-smiths, because that skill originated with them in the north-lands.'[50] This perspective on native poetry is very different from that of Snorri's nephew Óláfr Þórðarson:

> From this book one may clearly understand that that is all one art, the poetic art that the Roman sages learned in the city of Athens in Greece and later translated into the Latin speech, and that song-metre or poetry, which Óðinn and the other Asiamen brought north hither into the northern part of the world, and they taught the [native] men in their own speech art of the kind that they themselves used and learned in Asia, where there was the most beauty and power and learning in the world.[51]

While Óláfr was clearly influenced by his uncle's theories on the origins of Norse language and poetry, Klaus von See is correct to say that 'Snorri would in no way have agreed with this sentence.'[52] In Snorri's view, Norse and classical poetry stemmed from the same source and possessed equal dignity, but were not 'all one art.' Skaldic verse, as Thomas Krömmelbein notes, was for Snorri 'a genuine native' art, irreducible in form, function, or history to Latin poetry.[53] By linking native verse to Troy, Snorri did not want to raise its status by identifying it with classical poetry, but to represent it as a product of two worlds, with roots in the universally esteemed culture of the ancient Mediterranean, but also distinguished by its genetic connections to and evolution in the north. The historical Óðinn, as a concrete representation of the melding of north (wisdom, prophecy, and poetry) and east (power, beauty, and wealth), was of central importance to Snorri's attempts to affirm the equal venerability, singularity, and worth of the hybrid institutions of Scandinavian kingship and skaldic verse.

If, however, as I have suggested, Snorri concocted his migration tale and pedigrees of northern monarchy and culture with a royal audience in mind, why were his efforts to sell this package to Norway's king so fruitless? Trojan legends were certainly known to Hákon, and the same is true of the migration theories current on the continent and in Britain. And yet, nothing indicates that Snorri's (or anyone else's) theory of Trojan ancestry found favour in Hákon's cultural milieu. As Heusler observes: 'From Norway we have no evidence for a learned *Urheimatsfabel*, and for that our defective tradition is hardly to blame.'[54] Instead, what we find in Norway is an extreme promonarchical version of the ideology of 'monarchy by the grace of God,' the idea that the king is appointed by God as his representative and terrestrial counterpart without mediation by the church. This theory is most forcefully formulated in the *Konungs skuggsjá*, which in the form of a conversation between father and son seeks to impart all one must know to comport oneself as a proper merchant, courtier, or king. The following passage from this text exegetes the New Testament tale of Christ instructing Peter to hand over a coin found in a fish's mouth to Caesar:

> Now in this it shall be observed, that each man on earth is ... obliged to honour and exalt the royal title, that which an earthly man holds from God, because the son of God himself thought it befitting to honour the royal title so much that he made his very self subject to tribute ... along with that disciple of his, who he assigned to be chief over all of his apostles and over all priestly majesty ... God himself declares the king to be his anointed ... That one does not fear God, who does not give the king full honour.[55]

Historians agree that Hákon had great success in translating this ideology of kingship into political reality. As Bagge writes, there was

> a significant change in the position of the king and the central government during Hákon's reign: the doctrine of the king as God's representative on earth ... gained wider acceptance in the leading circles of the country ... A new kind

of government and a new ideology, based on continental European models, were introduced over a fairly short period.[56]

In light of Hákon's success in promoting this ideology, it is not surprising that he was uninterested in the argument for legitimacy based on Trojan descent offered by Snorri. Perhaps the main reason, however, that Hákon found so little to recommend in Snorri's migration fable is that it provided him with no ammunition in the most pressing political contest of the early years of his reign, the struggle to define his sphere of power against Skúli's. For Snorri, part of the appeal of the Trojan hypothesis was surely that it could apply simultaneously to both of Norway's corulers; each could use the genealogical tradition presented in the *Edda* to trace his own line of descent to Troy. A theory of kingship that could support multiple claims to the crown would have served Snorri's interests as a skaldic producer, and would have been unlikely to offend the jarl, for whom it could only provide additional support to his efforts to ascend to the throne. For Hákon, however, who already sat on one, things were different – joint kingship was an idea that neither he nor his supporters were any longer willing to tolerate. In the *Konungs skuggsjá* a divided monarchy is described as the worst calamity that can happen to a nation:

> Now if it thus evilly befalls any kingdom ... that kings' heirs are many, and moreover that ill counsel is taken, that all are at once adorned with royal rank and title, then that kingdom may be called a ship adrift or a ruined estate, and it then may nearly be deemed a destroyed kingdom, because it is then sown with the greatest seed of dearth and grain of dissension.[57]

Snorri's miscalculation, then, in positing a Trojan ancestry for Norway's elite seems to have lain in overestimating the value this would hold for a monarch, court, and church intent on enforcing the ideal of unitary kingship in their land.

Theological Afterthoughts

In addition to rejecting an antique origin for Danish monarchy, Saxo minimizes the role of pagan deities in his prehistory. In the *Gesta Danorum*, Othinus is a Byzantine ruler who often resides at Uppsala and is worshipped by kings of Europe. Saxo takes a dim view of this 'god' and those who revered him. After describing how a consort of Frigg helped her recast a golden statue of Othinus into ornaments, Saxo writes: 'Need I add anything but to say that such a god deserved such a wife? Men's intelligence was once made ridiculous by gullibility of this kind.'[58] For Saxo, these gods are apotheosized easterners guilty of promulgating paganism, and lacking any genealogical ties to northern kings.

For Snorri, things were again different. Because of the importance of Norse gods and their myths to skaldic poetry's comprehension, he was obliged to keep them at centre stage. Furthermore, because of Snorri's identification of the Asian *æsir* and especially Óðinn as the primordial link between the poetry and the kings who used (and ought still) to consume it, he could not so blithely dismiss them as contemptible charlatans. On the other hand, he could just as ill afford to ignore the infamous role to which Saxo reduced the gods – by continuing to trace Scandinavian kingship and the skaldic art to Óðinn, Snorri inextricably tied the origins of these institutions to that of pagan religion. The major task, then, remaining to Snorri after assembling the *Edda*'s historical frame was to ameliorate the damage that Óðinn and the *æsir* would seem to most readers to have inflicted upon the religious condition or progress of the north. It was in response to this problem of the *Edda*'s own making that Snorri started to think, for lack of a better term, theologically. The purpose, in short, of the frame's theological dimension was to depict the historical *æsir*'s introduction of false religion into the north as innocently as possible, so as to bring the king and other readers to a positive evaluation of the contributions of these figures to northern culture and politics.

In medieval thought, explaining pre-Christian religion typically involved a combination of euhemerism and demonization. Rather than deny reality to discredited gods, Christian writers, beginning with second-century apologists, interpreted them as heroes and rulers whose identities were assumed after their deaths by demons, who, performing 'miracles' and thereby sowing polytheism in defiance of God, were mistaken for deities. This theory was known and used in Iceland from at least the late 1100s, when it appears in sagas of Óláfrs Tryggvason and Haraldsson; in Oddr Snorrason's *Óláfs saga Tryggvasonar*, Óðinn is the devil himself.[59] Scholars are divided on whether Snorri employed 'demon theory' to understand the reality of the pagan gods. Baetke, who has done most to promote Snorri's acceptance of this theory, writes:

What for Oddr and *Fagrskinna*'s author is valid, naturally really holds true for Snorri, who as a history-writer stands on their shoulders ... [Although he] avoids, as much as possible, expressing theological judgments ... he probably did not really differ in his representation of the past from his forebears ... He also for his part took the apparition [of Óðinn that appears to Óláfr in Oddr's and Snorri's sagas] for a manifestation or an envoy of the devil.[60]

That Snorri nowhere explicitly equates Óðinn or any of the *æsir* with devils, nor attributes their power and success to demonic aid, does not trouble Baetke or his followers. Weber writes: 'That they [the *æsir*] herein – unbeknownst to themselves – are strengthened by the devil … is for the medieval Christian observer obvious, [and] therefore does not need – as the positivistic research holds necessary – to be expressly mentioned.'[61] Yet Weber also states in describing Snorri's historical method that 'historians prefer to add to knowledge and are reluctant to omit material found in other sources.'[62] This, however, is precisely what Snorri does whenever he encounters instances of demon theory in his predecessors' work – he omits them from his own. A clear example of this is his use of the aforementioned story from Oddr's saga. Both writers describe the king being visited by a mysterious old man who regales him with tales into the night, but vanishes by morning. Oddr has Óláfr exclaim upon learning of his guest's disappearance: 'God has rescued us from great danger, and it is clear that the devil has assumed the form of Óðinn, and wanted to deceive us.'[63] Snorri's text, alone of existing variants of this story, does not equate Óðinn with the devil, and merely reports Óláfr as saying: 'This must have been no man and it must have been Óðinn, the one whom heathen men had long believed in … [and who] would not succeed in deceiving them in any way.'[64] Given my understanding of the roles assigned by Snorri to Óðinn and the historical *æsir*, it is not difficult to see why statements that demonize these figures found no place in his work.

If Snorri rejected demon theory due to the pall it would cast over the origins of Scandinavian kingship and culture, however, he was willing to use a theory that could place paganism's introduction into the north in a more positive light. This was natural religion, the idea that pre- or non-Christian peoples were not wholly forsaken by God, but retained the capacity, through intuition or by applying reason to nature, to conceive of a single, all-powerful creator/controller of the cosmos. This theory was useful for configuring one's pagan ancestors as 'noble heathens' who knew, apart from revelation, that God existed. Snorri's version of this theory is presented mainly in the *Formáli*'s first half, where one reads that, after the flood, people

> forgot God's name and nearly everywhere in the world that man could not be found who knew details about his creator. But nonetheless God granted them earthly gifts, possessions and happiness, which they were to have in the world. He also distributed such knowledge that they understood all earthly things and all those particulars that they could see in the air and on the earth.[65]

Owing to this and similar passages in the *Formáli*, Snorri has often been seen as working in the *Edda* to redeem his pagan ancestors by crediting them with a pre-revelatory apprehension of Christian truth.[66] The question this claim raises, however, is which set of ancestors did Snorri wish to salvage: native northerners, Asian immigrants, or both? Many have supposed that the *Formáli*'s account of natural religion was meant to describe the Trojan *æsir*'s beliefs, which they carried with them and preserved in the north as skaldic diction. Based on the passage quoted above, however, there seems no reason to think that Snorri did not include everyone who had forgotten God's true name as recipients of natural religious knowledge. Thus, it is difficult to see why he should have accorded the language of the skalds any more value than the quotidian languages of Troy (of which he says there were twelve), or the native tongues of Scandinavia and Britain mentioned at the end of the *Formáli*. According to the liberal notion of God's generosity presented in this text, *all* 'non-Christian' languages could lay equal claim to being vehicles of natural religion.

Though I find nothing in Snorri's works to suggest that he regarded the *æsir* from Asia as exemplary proto-Christians, or their languages (skaldic or otherwise) as privileged carriers of natural religious insight, neither does it seem that this status can be assigned to the belief system or languages present in the north prior to their arrival. When in *Gylfaginning* Gylfi decides to visit the *æsir*, his stated purpose is to discover whether their success stems 'from their own nature, or if those divine powers to whom they sacrificed were the reason,' and the first question he asks them is: 'Who is the highest and oldest of all gods?'[67] While some have argued that we are meant to perceive in the course of Gylfi's questioning his conversion, and through him that of the north, from a reason-based belief in a creator god to erroneous polytheism, the Swedish king's initial concerns and query hardly seem those of a primitive monotheist. Gylfi seems already at the dialogue's inception prepared to accept the existence of multiple divinities.

The answer, then, to the question of which set of ancestors, the Trojan *æsir* or native northerners, Snorri intended to portray as carriers of a pure, natural religious monotheism is neither – or perhaps both. There are traces of this sort of belief in both Gylfi's questions and the *æsir*'s responses from the start of their conversation. Hár responds to Gylfi's question regarding the name of the highest god by stating: 'That one is called Alföðr according to our speech, but in Ásgarðr the old he had twelve names.'[68] After hearing these names, Gylfi then asks:

'Where is that god, and what can he do, and what wondrous works has he performed?' Hár says: 'He lives through all ages and rules all his kingdom and controls all things great and small.' Then says Jafnhár: 'He fashioned heaven and earth and the sky and all of their contents.' Then said Þriði: 'The greatest thing is when he made man and gave to him that spirit which shall live and never perish, though the body may rot into mould or burn to ashes. And all men who are right in morals shall live and will be with him in that place which is called Gimlé or Vingólf, but wicked men will fare to Hel and thence into Niflhel.'[69]

Many regard this passage's blend of pagan, Christian, and natural religious ideas as hopelessly confused; Sigurður Nordal calls it 'without doubt, the poorest that Snorri has written, and there would be nothing lost, even if it were altogether cut out.'[70] Others, however, Baetke above all, consider it the key to Snorri's 'Odinstheologie,' of his attempt to make Óðinn into the *æsir*'s god of natural religion.[71] For once, I am more in agreement with Baetke: in my view, this passage marks the beginning of Snorri's efforts to show that both the historical *æsir* and Gylfi continued, however contaminated by polytheism their beliefs might become, to retain insights into God's true nature through their notions of a supreme deity.

The god the *æsir* describe in this passage is clearly meant to harmonize with the natural religious deity with whom Gylfi (and, through the *Formáli*, the reader) is already acquainted. Like this nameless god, the *æsir*'s many-named Alföðr is not quite eternal, but has existed since before the beginning of the world, which he, as the *Formáli* states and *Gylfaginning* will soon narrate, 'fashioned out of certain material' and thereafter rules.[72] Having made this equation, Snorri has Hár and his associates begin to feed Gylfi what is essentially straight Norse myth, but not without a few further theological asides. The most important of these is the so-called confession of Hár, in which the fusion of natural religion and polytheism that the *æsir* are urging Gylfi to adopt is rendered most transparent. After describing the births of Óðinn, Vili, and Vé, Hár says: 'And that is my belief that Óðinn and his brothers must be the controllers of heaven and earth; we think that he must be called this. So that man is called whom we know to be the greatest and most excellent, and well may you let him be called thus.'[73] At this point, Óðinn is revealed to Gylfi as one and the same with Alföðr/the god of natural religion. If Gylfi was truly meant to embody the viewpoint of primitive monotheism, one might expect him at this point to object, not necessarily to the identification of Óðinn with the deity of natural religion, but to the decidedly god-filled cosmos over which he is supposed to reign. But this does not happen. Even when Hár makes the polytheistic character of the religion he is pushing more explicit, telling Gylfi that Óðinn 'may be called Alföðr because he is the father of all of the gods and of men,' Gylfi raises no protest.[74] Nor does he complain when Þriði declares that 'Óðinn is highest and oldest of the *æsir*,' a statement that not only echoes Gylfi's initial question to the historical *æsir*, but substitutes their own name for 'the gods' about whom he had first inquired.[75]

Thus, Snorri, rather than assigning natural religion in its pure and, to Christian minds, most praiseworthy form to either set of ancestors, deposits traces of this theology in the beliefs expressed by representatives of both cultures at the time when they are supposed to have met. It is their shared notion of a creator/controller of an ordered universe that provides the common ground for the melding of Gylfi's and the *æsir*'s religions and enables the latter to fill in the half-formed polytheism of the former with names and stories of their choosing. One of natural religion's functions in Snorri's frame is thus to enhance the verisimilitude of the establishment of the *æsir*'s more developed brand of polytheism in the north. It also, however, and more importantly serves to soften the spiritual injury caused by the triumph of Óðinn and the *æsir* in the north. Even if he was not himself too worried by the religious implications of his fabricated history, Snorri had good reason to fear that Hákon, a Christian king closely allied with and dependent upon his country's episcopal authorities, might have difficulty appreciating the contributions made to the founding of his monarchy by invaders who had maliciously disrupted his ancestors' spiritual maturation. By suggesting that the *æsir*'s subjugation of the north resulted in nothing worse than the displacement of one form of mixed natural religion/polytheism by another, Snorri presented the king and his clerics with a narrative of religious history that was not only feasible but also, to the extent that this was possible, theologically palatable.

Conclusions: Winning and Losing in the Game of Cultural Capital

What I have tried to do in this study is to confirm the value of an older way of understanding the *Edda*, to return to a view of Snorri's treatise as a pragmatic guide to the composition and comprehension of skaldic poetry. Where I have gone beyond this idea of the *Edda*'s purpose is mainly in my discussion of its producer's motivations. Rather than a desire to edify borne of scholarly antiquarianism or simple affection for his native culture, I have insisted that Snorri's interests in producing this text were overwhelmingly political in nature. I have argued, in sum, that the *Edda*, when situated in its social, historical, and biographical context, is best viewed as its author's response to the fact that a type of capital that he regarded as crucial to his success within the joint Icelandic-Norwegian field of power was, due to the shifting tastes of dominant agents within this market, losing its capacity to generate profit, or to function as a mechanism for converting cultural capital into more desirable forms.

Adopting this perspective on Snorri's cultural practice allows for an overdue reintegration of his biography and body of work. By seeing the *Edda* as the product, not of a general concern for safeguarding knowledge and culture in and of themselves, but of one man's compulsion to protect his stockpile of capital, we are no longer confronted with a paradoxical figure, alternately political and academic, but one whose political, social, legal, *and* literary practices were propelled by common interests and ambitions. We are also freed from having to account for many of the tensions and inconsistencies that this text has been accused of exhibiting. Scholars have too often treated the *Edda* as an exhaustively planned and meticulously implemented theoretical treatise, or else faulted it for failing to live up to this exacting (and quintessentially academic) standard. To do either, however, is to mistake Snorri's capabilities or intentions. 'The logic of practice,' writes Bourdieu, 'lies in being logical to the point at which being logical would cease being practical.'[76] In writing the *Edda*, Snorri must not be imagined to have operated as someone who has liberated himself from his social world in order to observe and comment upon it from outside and above. Nor can his product be regarded as a detached survey of skaldic verse and pagan myth, one assembled or reworked with the ideal of absolute logical or organizational consistency in mind. To judge Snorri's text (or his practice) by such standards is to demand 'of it more logic than it can give, thereby condemning oneself either to wring incoherences out of it or to thrust a forced coherence upon it.'[77] The logic employed in writing the *Edda* was a practical or strategic logic, that of an actor who remained invested in rather than abstracted from his social situation and the issues at stake therein, and the text itself was a series of responses to shifting challenges and circumstances, a set of interventions aimed at restoring the value of Snorri's poetic expertise.

When the *Edda* is viewed in this way, as a process rather than a thing, it becomes clear just how comprehensive an effort to reconstitute the market for skaldic verse it was. Over the course of writing this text, Snorri pinpointed and acted to redress every major point of weakness or vulnerability in this art form's continued capacity to function as capital: he fought his audience's ignorance of the conventions of skaldic metre and diction by developing a system of rules, terminology, and classificatory principles that could render the formal qualities of this poetry transparent; he sought, by compiling an unprecedented anthology of past masterpieces, to underscore skalds' historic contribution to the legitimation of Scandinavian kings and the memorialization of their reigns; by persistently equating poetry with praise (and honour) and through repeated reminders that poetry ought to be rewarded with gold (and honour), he drove home this product's capacity to generate, out of nothing more than words, a well-nigh inexhaustible stream of profits and benefits for those who were only willing to acknowledge its ability to do so; and by codifying and packaging the mythology of a dead religion, he worked to provide the scenic backdrop needed to give the language of the skalds renewed colour and significance in listeners' minds. The *Edda* even responded to problems of its own making, ones generated over the course of its production: so, for example, Snorri's retention of Óðinn as source and patron of the skaldic art led him to recast this figure as a Trojan culture-hero who, though ousted from the realm of the sacred, could still be revered as wellspring of the north's most distinctive artistic achievement, as well as its royal houses; and the theological musings of the *Edda*'s last written sections tried not only to reconcile the historical fiction of the *æsir*'s migration with the reality of pagan myth, but to cast the resulting fraud of the now-human *æsir* in as innocent a light as possible.

The scope and novelty of Snorri's efforts do nothing to alter the fact, however, that they were almost entirely ineffectual. By the time Snorri acted, the historical processes, structural forces, and events that conspired to rob skaldic verse of its cultural value had reached a point of critical mass and momentum that was probably impossible to counteract. That Snorri, in spite of the enormity of the obstacles he faced, remained fixated on rehabilitating this resource speaks to the power exerted by the habitus upon the practice of agents, a power that, under certain circumstances, can prove counterproductive to efforts to maximize social profit or position. A habitus, as Bourdieu describes it,

> is a potentiality, a desire to be which, in a certain way, seeks to create the conditions of its fulfilment, and therefore to create the conditions most favourable to what it is … And a number of behaviours can be understood as efforts to maintain or produce a state of the social world or of a field that is capable of giving to some acquired disposition … the possibility and opportunity of being actualized.[78]

In Snorri's case, his intense drive to exploit and often to overextend his capital resources can be attributed to his split habitus, to the fact that he was at a young age afforded access to the social, material, and cultural advantages of a family other than his own. Snorri was heir to a birthright that he had not actually been born to, and unlike the foster-father whose place as Iceland's leading figure he sought to arrogate, or the king of Norway whom he tried for so long to impress, his social worth and position were not perceived, by himself or others, as inborn and inalienable possessions, but rather as something that depended upon the resources that he controlled and the uses to which he put them. It should come as no surprise, then, that Snorri was uncommonly sensitive to challenges to the worth of his forms of politically relevant capital, or that he would expend considerable effort to squeeze every last bit of advantage from each one of them.

Snorri's failure to restore skaldic verse to its position as the favourite cultural product of Norway's royal court through the writing of the *Edda* had effects in his life that went well beyond his capacity to act and profit as a cultural producer. The cultural chasm that lay between Snorri and Hákon from their first meeting translated into a lifelong personal and political divide that Snorri never managed to bridge, and which helped set the stage for his fall alongside Skúli, the Norwegian agent whose tastes most closely matched his own. It would be a mistake, however, to think that Snorri's role as a player in the game of cultural capital ended along with his life in 1241. On the contrary, Snorri's unwitting participation in this game has continued into the modern era, in which this medieval Icelander has earned the admiration and gratitude of a community of scholars for whom apparent allegiance to the universal values of art and literature is esteemed over the blatant pursuit of wealth and power. As Sigurður Nordal remarked in an article in which he celebrated, along with the rest of Iceland, the seven-hundredth anniversary of Snorri's murder:

> We do not remember this anniversary of Snorri's on account of this, that he was a chieftain, a wealthy man, and bore great titles. We remain silent concerning the date of the deaths of Þorvaldr of the Vatnsfirðingar, Kolskeggr auðgi, and, what is more, jarl Gizurr. We do not feel the need to look to men such as these, long after centuries have passed ... But geniuses like Snorri are seldom born among such a small people and still less often do they get to mature and come into their own.[79]

Even if scholars have mostly been mistaken about Snorri's motives for preserving knowledge and culture, there is no sense in denying his enduring contribution to this enterprise. And so, in the end, it seems that Snorri won after all, even if in a different field of practice than he had intended, and one which he never could have imagined.

Appendix: Kennings
and Kenning-Types in *Háttatal*
and Explication in *Skáldskaparmál*

I here attempt to account in the left column for all kennings from *Háttatal*, and to indicate on the right the chapters where these are explicated and/or illustrated in *Skáldskaparmál* (with one reference to *Gylfaginning*, marked G27, for the kenning *Vindhlés hjálms fyllr*. G55–8 refer, following Faulkes, to the opening chapters of *Skáldskaparmál*, the so-called *Bragarœður* section; see p. 214, n. 6). The first chapters listed on the right are those in which a specific kenning is illustrated or the kenning-type in question is directly explicated. By 'kenning-type,' I mean a set of kennings for a common referent employing the same form or style of reference, e.g., all literal, non-mythological kennings for 'warrior' defined by action, an example of which is *skjaldar valdr*, 'shield-wielder.' For each kenning-type, I list all occurrences and give at least one example. In the case of mythological and legendary kennings, a separate kenning-type is listed for every specific entity referred to; so, for example, even though 'weather of Skögul' and 'storm-time of Hrist' are virtually identical in form and imagery, I have listed them as separate kenning-types owing to their use of different mythological figures/names. Chapters given in parentheses do not explain the kenning-type or kenning on the left, but contain references to mythological/legendary figures or stories used in their construction (complete listings are not provided for gods that are mentioned very often). Chapters in which extended narratives are offered in explanation of a kenning or kenning-type are printed in bold.

Kenning referents in *Háttatal* (total: 366)

Chapters in
Skáldskaparmál
where explicated

I   Kennings for Men (total: 132)

A   Warrior (51)

1   Literal/Non-Mythological/Def. by Action
   a. shield-wielder (skjaldar valdr, 5): 2, 5, 11, 16, 21,   Sk 31
       29, 30x2, 31x2, 32, 37, 39, 41x2, 42x2, 43, 44, 49,
       59, 61, 62, 64x2, 70, 83, 85, 86, 92x2

2   Metaphorical/Non-Mythological/Def. by Attribute, Possession, Relation
   a. trees of shields (randa viðir, 45): 24, 30x2, 45, 47,   Sk 31, 47
       53, 60, 63, 75
   b. shield-staves (gunnveggs stafar, 61)   Sk 47, 50

3   Metaphorical/Mythological/Def. by Attribute, Possession, Relation:
   a. rœki-Njörðr (13), sig-Njörðr (55)   Sk 1, 31, 49
                                          (G55, G56,
                                          6, **33,** 75)
   b. remmi-Týr (14), hjálm-Týr (35), hjaldr-Týr (53)   Sk 1, 2, 31,
                                            49, 53 (**G55,**
                                          9, **33,** 75)
   c. hjarar Baldr (43)   Sk 1, 2, 31,
                                          57 (**G56,** 5,
                                          45, 75)
   d. Gautr stála skúrar (55)   Sk 1, 2, 4,
                                          18, 31 (37,
                                          49, 54, 60,
                                          65, 75)
   e. rógálfr (75)   Sk 1, 31
   f. styrjar glóða støkkvi-Móði (85)   Sk 1, 31, 54,
                                            (4)
   g. maple of Hrist (Hristar hlynr, 61)   Sk 47 (75)

B   *King/Ruler* (40)

1   Literal/Non-Mythological/Def. by Action
   a. controller of hostility (styrjar stórlæti, 28): 2, 13, 26,   Sk 31, 53
       28x2, 29, 34, 39x2, 41, 49x2, 51, 53, 55x2, 59, 63,
       68, 77, 78, 81x2, 88, 90, 95

2   Literal/Non-Mythological/Def. by Attribute, Possession, Relation
   a. friend of men (gotna vinr, 11): 11, 14, 27,[1] 37x2, 54,   Sk 31
       58, 64, 83, 90
   b. son/brother of king (tiggja sonr, 18): 18, 33, 34, 69   Sk 31, 53

C   Generous Ruler (33)

1   Literal/Non-Mythological/Def. by Action
   a.   dealer of gold (gulls deilir, 2): 2, 3x3, 13, 16, 17x2,   Sk 31, 47
       29, 39, 43, 44, 45, 46x3, 47x4, 48, 60, 61, 63, 66,
       69, 71, 73, 86, 88, 95

2   Literal/Non-Mythological/Def. by Possession
   a.   man of bracelets (hringa skati, 90)   Sk 47

3   Metaphorical/Mythological/Def. by Possession
   a.   wealth-Týr (auð-Týr, 48)   Sk 1, 2, 31,
                                  47, 49, 53,
                                  (**G55**, 9, **33**,
                                  75)

D   Men (8)

1   Literal/Non-Mythological/Def. by Action
   a.   breaker of wealth (auðs brjótr, 27)   Sk 47
   b.   stem-deer steerer (stálhreins stýrir, 28): 28, 31, 59   Sk 31
   c.   spender of hoard (hoddspennir, 29)   Sk 31

2   Metaphorical/Non-Mythological/Def. by Possession
   a.   wealth-trees (auðviðir, 48): 17, 48, 80   Sk 47, 31

II   Kennings Related to Warfare (total: 109)

A   Battle (38)

1   Literal/Non-Mythological/Def. by Attribute, Relation
   a.   peace-destruction (friðlæ, 17)   —
   b.   time of wound-oars (sára ára tími, 61)   —

2   Metaphorical/Non-Mythological/Def. by Attribute, Possession, Relation:
   a.   song of swords (sveða söngr, 16): 2, 8, 16, 28, 32x2,   Sk 48
       39, 52, 53, 55x2, 57x2, 58x2, 59x2, 61x2, 62x3, 65
   b.   edge-þing (egg-þing, 36)   Sk 37, 64
   c.   meeting of steel (málms mót, 52), game of strife   Sk 47, 50
       (rógleikr, 14)

3   Metaphorical/Mythological-Legendary/Def. by Attribute, Relation,
    Possession

a.	resounding-storm of Hildr (Hildar hlemmidrífa, 54)	Sk 48, **50** (3, 48, 49, 64, 75)
b.	Högni's daughter (Högna mær, 49)	Sk 31, **50**
c.	Heðinn's beloved (Heðins mála, 49)	Sk 31, **50**
d.	lady of the Hjaðningar (Hjaðninga sprund, 49)	Sk 31, **50**
e.	din of Gungnir (Gungnis hlymr, 52)	Sk 48 (2, 35, 75)
f.	weather of Skögul (Sköglar veðr, 54)	Sk 48 (2, 64, 75)
g.	storm-time of Hrist (Hristar hreggöld, 59)	Sk 48 (47, 75)
h.	tempest of Göndul (Göndlar glygg, 59)	Sk 48 (2, 59, 61,[2] 75)
i.	rain of Mist (Mistar regn, 62)	Sk 48 (75)
j.	showers of Hlökk (Hlakkar skúrir, 64)	Sk 48 (49, 60, 64, 75)

B   Sword (29)

1   Literal/Non-Mythological/Def. by Action

a.	shield-damager (hlífgrandi, 17)	Sk 49

2   Metaphorical/Non-Mythological/Def. by Attribute, Relation, Possession

a.	fire of helmets (hjálma hyrr, 58): 2x2, 6x4, 13, 24, 28, 30, 50x2, 57, 58, 60x3, 61x2, 65, 85, 86	Sk 49, 50, 53

3   Metaphorical/Mythological/Def. by Attribute, Relation, Possession

a.	Vindhlér's head (Vindhlés hjálms fyllr, 7)	Sk 8, 69 (G27)
b.	fire of valkyrie (Yggs drósar eisa, 50)	Sk 49
c.	Hlökk's embers/fire (Hlakkar glóð, 50; Hlakkar eldr, 57)	Sk 49 (48, 60, 64, 75)
d.	frost/mast of Mist (Mistar frost, 61; Mistar laukr, 85)	Sk 49 (44, 75)

C   Shield (14)

1   Literal/Non-Mythological/Def. by Attribute, Relation, Possession
   a.   lime-woods of spear-winds (snarvinda lindar, 32)   —
   b.   fence of rims, i.e., shield-wall (jaðra garðr, 58)   —

2   Metaphorical/Non-Mythological/Def. by Attribute, Relation, Possession
   a.   land of spears (fleina land, 65): 30, 31, 49, 59, 61,   Sk 50
         65, 83, 85

3   Metaphorical/Mythological/Def. by Attribute, Relation, Possession
   a.   plank of Hrungnir's sole (þilja Hrungnis ilja, 30)   Sk **17**, 22, 49
   b.   gate of Þundr (Þundar grind, 58)   Sk 49 (3)
   c.   wall of Sigarr (Sigars veggr, 59)   Sk 49 (64)
   d.   ground of Hrund (Hrundar grund, 61)   Sk 49 (75)

D   Blood (10)

1   Metaphorical/Non-Mythological/Def. by Attribute, Relation
   a.   corpse-river (þjóðár hræs, 7): 6, 7, 11, 32, 54, 56,   Sk 58, 60³
         60x4

E   Raven/Eagle (5)

1   Metaphorical/Non-Mythological/Def. by Attribute, Relation, Possession
   a.   wound-gosling (undgagl, 62): 32, 62, 92x2   Sk 49, 60, 64

2   Metaphorical/Mythological/Def. by Relation
   a.   hawk of Hlökk (Hlakkar haukr, 5)   Sk 44 (48,
                                                              60, 64, 75)

F   Mailcoat (4)

1   Metaphorical/Non-Mythological/Def. by Relation
   a.   battle-shirt (styrs serkr, 7)   Sk 49

2   Metaphorical/Mythological/Def. by Relation
   a.   Hamðir's tunic (Hamðis fang, 2)   Sk 49 (**42**)

b. clothing of Hjarrandi (Hjarranda föt, 53)   Sk 49, 50
c. shirt of Skögul (Sköglar serkr, 64)   Sk 49 (2,
                                                       48, 64,
                                                       75)

G *Arrows* (2)

1 Metaphorical/Non-Mythological/Def. by Relation
   a. hail of battle (sóknar hagl, 62), snow of bows (boga   Sk 48, 49
       dript, 62)

H *Spear* (2)

1 Literal/Non-Mythological/Def. by Relation
   a. point of slaughter (valbroddr, 79)   —

2 Metaphorical/Non-Mythological/Def. by Relation
   a. corpse-adder (hrænaðr, 79)   Sk 58

I *Helmet* (1)

1 Metaphorical/Legendary/Def. by Relation
   a. battle-boar (hildigöltr, 2)   Sk **44**

J *Scabbard* (1):

1 Metaphorical/Non-Mythological/Def. by Relation
   a. baldric-slough (fetilhams, 6)   —

K *Ægishjálmr* (1)

1 Literal/Legendary/Def. by Relation
   a. helmet of dragon (gríma grundar gjaldseiðs, 15)   Sk **40**

L *Wound* (1)

1 Metaphorical/Non-Mythological/Def. by Relation
   a. window of breast (geðveggjar gluggi, 50)   —

M   Penant (1)

1   Literal/Non-Mythological/Def. by Relation
   a.   flag of battle (gunnfani, 52)   —

III   Kennings for Gold (total: 31)

1   Literal/Non-Mythological/Def. by Action
   a.   destroyer of unity (samþykkjar søkkvir, 43)   —

2   Metaphorical/Non-Mythological/Def. by Relation
   a.   rings' droplet/fragment (hringdropi, 42; hringa brot,   Sk 46
      45)
   b.   gleam of palm (spannar blik, 40): 40, 44x2, 86   Sk 32, 47
   c.   limb-skerry (liðar sker, 46)   Sk 32, 46

3   Metaphorical/Mythological/Def. by Attribute, Possession, Relation
   a.   fire of sea (ægis bál, 3): 3, 17x3, 22, 26, 44, 45x2,   Sk 32, **33**,
      46x2, 69, 93   46, 47
   b.   amber/fire of Rhine (Rínar röf, 26; Rínar bál, 91)   Sk 32, **33**,
                                                                                        (**42**, 45, 46,
                                                                                        47, 64)
   c.   otter's payment (otrgjöld, 41)   Sk 32, **39**, 45
   d.   burden of Grani (Grana þungfarmr, 41)   Sk **40**, 45, 47
   e.   loaded-metal of Gnita-heath (Gnitaheiðar   Sk **40**, 41
      reiðmálmr, 41)
   f.   treasure of Niflungar (Niflunga skattr, 41)   Sk **42**, 45
   g.   fair-rain of Mardöll's lids (fagrregn Mardallar   Sk 32, 37,
      hvarma, 42)   45, 75
   h.   joyful snow of Grotti (Grotta glaðdript, 43)   Sk **43**
   i.   peace-barley of Fróði (Fróða friðbygg, 43)   Sk 37, **43**
   j.   meal of Fenja (Fenju meldr, 43)   Sk 37, **43**, 45

IV   Kennings for Body-Parts (total: 27)

A   Arm/Hand (8)

1   Literal/Non-Mythological/Def. by Action
   a.   bow-forcer (boga nauðr, 48)   Sk 71

2   Literal/Non-Mythological/Def. by Relation
    a.   limb of shoulders (axla limr, 2)   Sk 71

3   Metaphorical/Non-Mythological/Def. by Relation
    a.   path of falcons (vala leið, 48): 2, 42, 44, 48x2, 86   Sk 71

B   *Head* (9)

1   Literal/Non-Mythological/Def. by Action:
    a.   helmet-filler (hjálms fyllr, 7)   —[4]

2   Metaphorical/Non-Mythological/Def. by Relation
    a.   brain-ground (heila grund, 63): 2, 57, 62, 63, 64,   Sk 69
         65x2
    b.   high-tower of life (aldrs gnapturn, 50)   —

C   *Breast* (6)

1   Metaphorical/Non-Mythological/Def. by Relation
    a.   thought's path (sefa stígr, 6): 6, 50x3, 51, 63   Sk 70

D   *Tongue* (2)

1   Metaphorical/Non-Mythological/Def. by Relation
    a.   oar of speech (tölu rœði, 81): 81, 85   Sk 69

E   *Hair* (1)

1   Metaphorical/Non-Mythological/Def. by Relation
    a.   wood of head (holt heila bæs, 2)   Sk 69

F   *Teeth* (1)

1   Metaphorical/Non-Mythological/Def. by Relation
    a.   skerry of words (orða sker, 87)   Sk 69

V   Kennings for Ships (total: 25)

1   Metaphorical/Non-Mythological/Def. by Relation

   a. animals of waves (unna dýr, 28): 19, 22, 28x2, 31,   Sk 51
       34, 35, 46, 59, 71, 73x2, 74x2, 77, 83
   b. dark-ski of prows (barða bláskíð, 79): 19, 74, 75,   Sk 51
       76, 79

2 Metaphorical/Mythological/Legendary/Def. by Relation
   a. Gyllir of waves (unna Gyllir, 19)   Sk 51 (58)
   b. stallion of Róði (Róða stóð, 21)   Sk 51 (37,
                                                       49, 75)
   c. horse of Haki (Haka blakkr, 38; Haka hnigfákr, 71) Sk 51 (17,
                                                       58, 62,
                                                          75)

VI   Kennings for Objects in Nature (total: 21):

A Sea (11)

1 Metaphorical/Non-Mythological/Def. by Attribute, Relation
   a. fish-home (lýsheimr, 22): 22, 35, 45x2, 74, 76x2, 83   Sk 25
   b. fetter of Mön (Manar hlekkr, 77)   —

2 Metaphorical/Legendary/Def. by Relation
   a. land of Røkkvi (Røkkva rein, 73)   Sk 25 (75)
   b. way of Haki (Haka vegr, 76)   Sk 25 (17,
                                                        58, 62,
                                                          75)

B Earth (4)

1 Metaphorical/Mythological/Def. by Relation
   a. wife/confidante of Óðinn (mála úlfs bága, 3; rúna   Sk 2, 24
       Míms vinar, 3)
   b. mother of Þórr (eiða orms váða, 3; móðir mellu   Sk 4, 24
       dólgs, 3)

C Winter (2)

1 Metaphorical/Non-Mythological/Def. by Attribute, Relation
   a. adder's terror (naðrs ógn, 83), worm's harm (orms   Sk 29
       galli, 83)

D   Shore (1)

1   Metaphorical/Non-Mythological/Def. by Relation
a.   earth's brow (brún Míms vinar rúnu, 3)   —[5]

E   Heaven (1)

1   Metaphorical/Non-Mythological/Def. by Relation
a.   wind's roof (vindræfur, 12)   —[6]

F   Fjörð (1)

1   Literal/Non-Mythological/Def. by Relation
a.   cleft of land (jarðar skarð, 17)   —

G   Wind (1)

1   Metaphorical/Non-Mythological/Def. by Relation
a.   branch-hound (limgarmr, 78)   Sk 27

VII   Other Kenning Referents (total: 21)

A   Óðinn (2)

1   Literal/Mythological/Def. by Relation
a.   wolf's enemy (úlfs bági, 3)   Sk 2
b.   Mímir's friend (Míms vinr, 3)   Sk 2

B   Þórr (2)

1   Literal/Mythological/Def. by Relation
a.   snake's attacker (orms váði, 3)   Sk 4
b.   troll-wife's enemy (mellu dólgr, 3)   Sk 4

C   Poetry (2)

1   Metaphorical/Mythological/Def. by Relation
a.   Yggr's booty (Yggs fengr, 31)   **G58**, Sk 3,
47, 54 (2,[7] 4,
64, 75)

   b.   waves of Hárr's hall-vat (hrannir Hárs saltunnu, 31)   **G58**, Sk 3 (48)

D *Mead* (2)

1 Metaphorical/Non-Mythological/Def. by Relation
   a.   waves of honey (hunangs öldur, 24)   —
   b.   speech's salvation (máls heilsa, 25)   —[8]

E *Ale* (2)

1 Metaphorical/Non-Mythological/Def. by Relation
   a.   current of yeast (jastar röst, 25)   —[8]
   b.   stream of cheerful-cup (blíðskálar bekkr, 87)   —

F *Drink* (1)

1 Metaphorical/Non-Mythological/Def. by Relation
   a.   pure lake of horns (horna hreintjörn, 24)   —

G *Beer* (1)

1 Metaphorical/Non-Mythological/Def. by Relation
   a.   horns' surf (horna brim, 25)   —[8]

H *Wine* (1)

1 Metaphorical/Non-Mythological/Def. by Relation
   a.   destruction of dignity (strúgs galli, 25)   —[8]

I *Valkyrie* (2)

1 Literal/Non-Mythological/Def. by Possession:
   a.   bow-woman (álmdrós, 60)   Sk 31, 49, 75

2 Literal/Mythological/Def. by Relation
   a.   Yggr's lady (Yggs drós, 50)   Sk 75 (2, 4, 64)

J   God (1)

1   Literal/Non-Mythological/Def. by Possession
   a.   lord of wind's roof (vindræfurs jöfurr, 12)   Sk 52

K   Norway (1)

1   Literal/Non-Mythological/Def. by Relation
   a.   seat of princes (stýra setr, 15)   —[9]

L   Dragon (1)

1   Metaphorical/Legendary/Def. by Relation
   a.   payment-fish of the ground (grundar gjaldseiðr, 15)   Sk **40**

M   Claw (1)

1   Literal/Non-Mythological/Def. by Relation
   a.   sole-stem of raven (hrafni ilstafn, 32)   —

N   Sail (1)

1   Metaphorical/Non-Mythological/Def. by Relation   —
   a.   yard-beard (ráskegg, 78)

O   Ring (1)

1   Literal/Non-Mythological/Def. by Relation
   a.   link of hands (handa hlekkr, 87)   —

VIII   Mythological/Legendary Figures Mentioned Outside of Kennings

A   Rán   = sea (19)   Sk 25, **33**, 61
                                      (50, 75)

B   Himinglæva   = waves (22)   Sk 25, 61
                                        (75)

C   Hildr   = battle (49)   Sk **50** (3, 48,
                                        49, 64, 75)

D *Fenrir*	Fenrir's paw (Fenris fit, 56)	Sk 58 (16, 75)
E *Geri*	Gerri's leg (Gera fótr, 64)	Sk 58 (60, 75)
F *Kraki (Hrólfr)*	94	Sk **44** (64)
G *Haki*	94	Sk 75 (17, 58, 62)
H *Sigurðr*	94	Sk **40, 41, 42** (58, 64)
I *Ragnarr loðbrók*	94	Sk 42, 50

Notes

1 The Paradox of Snorri Sturluson

1 Faulkes, Review of *Snorri Sturluson*, by Marlene Ciklamini, 306–7.
2 Hollander, introduction to *Heimskringla* by Snorri Sturluson, trans. Hollander, xv.
3 Ibid., ix.
4 Hollander, *Skalds*, 23.
5 Ciklamini, *Snorri Sturluson*, 25, 18.
6 Sigurður Nordal, *Snorri Sturluson*, 61: 'Þar sem ættin í bili virðist klofna í lygna kvísl og friðsama í Þórði og sonum hans, og stranga og stríðlynda í Sighvati og hans sonum, er skapferli Snorra á kvíslamótum. Hann er í aðra röndina höfðingi, ásælinn, stórhuga og metorðagjarn, en þó deigur til áræðis, íhugull og lítill skörungur, í hina röndina rithöfundur, lærður, djúpsær og listfengur, en þó með hugann við jarðneska muni.' Unless otherwise noted, all translations into English from primary or secondary sources are my own.
7 Ibid.: 'veikir slíkt marglyndi, þar sem andstæðar hvatir berjast um völdin, tilfinningar og viljaþrótt.' For another discussion of Snorri's many-sided nature, see Paasche, *Snorre Sturlason og Sturlungerne*, 307–15.
8 Einar Ól. Sveinsson, *Age of the Sturlungs*, 1.
9 Ibid., 4.
10 Schach, *Icelandic Sagas*, 97
11 Durrenberger, *Dynamics of Medieval Iceland*, 1, 5 (emphases added).
12 Einar Ól. Sveinsson, *Age of the Sturlungs*, 7. Stephen Norman Tranter has also puzzled over the Sturlung age's contradictions, writing that 'paradoxically, this age of disintegration left as its legacy the epitome of Icelandic literature' (*Sturlunga Saga*, 2), and Diana Whaley writes that Snorri's career 'vividly enacts the central paradox of the time' (*Heimskringla: An Introduction*, 9).
13 The term 'skaldic' and the form of poetry it identifies are discussed in chapter 4.

14 Faulkes, introduction to *Edda* by Snorri Sturluson, trans. Faulkes, xiii.
15 Ibid., xviii.
16 Davidson, *Gods and Myths of Northern Europe*, 24; Schier, 'Zur Mythologie der *Snorra Edda*,' 406: 'ein didaktisches Interesse'; Ciklamini, *Snorri Sturluson*, 62; Turville-Petre, *Origins of Icelandic Literature*, 227; Clunies Ross, 'Snorri's *Edda* as Narrative,' 10–11; Faulkes, introduction to *Edda* translation, xix.
17 Einar Ól. Sveinsson, *Age of the Sturlungs*, 6; Sigurður Nordal, *Snorri Sturluson*, 62: 'ótrufluð ró vísindamannsins sífelt er í baksýn.'
18 Fidjestøl, 'Snorri Sturluson – European Humanist and Rhetorician,' 346; Rosenblad and Rakel Sigurðardóttir-Rosenblad, *Iceland from Past to Present*, 28; Ciklamini, *Snorri Sturluson*, 17; Faulkes, introduction to *Edda: Prologue and Gylfaginning* by Snorri Sturluson, ed. Faulkes, xxii; and Stefán Einarsson, *History of Icelandic Literature*, 116, 119.
19 See Torfi H. Tulinius, 'Snorri og bræður hans,' 'Virðing í flóknu samfélagi,' 'Capital, Field, Illusio,' and *Skáldið í skriftinni*, 129–65.
20 Durrenberger, *Dynamics of Medieval Iceland*, 23.
21 Bourdieu, *Pascalian Meditations*, 98; and Bourdieu and Wacquant, *Invitation to Reflexive Sociology*, 235–6.
22 Bourdieu, *Pascalian Meditations*, 49, 53.
23 Bourdieu identifies this question as the starting point of his thinking in *In Other Words*, 65.
24 Given my emphasis on the importance of avoiding the unconsidered application of analysts' common-sense categories and ways of thinking to alien contexts, a potential objection must here be raised: namely, is not Bourdieu's theory, through its insistence that human action is universally motivated by agents' desire to maximize position within social fields, a gross application of the modern view of social systems as governed by market forces and utilitarian interests, a view that is essentially a legacy of Marx's critique of capitalist systems? Bourdieu's response to this objection has been to insist that to understand human practice as motivated by maximization of profit, in other words by agents' inclination to realize the social destiny inscribed in them through the formation of their habitus, is far from a common-sense assumption of most participants in modern society. Still, it must probably be conceded that, in order to accept Bourdieu's theory of practice, one must first accept that human practice is inherently and, for all practical purposes, universally interested.
25 Bourdieu, *Outline of a Theory of Practice*, 177.
26 Ibid.
27 Ibid.
28 Bourdieu, *Field of Cultural Production*, 163–4.
29 Geertz, *Interpretation of Cultures*, 89.

30 For example, the editors of a collection of essays on Bourdieu's theory write that '[e]conomic capital can be more easily and efficiently converted into symbolic (that is, social and cultural) capital than vice versa, although symbolic capital can ultimately be transformed into economic capital.' Postone, LiPuma, and Calhoun, 'Introduction: Bourdieu and Social Theory,' 5.

31 Randal Johnson, introduction to Bourdieu, *Field of Cultural Production*, 7; Bourdieu and Wacquant, *Invitation to Reflexive Sociology*, 119.

32 Bourdieu, *In Other Words*, 112 (original emphases).

33 Bourdieu, *Language and Symbolic Power*, 230.

34 Bourdieu, *Outline of a Theory of Practice*, 181.

35 Bourdieu, *Language and Symbolic Power*, 231.

36 Bourdieu, *Rules of Art*, 215; see also *Pascalian Meditations*, 103, and Bourdieu and Wacquant, *Invitation to Reflexive Sociology*, 76, n. 16. 'Field of power' is a concept that Bourdieu came to prefer to that of the 'dominant class' (which predominates in his studies up to *Distinction*), which he came to regard as overly reified and unsuited to express the relational perspective on social practice that he wished to encourage.

37 Bourdieu, *Language and Symbolic Power*, 231.

38 Bourdieu, *Outline of a Theory of Practice*, 184.

39 Bourdieu, *In Other Words*, 190; and Bourdieu and Wacquant, *Invitation to Reflexive Sociology*, 127.

40 Bourdieu, *Logic of Practice*, 53. It should be noted that a significant aspect of Bourdieu's concept of habitus will be neglected in this study, both because it is of little use in reconstructing agents' habitus through texts, and because it is one that I find problematic and often poorly formulated. Bourdieu often stressed the embodied nature of the habitus and its subdiscursive transmission. In such passages, habitus becomes another way to describe *hexis*, a complex of postures, movements, and bodily dispositions that mark and help to create ways of being and moving in social worlds. Bourdieu's identification of the body (as opposed to the brain or language) as the locus of habitus acquisition, transmission, and maintenance seems to me a strange move, particularly considering the criticisms he directs against Claude Lévi-Strauss and structural anthropologists for their tendency to locate the rules and structures that determine practice in a similarly inaccessible 'unconscious.' In this book, I will use habitus strictly to describe sets of *cognitive* dispositions, propensities, and capabilities acquired in formative experience owing to early access to and control over various forms of capital (admittedly, many such dispositions and capabilities, such as prowess in arms, must be acquired and enacted bodily, but the same could be said of speaking or writing). For a critique of Bourdieu's insistence on the embodied, prepredicative nature of the habitus (particularly in his analyses of 'traditional' societies) and its supposed impermeability to discursive or ideological manipulation, see Lane, *Pierre Bourdieu*, 135–8. For a similar 'intellectualization

of habitus' in another attempt to apply Bourdieu's concepts to medieval subjects and texts, see Discenza, *King's English*, esp. 152–3, n. 29.

41 Bourdieu, *Logic of Practice*, 56.

42 For statements of this position, see Bourdieu, *Outline of a Theory of Practice*, 164; and Bourdieu and Wacquant, *Invitation to Reflexive Sociology*, 133. For criticisms, see LiPuma, 'Culture and the Concept of Culture,' 24; and Brubaker, 'Social Theory as Habitus,' 228–9.

43 Bourdieu, 'Concluding Remarks,' 273–4.

44 See Bourdieu, *In Other Words*, 45, 90, 108, *Logic of Practice*, 60–1, and *Pascalian Meditations*, 150, 161; and Bourdieu and Wacquant, *Invitation to Reflexive Sociology*, 130–1.

45 See Bourdieu, *Logic of Practice*, 12; and Bourdieu and Wacquant, *Invitation to Reflexive Sociology*, 222.

2 *Snorra saga Sturlusonar*

1 On Sturla's authorship of *Íslendinga saga*, see Björn Magnússon Ólsen, 'Um Sturlungu,' 385–437; and Jón Jóhannesson, 'Um Sturlunga sögu,' xxxiv–xli.

2 Hákon died in 1263, and the saga was likely completed by 1265. On this saga and its manuscripts, see Guðbrandur Vigfússon's preface to *Hákonar Saga* by Sturla Þórðarson, xv–xxii. I cite chapter numbers and quote from Guðbrandur's normalized edition of this saga, which accords with the translation from *Saga of Hacon*, trans. Dasent.

3 Portions of versions of *Guðmundar saga byskups* relevant to Snorri's life are thought to have been adapted from *Íslendinga saga* and an early version of *Arons saga Hjörleifssonar*, which itself probably borrowed from *Íslendinga saga*; see Turville-Petre and Olszewska, introduction to *Life of Gudmund the Good*, xxvi–xxvii; and Guðrún Nordal, *Tools of Literacy*, 100–8.

4 *Gunnlaugs saga ormstungu*, ch. 1, p. 51, n. 3.

5 On this material, see Guðrún Nordal, *Tools of Literacy*, 50–1. Two versions of *Skáldatal* (designated A and B) are printed in *Edda Snorra Sturlusonar. Edda Snorronis Sturlæi*, 3:251–69.

6 *Íslendingasögur* (a modern label for what are sometimes also called 'family sagas') refers to sagas that, while mostly first recorded in the 1200s, tell of events in Iceland from approximately 930–1030.

7 Examples of studies taking this approach are Úlfar Bragason, '*Sturlunga saga*: Textar og rannsóknir'; and Tranter, *Sturlunga Saga*.

8 For an example of the first opinion, see Sigurður Nordal, *Snorri Sturluson*, 49, 85; for the second, see Guðrún Nordal, 'Skáldið Snorri Sturluson,' 55; and Jón

Jóhannesson, *History of the Old Icelandic Commonwealth*, 242; for the last,
see Ciklamini, *Snorri Sturluson*, 17–8.

9 On Sturla's bonds to Gizurr and Magnús, see Sturla Þórðarson, *Íslendinga saga*,
ch. 195, p. 527; and *Sturlu þáttr*, ch. 2, p. 235.

10 Those desiring a more comprehensive but still accessible account of the major
persons and events that shaped the last century of Icelandic independence should
consult Jón Jóhannesson's *History of the Old Icelandic Commonwealth*, in particular the excellent section 'The Death Throes of the Commonwealth' (222–87). My
account of Snorri's life is indebted to Jón's tracing of the complex lines of relation
and causation that link Snorri's conflicts and disputes with his wider social and
political context.

11 Faulkes, Review of *Snorri Sturluson*, by Marlene Ciklamini, 306–7.

12 Bourdieu, *Outline of a Theory of Practice*, 85.

13 These and other terms used in this chapter are defined and discussed in greater
detail in chapter 3. Þórðr Gilsson was descended from Snorri goði through his
mother's line; neither *Ættartölur* nor *Sturlu saga* bother to give his paternal genealogy (see ch. 2 in each, pp. 52–3, 64). For more genealogical information for Snorri,
see *Ættartölur*, ch. 2, pp. 52–3; and Sigurður Nordal, *Snorri Sturluson*, 1–2.

14 Or, possibly, in late 1178. See Sigurður Nordal, *Snorri Sturluson*, 1, n. 1, for a discussion of the uncertainty over the date of Snorri's birth.

15 According to *Ættartölur*, ch. 2, p. 52.

16 This entire episode is narrated in *Sturlu saga*, chs 31–4, pp. 109–14.

17 Stefán Einarsson, *History of Icelandic Literature* 115. Oddi's school was founded
by Jón's uncle Eyjólfr, son of the renowned *goði* and priest Sæmundr Sigfússon
(d. 1133). Sæmundr is the first Icelander known to have studied in France, and was
likely Iceland's first prose author, though he wrote in Latin rather than Norse, and
none of his work has survived.

18 *Íslendinga saga*, ch. 10, p. 237.

19 'Sigvatr' is sometimes spelled 'Sighvatr' (including in the edition of *Sturlunga
saga* used), but I use the former spelling throughout.

20 *Íslendinga saga*, ch. 11, pp. 237–8.

21 This poem is now lost; our only evidence for this composition is that in *Skáldatal*
Snorri is listed as a poet of King Sverrir (*Edda Snorra Sturlusonar. Edda Snorronis
Sturlæi*, 3:255).

22 See Gunnar Karlsson, 'Stjórnmálamaðurinn Snorri,' 30.

23 *Íslendinga saga*, ch. 15, p. 240.

24 Ibid., p. 241: 'Snorri sendi flugumenn þrjá saman, ok kómu þeir engu fram.'

25 Ibid., ch. 16, pp. 241–2: 'Egil dreymði, at Egill Skalla-Grímsson kæmi at honum,
ok var mjök ófrýnligr. Hann mælti: "Ætlar Snorri, frændi várr, í brott heðan?" "Þat
er mælt," segir Egill. "Brott ætlar hann, ok þat gerir hann illa," segir draummaðrinn,

"því at lítt hafa menn setit yfir hlut várum Mýramanna, þá er oss tímgaðist, ok þurf-
ti hann eigi ofsjónum yfir þessu landi at sjá." Egill kvað vísu:

> Seggr sparir sverði at höggva,
>
> snjóhvítt es blóð líta,
>
> skæruöld getum skýra,
>
> skarpr brandr fekk mér landa,
>
> skarpr brandr fekk mér landa.
>
> Ok sneri þá í brott. En Egill vaknar.'

26 Ibid., p. 242: 'Gerðist hann þá höfðingi mikill, því at eigi skorti fé. Snorri var inn
mesti fjárgæzlumaðr.'

27 Ibid.: 'Snorri var … fjöllyndr ok átti börn við fleirum konum en Herdísi. Hann átti
son, er Órækja hét. Þuríðr, dóttir Halls Órækjusonar, var móðir hans. Hann átti ok
börn við Guðrúnu, dóttur Hreins Hermundarsonar, ok komst Ingibjörg ein ór
barnæsku þeira barna. Þórdís var dóttir Snorra. Oddný hét hennar móðir.'
Ættartölur, ch. 2, p. 52, repeats this information. Snorri separated from Herdís
around the time of his move to Reykjaholt, and lived alone until 1224 (see Sigurður
Nordal, *Snorri Sturluson*, 68).

28 *Íslendinga saga*, ch. 18, p. 243.

29 Ibid., chs 24–7, pp. 251–7.

30 The *allsherjargoði* held the ancestral *goðorð* of Þorsteinn Ingólfsson, son of Iceland's reputed first settler, Ingólfr Arnarson. His chief duty was to open and in
pagan times hallow the *alþing*; despite its mainly ceremonial function, a great deal
of prestige was associated with this position.

31 That Snorri sent poetry to King Ingi is attested in *Skáldatal* (*Edda Snorra Sturlusonar. Edda Snorronis Sturlæi*, 3:256, 264).

32 *Íslendinga saga*, ch. 34, p. 269.

33 Ibid., ch. 35, p. 271.

34 Ibid., p. 270. See also *Hákonar saga*, ch. 38, pp. 37–8, and, for Ormr and Jón's
deaths, ch. 55, pp. 49–50. For the most part, I use city place-names as given in the
original texts rather than their modern equivalents.

35 *Íslendinga saga*, ch. 35, pp. 271–2. It is unclear whether Snorri sent this poem to
Kristín before 1218 or first delivered it to her in person; Bjarni Einarsson argues
that the latter is more likely ('Andvaka,' 28).

36 *Íslendinga saga*, ch. 38, p. 277.

37 *Hákonar saga*, ch. 59, pp. 51–2.

38 *Íslendinga saga*, ch. 38, pp. 277–8; and *Hákonar saga*, ch. 59, pp. 51–2.

39 *Íslendinga saga*, ch. 38, p. 278: 'Snorri skyldi senda útan Jón, son sinn, ok skyldi
hann vera í gíslingu með jarli, at þat endist, sem mælt var.' As Jón Jóhannesson
points out, the title of *lendr maðr* ordinarily signified 'a liege vassal with a lease on
royal property' (*History of the Old Icelandic Commonwealth*, 242, n. 54); since,

however, King Hákon technically possessed no land in Iceland that he could bestow on Snorri, it is difficult to see how this was anything more than 'an honorific title,' unless 'some royal estates in Norway were conferred upon him' (ibid., 242) or Snorri delivered some of his property to the king which was then made back over to him. It is known that Hákon claimed some of Snorri's property as his own after the latter's death.

40 *Íslendinga saga*, ch. 38, p. 278.

41 Ibid., ch. 50, p. 300: 'Fár varð Snorri um, er hann frétti kvánfang Sturlu, ok þótti mönnum sem hann hefði til annars ætlat.'

42 Ibid., chs 67–71, pp. 322–8.

43 Ibid., ch. 79, p. 342: 'Nú tók at batna með þeim Snorra ok Sturlu, ok var Sturla löngum þá í Reykjaholti ok lagði mikinn hug á at láta rita sögubækr eftir bókum þeim, er Snorri setti saman.'

44 Ibid., ch. 85, p. 357: 'Þá er þeir Sturla riðu heim hjá virki, var talat um, hversu Snorra myndi líka víg þessi eða hvárt hann myndi yrkja um.'

45 Jón Jóhannesson, *History of the Old Icelandic Commonwealth*, 245.

46 *Íslendinga saga*, ch. 86, p. 359.

47 *Hákonar saga*, ch. 180, p. 158: 'Konungr hafði Sturlu í boði með sér, ok talaði við hann marga hluti.'

48 Ibid., ch. 180, p. 158: 'vildu at hann bætti fyrir íll-virki [þau] sem Órækja, son hans, hafði gört.' These developments are also narrated, with some differences, in *Íslendinga saga*, chs 112–14, pp. 389–94.

49 *Íslendinga saga*, ch. 115, pp. 394–7. In *Hákonar saga*, Sturla Þórðarson is much less forthcoming about this incident between Sturla Sigvatsson and Órækja; see ch. 180, pp. 158–9.

50 Jón Jóhannesson (*History of the Old Icelandic Commonwealth*, 248–9) has interpreted Sigvatr's decision, which was clearly disadvantageous to Sturlungar interests, as evidence that he did not support his son's wish to carry out the king's program in Iceland. Þorleifr was the son of Þórðr Böðvarsson, the brother of Guðný, who was the mother of Snorri, Þórðr, and Sigvatr.

51 *Hákonar saga*, ch. 180, p. 158; and *Íslendinga saga*, ch. 139, p. 344.

52 According to *Hákonar saga*, ch. 190, p. 169, 'no one had received that title before in Norway' (Þat tignar-nafn hafði eingi fengit fyrri í Noregi).

53 Sturla also deprived Gizurr of his *goðorð*s; see *Íslendinga saga*, ch. 129, pp. 412–16.

54 Ibid., ch. 138, pp. 430–9.

55 Ibid., ch. 139, p. 439: 'þeir Sturla hefði þau ráð gert, at hann skyldi vinna land undir Hákon konung, en konungr skyldi gera hann höfðingja yfir landinu.'

56 Ibid., ch. 143, p. 444: 'konungr bannaði þeim öllum Íslendingum at fara út á því sumri. Þeir sýndu Snorra bréfin, ok svarar hann svá: "Út vil ek."'

57 Sigurður Nordal, *Snorri Sturluson*, 10.

58 Sturla describes the scene when Snorri takes his leave of Skúli: 'There were then few men at the talk between the duke and Snorri. Arnfinnr Þjófsson and Óláfr hvítaskáld were with the duke, and Órækja and Þorleifr with Snorri. And that was Arnfinnr's story, that the duke gave to Snorri the title of jarl, and so has Styrmir the learned written: "the anniversary of the death of Snorri the secret jarl" – , but none of those Icelanders [who were there] declared that to be true' (Váru þá fáir menn við tal þeira hertogans ok Snorra. Arnfinnr Þjófsson ok Óláfr hvítaskáld váru með hertoganum, en Órækja ok Þorleifr með Snorra. Ok var þat sögn Arnfinns, at hertoginn gæfi Snorra jarlsnafn, ok svá hefir Styrmir inn fróði ritat: 'Ártíð Snorra fólgsnarjarls' – , en engi þeira Íslendinganna lét þat á sannast. *Íslendinga saga*, ch. 143, p. 444). For other interpretations of the term *fólgsnarjarl* see Hallan, 'Snorri fólgsnarjarl'; and Hermann Pálsson, 'Hirðskáld í spéspegli,' 165–8.

59 *Hákonar saga*, ch. 241, pp. 233–4.

60 *Íslendinga saga*, ch. 151, p. 453: 'Var þar á, at Gizurr skyldi Snorra láta útan fara, hvárt er honum þætti ljúft eða leitt, eða drepa hann at öðrum kosti fyrir þat, er hann hafði farit út í banni konungs. Kallaði Hákon konungr Snorra landráðamann við sik. Sagði Gizurr, at hann vildi með engu móti brjóta bréf konungs, en kveðst vita, at Snorri myndi eigi ónauðigr útan fara.' On the dealings of Hallveig's sons with Snorri and Gizurr, see ibid., ch. 149, p. 452.

61 Ibid., ch. 151, p. 454: 'Eftir þat urðu þeir varir við, hvar Snorri var. Ok gengu þeir í kjallarann Markús Marðarson, Símon knútr, Árni beiskr, Þorsteinn Guðinason, Þórarinn Ásgrímsson. Símon knútr bað Árna höggva hann. "Eigi skal höggva," sagði Snorri. "Högg þú," sagði Símon. "Eigi skal höggva," sagði Snorri. Eftir þat veitti Árni honum banasár, ok báðir þeir Þorsteinn unnu á honum.' For an interesting analysis of Snorri's last words, see Lýður Björnsson, 'Eigi skal höggva.' Sturla gives a much briefer account of Snorri's death in *Hákonar saga*, ch. 243, p. 237.

62 Faulkes, Review of *Snorri Sturluson*, by Marlene Ciklamini, 307.

63 'Bók þessi heitir Edda. Hana hefir saman setta Snorri Sturluson eptir þeim hætti sem hér er skipat. Er fyrst frá Ásum ok Ymi, þar næst Skáldskaparmál ok heiti margra hluta, síðast Háttatal er Snorri hefir ort um Hákon konung ok Skúla hertuga.' Original quoted from Faulkes, introduction to *Edda: Prologue and Gylfaginning*, xiii. *Konungsbók* or *Codex Regius*, the basis of nearly all modern editions and translations of the *Edda*, is missing its first page, and so any information it may have provided regarding the text's producer is now lost. The beginning of the paper manuscript *Codex Trajectinus* (c. 1595), which is closely related to *Konungsbók*, is also missing. The third medieval manuscript containing the whole *Edda*, *Ormsbók* or *Codex Wormianus*, says nothing about the producer of the work as a whole, but the prologue to the grammatical treatises in this manuscript contains an apparent reference to Snorri as author of the prose commentary to *Háttatal*. Finally, the

manuscript AM 748 Ib 4to, compiled c. 1300–25, refers to Snorri's collection of skaldic verses that make up a large part of *Skáldskaparmál*. For a detailed description of the various ascriptions of parts of the *Edda* to Snorri, see Ólafur Halldórsson, 'Sagnaritun Snorra Sturlusonar,' 115–18.

64 The first is the meaning assigned to this term in relation to these passages by Richard Cleasby and Guðbrandur Vigfússon in their *Icelandic-English Dictionary* (524). For the second sense, see Guðrún Nordal, *Tools of Literacy*, 53. Lars Lönnroth has been the most persistent advocate of the third option; see *European Sources of Icelandic Saga-Writing*, 14–15.

65 On evidence for Snorri's authorship of *Heimskringla*, see Jakob Benediktsson, 'Hvar var Snorri nefndur höfundur Heimskringlu?'; Ólafur Halldórsson, 'Sagnaritun Snorra Sturlusonar,' 119–22; and Sigurður Nordal, *Snorri Sturluson*, 24–5. Snorri's authorship of *Heimskringla* and this text's traditional dating have been challenged in several articles by Alan J. Berger: see 'Sagas of Harald Fairhair,' '*Heimskringla* and the Compilations,' and '*Heimskringla* is an abbreviation of *Hulda-Hrokkinskinna*.' Nevertheless, most continue to accept Snorri's responsibility for this compilation; see, for example, Clunies Ross, *History of Old Norse Poetry*, 159; and Whaley, *Heimskringla: An Introduction*, 13–19.

66 Even so, nearly everyone who has examined this question to any extent has leaned towards ascribing *Egils saga* to Snorri. See, for example, Sigurður Nordal, 'Snorri Sturluson,' 29; Björn Magnússon Ólsen, 'Er Snorri Sturluson höfundur Egilssögu?'; Hallberg, *Snorri Sturluson och Egils saga Skallagrímssonar*; Vésteinn Ólason, 'Er Snorri höfundur Egils sögu?'; Jónas Kristjánsson, 'Egilssaga og konungasögur'; West, 'Snorri Sturluson and *Egils saga*'; and Torfi H. Tulinius, *Skáldið í skriftinni*. Though it is not included in this book, the final chapter of my dissertation addresses at length the question of Snorri's authorship of *Heimskringla* and *Egils saga*, and discusses the portraits of skalds offered in these texts and their possible motivations. I hope to revise this chapter for future publication.

67 Steblin-Kamenskij, *Saga Mind*, 54–5.

68 As Peter Foote notes, *setja saman* is most often used when the author being referred to 'would not be credited with invention' ('Sagnaskemtan: Reykjahólar 1119,' 72, n. 16).

69 Steblin-Kamenskij, *Saga Mind*, 52.

70 Clunies Ross, '*Mikill Skynsemi er at Rifja Vandliga þat Upp*,' 75.

71 Ibid.

72 Lindow, 'Mythology and Mythography,' 34.

73 Wessén, introduction to *Codex Regius of the Younger Edda*.

74 Faulkes, introduction to *Edda: Prologue and Gylfaginning*, xv; see also Clunies Ross, *History of Old Norse Poetry*, 161, 170.

75 The earlier date is suggested by Sigurður Nordal ('formáli' to *Egils Saga Skalla-grímssonar*, xciii; and 'Snorri Sturluson,' 27). Jónas Kristjánsson ('Egilssaga og konungasögur'), Berman (*'Egils Saga* and *Heimskringla'*), and Torfi H. Tulinius (*Matter of the North*, 234–89) have argued for the later date. Scholars have also speculated on occasion about Snorri's involvement in the collection of the so-called *Poetic Edda*, and Peter Hallberg has even argued that he composed one of them ('Om *Þrymskviða'*). Questions concerning Snorri's possible involvement with the eddic poems are not raised in this book.

76 Sigurður Nordal, 'Snorri Sturluson,' 23: 'þau 30 ár, sem hann átti heima í Reykholti og fekk að sitja þar í góðum friði, 1206–1236.'

3 Snorri at Home

1 Miller, *Bloodtaking and Peacemaking*, 13.

2 The most important sources for the period of Iceland's settlement are Ari Þorgilsson's *Íslendingabók* (c. 1122–3), and the anonymous *Landnámabók* (early 1100s).

3 'Commonwealth' is a common shorthand designation for Icelandic society from 870 to 1264. Although few are entirely satisfied with it, most find it preferable to more anachronistic labels such as 'freestate' or 'republic'; see Gísli Pálsson, *Textual Life of Savants*, 88; and Miller, *Bloodtaking and Peacemaking*, 312, n. 6.

4 Though the origin and meaning of the term have long been contested, it is generally agreed that *goði* derives from the word for deity, *goð*, and that prior to and for some time after Iceland's conversion *goðar* performed secular and religious duties.

5 *Íslendingabók*, ch. 10, pp. 55–7.

6 On the case that precipitated this modification, see ibid., ch. 5, pp. 50–1, and discussions in Byock, *Medieval Iceland*, 65; and Jón Jóhannesson, *History of the Old Icelandic Commonwealth*, 49–50. That quarter-courts were established at the same time as quarters is an assumption.

7 For discussion of original versus new *goðorð*s, see Barði Guðmundsson, 'Goðorð forn og ný.'

8 On the fifth-court, see Jón Jóhannesson, *History of the Old Icelandic Commonwealth*, 66–74.

9 Useful charts illustrating the post-1005 organization of the commonwealth's political/legal structure are found in Hastrup, *Culture and History*, 129; and Gunnar Karlsson, *History of Iceland*, 23.

10 See the medieval Icelandic law collection, *Grágás* Ia, ch. 89, p. 159; and II, p. 320.

11 Miller, *Bloodtaking and Peacemaking*, 219.

12 See Byock, *Medieval Iceland*, 165–7.

13 It was not, of course, necessary that one's advocate be a *goði* – the most famous
   (literary) example of a non-chieftain advocate is Njáll Þorgeirsson of *Njáls saga*
   (*Brennu-Njáls saga*) – but much of the time they were, and in the following discussion I will speak of advocacy strictly as a service performed by *goðar*.

14 *Sómi* and *sæmð* (or *sæmd*) are both translated as 'honour' in Cleasby and
   Guðbrandur Vigfússon's *Icelandic-English Dictionary*. As Miller points out, *sæmð*
   when plural can also refer to 'compensation payment,' an extension of meaning
   that illustrates the close connection between material outcomes of cases and the
   defence of one's honour (*Bloodtaking and Peacemaking*, 303). Of the three terms,
   virðing had the widest semantic range, encompassing the concrete sense of 'a valuation, taxing,' alongside those of 'worship, reputation, honour ... opinion, esteem'
   (Cleasby and Guðbrandur Vigfússon, *Icelandic-English Dictionary*, 710).

15 Miller, *Bloodtaking and Peacemaking*, 29.

16 *Görð* and *Jafnaðardómr* were terms for arbitration, while arbitrators were called
   görðamenn and *sáttarmenn* or *sættarmenn*; see Byock, *Feud*, 102, 219.

17 'Those desiring to dispose of a claim by compensation were for the most part con-
   strained to go to arbitration since compensation, according to the saga evidence,
   did not appear to have been a remedy available at law in any other than minor property claims' (Miller, *Bloodtaking and Peacemaking*, 263).

18 On *goðar*'s potential to gain property and land in return for mediation see Byock,
   Medieval Iceland, 165–82, and *Feud*, 43, 245–58; Bagge, *Society and Politics*, 78;
   and Miller, *Bloodtaking and Peacemaking*, 26, 239–41. The conclusions of such
   scholars that material gains for *goðar* from legal activities were substantial
   has been challenged; see Jón Viðar Sigurðsson, *Chieftains and Power*, 104; and
   Samson, '*Goðar*: Democrats or Despots?'

19 Miller, *Bloodtaking and Peacemaking*, 29.

20 Bourdieu, *Outline of a Theory of Practice*, 192.

21 Byock, *Medieval Iceland*, 125.

22 Many have stressed the importance attached to form and procedure in medieval
   Icelandic legal practice: see, for example, Sigurður Nordal, *Icelandic Culture*,
   83–6; and Byock, *Feud*, 216. A passage from *Grágás* suggests that in close cases
   those who presented their case more correctly ought to triumph (*Grágás* Ia, ch. 47,
   p. 83).

23 Bourdieu, *Language and Symbolic Power*, 56.

24 As Durrenberger writes, 'the Alþing was not primarily a legal institution but an
   arena for building coalitions, for making, breaking, and testing connections'
   (*Dynamics of Medieval Iceland*, 53).

25 Tranter, *Sturlunga Saga*, 59.

26 As Gunnar Karlsson writes: 'Sturla Þórðarson ... was a *goði* of this old style, and
   his saga is one of our best sources concerning how the power of *goðar* stood before

the days of the consolidation of authority and the rule of the *stórhöfðingjar*' (Sturla
Þórðarson … var goði af þessari fornu gerð, og saga hans er ein besta heimild
okkar um hvernig goðaveldinu var háttað fyrir daga valdasameiningar og
stórhöfðingjaveldis) ('Stjórnmálamaðurinn Snorri,' 28).

27 *Sturlu saga*, chs 4–5, pp. 65–8.

28 Ibid., ch. 13, p. 79: 'Einarr lézt vilja, at eigi ynni þeir oft á þingmönnum hans.'

29 Ibid., ch. 27, p. 102: 'Ok réðst Álfr þá at þingfesti undir Sturlu.'

30 Tranter, *Sturlunga Saga*, 105.

31 *Sturlu saga*, ch. 9, pp. 72–3.

32 Ibid., pp. 74–5: 'Sturla kvað eigi mundu þykkja haldit til jafns við Einar, ef hann
sæti heima ok hæði eigi féránsdóma, en kvað vant at vita, hvárir þar bæri hæra
hlut.'

33 Ibid., ch. 10, p. 75: 'at biskup ynni fimmtardómseið, at hann gerði jafnsætti.'

34 Ibid.: 'Svá virði ek eið biskups sem páskamessu. Má ek þat eigi til fjár meta, en
sómi er oss þat. En flestir munu kalla gjöldin eigi mikil ok gerðir eigi fésamar.'

35 See Byock, *Feud*, 155–60.

36 *Sturlu saga*, ch. 31, p. 109: 'Hví skal ek eigi gera þik þeim líkastan, er þú vill
líkastr vera, – en þar er Óðinn?'

37 Ibid., ch. 32, p. 111: 'þótti öllum mönnum mikil undr, er honum kom í hug at kveða
slíkt upp.'

38 For a medieval and a modern judgment, see *Sturlu saga*, ch. 29, p. 104; and Gunnar
Karlsson, 'Stjórnmálamaðurinn Snorri,' 29. Jón had found cause to intervene in
Sturla's affairs on a previous occasion; see *Sturlu saga*, ch. 29, pp. 103–5.

39 *Sturlu saga*, ch. 33, p. 112: 'Jón kvað með miklum ákafa farit á hendr Páli, en lét
eigi sama at etjast á við kennimenn gamla ok göfga ríkum höfðingjum.'

40 Ibid.

41 Foote, '*Sturlusaga* and Its Background,' 119.

42 *Sturlu saga*, ch. 34, p. 113: 'var sætzt á málit ok selt mér sjálfdæmi af Páli. En nú eru
sóttir at inir æðstu menn á Íslandi, at þetta mál skyli nú í gerð leggja, er áðr kom í
sjálfdæmi. Nú ef dæmi finnast til, at svá hafi menn fyrr gert, þá væri á at líta. En þeir
menn, er sik binda nú við málit, – nefni ek fyrst til þess Jón Loftsson, er dýrstr maðr
er á landi þessu ok allir skjóta sínum málaferlum til, – þá veit eigi ek, hvárt annat er
nú virðingar vænna en reyna, hvern sóma hann vill minn gera. Nú kann vera, at ek
hafa eigi vit til at sjá mér hlut til handa, en vilja mynda ek halda sæmð minni.'

43 Ibid.: 'Jón kvað Sturlu vitrliga mæla ok sjá fyrir margra hönd. "En fégjöld," segir
Jón, "af Páls hendi munu til vægðar snúast, þvi at þau váru hátt reist."'

44 *Laxdæla saga*, ch. 27, p. 75: 'ok er sá kallaðr æ minni maðr, er öðrum fóstrar barn.'

45 Ciklamini, *Snorri Sturluson*, 19.

46 On Sturla's fostering, see *Sturlu saga*, ch. 2, p. 64. Whether any of Snorri's siblings
were fostered is uncertain. Since, however, at the time of Sturla's death, his sons

Þórðr, aged eighteen, and Sigvatr, aged thirteen, 'were both at home' (váru þeir heima báðir. *Íslendinga saga*, ch. 1, p. 229), it seems unlikely that either was raised elsewhere. Parts of the following section, particularly my discussion of Snorri's and his brothers' divergent habitus, bear similarity to Torfi H. Tulinius's analyses in 'Capital, Field, Illusio,' and *Skáldið í skriftinni*, 132–65.

47 Ciklamini, *Snorri Sturluson*, 19; and Foote, '*Sturlusaga* and Its Background,' 230–1. For similar statements, see Hallberg, *Icelandic Saga*, 20; Meulengracht Sørensen, *Saga and Society*, 70; and Clunies Ross, *History of Old Norse Poetry*, 158.

48 Bourdieu, *Distinction*, 65–74.

49 Ciklamini, *Snorri Sturluson*, 20.

50 *Íslendinga saga*, ch. 10, p. 237.

51 Ibid., ch. 11, pp. 237–8: 'Sæmundr sendi Snorra Sturluson til Borgarfjarðar at kveðja upp þingmenn sína, er Jón, faðir hans, hafði átt, bæði marga ok góða bændr.'

52 Ibid., p. 238: 'Sæmundr hafði virðing af málum þessum. Kolbeini Tumasyni líkaði illa þessar málalyktir, en Sighvati verr.'

53 Bourdieu, *Rules of Art*, 388, n. 72.

54 *Íslendinga saga*, chs 6, 10, pp. 234, 237. A hundred approximated one cow's worth of wealth.

55 These families were, with major representatives and areas of influence, the following: 1) Svínfellingar (Sigurðr Ormsson, Ormr Jónsson; based in the east, but with *goðorð*s in the north); 2) Haukdælir (Þorvaldr Gizurarson, Gizurr and Björn Þorvaldssynir; the Árnessþing district in the southwest); 3) Vatnsfirðingar (Þorvaldr Snorrason; west quarter); 4) Ásbirningar (Kolbeinn Tumason, Kolbeinn ungi Arnórsson; Skagafjörðr in the north); 5) Oddaverjar (Jón Loptsson, Sæmundr and Páll Jónssynir; dominated the Rangarþing district of the south/southeast, with influence in Borgarfjörðr and Vestfirðir); and 6) Sturlungar (Snorri, Þórðr, and Sigvatr Sturlusynir; their power was initially centred in Hvammr, but spread over the entire west and into the north quarter). See further Gunnar Karlsson, *History of Iceland*, 72–8; and Jón Jóhannesson, *History of the Old Icelandic Commonwealth*, 230–6.

56 A sign that *goðar* were becoming increasingly territorial in the Sturlung age is contemporary sources' use of the term *ríki* to describe their spheres of influence. Usually translated as 'domain' or 'realm,' this term holds stronger geographical connotations than *goðorð*.

57 Jón Jóhannesson, *History of the Old Icelandic Commonwealth*, 226.

58 See Jón Viðar Sigurðsson, *Chieftains and Power*, 76–7.

59 Tranter, *Sturlunga Saga*, 25.

60 Miller, *Bloodtaking and Peacemaking*, 230.

61 While the sources are not explicit on this point, scholars agree that Snorri inherited the Mýramannagoðorð along with Bersi's other property in 1202. On Snorri's

reception of half of the Lundarmannagoðorð, see *Íslendinga saga*, ch. 15, p. 240, and on the Æverlingagoðorð, ibid., ch. 18, p. 243. Sturla also does not explicitly state that Snorri took possession of the Reykhyltingsgoðorð when he purchased the estate, though this too is generally assumed (ibid., ch. 16, p. 241). As for possible ownership of additional *goðorð*s, it is uncertain whether Snorri ever took over the two remaining in the Þverárþing district, the centre of his *ríki*, or the rest of those in which he owned partial shares; as Gunnar Karlsson observes, however, those who otherwise owned these *goðorð*s were in any case usually Snorri's followers ('Stjórnmálamaðurinn Snorri,' 29–30, 34).

62 On locations of Snorri's *goðorð*s, see Jón Jóhannesson, *History of the Old Icelandic Commonwealth*, 234.

63 *Grágás* Ia, ch. 84, pp. 141–2, and II, p. 278. Most believe this provision to have been in force in the early 1200s.

64 *Íslendinga saga*, ch. 33, p. 263: 'En Snorri Sturluson átti flesta þingmenn í hvárra tveggja heraði, ok þótti mönnum til hans koma at sætta þá.'

65 Ibid.: 'Snorri hét á þá, at þeir skyldi eigi berjast. Engi hirði, hvat er hann sagði. Þá gekk Þorljótr frá Bretalæk til Snorra ok bað hann milli ganga. Snorri kveðst eigi hafa lið til þess við heimsku þeira ok ákafa. Þorljótr veitti Snorra hörð orð. Síðan hljóp Þorljótr millum hrossana ok leysti ok rak millum þeira.'

66 Sigurður Nordal, *Snorri Sturluson*, 53.

67 *Íslendinga saga*, ch. 33, p. 264: 'Miðfirðingar eggjuðu þá Snorra til eftirreiðar, ok veitti Teitr honum mikit ámæli, er hann vildi eigi auka vandræði þeira.'

68 Ibid.: 'Snorri fekk sætta Miðfirðinga ok Víðdæli ok gerði um sakar allar, er gerzt höfðu.'

69 Helgi Þorláksson, 'Snorri Sturluson og Oddaverjar,' 71.

70 *Íslendinga saga*, ch. 34, p. 268: 'hefði enn einn virðing af málum þessum … "Hvat tjóir slíkt at mæla, því at bræðr þessir draga sik svá fram, at nær engir menn halda sik til fulls við þá."'

71 Ibid.: 'Eftir þetta fóru menn af þingi, ok Snorra líkaði illa.'

72 Ibid.: 'En hon var í þingi með Magnúsi, ok ætlaði hann sér fé hennar, en skipta frændum hennar til handa slíkt, sem honum sýndist.'

73 Ibid.: 'En er hann kom sunnan, hafði hann með sér þann mann, er Koðrán hét, strák einn, ok kallaði Snorri þann erfingja Jórunnar, ok tók hann þat fémál af Koðráni.'

74 Ibid: 'Ok stefndi Snorri Magnúsi skóggangsstefnu til Þverárþings. Magnús kallaðist þar útanþingsmaðr. En Snorri bað hann þar vörn fram færa. Eftir þat fór Snorri heim ok fór málum sínum fram á Þverárþingi, ok varð Magnús sekr skógarmaðr.'

75 Ibid., p. 269: 'Snorri reið upp með sex hundruð manna, ok váru átta tigir Austmanna í flokki hans alskjaldaðir. Bræðr hans váru þar báðir með miklu liði.' The text does not specify to whom rent was to be paid, but given the honour this case is said to have given Snorri (see next note), this is the logical conclusion.

76 Ibid.: 'Snorri hafði virðing af málum þessum. Ok í þessum málum gekk virðing hans við mest hér á landi.'

77 Helgi Þorláksson, 'Snorri Sturluson og Oddaverjar,' 77.

78 See Jón Jóhannesson, *History of the Old Icelandic Commonwealth*, 229–30; and Sigurður Nordal, *Snorri Sturluson*, 72.

79 *Íslendinga saga*, ch. 53, p. 304: 'hafði Snorri heim Hallveigu Ormsdóttur ok gerði við hana helmingarfélag, en tekit til varðveizlu fé sona hennar, Klængs ok Orms, átta hundruð hundraða. Hafði Snorri þá miklu meira fé en engi annarra á Íslandi.'

80 Torfi Tulinius suggests that Snorri was actually trying to marry Solveig to Jón murtr, and that she was of such interest to the Sturlungar mainly because of her relation through her father to Norwegian royalty (*Skáldið í skriftinni*, 137–9), though he admits that neither of these motives is explicit in the sources (ibid., 138).

81 Snorri in fact at one point blocked Jón from marrying (*Íslendinga saga*, ch. 75, p. 335); on Órækja, see ibid., ch. 86, pp. 358–9.

82 See Jón Jóhannesson, *History of the Old Icelandic Commonwealth*, 244.

83 Ibid., 246.

84 *Íslendinga saga*, ch. 64, pp. 319–20: 'Þat var eitt kveld, er Snorri sat í laugu, at talat var um höfðingja. Sögðu menn, at þá var engi höfðingi slíkr sem Snorri ok þá mátti engi höfðingi keppa við hann fyrir sakir mægða þeira, er hann átti. Snorri sannaði þat, at mágar hans væri eigi smámenni. Sturla Bárðarson hafði haldit vörð yfir lauginni, ok leiddi hann Snorri heim, ok skaut hann fram stöku þessi, svá at Snorri heyrði:

> Eiguð áþekkt mægi
> orðvitr sem gat forðum,
> – ójafnaðr gefsk jafnan
> illa – , Hleiðrar stillir.'

Hrólfr kraki, a semi-legendary figure, was betrayed and killed by a brother-in-law.

85 Ibid., ch. 86, p. 359: 'Snorri skyldi eiga helming goðorða þeira, er Kolbeinn átti at réttu, en Kolbeinn skyldi með fara ok veita Snorra á þingum.'

86 Aside from Einarr, the only grandchild of Snorri mentioned is Ingibjörg's and Gizurr's son, who, however, died in infancy (ibid.).

87 Miller, *Bloodtaking and Peacemaking*, 31.

88 This fine was tied for first place with that paid for the killing of Hallr Kleppjárnsson in 1213 (*Íslendinga saga*, ch. 29, pp. 258–9). Although by law the same fine, one *mörk*, was to have been assessed for any freeman's killing (*Grágás* Ia, ch. 88, p. 155), sums actually stipulated and paid varied widely according to the social standing of the persons involved.

89 Sigurður Nordal, *Snorri Sturluson*, 65, 63, 48: 'Jón sat á ættleifð forfeðra sinna, vald hans á þingi og í heraði stóð á gömlum merg, þingmenn hans voru fæddir fylgismenn hans og allur landslýður viðurkendi ríki Oddaverja. Jón var borinn til

valda, sem hann gat vel unað við'; 'En Snorri átti í eðli sínu framgirni, sem aldrei gat fengið fulla fróun'; 'Viðleitni hans að auka auð sinn og ríki er aðalefni alls þess, sem frá honum er sagt.'

90 See *Íslendinga saga*, chs 38–9, 73, 85, pp. 277–84, 330–2, 352–8.

4 Snorri Abroad

1 According to *Íslendinga saga*, it was not until after Snorri took control of Hallveig's wealth in 1224 that he had 'miklu meira fé en engi annarra á Íslandi' (ch. 53, p. 304).

2 See Jón Jóhannesson, *History of the Old Icelandic Commonwealth*, 222, 305–10; and Byock, *Feud*, 33–4.

3 Arguably, *riddarasögur*, or 'sagas of knights,' originated in Norway, where translations of French romances began in the 1220s; these are discussed in chapter 5. On the Norwegian synoptics, texts of the 1100s and (perhaps) early 1200s that, while not themselves sagas, may have inspired kings' sagas, see p. 198, n. 11; additionally, it is possible that one *konungasögur* collection, *Fagrskinna* (c. 1220), was produced by a Norwegian; for the debate, see Indrebø, *Fagrskinna*, 273–7; Jakobsen, 'Om Fagrskinna-forfattern'; and Bjarni Einarsson, 'formáli' to *Ágrip af Nóregskonunga sögum*, cxxvi–cxxx.

4 Bourdieu, *Distinction*, esp. 114–43.

5 Ibid., 116, 120.

6 Bourdieu, from lecture 'The Field of Power,' presented at the University of Wisconsin, Madison in April, 1989, quoted in Bourdieu and Wacquant, *Invitation to Reflexive Sociology*, 76, n. 16.

7 Saxo Grammaticus, *Gesta Danorum*, 3: 'Nec Tylensium industria silencio oblitteranda: qui cum ob natiuam soli sterilitatem luxurie nutrimentis carentes, officia continue sobrietatis exerceant, omniaque uite momenta ad excolendam alienorum operum noticiam conferre soleant, inopiam ingenio pensant. Cunctarum quippe nacionum res gestas cognosse memorieque mandare, uoluptatis loco reputant: non minoris glorie iudicantes alienas uirtutes disserere, quam proprias exhibere.' Translation from Henry Goddard Leach, *Angevin Britain and Scandinavia*, 129.

8 Clunies Ross, introduction to *Old Icelandic Literature and Society*, 1.

9 Schier, 'Iceland and the Rise of Literature,' 169–70.

10 Bourdieu, *Rules of Art*, 227.

11 'Skaldic' is the usual English equivalent for Icelandic *dróttkvæði*; both terms are used to differentiate a style of Norse poetry from another known as 'eddic' or 'eddaic.' These are modern coinages with no equivalents in Old Norse, which only used terms for poetry in general, such as *skáldskapr* and *bragr* (see Tranter, *Clavis Metrica*, 105).

12 For discussions of the poet and god, see Sigurður Nordal, *Icelandic Culture*, 187–8; and Turville-Petre, *Myth and Religion of the North*, 185–6, and *Scaldic Poetry*, xxiv–xxvi. On the full-blown appearance of skaldic verse's distinguishing features in Bragi's work, see Frank, *Old Norse Court Poetry*, 22; Gade, *Structure of Old Norse* Dróttkvætt, 3; Hollander, *Skalds*, 4; Kuhn, *Das Dróttkvætt*, 275–6; and Turville-Petre, *Origins of Icelandic Literature*, 34–5.

13 Of course, this does not mean that Norwegians no longer produced skaldic verse of any sort. Jónas Kristjánsson summarizes the evidence for skaldic activity in Norway after the mid-900s, none of which, however, points to court poetry (*Eddas and Sagas*, 97–8). Kari Ellen Gade has argued for a Norwegian presence among court skalds of later centuries, but the only evidence she points to is that some are not explicitly said to be Icelandic ('Poetry and Its Changing Importance,' 82 and 91, n. 15). Surveys of ninth- and tenth-century Norwegian skalds and their work include Hallberg, *Old Icelandic Poetry*; Hollander, *Skalds*; Kuhn, *Das Dróttkvætt*, 273–84; Reichardt, *Studien zu den Skalden*; and de Vries, *Altnordische Literaturgeschichte*, 1:99–208.

14 For an example of the first, see Hollander, *Skalds*, 4–5; for the second, see Sigurður Nordal, *Icelandic Culture*, 199. Among those who note this change without offering an explanation are Faulkes, introduction to *Edda* translation, xii–xiii; Frank, *Old Norse Court Poetry*, 23; Kuhn, *Das Dróttkvætt*, 284–5; and Turville-Petre, *Origins of Icelandic Literature*, 43.

15 Clunies Ross, 'Cognitive Approach to Scaldic Poetics,' 281.

16 Tranter, *Clavis Metrica*, 205. It should be noted that here, as throughout this book, Tranter confusingly uses the term 'Icelandic' to refer to all skaldic poets and poetic activity in the Middle Ages, even when discussing periods predating the existence of Icelandic society (ibid., 2).

17 Ibid., 205, 206.

18 Ström, 'Poetry as an Instrument of Propaganda,' 446.

19 Bourdieu, *Language and Symbolic Power*, 55 (original emphasis).

20 Ibid., 66.

21 Ibid., 76 (original emphasis). Of course, not only the poet but also the subject of his poetry profited when his praise was cast in an elaborate form. As Meulengracht Sørensen observes, 'It was a matter of prestige, both for the skald and for the king he served, to demonstrate the greatest possible control of the skaldic language' (*Saga and Society*, 89).

22 Edwards, 'Clause Arrangement in Skaldic Poetry,' 123; Hollander, *Skalds*, 20 (original emphasis); and Frank, *Old Norse Court Poetry*, 28, 33.

23 Much of what I describe here must be viewed as conventions rather than ironclad rules. Also, the temporal development of skaldic verse is lost in my brief overview. There is no lack of discussions of the formal qualities of skaldic verse and *dróttkvætt*; some of the most thorough include Einar Ól. Sveinsson, 'Dróttkvæða

þáttur'; Frank, *Old Norse Court Poetry*, 33–71; Gade, *Structure of Old Norse Dróttkvætt*, 12–51; Kuhn, *Das Dróttkvætt*, 33–214; Hollander, *Skalds*, 1–24; Turville-Petre, *Scaldic Poetry*, xi–lxvi; de Vries, *Altnordische Literaturgeschichte*, 1:99–121; and Clunies Ross, *History of Old Norse Poetry*, 23–4.

24 To make the characteristics of *dróttkvætt* clear I here adapt Hollander's helpful sample verse, in which he has marked all the pertinent features: 'Below is printed a typical *dróttkvætt* stanza – with rimes italicized, alliteration shown by bold type ... [all syllables that are marked are also stressed]

> **J***ór* rennr **a**ptansk*œ*ru
> **a**llsv*a*ngr gotur l*a*ng*a*r,
> v*öll* kná **h**ófr til **h**a*ll*ar
> **h**öfum l*í*tinn dag sl*í*ta;
> nú's, þat's **b**l*akk*r of **b**e*kk*i
> **b**e*rr* mik Dönum f*err*i;
> f*ák*r laust **d**rengs i **d***ík*i
> **d**œgr mœtask nú f*œt*i.'

Skalds, 10. The citation is st. 11 of Sigvatr Þórðarson's *Austrfaravísur*, for which see *Den norsk-islandske skjaldedigtning*, IB:220–5.

25 According to Peter Foote and David M. Wilson, 'the meaning of this name is not entirely certain. The best suggestion is that it got the name because such a poem was *drepit stefjum*, "fitted with refrains"' (*Viking Achievement*, 328; see also Gade, *Structure of Old Norse Dróttkvætt*, 246, n. 6).

26 See Edwards, 'Clause Arrangement in Skaldic Poetry,' 164.

27 For a full discussion of *heiti*, see Einar Ól. Sveinsson, 'Dróttkvæða þáttur,' 37–40. The terms *heiti* and *kenningar* may both have been invented by Snorri for use in his *Edda*. Uses of *heiti* are difficult to illustrate in translation; nevertheless, an example would be the substitution of the strictly poetic terms *hjaldr* or *storð* for the prosaic Norse word for battle, *orrosta*.

28 Adapted from Frank, *Old Norse Court Poetry*, 42.

29 Gade, *Structure of Old Norse Dróttkvætt*, 2.

30 For the first, see Meissner, *Die Kenningar der Skalden*, 201; the second is taken from *Skáldskaparmál* 48 (Snorri Sturluson, *Edda: Skáldskaparmál*, p. 66; all references to *Skáldskaparmál* are to volume 1).

31 Hollander, *Skalds*, 13.

32 The first kenning, *móðakarn*, is quoted from Einar Ól. Sveinsson, 'Dróttkvæða þáttur,' 49, the second, *unndýrs runnr*, from *Skáldskaparmál* 49, p. 68.

33 Einar Ól. Sveinsson, 'Dróttkvæða þáttur,' 49: 'eru allir hlutir aðrir en þeir sýnast eða segjast vera.'

34 Bourdieu, *Language and Symbolic Power*, 140.

35 Ibid., 141.

36 For examples of scholars who insist on the comprehensibility of skalds' verse to contemporaries and consumers, see Meulengracht Sørensen, *Saga and Society*, 89; and Kock, 'Skaldendichtung und Undeutlichkeit?' 79.

37 Lincoln, *Authority*, 4.

38 Bourdieu, *Distinction*, 323; and Lincoln, 'Culture,' 412.

39 Frank, 'Skaldic Poetry,' 183.

40 Fidjestøl, 'The Kenning System,' in *Selected Papers*, 41.

41 Lincoln, *Authority*, 10.

42 Bagge, *Society and Politics*, 31.

43 Fidjestøl, 'The King's Skald from Kvinesdal,' in *Selected Papers*, 77.

44 *Hávamál* st. 76, in *Edda. Die Lieder des Codex Regius*, p. 28: 'Deyr fé, deyia frændr, deyr siálfr it sama; en orztírr deyr aldregi, hveim er sér góðan getr.'

45 See Detienne, *Masters of Truth*, 43–8.

46 Ibid., 16, 74–5.

47 For a chart and discussion of all kennings for poetry in the extant skaldic corpus, see Kreutzer, *Die Dichtungslehre der Skalden*, 112–17; for *Hávamál*, see stt. 13–14, 104–10, and 140, in *Edda. Die Lieder des Codex Regius*, pp. 19, 33–4, 40.

48 Turville-Petre, *Origins of Icelandic Literature*, 38; see also Lindow, 'Mythology and Mythography,' 28.

49 Differentiation of eddic from skaldic verse according to these qualities is utterly conventional, though most caution against regarding the distinction as too absolute. Probably the clearest native criteria for generic differentiation is whether or not a poem is ascribed to a named author. As Carol Clover writes: 'The fact that men and women attached their names to skaldic poetry but retained anonymity in their Eddic verse is already a strong argument for the claim that the two types of poetic sensibility were distinct in the minds of the practitioners as far back as our records take us' ('Skaldic Sensibility,' 63).

50 See ibid., 63, n. 2; Fidjestøl, 'Icelandic Sagas and Poems on Princes,' in *Selected Papers*, 232–3; Frank, 'Scaldic Poetry,' 159–60; Gade, 'Poetry and Its Changing Importance,' 65; Lindow, 'Riddles, Kennings, and the Complexity of Skaldic Poetry,' 320 (Lindow seems later to have rethought his position on this issue, however; see the next note); and Skard, *Classical Tradition in Norway*, 23.

51 Lindow notes two telling contradictions: first, although Óðinn is the patron of poets no skaldic poems are expressly dedicated to this god; second, although eddic poetry is supposed to be the art form of the farmer and commoner, the favourite god of this class, Þórr, is often portrayed negatively in extant eddic compositions ('Mythology and Mythography,' 32–3).

52 See Fidjestøl, 'Icelandic Sagas and Poems on Princes,' in *Selected Papers*, 32; Fidjestøl, 'Skaldic Stanzas in Saga-Prose,' ibid., 260; and Steblin-Kamenskij, 'Attempt at a Semantic Approach,' 34.

53 This same point has been made by Tranter, 'Medieval Icelandic *artes poeticae*,' 140–1; see also Frank, *Old Norse Court Poetry*, 26, and 'Skaldic Poetry,' 180; Sigrún Davíðsdóttir, 'Old Norse Court Poetry,' 192–3; and Meulengracht Sørensen, *Saga and Society*, 89. For a discussion of representations of skaldic practice as inspired or as a craft, see Clunies Ross, *History of Old Norse Poetry*, 83–96.

54 *Egils saga Skalla-Grímssonar*, ch. 31, pp. 80–3.

55 See, for instance, *Hallfreðar saga vandræðaskálds*, ch. 2, p. 141; *Bjarnar saga Hítdœlakappa*, ch. 3, p. 116; *Gunnlaugs saga ormstungu*, ch. 4, p. 59; and *Sneglu-Halla þáttr*, chs 1, 3, pp. 415–16. This lack of description of skalds' training continues into the *samtíðarasögur*: see *Þorgils saga ok Hafliða*, ch. 3, p. 13, and *Sturlu saga*, ch. 30, p. 109.

56 In *Flateyjarbók*, Sigvatr Þórðarson becomes a skald by eating a magic fish (3:243), a story that is sometimes seen as involving Christian symbolism (Clunies Ross, *History of Old Norse Poetry*, 126–7), and in *Þorleifs þáttr jarlsskálds* an aspiring poet realizes his desire by sleeping on Þorleifr's grave, where he is visited in a dream by the skald's ghost and wakes a skilled verse-maker (*Flateyjarbók*, 1:215).

57 See Sigurður Nordal, *Icelandic Culture*, 209–10; and Clunies Ross, *History of Old Norse Poetry*, 63–4.

58 Clunies Ross, *History of Old Norse Poetry*, 119–22.

59 See Foote and Wilson, *Viking Achievement*, 333; Frank, *Old Norse Court Poetry*, 67; Hallberg, *Icelandic Saga*, 44; Hollander, *Skalds*, 22; and de Vries, *Altnordische Literaturgeschichte*, 2:12.

60 As Foote writes, this 'well-to-do group of clerical gentry ... by and large seem to have set the tone in matters of taste and propriety' ('Secular Attitudes in Early Iceland,' 32); see also Meulengracht Sørensen, *Saga and Society*, 2, 31–3.

61 Guðrún Nordal, *Tools of Literacy*, esp. 21–4.

62 Ibid., 131.

63 A majority of the *lausavísur* quoted in *Sturlunga saga* fall into this category.

64 Guðrún Nordal, *Tools of Literacy*, 119–20.

65 Like the early bishops, the founders of these centres of learning also spent considerable time studying on the continent. Sæmundr Sigfússon (1056–1133) is widely thought to have been the first Icelander to have studied in France, perhaps even in Paris; see Halldór Hermannsson, *Sæmund Sigfússon and the Oddaverjar*. Sæmundr's son Eyjólfr is credited with starting the school at Oddi (see Einar Ól. Sveinsson, *Sagnaritun Oddaverja*, 12). The school at Haukadalr was founded by Teitr (d. 1110), son of Bishop Ísleifr Gizurarson; Ari Þorgilsson was among those trained there.

66 Foote and Wilson, *Viking Achievement*, 63.

67 Turville-Petre, *Origins of Icelandic Literature*, 221.

68 *Diplomatarium Islandicum*, 291 (no. 72). This ban, issued by Archbishop Eiríkr Ívarsson, was preceded by a letter from Archbishop Eysteinn Erlendsson in 1173 which forbade Icelandic clergy from fighting or joining in lawsuits for personal or financial gain, and threatened any Icelander who attacked a clergyman with excommunication (ibid., 222), as well as an 1189 letter from Eiríkr which forbade clergy from carrying arms or participating in lawsuits likely to lead to violence (ibid., 283–4).

69 Jón Jóhannesson, *History of the Old Icelandic Commonwealth*, 190.

70 Faulkes, introduction to *Edda: Prologue and Gylfaginning*, xv.

71 Foote, '*Sturlusaga* and Its Background,' 233; see also Gísli Sigurðsson, *Medieval Icelandic Saga*, 63.

72 Faulkes, 'Sources of *Skáldskaparmál*'; see also Turville-Petre, *Origins of Icelandic Literature*, 221. Some of the works that Faulkes's position challenges are Ursula and Peter Dronke, 'Prologue of the Prose *Edda*'; Foote, 'Latin Rhetoric and Icelandic Poetry,' 257; Frank, 'Snorri and the Mead of Poetry,' 155; and Sigurður Nordal, *Snorri Sturluson*, 36. One scholar who agrees with Faulkes is Gísli Sigurðsson (*Medieval Icelandic Saga*, 8–9).

73 Faulkes, 'Sources of *Skáldskaparmál*,' 69.

74 Ibid., 70–1. I further agree with Faulkes's opinion that 'one only has to read the books of writers who did use Latin sources, such as Saxo Grammaticus and Óláfr hvítaskáld to see how different Snorri is, both in style and content, and the difference is presumably that he based most of his work on native traditions and had not read widely in Latin ... It would scarcely be possible for a writer trained in Latin grammar and rhetoric to write as Snorri does' (ibid., 70, 72).

75 Although sources give no hint as to who served as Snorri's couriers in these instances, there were more than enough Icelanders making the trip. Furthermore, his connections with Norwegian merchants place them among the more likely candidates.

76 Helgi Þorláksson, 'Snorri Sturluson og Oddaverjar,' 64–70. On relations between the Oddaverjar and the Orkneys in the late 1100s, see also Einar Ól. Sveinsson, *Sagnaritun Oddaverja*, esp. 16–17, 38–9. 'Birkibeinar' ('Birchlegs') was the originally disparaging label given to followers of Sverrir in his successful bid to usurp the kingship from Magnús Erlingsson in the 1170s and 80s.

77 For detailed accounts of these events, see Gjerset, *History of the Norwegian People*, 1:375–407; and Helle, *Norge blir en stat*, 74–93.

78 Snorri's aversion to mounting church influence is also attested to by his participation in the raid on the see of Hólar in 1209, an action taken to combat Bishop Guðmundr Arason's promotion of Gregorian ideals in Iceland (see chapter 2).

79 *Íslendinga saga*, ch. 34, p. 269: 'sverð ok skjöld ok brynju.' The skald who praised Snorri, Máni, was an Icelander who was probably at Hákon's court when Snorri

and the jarl exchanged gifts; he is also known to have composed for King Magnús Erlingsson, and is the only skald active in the thirteenth century who is quoted in Snorri's *Edda* (*Skáldskaparmál* 51, p. 75). Connections between Máni and Snorri are discussed further in chapter 5.

80 *Íslendinga saga*, ch. 34, p. 269: 'Jarlinn ritaði til Snorra, at hann skyldi fara útan, ok lézt til hans gera mundu miklar sæmðir. Ok mjök var þat í skapi Snorra. En jarl-inn andaðist í þann tíma, ok brá þat útanferð hans um nökkurra vetra sakir.'

81 On relations within Skúli's family, see Koht, 'Skule Jarl,' 432–3.

82 See Sturla Þórðarson, *Hákonar saga*, ch. 1, p. 2, and ch. 3, pp. 3–7.

83 Ibid., chs 41–6, pp. 40–4.

84 *Íslendinga saga*, ch. 35, p. 271: 'Tók jarl forkunnar vel við Snorra, ok fór hann til jarls.'

85 According to *Hákonar saga*, ch. 53, p. 51.

86 Kristín was the sister's daughter of Margrét, the widow of King Sverrir.

87 On this poem, see Bjarni Einarsson, 'Andvaka.'

88 *Íslendinga saga*, ch. 35, pp. 271–2: 'Ok tók hon sæmiliga við Snorra ok veitti honum margar gjafir sæmiligar. Hon gaf honum merki þat, er átt hafði Eiríkr Svíakonungr Knútsson. Þat hafði hann, þá er hann felldi Sörkvi konung á Gestilsreini.'

89 Helgi Þorláksson, 'Snorri Sturluson og Oddaverjar,' 80: 'Þetta eru óvenjuleg kvæðislaun. Birkibeinar munu hafa verið hlynntir Eiríki en Sörkvir hlaut stuðning Dana ... Kristín hefur e. t. v. talið að Snorri væri verðugur þess sem ákafur stuð-ningsmaður Birkibeina að bera merki Eiríks sem hafði dáið 1216.'

90 Sturla says only that his uncle 'var tvá vetr með Skúla' (*Íslendinga saga*, ch. 38, p. 277).

91 Ibid.: 'En þó váru Nóregsmenn miklir óvinir Íslendinga ok mestir Oddaverja.'

92 *Hákonar saga*, ch. 59, p. 51.

93 *Íslendinga saga*, ch. 38, p. 277: 'inir vitrari menn.'

94 Ibid., pp. 277–8: 'Snorri latti mjök ferðarinnar ok kallaði þat ráð at gera sér at vinum ina beztu menn á Íslandi ok kallaðist skjótt mega svá koma sínum orðum, at mönnum myndi sýnast at snúast til hlýðni við Nóregshöfðingja. Hann sagði ok svá, at þá váru aðrir eigi meiri menn á Íslandi en bræðr hans, er Sæmund leið, en kallaði þá mundu mjök eftir sínum orðum víkja ... En við slíkar fortölur slævaðist heldr skap jarlsins, ok lagði hann þat ráð til, at Íslendingar skyldi biðja Hákon konung, at hann bæði fyrir þeim, at eigi yrði herferðin. Konungrinn var þá ungr, en Dagfinnr lögmaðr, er þá var ráðgjafi hans, var inn mesti vinr Íslendinga. Ok var þat af gert, at konungr réð, at eigi varð herförin.'

95 *Hákonar saga*, ch. 59, p. 52: 'Snorri Sturluson ok þeir Íslenzkir menn sem þar vóru, báðu Dagfinn bónda flytja við konung at þessi ætlan félli niðr.'

96 Ibid.: 'Gaf þá jarl upp þessa ráða-görð. Var þat ráð gört, at Snorri Sturluson var út sendr at friða fyrir Austmönnum. Gaf Hákon konungr hónum lends manns nafn ... Var þá fyrsta sinni rætt um þat af jarli, at Snorri skyldi koma landi undir konung.'

 97 *Íslendinga saga*, ch. 38, p. 278: 'En þeir Hákon konungr ok Skúli jarl gerðu Snorra lendan mann sinn, var þat mest ráð þeira jarls ok Snorra.'
 98 Ibid.: 'Snorri hafði ort um jarl tvau kvæði.'
 99 Ibid.: 'Jarlinn hafði gefit honum skipit, þat er hann fór á, ok fimmtán stórgjafir.' Jón Jóhannesson, *History of the Old Icelandic Commonwealth*, 243.
100 See *Hallfreðar saga vandræðaskálds* and *Bjarnar saga Hítdœlakappa*, for example (both early 1200s).
101 Harris, 'Theme and Genre,' 16.
102 Ibid., 17. Lindow has labelled a subset of these *þættir* the 'poet's travel pattern,' wherein the Icelander 'relies on verbal skill to obtain, maintain, or regain a favoured position with the monarch' ('Skald Sagas in their Literary Context,' 219).
103 Andersson and Gade, introduction to *Morkinskinna*, 13–14; and Harris, 'Theme and Genre,' 2.
104 Sturla does quote three stanzas from *Háttatal*, but these are all taken from sections dedicated to Skúli, not Hákon (*Hákonar saga*, chs 74, 75, pp. 64–5).
105 Aside from three stanzas from *Háttatal* cited in *Hákonar saga* (see previous note), Sturla only quotes three lines from the *drápur* Snorri recited for Skúli before his departure from Norway in 1220 (*Íslendinga saga*, ch. 38, p. 278), and this mainly because they were lampooned by southlanders who objected to Snorri's dealings with Norway's rulers. Sturla's brother Óláfr hvítaskáld quotes parts of several stanzas of *Háttatal* (5, 15, 16, 28, 40, 73, 83) in his *Third Grammatical Treatise*; on Óláfr's use of the poetry of his uncle and other skalds, see Gísli Sigurðsson, 'Óláfr Þórðarson hvítaskáld and Oral Poetry,' and *Medieval Icelandic Saga*, 93–114.

5 A Poet in Search of an Audience

 1 *Íslendinga saga*, ch. 38, p. 278: 'En er Snorri kom í Vestmannaeyjar, þá spurðist brátt inn á land útkváma hans ok svá með hverjum sæmðum hann var út kominn.'
 2 Ciklamini, *Snorri Sturluson*, 27; and Sigurður Nordal, *Snorri Sturluson*, 62: 'Honum var ekki gefið skap Egils Skallagrímssonar og tilfinningar.'
 3 Turville-Petre, *Origins of Icelandic Literature*, 228–9; and Hollander, *Skalds*, 21.
 4 Bourdieu, *Distinction*, 67.
 5 Faulkes, introduction to *Edda: Háttatal*, xix.
 6 The earliest Icelandic text in which we find euhemeristic theory is the earliest surviving Icelandic text, Ari Þorgilsson's *Íslendingabók* (appendix III, p. 58); this, of course, makes it likely that euhemerism was known and applied in learned Icelandic circles before Ari's work appeared. Euhemeristic theory is discussed at greater length and in relation to Snorri's work in chapter 8.
 7 See Lindow, 'Mythology and Mythography,' 36–7.

8 See my discussion, however, in chapter 8 below, in the section 'Resurrecting Myth.'
9 Sæmundr is cited as such by Ari (*Íslendingabók*, *Prologus* and ch. 7, pp. 47, 52–4),
   in the poem *Nóregskonungatal* (*Den norsk-islandske skjaldedigtning*, IB:579–89),
   by Oddr Snorrason in his *Óláfs saga Tryggvasonar* (chs 15, 27, pp. 23, 30), and by
   Sturla Þórðarson in his version of *Landnámabók* (130).
10 Ari's *Prologus* to *Íslendingabók*, 47.
11 The synoptics include Theodoricus Monachus, *Historia de antiquitate regum Nor-*
   wagiensium (c. 1177–80), and the anonymous *Historia Norwegiæ* (1178–1220?)
   and *Ágrip af Nóregskonunga sögum* (c. 1190). On the use of this term, see Turville-
   Petre, *Origins of Icelandic Literature*, 169–75; and Andersson, 'Kings' Sagas
   (*Konungasögur*),' 201–11.
12 According to Kurt Schier, the first *konungasögur* compilation, Eiríkr Oddsson's
   lost *Hryggjarstykki*, was written between 1150 and 1170; this text was followed
   over the next half-century or so by several sagas of Óláfr Haraldsson and Óláfr
   Tryggvason, of which some are lost, and some are preserved in fragmentary states.
   No other genre of saga is thought by Schier to have emerged before 1200; see
   Sagaliteratur, esp. 9–33.
13 This according to the saga's prologue; see Karl Jónsson, *Sverris saga* 1.
14 Although the authors of some of the earliest *konungasögur* are not known, all are
   thought to have been churchmen, and several, like Oddr Snorrason and Gunnlaugr
   Leifsson, were also attached to Þingeyrar monastery. Sæmundr and Ari were
   priests as well as *goðar*.
15 See Frank, *Old Norse Court Poetry*, 121. This list includes, of course, Snorri
   himself. The two lines are found in Snorri Sturluson, *Edda: Skáldskaparmál* 29,
   p. 39; while Sverrir's name does not appear in this half-stanza, it is thought to
   have been taken from a long composition about this king by Ásgrímr Ketilsson;
   see Fidjestøl, *Det norrøne fyrstediktet*, 160; and Faulkes, n. to v139 in *Skáldskap-*
   armál, p. 183.
16 This is why, again, skaldic poems are nearly always and sagas hardly ever credited
   to named producers. It is important to note, however, that, of all saga genres, the
   names of the writers of *konungasögur* are the most likely to have been recorded.
   Steblin-Kamenskij suggests that this was because 'conscious authorship appeared
   first of all in the sagas representing incipient historical truth' (*Saga Mind*, 45).
   A clearer explanation, perhaps, is that since writers of kings' sagas were in many
   ways stepping into the role occupied by court poets, they sought to attach themselves more firmly to their work so as to receive at least some of the benefits and
   rewards enjoyed by their precursors.
17 Bagge, *From Gang Leader*, 93. Bagge also discusses this transition in 'Icelandic
   Uniqueness or a Common European Culture?' 'Norwegian Monarchy in the
   Thirteenth Century,' and *Political Thought of the King's Mirror*.

18 Primogeniture and legitimate birth first became privileged criteria in matters of
   royal succession during the reign of Magnús Erlingsson (1163/4–84); laws pertain-
   ing to these qualifications are preserved in the Gulaþing and Frostaþing law codes,
   printed in *Norges gamle love indtil 1387*, 1:3–4, and 4:31–2.

19 On this establishment, see Helle, *Norge blir en stat*, 45–52; and Johnsen, *Background for the Establishment of the Norwegian Church Province*, 3–19.

20 For accounts of Magnús's coronation, see *Fagrskinna*, ch. 109, p. 351, which dates
   it to September of 1163, and Snorri's *Magnúss saga Erlingssonar*, ch. 21, in *Heimskringla*, 3:397–8, which dates it to the summer of 1164.

21 See Wanner, '*At Smyrja Konung til Veldis.*'

22 Much of the following paragraph is taken or adapted from ibid., 28–9.

23 See Guðrún Nordal, 'Skáldið Snorri Sturluson,' 54.

24 *Hákonar saga*, chs 41–6, pp. 40–4.

25 See Koht, 'Skule Jarl,' 432.

26 *Fagrskinna*, ch. 2, p. 64:

> At leikurum ok trúðum
> hefi ek þik lítt fregit:
> hverr es ørgáti
> þeira Andaðar
> at húsum Haralds?
> At hundi elskar Andaðr
> ok heimsku drýgir
> eyrnalausum
> ok jöfur hlœgir;
> hinir eru ok aðrir,
> es of eld skulu
> brennanda spön bera,
> logöndum húfum
> hafa sér und linda drepit
> heldræpir halir.

This poem is called by Hans Kuhn the earliest true skaldic praise-poem that we
possess (*Das Dróttkvætt*, 281), and thus demonstrates that there was hardly a time
when skalds did not have to compete with other sorts of court entertainers. The
poem has also been attributed to Þjóðólfr of Hvinir, composer of *Haustlöng* and
Ynglingatal. On the history of enmity in Scandinavian courts between jugglers,
jesters, and minstrels and skaldic poets, see Lindow, 'Two Skaldic Stanzas in
Gylfaginning,' 118–24.

27 Frank, *Old Norse Court Poetry*, 102.

28 Ibid., 93; the verse (printed in ibid., 101) is from *Knýtlinga saga*, ch. 108, in *Danakonunga sögur*, p. 275.

29 Karl Jónsson, *Sverris saga*, ch. 85, p. 90.

30 Einar Ól. Sveinsson, *Age of the Sturlungs*, 37–8.

31 Meissner, *Die Strengleikar*, 132: 'Die bildung, die könig Hákon Hákonarson empfangen hatte, was eine geistlich-höfische, modern für seine zeit und sein land, wesentlich bestimmt durch ideen des auslandes.'

32 *Hákonar saga*, ch. 5, p. 11: 'Þá er Hákon konungs-son var sjau vetra gamall, lét jarl setja hann til bókar. En er hann hafði at námi verit um stund, spurði jarl: "Hvat nemr þú, Hákon?" … "Ek nem söng, mínn herra," sagði hann. Jarl svarar: "Ekki skaltú söng nema, þú skalt hvárki vera prestr né biskup."'

33 Ibid., ch. 13, p. 20.

34 Matthew Paris, *Chronica Majora*, 4:652. Matthew also describes Hákon as quoting Lucanus when the two met (ibid., 4:651). Fidjestøl calls Hákon his nation's 'first famous "grammar-school boy"' ('Romantic Reading at the court of Hákon Hákonarson,' in *Selected Papers*, 351). For arguments as to whether Hákon knew Old French, see Meissner, *Die Strengleikar*, 114–15 (pro), and Larsen, *History of Norway*, 188–9 (con).

35 See Snorri's *Magnússona saga*, ch. 3, in *Heimskringla*, 3:239–40; and *Fagrskinna*, ch. 86, p. 315.

36 This sentence summarizes material presented in Leach, *Angevin Britain and Scandinavia*, 48; see also Halvorsen, *The Norse Version of the* Chanson de Roland, 6–7.

37 For discussions of English and Norwegian trade during these years, see Bugge, 'Handeln mellem England og Norge'; Helle, 'Anglo-Norwegian Relations'; and Jón Jóhannesson, *History of the Old Icelandic Commonwealth*, 327–8.

38 Henry was born in 1207, three years after Hákon, and elected king a year earlier than Hákon, in 1216. Both also had uncommonly long reigns, Hákon from 1217 to 1263, and Henry from 1216 to 1272.

39 Helle, 'Anglo-Norwegian Relations,' 101.

40 Leach, *Angevin Britain and Scandinavia*, 50–1.

41 Helle, 'Anglo-Norwegian Relations,' 106.

42 See note 37 above for references.

43 Helle, *Norge blir en stat*, 104: 'Håkons saga gjør mye ut av disse kontaktene med utlandet og den angivelig smigrende oppmerksomhet som der ble kongen til del.'

44 *Hákonar saga*, chs 191, 247–55, 284, 294, 313, pp. 169–70, 239–51, 281, 299–303, 324–7. Scholars agree that there were more embassies between Hákon and foreign courts than what is described in his saga – his correspondence with Louis IX, for example, is described by Matthew Paris (see note 34 above), but not by Sturla.

45 Leach, *Angevin Britain and Scandinavia*, 72.

46 Schach, introduction to *The Saga of Tristram and Ísönd*, xvii.

47 *Tristrams saga ok Ísöndar*, 28: 'Var þá liðit frá hingatburði Christi 1226 ár, er þessi saga var á norrænu skrifuð eptir befalningu ok skipan virðuligs herra Hákonar kóngs. En Bróðir Robert efnaði ok upp skrifaði.'

48 These are *Strengleikar* (from the *lais* of Marie de France), *Ívens saga* (from Chrétien de Troyes's *Le chevalier au Lion* or *Yvain*), *Möttuls saga* (from *Le lai du cort mantel*), and *Elis saga ok Rósamundu* (from the *Elie de St. Gille*). There is some doubt over whether it is Hákon or his son of the same name who is mentioned as patron in several of these works. It makes little difference either way, since the younger Hákon's 'reign' was encompassed by that of his father, who outlived him by eight years. *Elis saga ok Rósamundu* names Robert as its author (ch. 59, p. 107).

49 These are *Parcevals saga*, *Erex saga*, and *Valvers þáttr* (all adapted from works of Chrétien de Troyes), *Bevis saga* (from *Buève de Hantone*), *Flóres saga ok Blanki-flúr* (from *Floire et Blancheflor*), and *Barlaams saga ok Jósafats*, a translation from Latin that may have been made by Hákon's own son Hákon before he died in 1255.

50 'Chivalry' is a term whose definition and application have been problematized by a growing number of scholars of the Middle Ages; see, for example, Bouchard, *Strong of Body, Brave and Noble*, 103–16; and Keen, *Chivalry*.

51 Einar Ól. Sveinsson, *Age of the Sturlungs*, 35.

52 Halvorsen, *The Norse Version of the* Chanson de Roland, 11.

53 Meissner, *Die Strengleikar*, 113, 134: 'erstens Hákon Norwegen, um einen modernen ausdruck zu gebrauchen, als europäische grossmacht anerkannt sehen wollte zweitens aber – und das war ihm gewiss das wichtigere – hoben diese verbindungen mit glänzenden höfen des auslandes das ansehen und die würde des norwegischen königtums in der heimat … sollte der hof des erstarkten norwegischen königtums den fremden höfen gleichstehen, so musste dort auch dieselbe geistige und gesellschaftliche bildung zu finden sein wie im auslande.'

54 Kramarz-Bein, 'Höfische Unterhaltung und ideologisches Ziel,' 81–2: 'Wie kein anderer norwegischer König vor ihm orientierte sich Hákon Hákonarson in seiner höfischen Kultur- und Bildungspolitik an England und dem europäischen Kontinent … hinter der didaktischen Absicht der Riddarasögur … steht ein ideologisches Ziel. Die übersetzten Riddarasögur leisten in fiktionaler Form ihren Beitrag zur Formulierung und Festigung der feudal-aristokratischen Königsidee.'

55 Barnes, 'Authors, Dead and Alive, in Old Norse Fiction,' 11; and Barnes, '*Riddarasögur* and Mediæval European Literature,' 147–8. See also Kramarz-Bein, 'Höfische Unterhaltung und ideologisches Ziel,' 70.

56 See Barnes, 'Parcevals Saga: Riddara Skuggsjá?' 62; and Barnes, 'Some Current Issues in *Riddarasögur* Research,' 80.

57 Sturla Þórðarson, *Hákonar saga*, chs 329–30, pp. 354–5: 'lét hann fyrst lesa sér Látínubækr. En þá þótti hónum sér mikil mæða í, at hugsa þar eptir hversu þat þýddi. Lét hann þá lesa fyrir sér Norænu-bækr, nætr ok daga; fyrst Heilagramannasögur; ok er þær þraut, lét hann lesa sér Konunga-tal frá Hálfdani Svarta, ok síðan frá öllum Noregskonungum, hverjum eptir annan … framan til Sverris … Nær miðri nátt var úti at lesa Sverris-sögu. En heldr at miðri nótt liðinni kallaði almáttigr Guð Hákon konung af þessa heims lífi.'

58 And he was not shy about making complaints; see note 29 above.

59 This same observation can be used to understand Kristín's attraction to Snorri's poetry. At the time of Snorri's visit, she had been the wife of one frustrated candidate for Norway's throne, and she would several years later become the mother of another: in 1227, her son by jarl Hákon, Knútr, was appointed 'king' of the Ribbungar, a band of rebels based in eastern Norway, whom Hákon and Skúli defeated in that same year (see *Hákonar saga*, chs 145–56, pp. 124–39).

60 By comparison, Haraldr hárfagri is listed as having had six skalds; the highest number for any king, twelve, is attached to Haraldr harðráði.

61 *Skáldatal* in the *Uppsalabók* manuscript contains all eight names, while the last is missing from *Kringla*; see *Skáldatal* A and B in *Edda Snorra Sturlusonar. Edda Snorronis Sturlæi*, 3:256, 265.

62 Guðrún Nordal, *Tools of Literacy*, 99, 143; see also her 'Contemporary Sagas and Their Social Context,' 238.

63 It is unlikely that Óláfr met Hákon during the former's trip to Norway in 1237–9. See *Íslendinga saga*, chs 126, 143, pp. 408–9, 444; and *Hákonar saga*, chs 180–1, 194, pp. 159, 171–3.

64 For Játgeirr's dealings with Hákon and Skúli, see *Hákonar saga*, chs 83, 196, 205, 216, 243, pp. 72, 175, 187, 198, 236.

65 Gizurr's only preserved skaldic stanza deals with Hákon's conflict with the Danes in 1257. Sturla does not say, however, that Gizurr composed or recited this verse in Hákon's presence or court, only that he was with the king at this time: 'This Gizurr Þorvaldsson composed, who then [i.e., at the time of the event, not of composition] was with the king' (Sem kvað Gizurr Þorvaldsson er þá var með konunginum. *Hákonar saga*, ch. 293, p. 297). There is no positive evidence that I am aware of to support Guðrún Nordal's claim that Gizurr 'gained a reputation for his poetry at the court of King Hákon' (*Tools of Literacy*, 138).

66 On Óláfr Leggsson, see *Íslendinga saga*, chs 79, 82, pp. 342–3, 346. Óláfr may have been the brother's son of Játgeirr Torfason (see Guðrún Nordal, *Tools of Literacy*, 180). If so, it is likely that he, like his uncle, was more closely associated with Skúli than with the king; and indeed, one of his few extant verses, preserved in the fifth grammatical treatise fragment, makes mention of Skúli (ibid.). On Guttormr Helgason, see *Íslendinga saga*, chs 187–8, pp. 511–12, 514; *Þorgils saga kakala*, ch. 4, p. 10; and *Þorgils saga skarða*, ch. 18, p. 133.

67 Another way to look at this question is to consider the kings to whom Snorri is attached as poet in *Skáldatal*: Sverrir, Ingi, and Hákon. Of these, Snorri never even met, let alone received signs of recognition, from two, and was basically ignored by the third in his capacity as poet; these facts alone show that evidence of poet-king associations in *Skáldatal* should be treated with caution, particularly in respect to the thirteenth century.

68 Helle, *Norge blir en stat*, 107–8, 112–13. The events themselves are recounted in
    Hákonar saga, chs 85–97, pp. 74–83, and chs 247–55, pp. 239–51.
69 *Íslendinga saga*, ch. 38, p. 278: 'Ýfðust Sunnlendingar þá mjök við honum ok mest
    tengðamenn Orms Jónssonar ... Var mest fyrir því Björn Þorvaldsson.'
70 Ibid., p. 279.
71 Ibid., p. 278:

> Harðmúlaðr vas Skúli
> rambliks framast miklu
> gnaphjarls skapaðr jarla.

72 Ibid., pp. 278–9: 'Sunnlendingar drógu spott mikit at kvæðum þeim, er Snorri
    hafði ort um jarlinn, ok sneru afleiðis. Þórrodr í Selvági keypti geldingi at manni,
    at þetta orti:

> Oss lízk illr at kyssa
> jarl, sás ræðr fyr hjarli,
> vörr es til hvöss á harra,
> harðmúlaðr es Skúli.
> Héfr fyr horska jöfra
> hrægamms komit sævar,
> – þjóð finnr löst á ljóðum –,
> leir aldrigi meira.'

73 See Helgi Þorláksson, 'Snorri Sturluson og Oddaverjar,' 83.
74 *Íslendinga saga*, ch. 39, p. 284: 'Snorri var allmjök snúinn á liðveizlu við Loft, því
    at illa hafði verit með þeim Birni. Líkaði honum ok illa spott þat, er Sunnlendingar
    höfðu gert af kvæðum hans.' Guðrún Nordal comments on this passage in 'Skaldið
    Snorri Sturluson,' 57.
75 The verse seems to stop just short of *níð* in its suggestion of impropriety between
    Snorri and Skúli. On *níð* or sexual defamation in medieval Iceland, see
    Meulengracht Sørensen, *Unmanly Man*; and Gade, 'Homosexuality and the
    Rape of Males.' The quotation is Frank's reference to this satire's composer
    (*Old Norse Court Poetry*, 125).
76 *Íslendinga saga*, ch. 39, p. 284:

> Björn frák brýndu járni,
> – bragð gótt var þat –, lagðan,
> gerði Guðlaugr fyrðum
> geysihark –, í barka.
> Auðkýfingr lét ævi
> óblíðr fyr Grásíðu,
> hvöss vas hon heldr at kyssa, –
> harðmúlaðr vas Skúli.

77 See Klingenberg, 'Hommage für Skúli Bárðarson,' 58.

78 *Jóns saga hins helga*, ch. 24, p. 237.

79 According to Stefán Einarsson (*History of Icelandic Literature*, 84–5), there are *danzar* mentioned in *Sturlunga saga* for the years 1119, 1121, 1220–1, 1232, 1245, 1255, 1258, and 1264. For a complete account of evidence for the production of *danzar* in Iceland in the 1100s and 1200s, see Jón Samsonarson, 'inngangur' to *Kvæði og Dansleikir*, 1:ix–xx.

80 Einar Ól. Sveinsson, *Age of the Sturlungs*, 38–9.

81 The last known Icelandic court poet was Jón murti Egilsson, Snorri's sister's grandson, who composed poetry for King Eiríkr Magnússon (r. 1280–99), Hákon Hákonarson's grandson. By this time, as Einar Sveinsson writes, skalds 'could well pack one half of their scrip with the product of their ancient art and the other with romances and "dances"' (ibid., 40). Cleasby and Guðbrandur Vigfússon, in their entry for '*danz*,' write that 'the Sturl. [*Sturlunga saga*] has by chance preserved two ditties ... sufficient to shew the flow and metre, which are exactly the same as those of the mod. ballads, collected in the west of Icel. (Ögr) in the 17th century under the name of Fornkvæði, *Old Songs*' (*Icelandic-English Dictionary*, 96).

82 Stefán Einarsson, *History of Icelandic Literature*, 85–8.

83 Sigurður Nordal, *Icelandic Culture*, 220.

84 It is told in *Sturlu saga*, ch. 20, p. 89, that in 1171 Sturla and his wife held a *hring-leikr*, a term used to denote *danz* performances paired with rehearsed movements (see Jón Samsonarson, 'inngangur' to *Kvæði og Dansleikir*, 1:xii–xiii). On Dansa-Bergr, see *Íslendinga saga*, ch. 46, p. 294.

85 Frank, *Old Norse Court Poetry*, 125.

86 *Íslendinga saga*, ch. 39, p. 279: 'færðu Breiðbælingar Loft í flimtan ok gerðu um hann dansa marga ok margs konar spott annat.'

87 Another instance of *danz* metres used to compose lampoons is attested in *Þórðar saga kakala*, ch. 38, p. 79. While few *flímvísur* ('mocking-verses') in *Sturlunga saga* are said to have been composed with *danz*-metres, scholars suspect that their use for this purpose was more common than explicit testimony suggests (Einar Ól. Sveinsson, *Age of the Sturlungs*, 93; Jón Samsonarson, 'inngangur' to *Kvæði og Dansleikir*, 1:xvii–xviii, xix–xx; and Stefán Einarsson, *History of Icelandic Literature*, 88).

88 *Íslendinga saga*, ch. 39, p. 284: 'Þá var þetta kveðit:
> Loftr er í eyjum,
> bítr lundabein,
> Sæmundr er á heiðum
> ok etr berin ein.'

89 See Sigurður Nordal, *Icelandic Culture*, 210; and *Grágás* Ib, pp. 183–4.

90 Bourdieu and Wacquant, *Invitation to Reflexive Sociology*, 133.

91 Bourdieu, *In Other Words*, 45; and Bourdieu and Wacquant, *Invitation to Reflexive Sociology*, 99.

6 *Háttatal*

1 Wessén, introduction to *Codex Regius of the Younger Edda*, 11.
2 Guðrún Nordal, *Tools of Literacy*, 41–2; Frank, *Old Norse Court Poetry*, 32; Tranter, 'Medieval Icelandic *artes poeticae*,' 142–3, 150, 153; and Weber, 'Edda, Jüngere,' 395.
3 Meulengracht Sørensen, 'Social Institutions and Belief Systems,' 20.
4 Gade, *Structure of Old Norse* Dróttkvætt, 239–40.
5 Gade, 'Poetry and Its Changing Importance,' 89.
6 Clunies Ross, 'Conservation and Reinterpretation of Myth,' 129.
7 Clunies Ross makes similar concessions to Snorri's political investment in his poetry in her recent *History of Old Norse Poetry* (140, 160). She still, however, describes his interest in skaldic verse as 'antiquarian,' and insists that 'he was by no means only a politician' (12, 159).
8 Guðrún Nordal, *Tools of Literacy*, 42.
9 On the dating of these manuscripts, see Seelow, 'Zur handschriftlichen Überlieferung der Werks Snorri Sturlusons,' 213.
10 Finnur Jónsson ('Edda Snorra Sturlusonar') and Boer ('Studien über die Snorra Edda') were among the first to make concerted cases for preferring R over other manuscripts, particularly U, which had been considered closer to Snorri's original by scholars such as Mogk ('Zur Bewertung des Codex Upsaliensis'). For summaries of this debate, see Lindow, 'Mythology and Mythography,' 35, and 'Two Skaldic Stanzas in *Gylfaginning*,' 107–8.
11 See Faulkes, introduction to *Edda: Prologue and Gylfaginning*, xxxi.
12 Ibid., xxxii.
13 Bragg, 'Generational Tensions in *Sturlunga Saga*,' 7.
14 The introduction to U states that Snorri *orti*, 'composed,' *Háttatal*, and he is named as its producer by his nephews Sturla (*Hákonar saga*, chs 74–5, pp. 64–5) and Óláfr (who quotes from seven of *Háttatal*'s stanzas, naming Snorri as their author six times; see *Den tredje og fjærde grammatiske afhandling*, 52, 79, 94, 95, 98, 107); he is also mentioned twice in the fourth grammatical treatise (ibid., 272–3).
15 Faulkes, introduction to *Edda: Háttatal*, xxvi.
16 Ibid., xxiv. T's text is close to R, but its end, following st. 61, is lost. W is missing the beginning and end, stt. 1–6 and 87–102, while U first records the names of the verse forms and initial lines only of most of stt. 1–36, and then begins over, recording whole stanzas and their commentary up to st. 56. There are also differences in placement of stanzas between manuscripts: in R, st. 38 is at the end of the poem, while in W stt. 43 and 44 are reversed, which most scholars and editors consider a more logical arrangement. For more detailed comparisons

of the manuscripts, see ibid., xxiv–xxvi; and *Háttatal Snorra Sturlusonar*, ed. Theodor Möbius, 1:17–18 (hereafter Möbius).

17 Konráð Gíslason, 'De ældste runeindskrifters sproglige stilling,' 147–8; see also Faulkes, introduction to *Edda: Háttatal*, xii; Hallberg, *Old Icelandic Poetry*, 2; Möbius, 1:33–4; and Wessén, introduction to *Codex Regius of the Younger Edda*, 14.

18 *Háttatal* 64, p. 28.

19 See *Hákonar saga*, ch. 84, pp. 73–4.

20 Finnur Jónsson writes in response to Konráð Gíslason's dating: 'There is yet nothing to hinder [the conclusion] that the poem may have been planned and begun earlier [than 1222]' (Der er dog intet til hinder for, at digtet kan være planlagt og påbegyndt för. 'Edda Snorra Sturlusonar,' 287). Others who support a somewhat earlier dating of *Háttatal* include Kuhn ('Das Háttatal muß bald nach 1220 gedichter sein,' *Das Dróttkvætt*, 324), Guðrún Nordal (*Tools of Literacy*, 5), and Hermann Pálsson ('Snorri Sturluson and the Everlasting Battle,' 35).

21 Sigurður Nordal, *Snorri Sturluson*, 23: 'slegið tvær flugur í einu höggi ... að bæta þriðja og síðasta hlutanum við Eddu sína og ... að mæra þá Hákon og Skúla.' See also ibid., 89.

22 Wessén, introduction to *Codex Regius of the Younger Edda*, 15–16, 29–32. This was a possibility that earlier scholars refused to entertain. Finnur Jónsson, for example, wrote that it 'is unnatural to suppose that lessons about theories should have been written after executions in practice' (det er unaturligt at forudsætte, at læren om teorien skulde være skreven bagefter udførelsen i praksis. 'Edda Snorra Sturlusonar,' 287).

23 Wessén, introduction to *Codex Regius of the Younger Edda*, 14.

24 See, *Mythos und Theologie*, 7–9, 13–17, and *Europa und der Norden im Mittelalter*, 275–7.

25 Baetke, 'Die Götterlehre der *Snorra-Edda*,' 214: 'nicht nur ein bedeutender Gelehrter ... sondern auch ein gläubiger Christ.'

26 Clunies Ross, *Skáldskaparmál: Snorri Sturluson's* ars poetica.

27 Lönnroth, 'Reception of Snorri's Poetics,' 144.

28 In her study on *Skáldskaparmál*, Clunies Ross writes that a 'separate analysis of *Háttatal* ... would be desirable to bring it out of its present obscurity' (*Skáldskaparmál: Snorri Sturluson's* ars poetica, 10). She provides something of one, though not along the same lines, in *Old Norse Poetry and Poetics*, 162–70.

29 Weber, 'Edda, Jüngere,' 406: 'Die Annahme, Snorri habe 1220 nach seiner Rückkehr aus Norwegen ... zuerst das *Háttatal* gedichtet, bevor er den Plan zu Gylf. und Skp. faßte ... ist unbeweisbar und angesichts der theoretischen und didaktischen Geschlossenheit der ganzen E. überflüssig.'

30 The only definite model for *Háttatal* that has been identified, however, is the Norse
Háttalykill, or 'Key of Metres,' a poem of 82 (extant) stanzas composed by jarl
Rögnvaldr kali Kolsson of the Orkneys and the Icelander Hallr breiðmagi
Þórarinsson in the 1140s; for an edition of and background on this text, see
Háttalykill enn forni. *Háttalykill* was certainly known to Snorri (Faulkes, introduction to *Edda: Háttatal*, xiv–xvii; and Sigurður Nordal, *Snorri Sturluson*, 91–2), and
was probably a model for his own more systematic and comprehensive enumera-
tion of skaldic metres. *Háttalykill* also, to an extent, shares *Háttatal*'s dual functions – while the former's subject matter is more genealogical and legendary than
strictly panegyric, consisting of tributes to the chief heroes of northern legend, one
of its purposes was probably to establish a storied ancestry for the Orkney jarls
(see Krömmelbein, 'Snorri als Skalde,' 298–9). *Háttalykill* has, however, no commentary that could have inspired Snorri to affix one to his own composition.
31 Hermann Pálsson, 'Snorri Sturluson and the Everlasting Battle,' 44.
32 See Krömmelbein, 'Snorri als Skalde,' 300; Möbius, 1:35; and Sigurður Nordal,
Snorri Sturluson, 23, 89. A variation on this argument is that Snorri was inspired by
his trip to Norway and the interest in old traditions and poetry that he encountered
there to write on these subjects; see Meulengracht Sørensen, 'Snorris frœði,' and
Saga and Society, 152; and Wessén, introduction to *Codex Regius of the Younger
Edda*, 31.
33 Faulkes, introduction to *Edda: Háttatal*, ix; Fidjestøl, *Det norrøne fyrstediktet*,
246–7; Klingenberg, 'Hommage für Skúli Bárðarson,' 61; Krömmelbein, 'Snorri als
Skalde,' 300–1; Möbius, 1:35; and Clunies Ross, *Old Norse Poetry and Poetics*, 163.
34 See Klingenberg, 'Hommage für Skúli Bárðarson,' 76–7.
35 Guðrún Nordal, 'Skáldið Snorri Sturluson,' 59: 'Það er ekki einasta hið óhagstæða
hlutfall lofsins sem borið er á Hákon, sem kann að hafa styggt hinn unga konung,
heldur er lofið mjög torfundið í fyrstu þrjátíu vísunum.'
36 Ibid.: 'Hann tekur því furðulega áhættu með því að sveipa lofið um Hákon í svo tor-
rætt form.'
37 *Háttatal* 1, pp. 3–4. All citations from *Háttatal* are from Faulkes's edition. I do not
reproduce his critical marks. All translations from *Háttatal* are my own unless otherwise noted, and are designed to be as literal and straightforward as possible. My
efforts owe, however, a great deal to Faulkes's work in his translation of the *Edda*
and the glossary to his edition of *Háttatal*, and frequent correspondence and simi-
larities between our renderings will be noticed. The same is true of my translations
of other parts of the *Edda*.
38 Ibid., pp. 4–5: 'Þetta er dróttkvæðr háttr. Með þeima hætti er flest ort þat er vandat
er. Þessi er upphaf allra hátta.' *Dróttkvætt*'s basic characteristics are described in
chapter 4.

39 Ibid., p. 5: 'Hvern<i>g skal breyta háttunum ok halda sama hætti?'

40 See Faulkes's n. to *Háttatal* 1/44 (ibid., p. 49).

41 *Háttatal* 27, p. 16: 'Þessi er hinn fyrsti háttr er ritaðr sé þeira er breytt er af drótt-kvæðum hætti með fullu háttaskipti … með hljóðum ok hendingaskipti eða orða-lengð'; and Kuhn, *Das Dróttkvætt*, 324.

42 As de Vries has observed in *Altnordische Literaturgeschichte*, 2:80, 'In str. 1–68 the various types of *dróttkvætt*-strophe are handled, and clearly in str. 1–30 the rhetorical, in str. 31–68 the metrical varieties' (In Str. 1–68 behandelt er die verschiedenen Abarten der dróttkvætt-Strophe, und zwar in Str. 1–30 die rhetorischen, in Str. 31–68 die metrischen Sonderformen).

43 Faulkes, introduction to *Edda: Háttatal*, xiii; Fidjestøl, *Det norrøne fyrstediktet*, 247; and Möbius, 1:40–2.

44 Guðrún Nordal, 'Skáldið Snorri Sturluson,' 61: 'Snorri virðist storka Hákoni'; 'að slá í brýnu milli Hákonar og Skúla.'

45 Snorri Sturluson, *Heimskringla*, 1:5: 'En þat er háttr skálda at lofa þann mest, er þá eru þeir fyrir, en engi myndi þat þora at segja sjálfum honum þau verk hans, er allir þeir, er heyrði, vissi, at hégómi væri ok skrök, ok svá sjálfr hann. Þat væri þá háð, en eigi lof.'

46 *Háttatal* 7, p. 7:

> Hjálms fylli spekr hilmir
> hvatr Vindhlés skatna;
> hann kná hjörvi þunnum
> hræs þjóðár ræsa;
> ýgr hilmir lætr eiga
> öld dreyrfá skjöldu;
> styrs rýðr stillir hersum
> sterkr járngrá serki.

47 Ibid. 4, p. 6:

> Stinn sár þróask stórum,
> sterk egg frömum seggjum
> hvast skerr hlífar traustar;
> hár gramr lifir framla.
> Hrein sverð litar harða
> hverr drengr; göfugr þengill
> (ítr rönd furask undrum)
> unir bjart<r> snöru hjarta.

The translation is Faulkes's (*Edda* translation, 169). See also *Háttatal* 9, p. 9.

48 *Háttatal* 6, p. 6:

> Sviðr lætr sóknar naðra
> slíðrbraut jöfurr skríða;

and ibid. 18, p. 13:

> fal lætr <of> her hvítan
> hollr gramr rekinn framðan.

See also stt. 1, 7, 11, pp. 3–4, 7, 9–10.

49 In contrast, stanzas praising Skúli for his prowess in battle typically ascribe action directly to the jarl and place him in the midst of the fray. A good example of this is st. 32, p. 17. Snorri often speaks of battle raging *of Skúla* or *of jarli*, 'around the jarl,' in *kvæði* two; see stt. 52–4, 57, 59, 61, 62, 65, pp. 24–8.

50 Ibid. 10, p. 9:

> Jörð verr siklingr sverðum.
> Sundr rjúfa spjör undir.
> Lind skerr í styr steinda.
> Støkkr hauss af bol lausum.
> Falla fólk á velli.
> Fremr mildr jöfurr hildi.
> Egg bítr á lim lýti.
> Liggr skör sniðin hjörvi.

51 Ibid., p. 5.

52 These kennings are found in stt. 21, 26, 5, 19, pp. 14, 15, 6, 13.

53 Ibid. 15, p. 11. On the *ægishjálmr*, see *Skáldskaparmál* 40, p. 46.

54 *Háttatal* 3, p. 5.

55 Ibid. 6, p. 7: 'því at kenningar auka orðfjölða.'

56 Ibid. 28, 29, p. 16. The ship-levy estate may refer to lands bestowed on Snorri (which he may, however, already have owned; see pp. 180–1, n. 39 above) by the king. Alternatively, the word that Snorri meant to use may have been *skipreiði*, as T's and W's readings suggest, in which case the meaning is 'ship-rigging,' and would constitute another reference to the gift of a physical ship (see Faulkes's note to st. 28/4, p. 56).

57 *Íslendinga saga*, ch. 38, p. 278: 'Jarlinn hafði gefit honum skipit, þat er hann fór á.' Although *dýr* is plural in *Háttatal* 28, I agree with Faulkes that 'it seems unlikely that Snorri was given more than one' ship (see his note to st. 28/6, pp. 56–7).

58 *Háttatal* 27, p. 15: 'hersis heiti hátt.' Although *hersir* was not in fact one of the titles received by Snorri while in Norway, his use of the term was probably dictated by metrical considerations.

59 Faulkes, *Edda* translation, 184; and *Edda: Háttatal*, p. 133. Finnur Jónsson (*Den norsk-islandske skjaldedigtning*, IB:68) and Sveinbjörn Egilsson (*Lexicum poeticum antiquæ linguæ septentrionalis*, 453) both choose *prýðir*, and Möbius *prýði* (1:109).

60 *Íslendinga saga*, ch. 38, p. 278: 'En þeir Hákon konungr ok Skúli jarl gerðu Snorra lendan mann sinn, var þat mest ráð þeira jarls ok Snorra.'

61 *Skáldskaparmál* 64, p. 101. See Klingenberg, 'Hommage für Skúli Bárðarson,' 59–60.

62 *Háttatal* 30, pp. 16–17:
    Þoll bið ek hilmis hylli
    halda grœnna skjalda,
    askr beið af því þroska
    þilju Hrungnis ilja;
    vígfoldar njót valdi
    vandar margra landa –
    nýtr vartu oss – til ítrar
    elli dólga fellir.
Translation slightly adapted from Faulkes's (*Edda* translation, 185–6).

63 *Háttatal* 31, p. 17. Translation slightly adapted from Faulkes's (*Edda* translation, 186).

64 *Lof* can refer to a panegyric or the praise it conveys; see Fidjestøl, *Det norrøne fyrstediktet*, 253–4.

65 *Háttatal* 67, p. 29: 'Nú skal upp hefja it þriðja kvæði þat er ort er eptir inum smærum háttum, ok eru þeir hættir þó margir áðr í lofkvæðum.'

66 Ibid. 70, p. 30:
    [Mitt] er of mœti
    [mart lag bra]gar
    áðr ókveðit
    oddbraks spakan.
The translation is Faulkes's (*Edda* translation, 207). On Snorri's invention of metres and his systematization of metres already found in the poetic corpus, see Faulkes, 'Use of Snorri's Verse-Forms by Earlier Norse Poets.'

67 *Háttatal* 100, p. 39:
    hróðrs ørv<er>ðr
    skala maðr heitinn vera
    ef sá fær alla háttu ort.
The translation is Faulkes's (*Edda* translation, 220).

68 See Faulkes, introduction to *Edda: Háttatal*, xi–xii.

69 *Háttatal* 39, p. 19.

70 Take, for instance, his praise of the jarl's generosity with gold that climaxes in st. 47, p. 22:
    Seimþverrir gefr seima
    seimörr liði beima,
    hringmildan spyr ek hringum
    hringskemmi brott þinga;
    baugstøkkvir fremr baugum
    bauggrimmr hjarar draug<a>,

viðr gullbroti gulli

gullhættr skaða fullan

(The gold-liberal diminisher of gold gives gold to the troop of men, I hear that the ring-generous ring-damager throws rings away; the arm-ring hating flinger of arm-rings benefits sword-trunks [men] with arm-rings, the gold-hating gold-flinger causes complete damage to gold).

To be fair, it should be noted that this stanza demonstrates the verse-form *iður-mæltr*, 'repeatedly said.' For use of superlatives in praising Skúli, as well as instances where Snorri states that there are 'none greater' than the jarl in terms of courage, generosity, etc., see stt. 35, 55, 68, 82, 84, 88, 90–4, pp. 18, 25, 29, 34, 35–7. By comparison, Snorri once calls Hákon *ofrhugaðr*, 'most bold' (*Háttatal* 5, p. 6), and applies superlatives to him only when he uses the same adjective to praise the king and jarl together; see ibid. 67, p. 29, and esp. 99, pp. 38–9, in which seven superlatives are found.

71 Ibid. 41, p. 20.

72 Ibid., pp. 20–1. This stanza is 43 in Faulkes's edition, 44 in his translation; see note 16 above.

73 Ibid. 41 and 43, p. 23.

74 Ibid. 35, 43, 48, 53, 55, pp. 18, 21–5.

75 Ibid. 94, p. 37.

76 Ibid. 67, p. 29:

> Ortak öld at minnum
> þá er alframast vissak
> of siklinga snjalla
> með sex tøgum hátta.
> Sízt hafa veg né vellum
> er virðan mik létu
> á aldinn mar orpit
> (þat er oss frami) jöfrar.

77 Fidjestøl, *Det norrøne fyrstediktet*, 255: 'Lovkvadet over fyrstane endar med å bli eit lovkvad over lovkvadet.'

78 *Háttatal* 95, p. 37:

> Munða ek mildingi,
> þá er Mœra hilmi
> fluttak fjögur kvæði,
> fimtán stórgjafar.
> Hvar viti áðr orta
> með œðra hætti
> mærð of menglötuð
> maðr und himins skautum?

79 Snorri here refers to the two *drápur* that he delivered to Skúli before his departure in 1220 and the two that form part of *Háttatal*. The fifteen gifts, therefore, were really given in response to just the first two poems. As Faulkes observes (note to *Háttatal* 95, p. 73), it is likely that this stanza is the basis of Sturla's statement in *Íslendinga saga* (ch. 38, p. 278) that the jarl had given Snorri *fimmtán stórgjafir* in 1220.

80 *Háttatal* 96, p. 38:
> þat mun æ lifa
> nema öld farisk,
> bragni<n>ga lof,
> eða bili heimar.

81 Ibid. 102, p. 39:
> Njóti aldrs
> ok auðsala
> konungr ok jarl.
> Þat er kvæðis lok.
> Falli fyrr
> fold í ægi
> steini studd
> en stillis lof.

82 Ibid. 97, p. 38:
> Lypta ek ljósu
> lofi þjóðkonungs,
> upp er fyrir ýta
> jarls mærð borin;
> hverr muni heyra
> hróðr gjöflata
> seggr svá kveðinn
> seims ok hnossa?

83 Fidjestøl, '"Have You Heard of a Poem Worth More?"' in *Selected Papers*, 117–32.

84 See Boer, 'Om kommentaren,' 280–1, 301–7; Faulkes, introduction to *Edda: Háttatal*, ix–x; and Finnur Jónsson, 'Snorre Sturlusons *Háttatal*,' 232–43.

85 R contains the most complete version of the commentary, although it lacks the comments to st. 38, which it places at the end of the poem. W and T have the commentary to the stanzas which they preserve (for W, 7–86, and for T, 1–61), though with many differences from R. U has a peculiar arrangement: it first supplies the verse-form names and initial lines of most of stt. 1–36, then offers the entire text of the poem and commentary, though with many alterations and seeming omissions, until st. 56.

86 *Háttatal* 100, p. 39:

> Gløggva grein
>
> hefi ek gert til bragar,
>
> svá er tíroett hundrað talit

(I have given a precise account of poetic-form, so that a hundred counted in tens are told).

As Faulkes suggests, 'This could be taken to refer to the commentary to *Háttatal*, thus confirming that it is by the poet' (n. to *Háttatal* 100/1–3, p. 74).

87 See Ólafur Halldórsson, 'Sagnaritun Snorra Sturlusonar,' 115. That U does not ascribe the commentary to Snorri along with the *Edda*'s other parts might seem strong contrary evidence, except that, as Möbius points out, U's scribe would likely have named its author had it been anyone other than Snorri (1:83).

88 Faulkes, introduction to *Edda: Háttatal*, xv; and Tranter, 'Das *Háttatal*,' 183.

89 *Háttatal* 0, p. 3: 'Hvat eru hættir skáldskapar? Þrent. Hverir? Setning, leyfi, fyrir-boðning. Hvat er setning háttanna? Tvent. Hver? Rétt ok breytt.' As some have noted, this and other passages in the commentary (such as those preceding stt. 2 and 9, pp. 5, 9) resemble the opening of Fortunatianus's *Ars rhetorica*. As Faulkes, however, observes, 'Fortunatianus is concerned with rhetoric, not metre, and his categories are different; only the manner is similar, and no direct influence is likely' (introduction to *Edda: Háttatal*, xv).

90 Frank, 'Snorri and the Mead of Poetry,' 156, n. 3.

91 As Faulkes writes: 'While *Háttatal* more than any other of the writings attributed to Snorri is reminiscent in manner and style and approach of the learned Latin treatises (particularly in its opening), the influence of any specific work cannot be demonstrated either on its form or its actual scheme of categorization and vocabulary' (introduction to *Edda: Háttatal*, xiv–xv). As some of those most convinced of Snorri's indebtedness to Latin learning have admitted, his treatment of native poetry is a good deal more original (or, depending on how one looks at it, traditional) than those found in the grammatical treatises; see Guðrún Nordal, *Tools of Literacy*, 209–10, 239; and Tranter, 'Medieval Icelandic *artes poeticae*,' 147, 153.

92 Tranter, 'Das *Háttatal*,' 180: 'Produkt einer christlich-lateinischen Schrift-gelehrsamkeit.'

93 Ibid., 192: 'Die Vitalität dieser Tradition wird dadurch bezeugt, daß sie noch in der Analyse der Schriftgelehrten weiterlebte.'

94 For a similar judgment on this matter, see Gísli Sigurðsson, *Medieval Icelandic Saga*, 16.

95 See note 91 above.

7 *Skáldskaparmál*

1 Bourdieu, *Language and Symbolic Power*, 57 (original emphasis).

2 *Skáldskaparmál* 1, p. 5: 'En þetta er nú at segja ungum skáldum þeim er girnask at nema mál skáldskapar ok heyja sér orðfjölða með fornum heitum eða girnask þeir at kunna skilja þat er hulit er kveðit: þá skili hann þessa bók til fróðleiks ok skemtunar.'

3 Mogk, *Novellistiche Darstellung*, 4–10; see also Sigurður Nordal, 'Snorri Sturluson,' 23–4. On Eyjólfr, see Einar Ól. Sveinsson, *Sagnaritun Oddaverja*, 12; and Haugen, introduction to *First Grammatical Treatise*, 78. On Óláfr, see Krömmelbein, 'Einführung' to Óláfr Þórðarson Hvítaskáld, *Dritte grammatische Abhandlung*, 9–10.

4 On the fragmentary manuscripts, see Guðrún Nordal, *Tools of Literacy*, 57–68.

5 See p. 205, n. 10 above, as well as Faulkes, introduction to *Edda: Skáldskaparmál*, xii.

6 This section's title, like that of the *Eptirmáli*, was provided by early modern editors, who viewed it as a continuation of *Gylfaginning* rather than part of *Skáldskaparmál*, a judgment that is not without merit. It is so named in Rask's 1818 edition (Snorri Sturluson, *Snorra-Edda ásamt Skáldu og þarmeð fylgjandi ritgjörðum*) and the Arnamagnæan edition (*Edda Snorra Sturlusonar. Edda Snorronis Sturlæi*). Faulkes keeps the numbering system of some earlier editions, and so designates the material in *Bragarœður* as G55–8; see his introduction to *Edda: Skáldskaparmál*, vii.

7 On these lists, see Boer, 'Studier over Snorra Edda,' 182–3; Krömmelbein, 'Creative Compilers,' 121–3; and Mogk, 'Zur Bewertung des Codex Upsaliensis,' 404–5.

8 For examples, see Boer, 'Studier over Snorra Edda,' 237, 263; Finnur Jónsson, 'inledning' to *Edda Snorra Sturlusonar*, xxxviii; Mogk 'Untersuchungen über die Gylfaginning,' 537; Eeden, 'inleiding' to *De Codex Trajectinus van de Snorra Edda*, cxxvi; and Zetterhölm, *Studier i en Snorre-Text*, 10–11.

9 The only portions of *Skáldskaparmál* not included in these modules are ch. 75's *þulur*, which virtually all agree are interpolated, and the three lists in U, which, even if they originated with Snorri, cannot be considered parts of the *Edda*. To my knowledge, no one who has considered the authorship of *Skáldskaparmál*'s components has refused to attribute its narrative portions to Snorri. Finnur Jónsson ('inledning' to *Edda Snorra Sturlusonar*, xx), Hans Kuhn ('Das nordgermanische Heidentum,' 162) and Heinrich Beck ('Zum Wahrheitsbegriff bei Snorri Sturluson,' 5–6) are among those who have doubted Snorri's responsibility for all or part of the *Eptirmáli*. Boer rejected all of *Skáldskaparmál* proper as Snorri's work, assigning it to his nephew Óláfr Þórðarson ('Studien über die Snorra Edda,' 141, 147–50).

10 Weber, 'Edda, Jüngere,' 404: 'hohe theoretische Geschlossenheit.'

11 Clunies Ross, *Skáldskaparmál: Snorri Sturluson's* ars poetica, esp. 19–21, 31–4, 141–73.

12 Sigurður Nordal, *Snorri Sturluson*, 98; and Faulkes, introduction to *Edda: Skáldskaparmál*, xi, xvi. This is a view that Clunies Ross herself seems to assent to in her recent *History of Old Norse Poetry* (161, 170), though she does not attempt to reconcile these statements with her earlier position.

13 For others who have proposed this sequence, see Wessén, introduction to *Codex Regius of the Younger Edda*, 15–16, 29–32; de Vries, *Altnordische Literaturgeschichte*, 2:227–31; and Faulkes, introduction to *Edda: Prologue and Gylfaginning*, xix; and introduction to *Edda: Skáldskaparmál*, x–xi.

14 For rejection of this idea, see Finnur Jónsson, 'inledning' to *Edda Snorra Sturlusonar*, xxviii, xxxi; and Sigurður Nordal, *Snorri Sturluson*, 82. For support for it, see Müller, *Untersuchungen zur Uppsala-Edda*, 148–9; and Faulkes, introduction to *Edda: Skáldskaparmál*, xii, xxxv, xliii–xliv.

15 *Skáldskaparmál* 1, p. 5: 'Þá mælir Ægir: "Hversu á marga lund breytið þér orðtökum skáldskapar, eða hversu mörg eru kyn skáldskaparins?" Þá mælir Bragi: "Tvenn eru kyn þau er greina skáldskap allan." Ægir spyrr: "Hver tvenn?" Bragi segir: "Mál ok hættir." "Hvert máltak er haft til skáldskapar?" "Þrenn er grein skáldskaparmáls." "Hver?"'

16 On *Háttatal*, see pp. 115–18. On scholars' failure to identify Latin models for *Skáldskaparmál*, see Faulkes, 'Sources of *Skáldskaparmál*.'

17 *Skáldskaparmál* 1, p. 5: 'at nefna hvern hlut sem heitir; önnur grein er sú er heitir fornöfn; in þriðja málsgrein er kölluð er kenning.'

18 Ibid., pp. 107–8. For different understandings of Snorri's use of *fornöfn*, see Meissner, *Die Kenningar der Skalden*, 1; Brodeur, 'Meaning of Snorri's Categories,' 132; Clunies Ross, *Skáldskaparmál: Snorri Sturluson's* ars poetica, 67–77; and Faulkes, introduction to *Edda: Skáldskaparmál*, xxvi–xxvii.

19 Clunies Ross, *Skáldskaparmál: Snorri Sturluson's* ars poetica, 29.

20 This distinction is not absolute, since kennings such as 'son of Óðinn = Þórr' do refer to themselves. Many kennings, in other words, stand in a literal rather than metaphoric relationship to their referent. While some refuse to identify circumlocutions of this type as kennings (see Heusler, *Die altgermanische Dichtung*, 136–7; and Brodeur, 'Meaning of Snorri's Categories,' 136–7), Snorri nowhere requires a kenning to be metaphorical (see Fidjestøl, 'The Kenning System,' in *Selected Papers*, 28–30).

21 *Skáldskaparmál* 1, p. 5: 'ok <er> sú grein svá sett at vér köllum Óðin eða Þór eða Tý eða einnhvern af Ásum eða álfum, at hverr þeira er ek nefni til, þá tek ek með heiti af eign annars Ássins eða get ek hans verka nokkvorra. Þá eignask hann nafnit en eigi hinn er nefndr var, svá sem vér köllum Sigtý eða Hangatý eða Farmatý, þat er þá Óðins heiti, ok köllum vér þat kent heiti.'

22 See ibid. 2, pp. 7–10.

23 Ibid. 22, 31, pp. 33, 40.

24 Clunies Ross, *Skáldskaparmál: Snorri Sturluson's* ars poetica, 103, 134–5, 175.

25 Faulkes, introduction to *Edda: Skáldskaparmál*, xxx.

26 *Skáldskaparmál* 31, p. 40: 'Mann er ok rétt at kenna til allra Ása heita.' The kennings for Hákon and Skúli employing this technique are in *Háttatal* 13, 14, 35, 43, 48, 53, 55, 85, pp. 10–11, 18, 21, 22, 24, 25, 35. Snorri also calls warriors *sig-Njörðum* (ibid. 55, p. 25).

27 For the former opinion, see Faulkes, introduction to *Edda: Skáldskaparmál*, x–xi, xvi; and Sigurður Nordal, *Snorri Sturluson*, 100–1. For the latter, see Boer, 'Studien über die Snorra Edda,' 131, 136; and Finnur Jónsson, 'Edda Snorra Sturlusonar,' 321–4.

28 Finnur Jónsson, 'inledning' to *Edda Snorra Sturlusonar*, xxiv.

29 *Háttatal* 2, p. 5; and *Skáldskaparmál* 69, p. 108: 'Hár er svá kent at kalla skóg eða viðar heiti nokkvoru, kenna til hauss eða hjarna eða höfuðs.'

30 Boer, 'Studien über die Snorra Edda,' 99.

31 *Háttatal* 7, p. 7.

32 *Skáldskaparmál* 8, p. 19: 'Hann heitir ok Vindlér.'

33 *Gylfaginning* 27, p. 26: 'Heimdalar sverð er kallat höfuð'; Mogk, 'Untersuchungen über die Gylfaginning,' 512; and Faulkes, n. to p. 26, 1.1 of *Gylfaginning*, p. 64.

34 *Háttatal* 21, 42, pp. 14, 20.

35 This number includes all simple kennings, even those forming parts of extended kennings. So, for example, *mála úlfs bága* (*Háttatal* 3, p. 5) counts as two discrete kennings: *úlfs bági* (wolf's enemy = Óðinn) and *Óðins mála* (Óðinn's wife = Jörð). It should be noted that it is impossible to determine the precise number of kennings in *Háttatal* owing to uncertainty over what exactly qualifies as a kenning: for example, *alinveldi*, 'field of the forearm' (ibid. 43, p. 21) could be counted as a kenning, even though its referent, 'forearm,' is named within it. Faulkes estimates 382 kennings in *Háttatal* (introduction to *Edda: Skáldskaparmál*, xxx).

36 *Skáldskaparmál* 53, p. 78: 'Konunga alla er rétt at kenna svá at kalla þá landráðendr eða lands vörðu eða lands sœki.'

37 I have not included in this number the four kennings for intoxicating beverages from *Háttatal* 25, p. 15, which are explicated within the stanza itself. It is perhaps for this reason that Snorri does not dedicate a section of *Skáldskaparmál* to kennings for kinds of drink.

38 Ibid. 43, 17, 24, pp. 21, 12, 15.

39 The only literal kenning given a narrative background is 'helmet of dragon' (*gríma grundar gjaldseiðs*; ibid. 15, p. 11), a reference to the *œgishjálmr* (helm of terror) claimed by Sigurðr from Fáfnir. This may not even qualify as a kenning, since *gríma* is a *heiti* for 'helmet.'

40 Ibid. 2, 15, pp. 5, 11.
41 Ibid. 50, 3, pp. 23, 5.
42 The only truly mythological kenning in *Háttatal* that does not receive more than one instance of explication in *Skáldskaparmál* is *Grotta glaðdript* (joyful snow of Grotti = gold; ibid. 43, p. 21). Still, *Skáldskaparmál* 43, pp. 51–8, contains not only a prose version of the story that supplies this kenning's background, but also, in several manuscripts, *Grottasöngr*, the eddic poem from which it derives.
43 *Háttatal* 59, p. 26; *Skáldskaparmál* 48, p. 66: 'Hvernig skal kenna orrostu? Svá at kalla veðr vápna eða hlífa eða Óðins eða valkyrju'; and ibid. 59, p. 90.
44 *Skáldskaparmál* 2, pp. 8–9: 'Hér er þess dœmi at jörð er kölluð kona Óðins í skáldskap ... Hér er hann kallaðr guðjaðarr ok Míms vinr ok úlfs bági.'
45 *Háttatal* 3, p. 5; and *Skáldskaparmál* 4, p. 14.
46 *Háttatal* 2, p. 5, and *Skáldskaparmál* 4, p. 49; *Háttatal* 30, pp. 16–17, and *Skáldskaparmál* 49, pp. 67, 69, and 17, pp. 21–2. *Skáldskaparmál* 22's excerpt from *Haustlöng* also contains a variation on this kenning: *fjalla Finns ilja brú* (p. 33).
47 *Skáldskaparmál* 64, p. 99: 'It fyrsta ok it œzta heiti manns er kallat maðr keisari, því næst konungr, þar næst jarl.'
48 Ibid.: 'Þessir þrír menn eigu saman þessi heiti öll.'
49 Ibid. 53, p. 79: 'Þar næst eru þeir menn er jarlar heita eða skattkonungar, ok eru þeir jafnir í kenningum við konung nema eigi má þá kalla þjóðkonunga er skattkonungar eru.'
50 Ibid., pp. 79–80: 'Þar næst eru í kenningum í skáldskap þeir menn er hersar heita. Kenna má þá sem konung eða jarl svá at kalla þá gullbrjóta ok auðmildinga ... fyrir því at þjóðkonungr hverr sá er ræðr mörgum löndum þá setr hann til landstjórnar með sér skattkonunga ok jarla at dœma lands lög ... ok skulu þeir dómar ok refsingar vera þar jafnréttir sem sjálfs konungs.'
51 *Háttatal* 27, p. 15.
52 *Skáldskaparmál* 64, p. 101: 'Þessir níu brœðr urðu svá ágætir í hernaði at í öllum frœðum síðan eru nöfn þeira haldin fyrir tignarnöfn svá sem konungs nafn eða nafn jarls.'
53 Klingenberg, 'Hommage für Skúli Bárðarson'; and *Skáldskaparmál* 64, p. 101.
54 See Faulkes, 'Descent from the Gods,' 102–3; and Guðrún Nordal, *Tools of Literacy*, 53–4. On Snorri and the lists in U, see Boer, 'Studien über die Snorra Edda,' 79.
55 *Skáldskaparmál* 1, p. 5.
56 On Snorri and the eddic poems, see Hallberg, *Icelandic Saga*, 44; and Meulengracht Sørensen, *Saga and Society*, 80.
57 In *Háttatal*, there are thirty-one kennings that refer to gold, and thirty-four that refer to rulers as givers, destroyers, dispensers, etc. of gold, rings, etc., and numerous direct references to gold and treasure.

58 Turville-Petre, 'On Scaldic Poetry,' 12.

59 For *gull*, see stt. 2, 23, 47(x3), 48, 61, 72, 89, 90, 91, 94; for *seimr*, stt. 29, 47(x3), 71, 90, 97; and *vell*, stt. 16, 46(x2), 67, 98, 99.

60 *Háttatal* 49, p. 23; and *Skáldskaparmál* 50, p. 72.

61 Comprehension of the kenning *ægis bál* (sea's [Ægir's] fire = gold; *Háttatal* 3, p. 5) is facilitated by information provided in narrative 3; and in *Háttatal* 94, p. 37, Snorri writes that 'bold Kraki sowed gold' (gull<i> søri Kraki fram<r>), a reference to the story in *Skáldskaparmál* 44, pp. 58–9.

62 'Here begins the language of poetry and *heiti* for many things.' Quoted from Faulkes, introduction to *Edda: Skáldskaparmál*, vii.

63 Ibid., xxxv.

64 *Gylfaginning* 23, pp. 23–4.

65 U lacks this excerpt.

66 *Skáldskaparmál* G56, p. 3.

67 Ibid.

68 Many doubt that the excerpts from *Haustlöng* and *Þórsdrápa* in *Skáldskaparmál* 17, 18, and 22 were put there by Snorri (Boer, 'Studien über die Snorra Edda,' 100–2; Finnur Jónsson, 'Edda Snorra Sturlusonar,' 313–14; and Faulkes, introduction to *Edda: Skáldskaparmál*, xv), but this is not certain, and it is in any case certain that Snorri used both poems as sources.

69 See *Skáldskaparmál* 10, 22, 25, 32–3, pp. 19, 30, 36–8, 40–1.

70 Ibid. 1, p. 5: 'En ekki er at gleyma eða ósanna svá þessar sögur at taka ór skáldskapinum for[nar ke]nningar þær er höfuðskáld hafa sér líka látit. En eigi skulu kristnir menn trúa á heiðin goð ok eigi á sannyndi þessar sagnar annan veg en svá sem hér finnsk í upphafi bókar.'

71 References in illustrative stanzas outside of chapters specifically dedicated to this concept are here given according to Faulkes's numbering of *Skáldskaparmál*'s verses: 1, 4, 12, 13, 15, 16, 17, 18, 23, 26 (all so far are in stanzas illustrating Óðinn kennings), 141, 197, 207, 216, 292, 307, 308, 341, 350.

72 *Skáldskaparmál* G58, p. 5: 'hann sendi aptr suman mjöðinn, ok var þess ekki gætt. Hafði þat hverr er vildi, ok köllum vér þat skáldfífla hlut. En Suttunga mjöð gaf Óðinn Ásunum ok þeim mönnum er yrkja kunnu. Því köllum v[ér] skáldskapinn feng Óðins ok fund ok drykk hans ok gjöf hans ok drykk Ásanna.'

73 Especially sceptical are Mogk, *Novellistiche Darstellung*, 14; and Frank, 'Snorri and the Mead of Poetry,' 159–65, 168. See also, and for differing opinions, Edwards, 'Alcohol into Art'; Stephens, 'Mead of Poetry'; Hamel, 'Gods, Skalds and Magic,' and 'Mastering of the Mead'; and Svava Jakobsdóttir, 'Gunnlöð and the Precious Mead.'

74 Hallberg, *Old Icelandic Poetry*, 5; and Kreutzer, *Die Dichtungslehre der Skalden*, 186.

75 *Yggs fengr* (Yggr's booty) and *hrannir Hárs saltunnu* (waves of Hárr's hall-vat), both in *Háttatal* 31, p. 17.

76 For *mærð*, see stt. 68, 85, 92, 95, 97; *lof*, stt. 31, 68, 80, 96, 97, 102; and *hróðr*, stt. 81, 97.

77 Brodeur, 'Meaning of Snorri's Categories,' 130–1.

78 *Skáldskaparmál* G57, p. 3: 'mjöðr sá er hverr er af drekkr verðr skáld eða frœðamaðr.'

79 Stephens, 'Mead of Poetry,' 259.

80 Frank, 'Snorri and the Mead of Poetry,' 169–70; and Stephens, 'Mead of Poetry,' 261.

81 Faulkes writes: 'Although Snorri includes the story of Óðinn's winning of the mead of poetry from the giants and giving it to the Æsir and to poets and scholars ... there is little other indication that he regarded poetry as an inspirational activity' (introduction to *Edda: Skáldskaparmál*, xxxvi).

82 For texts, see *Den norsk-islandske skjaldedigtning*, IB:548–65 (*Harmsól*), 622–33 (*Leiðarvísan*), and 427–45 (*Geisli*).

83 See, for example, Jón Helgason, 'Norges og Islands digtning,' 25.

84 Kreutzer *Die Dichtungslehre der Skalden*, 187: 'Es ist auch kaum anzunehmen, daß Snorri oder ein anderer Skalde so weit in christlicher Zeit sich Odin tatsächlich noch verpflichtet fühlte.'

8 *Gylfaginning* and *Formáli*

1 *Ragnarøkr* = 'twilight of the powers,' *ragnarök* = 'doom of the powers.' The former spelling is used by Snorri, while the latter is more usual in eddic poetry.

2 Both names are provided by modern editors. I use the Icelandic title throughout; all page number references for the *Formáli* are to Snorri Sturluson, *Edda: Prologue and Gylfaginning*.

3 These parts include *Gylfaginning* ch. 1, the Trojan material after the *Formáli* (such as the equation of Ásgarðr with Troy in ch. 9, p. 13), and the end of ch. 54.

4 Of those who have argued against Snorri's authorship of the *Formáli*, the work of two scholars, Andreas Heusler ('Die gelehrte Urgeschichte,' esp. 88, 99–108, 135–7) and Klaus von See (*Mythos und Theologie*, and 'Zum Prolog der Snorra Edda') has been particularly important as well as ardent. A synopsis of older scholars' positions on this question is found in Breiteig, 'Snorre Sturlason og æsene,' 118.

5 Klaus von See's work alone has generated many challenges: see Clunies Ross, '*Mikill Skynsemi er at Rifja Vandliga þat Upp*'; Lönnroth, Review of *Mythos und Theologie*; and Weber, 'Snorri Sturlusons Verhältnis zu seinen Quellen,' 237–8, n. 57.

6 Above all, see Baetke, 'Die Götterlehre der *Snorra-Edda*,' 206.

7 Faulkes, introduction to *Edda: Prologue and Gylfaginning*, xx.

8 Ibid.

9 Of the fifty-one chapters within *Gylfaginning*'s frame (excluding, that is, 1, 2, and 54, which describe Gylfi meeting and departing from the *æsir*), only fourteen are truly narrative: these are chs 34 (Fenrisúlfr and Týr), 37 (Freyr and Gerðr), 42 (giant-builder), 44–8 (Þórr and Útgarða-Loki and Hymir), 49–50 (Baldr's death and Loki's punishment), and, to a certain extent, 51–4 (*ragnarøkr*). Of course, many of these chapters are among *Gylfaginning*'s longest; still, even in terms of space, narratives account for somewhat less than half of this text.

10 Wessén, introduction to *Codex Regius of the Younger Edda*, 32.

11 Two well-known accounts of oral narrative performance in twelfth- and thirteenth-century Iceland are found in ch. 10 of *Þorgils saga ok Hafliða*, where several prose pieces are said to have been performed at a wedding at Reykjahólar in 1119 (*Sturlunga saga*, 1:27), and ch. 2 of *Sturlu þáttr* (pp. 232–3), in which Snorri's nephew Sturla Þórðarson is said to have gained the favour of Magnús Hákonarson and his queen through performance of prose rather than poetic material. These and other pieces of evidence for oral narrative are discussed in Gísli Sigurðsson, *Medieval Icelandic Saga*, 35–7.

12 On Snorri's use of eddic poems in *Gylfaginning*, and the state in which he probably knew them, see Finnur Jónsson, 'inledning' to *Edda Snorra Sturlusonar*, li–liv; Mogk, 'Untersuchungen über die Gylfaginning II'; Müller, *Untersuchungen zur Uppsala-Edda*, 54–6; and Sigurður Nordal, *Snorri Sturluson*, 117–22.

13 See Hamel, 'Mastering of the Mead,' 81–3; Harris, 'Masterbuilder Tale'; Mogk, *Novellistiche Darstellung*, 15–19, 31–2; Óskar Halldórsson, 'Snorri og Edda,' 108; Meulengracht Sørensen, 'Snorris frœði,' 281–2; Zetterhölm, *Studier i en Snorre-Text*, 43–4; and Gísli Sigurðsson, *Medieval Icelandic Saga*, 13–17, 115.

14 While some have argued that Snorri was responsible for the first written collection of eddic poems, it is more likely that this was compiled by others after his work had appeared; see p. 184, n. 75 above.

15 The exact dating of the *Gesta Danorum* is uncertain. Saxo may have begun writing before 1185, the year at which his history ends, and probably finished sometime between 1208–16; see Friis-Jensen, *Saxo Grammaticus as Latin Poet*, 11–12; and Davidson, introduction to Saxo Grammaticus, *History of the Danes: Books I–IX*, 2:12.

16 *Gesta Danorum*, 2–3: 'Danorum antiquiores conspicuis fortitudinis operibus editis, glorie emulacione suffusos, Romani stili imitacione, non solum rerum a se magnifice gestarum titulos exquisito contextus genere, ueluti poetico quodam opere, perstrinxisse, uerum eciam maiorum acta patrii sermonis carminibus uulgata,

lingue sue literis, saxis ac rupibus insculpenda curasse. Quorum uestigiis ... metra metris reddenda curaui.' *History of the Danes*, trans. Fisher, 5.

17 *Historia Norwegiae*, 97. This text has proven impossible to date, having been written, as Andersson states, 'perhaps before 1178, but perhaps as late as 1220' ('Kings' Sagas (*Konungasögur*),' 201).

18 On these influences, see Andersson, 'Kings' Sagas (*Konungasögur*),' 201–11.

19 None of the kings' sagas or compilations produced before *Heimskringla*, which include Eiríkr Oddsson's lost *Hryggjarstykki*, various sagas of St Óláfr and Óláfr Tryggvason, *Sverris saga*, *Fagrskinna*, and *Morkinskinna*, deal with myth or pre-history. One Icelandic saga that did deal with pre-history and euhemerized pagan gods was *Skjöldunga saga*, but this was concerned with Danish rather than Norwegian royal history.

20 Gísli Sigurðsson, *Medieval Icelandic Saga*, 45–6, referring to Clover, 'Long Prose Form.'

21 Heusler, 'Die gelehrte Urgeschichte,' 104: 'sich der Frömmste dabei beruhigen konnte, und doch standen die Geschichten in ihrer heidnischen Frische da.'

22 Ibid., 88–94; and Faulkes, 'Descent from the Gods,' esp. 96–105.

23 *Íslendingabók,* appendix III, p. 58. This tradition is also represented in the *Historia Norwegiae*, and was probably present in the lost beginning of *Ynglingatal*; see Faulkes, 'Descent from the Gods,' 96.

24 *Formáli* 11, p. 6: 'þess ríkis er nú heitir Nóregr. Sá er Sæmingr kallaðr, ok telja þar Nóregskonungar sínar ættir til hans ok svá jarlar ok aðrir ríkismenn.' Snorri goes on to say that he derives this information from *Háleygjatal*, a poem composed by Eyvindr Finnsson c. 985.

25 See Bjarni Guðnason, *Um Skjöldungasögu*.

26 On the sources for this tradition, see Faulkes, 'Genealogies and Regnal Lists in a Manuscript in Resen's Library'; and his 'Descent from the Gods,' 99.

27 *Formáli* 3, p. 4: 'er heitr ok brunninn af sólu ... Hinn nyrðri hlutr er þar kaldr svá at eigi vex gras ok eigi má byggja ... er öll fegrð ok prýði ok eign jarðar ávaxtar, gull ok gimsteinar. Þar er ok mið veröldin.'

28 The idea that the *æsir* were from Tyrkland was seemingly borrowed by Snorri from Ari, who begins his genealogy with *Yngvi Tyrkja konungr* (*Íslendingabók*, appendix III, p. 58). Troy is not mentioned, however, in Ari's surviving work.

29 *Formáli* 9, pp. 4–5: 'þann köllum vér Þór ... Þat köllum vér Þrúðheim.'

30 Ibid., p. 5: 'kannaði allar heims hálfur ok sigraði einn saman alla berserki ok risa ok einn hinn mesta dreka ok mörg dýr. Í norðrhálfu heims fann hann spákonu þá er Sibil hét, er vér köllum Sif, ok fekk hennar.'

31 Ibid.: 'Voden, þann köllum vér Óðin.'

32 Ibid.: 'Hann var ágætr maðr af speki ok allri atgervi.'

33 Ibid. 11, p. 6: 'slíkt vald hafa í hans ríki sem hann vildi sjálfr.'

34 Ibid.: 'var eigintunga um öll þessi lönd.'

35 Ibid. 10–11, pp. 5–6.

36 As Heusler writes: 'Above all it should please me … to cleanse the image of the writer Snorri of the stain of the transmitted *Edda* Prologue' (Vor allem soll es mich freuen … das Bild des Schriftstellers Snorri zu reinigen von dem Makel des überlieferten Eddaprologs. 'Die gelehrte Urgeschichte,' 88).

37 Faulkes, 'Descent from the Gods,' 123; see also 101.

38 On Roman, Frankish, and British historians' attempts to trace the origins of their cultures and/or rulers to Troy, see ibid., 116–18; and Heusler, 'Die gelehrte Urgeschichte,' 82–6.

39 Faulkes, 'Sources of *Skáldskaparmál*,' 62–3; and Leach, *Angevin Britain and Scandinavia*, 147–8.

40 Faulkes, 'Descent from the Gods,' 101–2; and Heusler, 'Die gelehrte Urgeschichte,' 130.

41 Leach, *Angevin Britain and Scandinavia*, 145.

42 Ibid., 147. These texts include the Sturlungar genealogy in U and an expanded prologue to *Sverris saga* found in *Flateyjarbók*, an Icelandic manuscript of the late 1300s (2:535–6; see also Heusler, 'Die gelehrte Urgeschichte,' 92–4, 137).

43 Larson, introduction to *The King's Mirror*, 64–5. This dating is not entirely certain; Bagge, for example, argues for this text having been written between 1247 and 1263 (*Political Thought of the King's Mirror*, 12–14).

44 Friis-Jensen, 'Saxo Grammaticus's Study of the Roman Historiographers,' 71. For a summary of scholarly opinion on Saxo's typological treatment of Danish history, see Davidson, introduction to Saxo Grammaticus, *History of the Danes*, 2:4–7.

45 *Gesta Danorum*, p. 10: 'Dan igitur et Angul, a quibus Danorum cepit origo … non solum conditores gentis nostre, uerum eciam rectores fuere. Quanquam Dudo, rerum Aquitãnicarum scriptor, Danos a Danais ortos nuncupatosque recenseat … Verum a Dan (ut fert antiquitas) regum nostrorum stemmata, ceu quodam deriuata principio, splendido, successionis ordino profluxerunt.' *History of the Danes*, trans. Fisher, 14.

46 Skovgaard-Petersen, 'Saxo, Historian of the Patria,' 75.

47 Mortensen, 'Saxo Grammaticus' View of the Origins of the Danes,' 172, 174–5.

48 *Formáli* 9, p. 5: 'Engi kann at segja ætt Sifjar.'

49 Ibid. 10, p. 5: 'Óðinn hafði spádóm ok svá kona hans, ok af þeim vísindum fann hann þat at nafn hans mundi uppi vera haft í norðrhálfu heimsins ok tignat um fram alla konunga. Fyrir þá sök fýstisk hann at byrja ferð sína af Tyrklandi ok hafði með sér mikinn fjölða liðs … En hvar sem þeir fóru yfir lönd, þá var ágæti mikit frá þeim sagt, svá at þeir þóttu líkari goðum en mönnum.' Translation slightly adapted from Faulkes's *Edda* translation, 3–4.

50 *Ynglinga saga*, ch. 6, in Snorri Sturluson, *Heimskringla*, 1:17: 'Mælti hann allt
   hendingum, svá sem nú er þat kveðit, er skáldskapr heitir. Hann ok hofgoðar hans
   heita ljóðasmiðir, því at sú íþrótt hófsk af þeim í Norðrlöndum.'

51 Óláfr hvítaskáld Þórðarson, *Dritte grammatische Abhandlung*, 96: 'Jþæssi bok ma
   gerla skilia, at öll ær æin listin skalld skapr sa, ær romverskir spækingar namv
   iathænis borg a griklandi ok snerv siþan i latinv mal, ok sa lioða háttr æða skalld-
   skapr, ær oðinn ok aðrir asiamenn flvttv norðr higat I norðr halfv heimsins, ok
   kendv monnvm a sina tvngv þæsskonar list, sva sæm þeir höföv skipat ok nvmit
   isialfv asia landi, þar sæm mæst var fregð ok rikdomr ok froðlæikr veralldarinnar.'
   I have not reproduced this edition's critical marks.

52 See, 'Snorris Konzeption einer nordischen Sonderkultur,' 150: 'diesem Satz würde
   Snorri keineswegs zugestimmt haben.'

53 Krömmelbein, 'Einführung' to Ólafr Þórðarson hvítaskáld, *Dritte grammatische
   Abhandlung*, 30: 'eine genuin einheimische Dichtungsart.' See also his 'Creative
   Compilers,' 117–19.

54 Heusler, 'Die gelehrte Urgeschichte,' 86: 'Aus Norwegen haben wir keine Zeug-
   nisse für eine gelehrte Urheimatsfabel, und daran wird schwerlich unsre lücken-
   hafte Überlieferung schuld sein.'

55 *Konungs skuggsjá*, chs 43, 44, pp. 104–5: 'Nú skal í þessu merkja, at hverr maðr á
   jörðu er … skyldr at sœma ok tigna konungligt nafn, þat sem jarðligr maðr heldr af
   guði; þvíat sjálfr guðs son lét sér sama at tigna svá mjök konungligt nafn, at hann
   gerði sjálfan sik skattgildan … ok þann lærisvein sinn, er hann skipaði at vera
   höfðingja yfir öllum postolum sínum ok allri kennimannligri tign … guð sjálfr kal-
   lar konung vera krist sinn … sá hræðisk eigi guð, er eigi veitir konungi fulla tign.'

56 Bagge, *From Gang Leader*, 159–60.

57 *Konungs skuggsjá*, ch. 36, p. 75: 'nú ef svá illa berr einuhverju ríki … at mörg eru
   konunga efni, enda verðr svá ilt ráð tekit, at öll verða senn skrýdd konungligri tign
   eða nafni; þá má þat ríki kalla hömlubarða eða auðnaróðal, ok má þat þá náliga
   virðask sem týnt ríki, þvíat þat er þá sáit með hinu mesta úárans fræi ok úfriðar
   korni.'

58 *Gesta Danorum*, p. 25 'Hoc loci quid aliud adiercerim, quam tale numen hac coni-
   uge dignum extitisse? Tanto quondam errore mortalium ludificabantur ingenia.'
   History of the Danes, trans. Fisher, 26.

59 Oddr Snorrason, *Saga Olafs Konungs Tryggvasunar*, ch. 32, p. 35. Another Latin
   saga of Óláfr Tryggvason that likely used a combination of euhemerism and
   demon theory was that of Gunnlaugr Leifsson from the 1190s. While none of
   the sagas of St Óláfr that predate Snorri's survive, traces of them are preserved
   in compilations like *Flateyjarbók*, where Óðinn is identified with the devil
   (2:134–5). It is likely, moreover, that Saxo adopted this theory; see Weber,
   'Intellegere Historiam,' 107–8.

60 Baetke, 'Die Götterlehre der *Snorra-Edda*,' 213–14: 'Was für Oddr und den Ver-
fasser der Fagrsk. gilt, trifft natürlich erst recht für Snorri zu, der als Geschichts-
schreiber auf ihren Schultern steht … vermeidet soviel wie möglich, theologische
Urteile abzugeben … Wahrscheinlich hat er sich in der Auffassung des Vorgangs
überhaupt nicht von seinem Vorgänger unterschieden … er die Erscheinung auch
seinerseits für eine Verkörperung oder einen Abgesandten des Teufels gehalten hat.'

61 Weber, 'Snorri Sturlusons Verhältnis zu seinen Quellen,' 238–9: 'Daß sie hierin –
ihnen selbst unbewußt – vom Teufel bestärkt werden … ist für den mittelalterlichen
christlichen Betrachter selbstverständlich, braucht also nicht eigens – wie positivis-
tische Forschung für nötig hält – erwähnt zu werden.'

62 Weber, 'Intellegere Historiam,' 109.

63 Oddr Snorrason, *Saga Olafs Konnungs Tryggvasunar*, ch. 32, p. 35: 'Miok hefir
guð leyst oss af miklom haska en avðsett er at fiandin hefir brvgðiz ilike Oðens. ok
villdi blekia oss.'

64 *Óláfs saga Tryggvasonar*, ch. 64, in Snorri Sturluson, *Heimskringla*, 1:314: 'þetta
myndi engi maðr verit hafa ok þar myndi verit hafa Óðinn, sá er heiðnir menn
höfðu lengi á trúat … engu áleiðis koma at svíkja þá.'

65 *Formáli* 1, p. 3: 'þeir týndu guðs nafni ok víðast um veröldina fansk eigi sá maðr er
deili kunni á skapara sínum. En eigi at síðr veitti guð þeim jarðligar giptir, fé ok
sælu, er þeir skyldu við vera í heiminum. Miðlaði hann ok spekina svá at þeir
skilðu alla jarðliga hluti ok allar greinir þær er sjá mátti loptsins ok jarðarinnar.'

66 See, for example, Beyschlag, 'Die Betörung Gylfis,' 176–7; Ursula and Peter
Dronke 'Prologue of the Prose *Edda*,' 153, 157–8; Einar Ól. Sveinsson, 'Snorri
Sturluson,' 156; Klingenberg, 'Gylfaginning. Tres vidit unum adoravit,' 650–8;
Strerath-Bolz, *Kontinuität statt Konfrontation*, 45–6, 51; and Weber, 'Edda, Jüng-
ere,' 397–403. Even some who have argued that Snorri did not write the *Formáli*
have seen this as its author's primary goal: see especially See, 'Zum Prolog der
Snorra Edda,' 113–15.

67 *Gylfaginning* 2, 3, pp. 7, 8: 'af eðli sjálfra þeira, eða mundi því valda goðmögn þau
er þeir blótuðu'; 'Hverr er œztr eða elztr allra goða?'

68 Ibid. 3, p. 8: 'Sá heitir Alföðr at váru máli, en í Ásgarði inum forna átti hann tólf
nöfn.'

69 Ibid. 3, pp. 8–9: '"Hvar er sá guð, eða hvat má hann, eða hvat hefir hann unnit fra-
maverka?" Hár segir: "Lifir hann of allar aldir ok stjórnar öllu ríki sínu ok ræðr
öllum hlutum stórum ok smám." Þá mælir Jafnhár: "Hann smíðaði himin ok jörð
ok loptin ok alla eign þeira." Þá mælti Þriði: "Hitt er mest er hann gerði manninn
ok gaf honum önd þá er lifa skal ok aldri týnask, þótt líkaminn fúni at moldu eða
brenni at ösku. Ok skulu allir menn lifa þeir er rétt eru siðaðir ok vera með honum
sjálfum þar sem heitir Gimlé eða Vingólf, en vándir menn fara til Heljar ok þaðan í
Niflhel."'

70 Sigurður Nordal, *Snorri Sturluson*, 116: 'Þessi kapítuli er vafalaust það lakasta, sem Snorri hefur skrifað, og væri engin missa í, þótt honum væri alveg burtu kipt.'

71 Baetke, 'Die Götterlehre der *Snorra-Edda*,' esp. 236–9.

72 *Formáli* 2, p. 4: 'væri smíðaðir af nokkuru efni.'

73 *Gylfaginning* 6, p. 11: 'Ok þat er mín trúa at sá Óðinn ok hans brœðr munu vera stýrandi himins ok jarðar; þat ætlum vér at hann muni svá heita. Svá heitir sá maðr er vér vitum mestan ok ágæztan, ok vel megu þér hann láta svá heita.'

74 Ibid. 9, p. 13: 'má hann heita Alföðr at hann er faðir allra goðanna ok manna.'

75 Ibid. 20, p. 21: 'Óðinn er œztr ok elztr Ásanna.'

76 Bourdieu, *In Other Words*, 79.

77 Bourdieu, *Logic of Practice*, 86.

78 Bourdieu, *Pascalian Meditations*, 150.

79 Sigurður Nordal, 'Snorri Sturluson,' 7–8: 'Vér minnumst ekki þessarar ártíðar Snorra vegna þess, að hann var höfðingi, auðmaður og bar mikil tignarnöfn. Vér látum hljótt um dánarafmæli Þorvalds Vatnsfirðings, Kolskeggs auðga og meira að segja Gissurar jarls. Vér þykjumst ekki þurfa að leita að mönnum, sem svipar til þeirra, langt aftur í aldir … En snillingar eins og Snorri fæðast sjaldan hjá smárri þjóð og fá enn sjaldnar að þroskast og njóta sín.'

Appendix

1 This kenning is possibly defined by action; see my discussion of it in chapter 6, pp. 109–10.

2 Found only in two partial *Edda* manuscripts; see Faulkes's n. to v357 (*Skáldskaparmál*, p. 215).

3 While the referent 'blood' is not given its own section in *Skáldskaparmál*, numerous illustrations of kennings for this term are found in these chapters dedicated to carrion beasts.

4 In *Skáldskaparmál* 69, Snorri says that a head can be referred to as *hjálms land*, 'land of helmet' (p. 108).

5 *Brún* means 'edge, shore' as well as 'eyebrow,' and so this kenning could be regarded as literal.

6 There are, however, close parallels to this kenning in *Skáldskaparmál* 52: *glyggrann*, 'hall of winds,' and *heims hrót*, 'world's roof' (p. 77).

7 One of the illustrations found here is repeated in *Skáldskaparmál* 49, pp. 67–8.

8 The four kennings from st. 25 are explained in the verse itself; see p. 216, n. 37 above.

9 While this kenning is nowhere directly explicated, *setr* is used in three kennings in *Skáldskaparmál* to denote a place (chs 18, 64, pp. 26–7, 99).

Works Cited

Names of Icelandic authors (medieval and modern) are alphabetized according to first name. Titles of works beginning with 'Þ' are found at the end of the list of primary sources. Accents and other vowel markings are ignored for purposes of alphabetization.

Primary Sources

Ættartölur. In *Sturlunga saga*, 1:51–6.

Ágrip af Nóregskonunga sögum: Fagrskinna – Nóregs konunga tal. Edited by Bjarni Einarsson. Íslenzk fornrit 29. Reykjavík: Hið íslenzka fornritafélag, 1984.

Ari Þorgilsson. *The Book of the Icelanders* (*Íslendingabók*). Edited and translated by Halldór Hermannsson. Islandica 20. Ithaca: Cornell University Press, 1930.

Biskupa sögur. Edited by Guðbrandur Vigfússon and Jón Sigurðsson. 2 vols. Copenhagen: Hið íslenzka bókmentfélag, 1856–78.

Bjarnar saga Hítdœlakappa. In *Borgfirðingar sögur*, 109–211

Borgfirðingar sögur. Edited by Sigurður Nordal and Guðni Jónsson. Íslenzk fornrit 3. Reykjavík: Hið íslenzka fornritafélag, 1938.

Brennu-Njáls saga. Edited by Einar Ól. Sveinsson. Íslenzk fornrit 12. Reykjavík: Hið íslenzka fornritafélag, 1954.

Danakonunga sögur: Skjöldunga saga, Knýtlinga saga, Ágrip af sögu Danakonunga. Edited by Bjarni Guðnason. Íslenzk fornrit 35. Reykjavík: Hið íslenzka fornritafélag, 1982.

Den norsk-islandske skjaldedigtning. Edited by Finnur Jónsson. 4 vols. Vols IA, IIA, Tekst efter håndskrifterne. Vols IB, IIB, Rettet tekst. Copenhagen: Rosenkilde og Bagger, 1912–15.

Den tredje og fjærde grammatiske afhandling i Snorres Edda tilligemed de grammatiske afhandlingers prolog og to andre tillæg. Edited by Björn Magnússon Ólsen. Copenhagen: G. Knudtzon, 1884.

Diplomatarium Islandicum: Íslenzkt fornbréfasafn, vol. 1, *834–1264*. Edited by Jón Sigurðsson. Copenhagen: S.L. Møller, 1857.

Edda. Die Lieder des Codex Regius nebst verwandten Denkmälern. Edited by Gustav Neckel. 5th ed. Revised by Hans Kuhn. Heidelberg: Carl Winter, 1983.

Egils saga Skalla-Grímssonar. Edited by Sigurður Nordal. Íslenzk fornrit 2. Reykjavík: Hið íslenzka fornritafélag, 1933.

Elis saga ok Rósamundu. In *Riddarasögur*, edited by Bjarni Vilhjálmsson, 4:1–135. Reykjavík: Íslendingasagnaútgáfan, 1954.

Fagrskinna. In *Ágrip af Nóregskonunga sögum: Fagrskinna – Nóregs konunga tal*, 57–373.

First Grammatical Treatise: The Earliest Germanic Phonology. Edited and translated by Einar Haugen. 2nd ed. London: Longman, 1972.

Flateyjarbók: En samling af norske konge-sagaer. Edited by Guðbrandur Vigfússon and C.R. Unger. 3 vols. Oslo: P.T. Malling, 1860–8.

Grágás Ia, Ib: *Grágás: Islændernes lovbog i fristatens tid, udgivet efter det Konge-lige bibliotheks haandskrift*. Edited by Vilhjálmur Finsen. Copenhagen: Berling, 1852.

Grágás II: *Grágás efter det Arnamagnæanske haandskrift Nr. 334 fol., Staðarhólsbók*. Edited by Vilhjálmur Finsen. Copenhagen: Gyldendal, 1879.

Gunnlaugs saga ormstungu. In *Borgfirðinga sögur*, 49–107.

Hallfreðar saga vandræðaskálds. In *Vatnsdæla saga*, edited by Einar Ól. Sveinsson, 133–200. Íslenzk fornrit 8. Reykjavík: Hið íslenzka fornritafélag, 1939.

Háttalykill enn forni. Edited by Jón Helgason and Anne Holtsmark. Bibliotheca Arnamagnæana 1. Copenhagen: Ejnar Munksgaard, 1941.

Historia Norwegiae. In *Monumenta Historica Norvegiae: Latinske kildeskrifter til Norges historie i middelalderen*, edited by Gustav Storm, 69–124. Oslo: A.W. Brøgger, 1880.

Jóns saga hins helga. In *Biskupa sögur*, 1:213–60.

Karl Jónsson. *Sverris saga etter Cod. AM 327 4o*. Edited by Gustav Indrebø. Christiania: Emil Moestne, 1920.

The King's Mirror: Speculum Regale – Konungs Skuggsjá. Translated by Laurence Marcellus Larson. Scandinavian Monographs 3. New York: The American-Scandinavian Foundation, 1917.

Konungs Skuggsjá. Konge-Speilet. Speculum Regale. Edited by R. Keyser, P.A. Munch, and C.R. Unger. Christiania: Carl C. Werner, 1848.

Kvæði og Dansleikir. Edited by Jón Samsonarson. 2 vols. Reykjavík: Almenna bóka-félagið, 1964.

Landnámabók I-III: Hauksbók. Sturlubók. Melabók. Edited by Finnur Jónsson. Copen-hagen: Thiele, 1900.

Laxdæla saga. Edited by Einar Ól. Sveinsson. Íslenzk fornrit 5. Reykjavík: Hið íslenz-ka fornritafélag, 1934.

The Life of Gudmund the Good, Bishop of Holar. Translated by E.O.G. Turville-Petre and E.S. Olszewska. Coventry, Great Britain: Viking Society for Northern Research, 1942.

Matthew Paris. *Chronica Majora.* Edited by Henry Richards Luard. 7 vols. London: Longman, 1877.

Morkinskinna: The Earliest Icelandic Chronicle of the Norwegian Kings (1030–1157). Translated by Theodore M. Andersson and Kari Ellen Gade. Islandica 51. Ithaca: Cornell University Press, 2000.

Nóregskonungatal. In *Den norsk-islandske skjaldedigtning,* edited by Finnur Jónsson, vol. 1A:579–89.

Norges gamle love indtil 1387. Edited by R. Keyser and P.A. Munch. 4 vols. Christiania: Chr. Gröndahl, 1846–85.

Oddr Snorrason. *Saga Olafs Konungs Tryggvasunar: Kong Olaf Tyrggvesöns Saga.* Edited by P.A. Munch. Christiania: Brøgger and Christie, 1853.

Óláfr Þórðarson hvítaskáld. *Dritte grammatische Abhandlung: Der isländische Text nach den Handschriften AM 748 I, 4° und Codex Wormianus.* Edited by Björn Magnússon Ólsen. Translated and edited by Thomas Krömmelbein. Oslo: Novus Forlag, 1998.

The Saga of Tristram and Ísönd. Translated by Paul Schach. Lincoln: University of Nebraska Press, 1973.

Saxo Grammaticus. *Gesta Danorum.* Edited by Alfred Holder. Strassburg: Karl J. Trübner, 1886.

– *The History of the Danes: Books I-IX.* Edited by H.R. Ellis Davidson. Translated by Peter Fisher. 2 vols. Cambridge: D.S. Brewer, 1996.

Skáldatal A and B. In *Edda Snorra Sturlusonar. Edda Snorronis Sturlæi,* 3:251–69. Copenhagen: Legatus Arnamagnæani, 1848–87.

Sneglu-Halla þáttr. In *Flateyjarbók,* 3:261–95.

Snorri Sturluson. *Edda.* Translated by Anthony Faulkes. London: Everyman, 1987.

– *Edda: Háttatal.* Edited by Anthony Faulkes. Oxford: Clarendon Press, 1991.

– *Edda: Prologue and Gylfaginning.* Edited by Anthony Faulkes. Oxford: Clarendon Press, 1982.

– *Edda: Skáldskaparmál.* Edited by Anthony Faulkes. 2 vols. Oxford: Viking Society for Northern Research, 1998.

– *Edda Snorra Sturlusonar.* Edited by Finnur Jónsson. Copenhagen: Gyldensdal, 1931.

– *Háttatal Snorra Sturlusonar.* Edited by Theodor Möbius. 2 vols. Halle: Waisenhause, 1879–81.

– *Heimskringla.* Edited by Bjarni Aðalbjarnarson. 3 vols. Íslenzk fornrit 26–8. Reykjavík: Hið íslenzka fornritafélag, 1941–51.

– *Heimskringla: History of the Kings of Norway.* Translated by Lee M. Hollander. Austin: University of Texas Press, 1964.

– *Snorra-Edda ásamt Skáldu og þarmeð fylgjandi ritgjörðum*. Edited by R.Kr. Rask. Stockholm: Elménska prentsmiðja, 1818.

Sturla Þórðarson. *Íslendinga saga*. In *Sturlunga saga*, 1:229–534.

– *Hákonar saga Hákonarsonar: Hakonar Saga and a Fragment of Magnús Saga*. Edited by Guðbrandur Vigfússon. Rerum Britannicarum Medii Ævi Scriptores 88. Icelandic Sagas 2. London: Eyre and Spottiswoode, 1887.

– *The Saga of Hacon and a Fragment of The Saga of Magnus with Appendices*. Translated by G.W. Dasent. Rerum Britannicarum Medii Ævi Scriptores 88. Icelandic Sagas 4. London: Eyre and Spottiswoode, 1894.

Sturlunga saga. Edited by Jón Jóhannesson, Magnús Finnbogason, and Kristján Eldjárn. 2 vols. Reykjavík: Sturlunguútgáfan, 1946.

Sturlu saga. In *Sturlunga saga*, 1:63–114.

Sturlu þáttr. In *Sturlunga saga*, 2:227–36.

Theodoricus Monachus. *Historia de antiquitate regum Norwagiensium*. In *Monumenta Historica Norvegiae: Latinske kildeskrifter til Norges historie i middelalderen*, edited by Gustav Storm, 1–68. Oslo: A.W. Brøgger, 1880.

Tristrams saga ok Ísöndar. Edited and translated by Peter Jorgensen. In *Norse Romance*, vol. 1: *The Tristan Legend*, edited by Marianne E. Kalinke, 23–226. Cambridge: D.S. Brewer, 1999.

Þórðar saga kakala. In *Sturlunga saga*, 2:1–86.

Þorgils saga ok Hafliða. In *Sturlunga saga*, 1:12–50.

Þorgils saga skarða. In *Sturlunga saga*, 2:104–226.

Þorleifs þáttr jarlsskálds. In *Flateyjarbók*, 1:207–15.

Secondary Sources

Andersen, Stig Toftgaard, ed. *Die Aktualität der Saga: Festschrift für Hans Schottmann*. Berlin: Walter de Gruyter, 1999.

Andersson, Theodore M. 'Kings' Sagas (*Konungasögur*).' In *Old Norse-Icelandic Literature: A Critical Guide*, edited by Clover and Lindow, 197–238.

Baetke, Walter. 'Die Götterlehre der *Snorra-Edda*.' In his *Kleine Schriften: Geschichte, Recht und Religion in germanischen Schrifttum*, edited by Kurt Rudolph and Ernst Walter, 206–46. Weimar: H. Böhlau, 1973.

Bagge, Sverre. *From Gang Leader to the Lord's Anointed: Kingship in* Sverris saga *and* Hákonar saga Hákonarsonar. The Viking Collection 8. Odense: Odense University Press, 1996.

– 'Icelandic Uniqueness or a Common European Culture? The Case of the Kings' Sagas.' *Scandinavian Studies* 69 (1997): 418–42.

– 'The Norwegian Monarchy in the Thirteenth Century.' In *Kings and Kingship in Medieval Europe*, edited by Anne J. Duggan, 159–76. Exeter: Short Run Press, 1993.

– *The Political Thought of the King's Mirror*. Mediaeval Scandinavia Supplements 3. Odense: Odense University Press, 1987.

– *Society and Politics in Snorri Sturluson's* Heimskringla. Berkeley: University of California Press, 1991.

Barði Guðmundsson. 'Goðorð forn og ný.' *Skírnir* 11 (1937–8): 56–83.

Barnes, Geraldine. 'Authors, Dead and Alive, in Old Norse Fiction.' *Parergon* 8 (1990): 5–22.

– '*Parcevals Saga*: Riddara Skuggsjá?' *Arkiv för nordisk filologi* 99 (1984): 49–62.

– 'The *Riddarasögur* and Mediæval European Literature.' *Mediaeval Scandinavia* 8 (1975): 140–58.

– 'Some Current Issues in *Riddarasögur* Research.' *Arkiv för nordisk filologi* 104 (1989): 73–88.

Beck, Heinrich. 'Zum Wahrheitsbegriff bei Snorri Sturluson.' In *Die Aktualität der Saga*, edited by Andersen, 1–11.

Berger, Alan. '*Heimskringla* and the Compilations.' *Arkiv för nordisk filologi* 114 (1999): 5–15.

– '*Heimskringla* is an abbreviation of *Hulda-Hrokkinskinna*.' *Arkiv för nordisk filologi* 116 (2001): 65–70.

– 'The Sagas of Harald Fairhair.' *Scripta Islandica* 31 (1980): 14–29.

Berman, Melissa A. '*Egils Saga* and *Heimskringla*.' *Scandinavian Studies* 54 (1982): 21–50.

Beyschlag, Siegfried. 'Die Betörung Gylfis.' *Zeitschrift für deutsches Altertum und deutsche Literatur* 85 (1954–5): 163–81.

Bjarni Einarsson. 'Andvaka.' In *Afmælisrit Jóns Helgasonar 30. júní 1969*, edited by Jakob Benediktsson, Jón Samsonarson, Jónas Kristjánsson, Ólafur Halldórsson, and Stefán Karlsson, 27–33. Reykjavík: Heimskringla, 1969.

Bjarni Guðnason. *Um Skjöldungasögu*. Reykjavík: Bókaútgáfa menningarsjóðs, 1963.

Björn Magnússon Ólsen. 'Er Snorri Sturluson höfundur Egilssögu?' *Skírnir* 79 (1905): 363–8.

– 'Um Sturlungu.' In *Safn til sögu Íslands og íslenzkra bókmenta að fornu og nýju*, 3:193–509. Copenhagen: S.L. Møller, 1896.

Boer, R.C. 'Om kommentaren til *Háttatal*.' *Arkiv för nordisk filologi* 43 (1927): 262–309.

– 'Studien über die Snorra Edda: Die Geschichte der Tradition bis auf den Archetypus.' *Acta Philologica Scandinavica* 1 (1926–7): 54–150.

– 'Studier over Snorra Edda.' *Aarböger for nordisk oldkyndighed og historie* 48 (1924): 145–272.

Bouchard, Constance Brittain. *Strong of Body, Brave and Noble: Chivalry and Society in Medieval France*. Ithaca: Cornell University Press, 1998.

Bourdieu, Pierre. 'Concluding Remarks: For a Sociogenetic Understanding of Intellectual Works.' In *Bourdieu: Critical Perspectives*, edited by Calhoun, LiPuma, and Postone, 263–75.
– *Distinction: A Social Critique of the Judgement of Taste*. Translated by Richard Nice. Cambridge, MA: Harvard University Press, 1984.
– *The Field of Cultural Production: Essays on Art and Literature*. Edited and introduced by Randal Johnson. New York: Columbia University Press, 1993.
– *In Other Words: Essays Towards a Reflexive Sociology*. Translated by Matthew Adamson. Stanford: Stanford University Press, 1990.
– *Language and Symbolic Power*. Edited and introduced by John B. Thompson. Translated by Gino Raymond and Matthew Adamson. Cambridge, MA: Harvard University Press, 1991.
– *The Logic of Practice*. Translated by Richard Nice. Stanford: Stanford University Press, 1990.
– *Outline of a Theory of Practice*. Translated by Richard Nice. Cambridge: Cambridge University Press, 1977.
– *Pascalian Meditations*. Translated by Richard Nice. Stanford: Stanford University Press, 2000.
– *The Rules of Art: Genesis and Structure of the Literary Field*. Translated by Susan Emanuel. Stanford: Stanford University Press, 1996.
Bourdieu, Pierre, and Loïc J.D. Wacquant. *An Invitation to Reflexive Sociology*. Chicago: University of Chicago Press, 1992.
Bragg, Lois. 'Generational Tensions in *Sturlunga Saga*.' *Arkiv för nordisk filologi* 112 (1997): 5–34.
Breiteig, Byrge. 'Snorre Sturlason og æsene.' *Arkiv för nordisk filologi* 79 (1963): 117–53.
Brodeur, Arthur G. 'The Meaning of Snorri's Categories.' *University of California Publications in Modern Philology* 36 (1952): 129–47.
Brubaker, Rogers. 'Social Theory as Habitus.' In *Bourdieu: Critical Perspectives*, edited by Calhoun, LiPuma, and Postone, 212–34.
Bugge, Alexander. 'Handeln mellem England og Norge indtil begyndelsen af det 15de aarhundrede.' *Historisk tidsskrift* 3 (1898): 9–22.
Byock, Jesse L. *Feud in the Icelandic Saga*. Berkeley: University of California Press, 1982.
– *Medieval Iceland: Society, Sagas and Power*. Berkeley: University of California Press, 1988.
Calhoun, Craig, Edward LiPuma, and Moishe Postone, eds. *Bourdieu: Critical Perspectives*. Chicago: University of Chicago Press, 1993.
Ciklamini, Marlene. *Snorri Sturluson*. Boston: Twayne Publishers, 1978.
Cleasby, Richard, and Guðbrandur Vigfússon. *An Icelandic-English Dictionary*. 2nd ed. With a supplement by William A. Craigie. Oxford: Clarendon Press, 1874.

Clover, Carol J. 'The Long Prose Form.' *Arkiv för nordisk filologi* 101 (1986): 10–39.
– 'Skaldic Sensibility.' *Arkiv för nordisk filologi* 93 (1978): 63–81.
Clover, Carol J., and John Lindow, eds. *Old Norse-Icelandic Literature: A Critical Guide*. Islandica 45. Ithaca: Cornell University Press, 1985.
Clunies Ross, Margaret. 'The Cognitive Approach to Scaldic Poetics, from Snorri to Vigfússon and Beyond.' In *Úr Dölum til Dala: Guðbrandur Vigfússon Centenary Essays*, edited by Rory McTurk and Andrew Wawn, 267–86. Leeds: School of English, University of Leeds, 1989.
– 'The Conservation and Reinterpretation of Myth in Medieval Icelandic Writings.' In *Old Icelandic Literature and Society*, edited by Clunies Ross, 116–39.
– *A History of Old Norse Poetry and Poetics*. Cambridge: D.S. Brewer, 2005.
– '*Mikill Skynsemi er at Rifja Vandliga þat Upp*: A Response to Klaus von See.' *Saga-Book* 23 (1990): 73–9.
– ed. *Old Icelandic Literature and Society*. Cambridge Studies in Medieval Literature 42. Cambridge: Cambridge University Press, 2000.
– *Skáldskaparmál: Snorri Sturluson's* ars poetica *and Medieval Theories of Language*. The Viking Collection 4. Odense: Odense University Press, 1977.
– 'Snorri's *Edda* as Narrative.' In *Snorri Sturluson: Beiträge zu Werk und Rezeption*, edited by Fix, 9–22.
Davidson, H.R. Ellis. *Gods and Myths of Northern Europe*. London: Penguin Books, 1964.
Detienne, Marcel. *The Masters of Truth in Archaic Greece*. Translated by Janet Lloyd. New York: Zone Books, 1999.
Discenza, Nicole Guenther. *The King's English: Strategies of Translation in the Old English* Boethius. Albany: State University of New York Press, 2005.
Dronke, Ursula, and Peter Dronke. 'The Prologue of the Prose *Edda*: Explorations of a Latin Background.' In *Sjötíu ritgerðir helgaðar Jakobi Benediktssyni 20. júlí 1977*, edited by Einar G. Pétursson and Jónas Kristjánsson, 1:153–76.
Dronke, Ursula, Guðrún P. Helgadóttir, Gerd Wolfgang Weber, and Hans Bekker-Nielson, eds. *Speculum Norroenum: Norse Studies in Memory of Gabriel Turville-Petre*. Odense: Odense University Press, 1981.
Durrenberger, E. Paul. *The Dynamics of Medieval Iceland: Political Economy and Literature*. Iowa City: University of Iowa Press, 1992.
Edwards, Diana C. 'Clause Arrangement in Skaldic Poetry. I. Clause Arrangment in the *Dróttkvætt* Poetry of the Ninth to Fourteenth Centuries. II. Clause Arrangment in the Poetry of Arnórr jarlaskáld.' *Arkiv för nordisk filologi* 98 (1983): 123–75.
Edwards, Paul. 'Alcohol into Art: Drink and Poetry in Old Icelandic and Anglo-Saxon.' In *Sagnaskemmtun: Studies in Honour of Hermann Pálsson on his 65th Birthday, 25th May 1986*, edited by Rudolf Simek, Jónas Kristjánsson, and Hans Bekker-Nielsen, 85–98. Vienna: H. Böhlau, 1986.

Eeden, Willem van, Jr. 'Inleiding' to *De Codex Trajectinus van de Snorra Edda.* Leiden: Eduard Ijdo, 1913.

Einar G. Pétursson, and Jónas Kristjánsson, eds. *Sjötíu ritgerðir helgaðar Jakobi Benediktssyni 20. júlí 1977.* 2 vols. Reykjavík: Stofnun Árna Magnússonar, 1977.

Einar Ól. Sveinsson. *The Age of the Sturlungs: Icelandic Civilization in the 13th Century.* Translated by Jóhann S. Hannesson. Islandica 36. Ithaca: Cornell University Press, 1953.

– 'Dróttkvæða þáttur.' In *Við uppspretturnar*, 34–63.

– *Sagnaritun Oddaverja: Nokkrar athuganir.* Íslenzk fræði I. Reykjavík: Ísafoldarprentsmiðja, 1937.

– 'Snorri Sturluson.' In *Við uppspretturnar*, 153–60.

– *Við uppspretturnar.* Reykjavík: Helgafell, 1956.

Faulkes, Anthony. 'Descent from the Gods.' *Mediaeval Scandinavia* 11 (1978–9): 92–125.

– 'The Genealogies and Regnal Lists in a Manuscript in Resen's Library.' In *Sjötíu ritgerðir helgaðar Jakobi Benediktssyni 20. júlí 1977*, edited by Einar G. Pétursson and Jónas Kristjánsson, 2:177–90.

– Review of *Snorri Sturluson*, by Marlene Ciklamini. *Saga-Book* 20 (1981): 306–9.

– 'The Sources of *Skáldskaparmál*: Snorri's Intellectual Background.' In *Snorri Sturluson: Kolloquium anlässlich der 750. Wiederkehr seines Todestages*, edited by Wolf, 59–76.

– 'The Use of Snorri's Verse-Forms by Earlier Norse Poets.' In *Snorrastefna: 25.–27. júlí 1990*, edited by Úlfar Bragason, 35–51.

Fidjestøl, Bjarne. *Det norrøne fyrstediktet.* Øvre Ervik: Alvheim and Eide, 1982.

– *Selected Papers.* Edited by Odd Einar Haugen and Else Mundal. Translated by Peter Foote. The Viking Collection 9. Odense: Odense University Press, 1997.

Finnur Jónsson. 'Edda Snorra Sturlusonar, dens oprindelige form og sammensætning.' *Aarbøger for nordisk oldkyndighed og historie* 11 (1898): 283–357.

– 'Snorre Sturlusons *Háttatal.' Arkiv för nordisk filologi* 45 (1929): 229–69.

Fix, Hans, ed. *Snorri Sturluson: Beiträge zu Werk und Rezeption.* Berlin: Walter de Gruyter, 1998.

Foote, Peter. *Aurvandilstá: Norse Studies.* The Viking Collection 2. Odense: Odense University Press, 1984.

– 'Secular Attitudes in Early Iceland.' *Mediaeval Scandinavia* 7 (1974): 31–44.

– '*Sturlusaga* and Its Background.' *Saga-Book* 13 (1946–53): 207–37.

Foote, Peter, and David M. Wilson. *The Viking Achievement: The Society and Culture of Early Medieval Scandinavia.* London: Sidgwick and Jackson, 1970.

Frank, Roberta. *Old Norse Court Poetry: The* Dróttkvætt *Stanza.* Islandica 42. Ithaca: Cornell University Press, 1978.

– 'Skaldic Poetry.' In *Old Norse-Icelandic Literature: A Critical Guide*, edited by Clover and Lindow, 157–96.

– 'Snorri and the Mead of Poetry.' In *Speculum Norroenum: Norse Studies in Memory of Gabriel Turville-Petre*, edited by Dronke, Guðrún P. Helgadóttir, Weber, and Bekker-Nielson, 155–70.

Friis-Jensen, Karsten. *Saxo Grammaticus as Latin Poet: Studies in the Verse Passages of the* Gesta Danorum. Analecta Romana Instituti Danici, Supplementa 14. Rome: Bretschneider, 1987.

– 'Saxo Grammaticus's Study of the Roman Historiographers and His Vision of History.' In *Saxo Grammaticus: Tra storiographia e letteratura, Bevagna, 27–29 settembre 1990*, edited by Carlo Santini, 61–81. Rome: Editrice, 1992.

Gade, Kari Ellen. 'Homosexuality and the Rape of Males in Old Norse Law and Literature.' *Scandinavian Studies* 60 (1986): 124–41.

– 'Poetry and Its Changing Importance in Medieval Icelandic Culture.' In *Old Icelandic Literature and Society*, edited by Clunies Ross, 61–95.

– *The Structure of Old Norse* Dróttkvætt *Poetry*. Islandica 49. Ithaca: Cornell University Press, 1995.

Geertz, Clifford. *The Interpretation of Cultures*. New York: Basic Books, 1973.

Gísli Pálsson. *The Textual Life of Savants: Ethnography, Iceland, and the Linguistic Turn*. Chur, Switzerland: Harwood Academic Publishers, 1995.

Gísli Sigurðsson. *The Medieval Icelandic Saga and Oral Tradition: A Discourse on Method*. Translated by Nicholas Jones. Publications of the Milman Parry Collection of Oral Literature 2. Cambridge, MA: Harvard University Press, 2004.

– 'Óláfr Þórðarson hvítaskáld and Oral Poetry in the West of Iceland c. 1250: The Evidence of References to Poetry in *The Third Grammatical Treatise*.' In *Old Icelandic Literature and Society*, edited by Clunies Ross, 96–115.

Gjerset, Knut. *History of the Norwegian People*. 2 vols. New York: Macmillan, 1932.

Guðrún Nordal. 'The Contemporary Sagas and Their Social Context.' In *Old Icelandic Literature and Society*, edited by Clunies Ross, 221–40.

– 'Skáldið Snorri Sturluson.' In *Snorrastefna: 25.–27. júlí 1990*, edited by Úlfar Bragason, 52–69.

– *Tools of Literacy: The Role of Skaldic Verse in Icelandic Textual Culture of the Twelfth and Thirteenth Centuries*. Toronto: University of Toronto Press, 2001.

Gunnar Karlsson. *The History of Iceland*. Minneapolis: University of Minnesota Press, 2000.

– 'Stjórnmálamaðurinn Snorri.' In *Snorri: Átta alda minning*, edited by Gunnar Karlsson and Helgi Þórlaksson, 23–51.

Gunnar Karlsson, and Helgi Þórlaksson, eds. *Snorri: Átta alda minning*. Reykjavík: Sögufélag, 1979.

Hallan, Nils. 'Snorri fólgsnarjarl.' *Skírnir* 146 (1972): 159–76.

Hallberg, Peter. *The Icelandic Saga.* Translated by Paul Schach. Lincoln: University of Nebraska Press, 1962.

– *Old Icelandic Poetry: Eddic Lay and Skaldic Verse.* Translated by Paul Schach and Sonja Lindgrenson. Lincoln: University of Nebraska Press, 1975.

– 'Om Þrymskviða.' *Arkiv för nordisk filologi* 69 (1954): 51–77.

– *Snorri Sturluson och Egils saga Skallagrímssonar: Ett försök till språklig författarbestämning.* Studia Islandica 20. Reykjavík: H.F. Leiftur, 1962.

Halldór Hermannsson. *Sæmund Sigfússon and the Oddaverjar.* Islandica 22. Ithaca: Cornell University Library, 1932.

Halvorsen, E.F. *The Norse Version of the* Chanson de Roland. Bibliotheca Arnamagnæana 19. Copenhagen: Ejnar Munksgaard, 1959.

Hamel, A.G. van. 'Gods, Skalds and Magic.' *Saga-Book* 11 (1935): 129–52.

– 'The Mastering of the Mead.' In *Studia Germanica tillägnade Ernst Albin Kock den 6 december 1934,* 76–85. Lund: C.W. Gleerup, 1934.

Harris, Joseph. 'The Masterbuilder Tale in Snorri's *Edda* and Two Sagas.' *Arkiv för nordisk filologi* 91 (1976): 66–101.

– 'Theme and Genre in Some *Íslendinga Þættir.*' *Scandinavian Studies* 48 (1976): 1–28.

Hastrup, Kirsten. *Culture and History in Medieval Iceland: An Anthropological Analysis of Structure and Change.* Oxford: Clarendon Press, 1985.

Helgi Þorláksson. 'Snorri Sturluson og Oddaverjar.' In *Snorri: Átta alda minning,* edited by Gunnar Karlsson and Helgi Þórlaksson, 53–88.

Helle, Knut. 'Anglo-Norwegian Relations in the Reign of Håkon Håkonsson (1217–63).' *Mediaeval Scandinavia* 1 (1968): 101–14.

– *Norge blir en stat 1130–1319.* Oslo: Universitetsforlaget, 1974.

Hermann Pálsson. 'Hirðskáld í spéspegli.' *Skáldskaparmál* 2 (1992): 148–69.

– 'Snorri Sturluson and the Everlasting Battle.' In *Snorri Sturluson: Beiträge zu Werk und Rezeption,* edited by Fix, 44–56.

Heusler, Andreas. *Die altgermanische Dichtung.* 2nd ed. Potsdam: Akademische Verlagsgesellschaft Athenaion, 1941.

– 'Die gelehrte Urgeschichte im isländischen Schrifttum.' In his *Kleine Schriften,* edited by Helga Reuschel and Stefan Sonderegger, 2:80–161. Berlin: Walter de Gruyter, 1969.

Hollander, Lee M. *The Skalds.* Princeton: Princeton University Press, 1945.

Indrebø, Gustav. *Fagrskinna.* Avhandlinger fra universitetets historiske seminar 4. Oslo: Grøndahl and Son, 1917.

Jakob Benediktsson. 'Hvar var Snorri nefndur höfundur Heimskringlu?' *Skírnir* 129 (1955): 118–27.

Jakobsen, Alfred. 'Om Fagrskinna-forfattern.' *Arkiv för nordisk filologi* 85 (1970): 88–124.

Johnsen, Arne Odd. *On the Background for the Establishment of the Norwegian Church Province: Some New Viewpoints*. Avhandlinger utgitt av Det norske videnskaps-akademi i Oslo. Ny serie 11. Oslo: Universitetsforlaget, 1967.

Jón Helgason. 'Norges og Islands digtning.' In *Litteraturhistorie: Norge og Island*, edited by Sigurður Nordal, 3–179. Nordisk Kultur 8B. Stockholm: Albert Bonnier, 1953.

Jón Jóhannesson. *A History of the Old Icelandic Commonwealth: Íslendinga saga*. Translated by Haraldur Bessason. University of Manitoba Icelandic Studies 2. Winnipeg: University of Manitoba Press, 1974.

– 'Um Sturlunga sögu.' In *Sturlunga saga*, 2:vii–lvi.

Jón Viðar Sigurðsson. *Chieftains and Power in the Icelandic Commonwealth*. Translated by Jean Lundskær-Nielsen. The Viking Collection 12. Odense: Odense University Press, 1999.

Jónas Kristjánsson. *Eddas and Sagas: Iceland's Medieval Literature*. Translated by Peter Foote. Reykjavík: Hið íslenzka bókmenntafélag, 1988.

– 'Egilssaga og konungasögur.' In *Sjötíu ritgerðir helgaðar Jakobi Benediktssyni 20. júlí 1977*, edited by Einar G. Pétursson and Jónas Kristjánsson, 2:449–72.

Keen, Maurice. *Chivalry*. New Haven: Yale University Press, 1984.

Klingenberg, Heinz. 'Gylfaginning. Tres vidit unum adoravit.' In *Germanic Dialects: Linguistic and Philological Investigations*, edited by Bela Brogyanyi and Thomas Krömmelbein, 627–89. Amsterdam Studies in the Theory and History of Linguistic Science 4. Current Issues in Linguistic Theory 38. Amsterdam: John Benjamins, 1986.

– 'Hommage für Skúli Bárðarson.' In *Snorri Sturluson: Beiträge zu Werk und Rezeption*, edited by Fix, 57–96.

Kock, Ernst A. 'Skaldendichtung und Undeutlichkeit?' In *Festschrift Eugen Mogk zum 70. Geburtstag 19. Juli 1924*, 78–80. Halle: Max Niemeyer, 1924.

Koht, Halvdan. 'Skule Jarl.' *Historisk tidsskrift* 5 (1924): 428–52.

Konráð Gíslason. 'De ældste runeindskrifters sproglige stilling.' *Aarbøger for nordisk oldkyndighed og historie* (1869): 35–148.

Kramarz-Bein, Susanne. 'Höfische Unterhaltung und ideologisches Ziel: Das Beispiel der altnorwegischen *Parcevals saga*.' In *Die Aktualität der Saga*, edited by Andersen, 63–84.

Kreutzer, Gert. *Die Dichtungslehre der Skalden: Poetologische Terminologie und Autorenkommentare als Grundlagen einer Gattungspoetik*. Kronberg: Scriptor Verlag, 1974.

Krömmelbein, Thomas. 'Creative Compilers: Observations on the Manuscript Tradition of Snorri's *Edda*.' In *Snorrastefna: 25.-27. júlí 1990*, edited by Úlfar Bragason, 113–29.

– 'Snorri als Skalde. Studien zum *Háttatal*.' In *Germanic Dialects: Linguistic and Philological Investigations*, edited by Bela Brogyanyi and Thomas Krömmelbein,

295–331. Amsterdam Studies in the Theory and History of Linguistic Science 4. Current Issues in Linguistic Theory 38. Amsterdam: John Benjamins, 1986.

Kuhn, Hans. *Das Dróttkvætt*. Heidelberg: Carl Winter, 1983.

– 'Das nordgermanische Heidentum in den ersten christlichen Jahrhunderten.' *Zeitschrift für deutsches Altertum und deutsche Literatur* 79 (1942): 133–66.

Lane, Jeremy F. *Pierre Bourdieu: A Critical Introduction*. London: Pluto Press, 2000.

Larsen, Karen. *A History of Norway*. Princeton: Princeton University Press, 1948.

Leach, Henry Goddard. *Angevin Britain and Scandinavia*. Cambridge, MA: Harvard University Press, 1921.

Lincoln, Bruce. *Authority: Construction and Corrosion*. Chicago: University of Chicago Press, 1994.

– 'Culture.' In *Guide to the Study of Religion*, edited by Russell McCutcheon and Willi Braun, 409–22. London: Cassell Academic, 2000.

Lindow, John. 'Mythology and Mythography.' In *Old Norse-Icelandic Literature: A Critical Guide*, edited by Clover and Lindow, 21–67.

– 'Riddles, Kennings, and the Complexity of Skaldic Poetry.' *Scandinavian Studies* 47 (1975): 311–27.

– 'Skald Sagas in their Literary Context 1: Related Icelandic Genres.' In *Skaldsagas: Text, Vocation, and Desire in the Icelandic Sagas of Poets*, edited by Russell Poole, 218–31. Berlin: Walter de Gruyter, 2000.

– 'The Two Skaldic Stanzas in *Gylfaginning*: Notes on Sources and Text History.' *Arkiv för nordisk filologi* 92 (1977): 106–24.

LiPuma, Edward. 'Culture and the Concept of Culture in a Theory of Practice.' In *Bourdieu: Critical Perspectives*, edited by Calhoun, LiPuma, and Postone, 14–34.

Lönnroth, Lars. *European Sources of Icelandic Saga-Writing: An Essay Based on Previous Studies*. Stockholm: Boktryckeri Aktiebolaget Thule, 1965.

– 'The Reception of Snorri's Poetics: An International Research Project.' In *Snorrastefna: 25.-27. júlí 1990*, edited by Úlfar Bragason, 143–54.

– Review of *Mythos und Theologie im skandinavischen Hochmittelalter*, by Klaus von See. *Skandinavistik* 20 (1990): 43–7.

Lýður Björnsson. 'Eigi skal höggva.' *Skírnir* 152 (1978): 162–5.

Meissner, Rudolf. *Die Kenningar der Skalden: Ein Beitrag zur skaldischen Poetik*. Bonn: Kurt Schroeder, 1921.

– *Die Strengleikar: Ein Beitrag zur Geschichte der altnordischen Prosalitteratur*. Halle: Max Niemeyer, 1902.

Meulengracht Sørensen, Preben. *Saga and Society: An Introduction to Old Norse Literature*. Translated by John Tucker. Odense: Odense University Press, 1993.

– 'Snorris frœði.' In *Snorrastefna: 25.-27. júlí 1990*, edited by Úlfar Bragason, 270–83.

– 'Social Institutions and Belief Systems of Medieval Iceland (c. 870–1400) and Their Relations to Literary Production.' In *Old Icelandic Literature and Society*, edited by Clunies Ross, 8–29.

– *The Unmanly Man: Concepts of Sexual Defamation in Early Northern Society.* Translated by Joan Turville-Petre. The Viking Collection 1. Odense: Odense University Press, 1983.

Miller, William Ian. *Bloodtaking and Peacemaking: Feud, Law, and Society in Saga Iceland.* Chicago: University of Chicago Press, 1990.

Mogk, Eugen. *Novellistiche Darstellung mythologischer Stoffe Snorris und seiner Schule.* Folklore Fellows Communications 51. Helsinki: Suomalainen tiedeakatemia, 1923.

– 'Untersuchungen über die Gylfaginning.' *Beiträge zur Geschichte der deutschen Sprache und Literatur* 6 (1879): 477–537.

– 'Untersuchungen über die Gylfaginning II.' *Beiträge zur Geschichte der deutschen Sprache und Literatur* 7 (1880): 203–318.

– 'Zur Bewertung des Codex Upsaliensis der Snorra-Edda.' *Beiträge zur Geschichte der deutschen Sprache und Literatur* 49 (1925): 402–14.

Mortensen, Lars Boje. 'Saxo Grammaticus' View of the Origins of the Danes and His Historiographical Models.' *Cahiers de l'Institute du Moyen-âge Grec et Latin* 55 (1987): 169–83.

Müller, Friedrich W. *Untersuchungen zur Uppsala-Edda.* Dresden: M. Dittert, 1941.

Nordal, Guðrún. *See* Guðrún Nordal.

Nordal, Sigurður. *See* Sigurður Nordal.

Ólafur Halldórsson. 'Sagnaritun Snorra Sturlusonar.' In *Snorri: Átta alda minning*, edited by Gunnar Karlsson and Helgi Þórlaksson, 113–38.

Óskar Halldórsson. 'Snorri og Edda.' In *Snorri: Átta alda minning*, edited by Gunnar Karlsson and Helgi Þórlaksson, 89–112.

Paasche, Fredrik. *Snorre Sturlason og Sturlungerne.* Christiania: H. Aschehoug, 1922.

Postone, Moishe, Edward LiPuma, and Craig Calhoun. 'Introduction: Bourdieu and Social Theory.' In *Bourdieu: Critical Perspectives*, edited by Calhoun, LiPuma, and Postone, 1–13.

Reichardt, Konstantin. *Studien zu den Skalden des 9. und 10. Jahrhunderts.* Leipzig: Mayer & Müller, 1928.

Rosenblad, Esbjörn, and Rakel Sigurðardóttir-Rosenblad. *Iceland from Past to Present.* Translated by Alan Crozier. Reykjavík: Mál og menning, 1993.

Samson, Ross. '*Goðar*: Democrats or Despots?' In *From Sagas to Society: Comparative Approaches to Early Iceland*, edited by Gísli Pálsson, 167–88. Enfield Lock, UK: Hisarlik Press, 1992.

Schach, Paul. *Icelandic Sagas.* Boston: Twayne Publishers, 1984.

Schier, Kurt von. 'Iceland and the Rise of Literature in "terra nova": Some Comparative Reflections.' *Grípla* 1 (1975): 168–81.
– *Sagaliteratur*. Stuttgart: J.B. Metzler, 1970.
– 'Zur Mythologie der *Snorra Edda*: Einige Quellenprobleme.' In *Speculum Norroenum: Norse Studies in Memory of Gabriel Turville-Petre*, edited by Dronke, Guðrún P. Helgadóttir, Weber, and Bekker-Nielson, 405–20.
See, Klaus von. *Europa und der Norden im Mittelalter*. Heidelberg: Carl Winter, 1999.
– *Mythos und Theologie im skandinavischen Hochmittelalter*. Skandinavistische Arbeiten 8. Heidelberg: Carl Winter, 1988.
– 'Snorris Konzeption einer nordischen Sonderkultur.' In *Snorri Sturluson: Kolloquium anlässlich der 750. Wiederkehr seines Todestages*, edited by Wolf, 141–77.
– 'Zum Prolog der Snorra Edda.' *Skandinavistik* 20 (1990): 111–26.
Seelow, Hubert. 'Zur handschriftlichen Überlieferung der Werks Snorri Sturlusons.' In *Snorri Sturluson: Beiträge zu Werk und Rezeption*, edited by Fix, 246–54.
Sigrún Davíðsdóttir. 'Old Norse Court Poetry: Some Notes on Its Purpose, Transmission and Historical Value.' *Grípla* 3 (1979): 186–203.
Sigurður Nordal. *Icelandic Culture*. Translated by Vilhjálmur T. Bjarnar. Ithaca: Cornell University Press, 1990.
– *Snorri Sturluson*. Reykjavík: Þór B. Þórlaksson, 1920.
– 'Snorri Sturluson: Nokkurar hugleiðingar á 700. ártíð hans.' *Skírnir* 15 (1941): 5–33.
Skard, Sigmund. *Classical Tradition in Norway*. Oslo: Universitetsforlaget, 1980.
Skovgaard-Petersen, Inge. 'Saxo, Historian of the Patria.' *Mediaeval Scandinavia* 2 (1969): 54–77.
Steblin-Kamenskij, M.I. 'An Attempt at a Semantic Approach to the Problem of Authorship in Old Icelandic Literature.' *Arkiv för nordisk filologi* 81 (1966): 24–34.
– *The Saga Mind*. Translated by Kenneth H. Ober. Odense: Odense University Press, 1973.
Stefán Einarsson. *A History of Icelandic Literature*. New York: Johns Hopkins Press for the American Scandinavian Foundation, 1957.
Stephens, John. 'The Mead of Poetry: Myth and Metaphor.' *Neophilologus* 56 (1972): 259–68.
Strerath-Bolz, Ulrike. *Kontinuität statt Konfrontation: Der Prolog der Snorra Edda und die europäische Gelehrsamkeit des Mittelalters*. Frankfurt: Peter Lang, 1991.
Ström, Folke. 'Poetry as an Instrument of Propaganda: Jarl Hákon and His Poets.' In *Speculum Norroenum: Norse Studies in Memory of Gabriel Turville-Petre*, edited by Dronke, Guðrún P. Helgadóttir, Weber, and Bekker-Nielson, 440–58.
Svava Jakobsdóttir. 'Gunnlöð and the Precious Mead (*Hávamál*).' Translated by Katrina Attwood. In *The Poetic Edda: Essays on Old Norse Mythology*, edited by Paul Acker and Carolyne Larrington, 27–58. New York: Routledge, 2002.

Sveinbjörn Egilsson. *Lexicum poeticum antiquæ linguæ septentrionalis. Ordbog over det norsk-islandske skjaldesprog*. 2nd ed. Revised by Finnur Jónsson. Copenhagen: S.L. Møller, 1931.

Torfi H. Tulinius. 'Capital, Field, Illusio. Can Bourdieu's Sociology Help Us Understand the Development of Literature in Medieval Iceland?' In *Sagas and Societies: International Conference at Borgarnes, Iceland, September 5–9, 2002*, edited by Stefanie Würth, Tõnno Jonuks, and Axel Kristinsson, 18 pp. Tübingen: Universitätsbibliothek Tübingen, 2004. http://w210.ub.uni-tuebingen.de/dbt/volltexte/ 2004/1080/ (accessed 6 April 2007).

– *The Matter of the North: The Rise of Literary Fiction in Thirteenth-Century Iceland*. Translated by Randi C. Eldevik. The Viking Collection 13. Odense: Odense University Press, 2002.

– *Skáldið í skriftinni: Snorri Sturluson og* Egils saga. Reykjavík: Hið íslenska bókmenntafélag, 2004.

– 'Snorri og bræður hans. Framgangur og átök í félagslegu rými þjóðveldisins.' *Ný Saga* 12 (2000): 49–60.

– 'Virðing í flóknu samfélagi. Getur félagsfræði Pierre Bourdieu skýrt hlutverk og eðli virðingar í íslensku miðaldasamfélagi?' In *Sæmdarmenn. Um heiður á þjóðveldisöld* 57–89. Reykjavík: Hugvísindastofnun, 2001.

Tranter, Stephen Norman. *Clavis Metrica:* Háttatal, Háttalykill *and the Irish Metrical Tracts*. Basel: Helbing and Lichtenhahn, 1997.

– 'Das *Háttatal* von Snorri Sturluson, mündlich trotz Schriftlichkeit?' In *Snorri Sturluson: Kolloquium anlässlich der 750. Wiederkehr seines Todestages*, edited by Wolf, 179–92.

– 'Medieval Icelandic *artes poeticae*.' In *Old Icelandic Literature and Society*, edited by Clunies Ross, 140–60.

– *Sturlunga Saga: The Rôle of the Creative Compiler*. Frankfurt: Peter Lang, 1987.

Tulinius, Torfi H. *See* Torfi H. Tulinius.

Turville-Petre, E.O.G. *Myth and Religion of the North: The Religion of Ancient Scandinavia*. London: Wiedenfeld and Nicolson, 1964.

– 'On Scaldic Poetry.' *Mediaeval Scandinavia* 7 (1974): 7–14.

– *Origins of Icelandic Literature*. Oxford: Clarendon Press, 1953.

– *Scaldic Poetry*. Oxford: Clarendon Press, 1976.

Úlfar Bragason, ed. *Snorrastefna: 25.–27. júlí 1990*. Reykjavík: Stofnun Sigurðar Nordals, 1992.

– '*Sturlunga saga*: Textar og rannsóknir.' *Skáldskaparmál* 2 (1992): 176–206.

Vésteinn Ólason. 'Er Snorri höfundur Egils sögu?' *Skírnir* 142 (1968): 48–67.

Vries, Jan de. *Altnordische Literaturgeschichte*. 2 vols. Berlin: Walter de Gruyter, 1964–7.

Wanner, Kevin J. '*At Smyrja Konung til Veldis*: Royal Legitimation in Snorri Sturluson's *Magnúss saga Erlingssonar*.' *Saga-Book* 30 (2006): 5–38.

Weber, Gerd Wolfgang. 'Edda, Jüngere.' In *Reallexikon der germanischen Altertums-kunde*, edited by Heinrich Beck, Herbert Jankuhn, Kurt Ranke, and Reinhard Wenskus, 6:394–412. Berlin: Walter de Gruyter, 1986.

– 'Intellegere Historiam: Typological Perspectives of Nordic Prehistory.' In *Tradition og historieskrivning: Kilderne til Nordens ældste historie*, edited by Kirsten Hastrup and Preben Meulengracht Sørensen, 95–141. Acta Jutlandica 63. Aarhus: Universitetsforlag, 1987.

– 'Snorri Sturlusons Verhältnis zu seinen Quellen und sein Mythos Begriff.' In *Snorri Sturluson: Kolloquium anlässlich der 750. Wiederkehr seines Todestages*, edited by Wolf, 193–244.

Wessén, Elias. Introduction to *Codex Regius of the Younger Edda: MS No. 2367 4o in the Old Royal Library of Copenhagen*. Corpus Codicum Islandicorum Medii Ævi 14. Copenhagen: E. Munksgaard, 1940.

West, Ralph. 'Snorri Sturluson and *Egils Saga*: Statistics of Style.' *Scandinavian Studies* 52 (1980): 163–93.

Whaley, Diana. *Heimskringla: An Introduction*. London: Viking Society for Northern Research, 1991.

Wolf, Alois, ed. *Snorri Sturluson: Kolloquium anlässlich der 750. Wiederkehr seines Todestages*. Tübingen: G. Narr, 1993.

Zetterhölm, D.O. *Studier i en Snorre-Text: Tors färd till Utgård i Codices Upsaliensis DG 11 4o och Regius hafn. 2367 4o*. Nordiska texter och undersökningar 17. Stockholm: Hugo Geber, 1949.

Index

Modern Icelandic and medieval Norse persons are alphabetized according to first name. Items beginning with 'æ,' 'ö,' 'ø,' and 'þ' appear at the end of the alphabet; 'ð' appears with 'd.' Accents are ignored for purposes of alphabetization. Writers or works referenced in the notes are indexed only in cases where they are discussed or where a substantial quotation from them appears.

Toronto Old Norse–Icelandic Series

General Editor
Andy Orchard

Editorial Board
Robert E. Bjork
Roberta Frank